D. L. Moody was a towering giant of  *ful communicator of the gospel, and, mos_____ he humility and love of Christ. He is truly _____ is book is an insightful look at a great mc_____*

Bill Bright
Founder and Former President
Campus Crusade for Christ International

D. L. Moody may have lived 100 years ago, but his life's story speaks to this generation with the same power that it did in the 19th century. Here is the story of an ordinary man who rose from poverty with only a minimum of education to bring two continents, Europe and North America, to repentance. No one can read this book without getting tremendously excited, motivated, and deeply moved by God.

Luis Palau
International Evangelist

To our desperate world struggling with broken families, poverty, and hopelessness, D. L. Moody brings visionary inspiration. To our jaded world looking on men of God with skepticism, and even cynicism, D. L. Moody brings integrity. To our self-centered world starving for love, D. L. Moody brings a Christ-centered passion for souls.

Gene Getz
Author, *MBI: The Story of Moody Bible Institute*

Biographers of D. L. Moody have tended to praise him as a spiritual hero or reduce his efforts to a function of historical circumstance. The great merit of Lyle Dorsett's new biography is to combine spiritual insight with unusually wide research. The result is a book that positions Moody in his times, but which also provides Christian reasons for why he was so important in those times, and since.

Mark A. Noll
McManis Professor of Christian Thought
Wheaton College

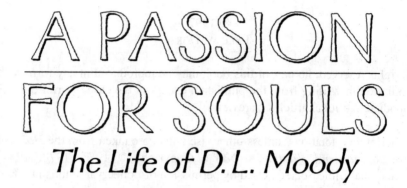

A PASSION FOR SOULS

The Life of D. L. Moody

LYLE W. DORSETT

Foreword by Joseph Stowell

MOODY PUBLISHERS
CHICAGO

© 1997 by
LYLE W. DORSETT

All rights reserved. no part of this book may be reproduced in any form without permission in writing from the publisher, except in the case of brief quotations embodied in critical articles or reviews.

All Scripture quotations, unless otherwise noted, are taken from the *Holy Bible: New International Version* ®. NIV®. Copyright © 1973, 1978, 1984 by International Bible Society. Used by permission of Zondervan Publishing House. All rights reserved.

The "NIV" and "New International Version" trademarks are registered in the United States Patent and Trademark Office by International Bible Society. Use of either trademark requires permission of International Bible Society.

Scripture quotations marked KJV are taken from the King James Version.

ISBN: 0-8024-5181-0

1 3 5 7 9 10 8 6 4 2

Printed in the United States of America

*I dedicate this book with love
to my son and daughter-in-law, Mike and Connie;
to my grandsons, Michael William and Daniel Wesley;
and to my beloved wife, Mary.*

If God calls a man to a work, He will be with him in that work, and he will succeed no matter what the obstacles may be.

D. L. Moody

CONTENTS

FOREWORD

Shakespeare asked, through the lips of Juliet, "What's in a name?" Some names hold more significance for us than others, and for me few names are as meaningful as that of Dwight Lyman Moody. I am honored to serve as President of Moody Bible Institute, which proudly remains "the school that D. L. Moody founded." Each time I walk through our visitor reception area in Smith Hall, I am reminded of Moody's life and ministry as I see the photographs, newspaper articles, miniature-scale rooms, and other memorabilia. Several of my books are published by Moody Press. The first button of my car radio (both AM and FM) is tuned to WMBI, the Moody station that broadcasts from the college. My life's work and ministry is engulfed in his vision to reach the world for Christ. So I can honestly say that had it not been for D. L. Moody, my life would be considerably different today.

D. L. Moody is a man whose life is worthy of our attention. To some, he might be just another name in the list of those who influenced church history, along with Spurgeon, Calvin, Wesley, and others about whom little is known. But regardless of how much or how little you know about D. L. Moody, you will find this book to be a fascinating read and highly motivational. Lyle Dorsett has done an outstanding job of researching his life. My friend Lyle makes D. L. Moody come to life all over again and tells a story that compels the reader to turn to the next page.

With all the recent talk about building a bridge to the twenty-first century, you may be surprised to discover how progressive some of Moody's opinions were for someone who lived a century and a half ago. For example, he was eager to provide opportunities for women in ministry. He emphasized unity between believers and was greatly saddened when divisions threatened to hurt believers' testimony to the secular world.

This book is a biography, not a theological treatise. Moody never received formal theological training, yet no one can question his down to earth spiritual wisdom. His beliefs were based on his personal Bible study and experience combined with the training of others he chose as mentors.

The Institute is blessed today with legacies he left. Moody Press was birthed as his vision. Our tuition-paid policy reflects his heart that no student be denied training for Christ's work because of a lack of funds. Training costs continue to be underwritten by faithful Christians who feel called to support the training of young men and women for effective ministry.

As you learn more about Dwight L. Moody, I believe you'll come to appreciate this dedicated and sincere man of God. His message of the good news of Jesus Christ came during a time of severe natural conflict and disruption. He was born in 1837, and Moody's early years of ministry took place during the Civil War. Later, in the fall of 1871, his work was affected by the great Chicago fire. But by then two fires were burning in Chicago. One destroyed nearly four square miles of the city, but was eventually contained and extinguished. The other fire, burning in the heart of a faithful servant of God, had an even greater effect on the city. It continues to burn to this day, being passed from person to person willing to carry on the legacy of D. L. Moody.

It is my prayer that by the time you finish reading this book, the fire will burn in your heart as well.

Joseph Stowell
President of Moody Bible Institute

ANCESTRY OF DW

Edmund
B Abt. 1495, granted coat-of

Rev. Thomas Moody, Rector of Moulton, Suffolk, 1545–1556
later Chaplain at Islington, B 1520, D 1569, UNM

Thomas	John	Thomasine	Grace		Margaret Newce	1581	George Moo
B 1552	B 1554	B 1556, M	B 1556		B abt 1561		of Moulton
D 1552	D 1554	Henry Smith			D 1603		BP 1560, Bu

Elizabeth	Frances	George Moody	Lydia Hovill	Sarah	Samuel Moo
B 1562, M	B 1584, M	of Moulton, Gent.	Als. Smith	B 1589	Bury St. Edm
John Pratt	Thomas Kilborne	B 1587, D 1653			B 1592, D 1
					M.P. 1654–1

John	John	Hannah	Sar
B 1619	B 1622	B 1624	B 1
D 1619	D 1622	D 1624	D

Sarah	John	Hannah	Mary
B 1659	B 1661	B 1663	B 1666

Jonathan	Mary	Ebenezer	Sarah	Joseph Moody
B 1703	B 1705	B 1707	B 1709	of So. Hadley M
				B 1711/12, D 1

Joseph	Louis	Noah Moody	Susa
B 1738	B 1740	of So. Hadley Mass.	D 17
		B 1742	

Silence	Joseph	Cloe	Eunice	Noah
B 1762	B 1764	B 1765	B 1767	B 1769

Edwin Moody	1828	Betsey Holton	Isaiah	Lucius
of Northfield, Mass.		B 1805, D 1896	B 1803	B 1805
B 1800, D 1841				

Isaiah	Cornelia M.	George F.	Edwin J.	Luther H.	Dv
B 1828	B 1830	B 1832	B 1834	B 1835	B 5
					D

Arthur Percy Fitt	1894	Emma Moody	William Revell Moody
of Northfield, Mass.		B 24 Oct. 1864	President of the Northfi
B 1869, D 1949		D 17 Sept. 1942	B 25 Mar. 1869, D 12 O

1917	Emma Moody Fitt	Irene Moody	Dwight Lyman Moody	Mary Whittle Moody	1928	Arthur Worthington Packard	Constance Annie Moody
	B 16 Dec. 1895	B 20 Aug. 1895	B 7 Nov. 1897	B 13 Nov. 1899		B 1901	B 25 Apr. 1901
	D 22 Aug. 1970	D 22 Aug. 1899	D 30 Nov. 1898			D 24 Jan. 1953	

Virginia Moody Powell	Edward Merriam Powell, II	John Douglas and David Stephen Powell	David Bruce Packard	William Moody Packard
B 8 Feb. 1919	B 17 Dec. 1924	B 31 Mar. 1930	B 8 Mar. 1931	B 2 Sept. 1933

GHT LYMAN MOODY

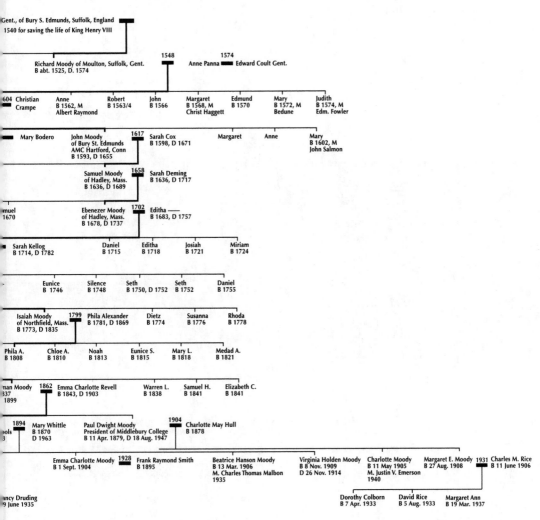

Gent., of Bury S. Edmunds, Suffolk, England
1540 for saving the life of King Henry VIII

Richard Moody of Moulton, Suffolk, Gent.
B abt. 1525, D. 1574

1548

1574
Anne Panna ■■ Edward Coult Gent.

| 604 Christian Crampe | Anne B 1562, M Albert Raymond | Robert B 1563/4 | John B 1566 | Margaret B 1568, M Christ Haggett | Edmund B 1570 | Mary B 1572, M Bedune | Judith B 1574, M Edm. Fowler |

Mary Bodero

John Moody
of Bury St. Edmunds
AMC Hartford, Conn
B 1593, D 1655

1617 Sarah Cox
B 1598, D 1671

Margaret   Anne

Mary
B 1602, M
John Salmon

Samuel Moody
of Hadley, Mass.
B 1636, D 1689

1658 Sarah Deming
B 1636, D 1717

muel
670

Ebenezer Moody
of Hadley, Mass.
B 1678, D 1737

1702 Editha ——
B 1683, D 1757

Sarah Kellog
B 1714, D 1782

| Daniel B 1715 | Editha B 1718 | Josiah B 1721 | Miriam B 1724 |

| Eunice B 1746 | Silence B 1748 | Seth B 1750, D 1752 | Seth B 1752 | Daniel B 1755 |

Isaiah Moody
of Northfield, Mass.
B 1773, D 1835

1799 Phila Alexander
B 1781, D 1869

| Dietz B 1774 | Susanna B 1776 | Rhoda B 1778 |

| Phila A. B 1808 | Chloe A. B 1810 | Noah B 1813 | Eunice S. B 1815 | Mary L. B 1818 | Medad A. B 1821 |

man Moody
337
1899

1862 Emma Charlotte Revell
B 1843, D 1903

| Warren L. B 1838 | Samuel H. B 1841 | Elizabeth C. B 1841 |

1894 Mary Whittle
B 1870
D 1963

Paul Dwight Moody
President of Middlebury College
B 11 Apr. 1879, D 18 Aug. 1947

1904 Charlotte May Hull
B 1878

Emma Charlotte Moody
B 1 Sept. 1904

1928 Frank Raymond Smith
B 1895

Beatrice Hanson Moody
B 13 Mar. 1906
M. Charles Thomas Malbon
1935

Virginia Holden Moody
B 8 Nov. 1909
D 26 Nov. 1914

Charlotte Moody
B 11 May 1905
M. Justin V. Emerson
1940

Margaret E. Moody
B 27 Aug. 1908

1931 Charles M. Rice
B 11 June 1906

ancy Druding
9 June 1935

Dorothy Colborn
B 7 Apr. 1933

David Rice
B 5 Aug. 1933

Margaret Ann
B 19 Mar. 1937

ACKNOWLEDGMENTS

J im Bell, my friend and Editorial Director at Moody Press, stands at the beginning of a long list of people who have helped me produce this book. Jim urged me to undertake the project, and he consistently offered encouragement. I am also grateful to Greg Thornton, Vice President for Publications, Moody Press, for his confidence in me and his commitment to this project. Managing Editor Julie-Allyson Ieron, General Editor Cheryl Dunlop, and the rest of the staff provided invaluable assistance once they received a completed manuscript.

During the research phase of my work, numerous people provided help. Pheg Callaway, a Moody Bible Institute student, photocopied more than a thousand pages of Moody letters. Several Wheaton College students—Jenny Hong, Bill Search, David Rendall, and Christine Yu—searched for and copied reams of material. Three graduate assistants at Wheaton provided invaluable aid: Nathan Oates combed many files of primary sources; David Setran located biographical data on scores of Moody's associates, and he prepared working papers on several topics; Rebecca Litfin sifted through countless primary sources, and she did a masterful task of transcribing Moody letters.

The head of Archives and Special Collections at Wheaton College, Larry Thompson, was always helpful. Likewise generous with their resources were Ferne Weimer, Director, and Kenneth Gill, Associate Director, Billy Graham Center Library; Robert D. Shuster, Director, Paul Ericksen, Associate Director, and Janyce Nasgowitz, Reference Archivist, Billy Graham Center Archives, Wheaton College.

Moody Bible Institute's Library Director, Roger Van Oosten, was unusually generous with his time and resources. He and his able archivist, Walter Osborn, served me extremely well. Conservatively speaking, they reduced my research time by six months.

Linda Batty, Archivist and Librarian at the Northfield Mount Hermon School, opened her files. She was particularly talented at helping me find previously overlooked primary sources in the archives and the Moody Museum collection. Other helpful people at Northfield, Massachusetts, were Joanne and David Dowdy. They provided hospitality and a tour of the Northfield and Mount Hermon campuses. They also introduced me to Lawrence and Hazel Marcy, who shared their memories and knowledge of Northfield historic places. Pal and Margaret Turner and their daughters, Keri and Kristi, provided splendid hospitality in Brattleboro, Vermont.

Access to Yale Divinity School Archives was given by Martha Lund Smalley, Curator. Joan Duffy, Assistant Curator, helped during my extended visit. She also arranged to have materials copied and mailed to me.

University of Rhode Island Professor of History, James F. Findlay, Jr., author of a first-rate biography of Moody, offered wise counsel about sources and interpretations. He also introduced me to Moody's granddaughter, Virginia Powell McDonald, who shared some important family lore. Dr. Findlay also put me in contact with Mrs. Margaret Stout. Peggy Stout is Moody's great-granddaughter. Her counsel was useful, and her willingness to photocopy previously unresearched Moody family correspondence proved to be essential for my understanding of Moody and his family's interrelationships.

Special thanks goes to Jim Lutzweiler, a North Carolina historian who faithfully shared all Moody-related sources he found during his archival research into the history of revivalism in North America. The Reverend Richard Dickinson, my friend in Syracuse, New York, gave up valuable time to photocopy the Moody correspondence at Syracuse University's Archives.

I owe gratitude to archival assistants at the University of Wisconsin-Eau Claire, the State Historical Society of Wisconsin, and the Library of Congress.

Longtime friend and fellow historian, Bruce Clayton, the Harry A. Logan, Sr., Professor of History at Allegheny College, read the entire manuscript with care. Although he is in no way responsible for the book's shortcomings, he markedly improved the manuscript by his critical review.

Linda Kacena, my Wheaton College colleague who serves on the staff of the Institute of Evangelism, Billy Graham Center, spent many hours typing revisions and additions. Her friendship and assistance will always be cherished.

Finally, my wife, Mary, an able author and historian, provided encouragement, advice, and critical evaluations of the manuscript. She typed two drafts, shared her knowledge of revival history, and offered expertise on material related to Emma Dryer and the Blanchard family. Mary Dorsett's contributions to this book and my life are beyond measure.

INTRODUCTION

At least a decade and a half before Woodrow Wilson became president of the United States, he described an unusual encounter in a barber shop. While "sitting in a chair . . . I became aware that a personality had entered the room. A man had come quietly in upon the same errand as myself and sat in the chair next to me. Every word he uttered . . . showed a personal and vital interest in the man who was serving him." Wilson recalled that before leaving, "I was aware that I had attended an evangelistic service, because Mr. Moody was in the next chair. I purposely lingered in the room after he left and noted the singular effect his visit had upon the barbers in that shop. They talked in undertones. They did not know his name, but they knew that something had elevated their thought. And I felt that I left that place as I should have left a place of worship."[1]

Woodrow Wilson witnessed and experienced Mr. Dwight L. Moody's extraordinary ability—many said supernatural ability—to captivate people and usher them into the presence of Jesus Christ.

Moody's power to communicate with souls at the deepest levels transcended all natural boundaries, including those of class and nationality. One night in the early spring of 1884 in London, a medical student named Wilfred Thomason Grenfell slipped into the back of a religious meeting, strictly out of curiosity. Grenfell enjoyed a privileged place in English society. His father, an ordained Anglican priest, served as headmaster of a fashionable college preparatory school; his mother was the daughter of a high-ranking British army officer. Wilfred Grenfell had attended the exclusive Marlborough School, and then he went on to Queen's College, Oxford.

This particular night, on his way home from observing some hospital patients, he decided to see what attracted the crowd. Inside the lecture hall a local man stood offering prayer. Grenfell recalled that the fellow seemed to pray forever in a sanctimonious tone. "The prayer bored me, and I started to leave as he droned on." Before Grenfell could get out of the door, "a vivacious person [on the platform] jumped up and shouted: 'Let us sing a hymn while our brother finishes his prayer.'" Grenfell was astounded. He confessed that "unconventionality, common sense, or humor in anything 'religious' was new to me. Brawling or disturbing the order of ritual is criminal in the Established Church."

In those days Grenfell was a Christian in form only. In fact, he was rather agnostic, finding little of power or magnetism in the professed faith of his family. Turning to a person nearby, he inquired as to the identity of this unorthodox man. Grenfell learned that "the interrupter was the speaker of the evening," so he decided to stay and hear him out. "I did not know anything about this man, nor did I see him again till fourteen years later. But he left a new idea in my mind, the idea that loyalty to a living leader was religion, and that knightly service in the humblest life was the expression of it."[2]

Wilfred Grenfell, ushered into the presence of Jesus Christ that night by an unlettered American named Dwight L. Moody, soon found himself with a new worldview and ambition for life. Grenfell felt as though Moody spoke directly to him, saying, "Why don't you turn your life over to Christ? He can do more with it than you can." Moody's message was full of simple illustrations, "much as Christ's were," and it "touched everyone's heart." The American preacher said Christianity is not an insurance ticket that provides eternal life; rather, it is a personal relationship with a Leader who wants you to follow Him and not go your own way. He wants you to devote your life to Him as a knight would be completely devoted to his king.[3]

As Grenfell left the hall, he took one of Moody's booklets, *How to Read the Bible*. He followed the author's prescription and imbibed large doses of Scripture. After a few spells of doubt, he met up with some Christian athletes, the "Cambridge Seven," who reiterated Moody's message. Consequently, Grenfell turned his back on the lucrative London medical practice he had planned for himself and followed Christ's call to medical missions. Eventually Dr. Grenfell landed on the coast of Labrador. The enormous medical needs of these English-speaking people, who did not have even one doctor in their country, moved him with compassion. For the next forty years he built clinics and hospitals, tended to medical needs, and did evangelism and disciple-making among this long-neglected population of Indians, Eskimos, and whites. Before he died in 1940, Grenfell received numerous honors and enjoyed international acclaim. He always gave credit to Mr. Dwight L. Moody as the man God used to get him with Christ and into missions.[4]

In the wake of Moody's lifetime of travels and ministry, the story is much the same everywhere. Whether he ministered among barbers, future political leaders, university students, or impoverished slum dwellers, souls were always stirred, spirits changed, and lives utterly transformed. This depth of ministry became all the more significant because it reached so many people. Except for two twentieth-century evangelists, Billy Sunday and Billy Graham, no American has had the privilege of personally presenting the gospel of Jesus Christ to so many people. Indeed, by the time of Moody's death in 1899, the secretary of the International Committee of the Young Men's Christian Association declared that "Mr. Moody delivered the gospel message in a larger number of places, to a larger number of persons, a larger number of times than any man who ever lived."[5] One of Moody's critics caustically admitted, "In his rage to save souls he traveled more than a million miles, addressed more than a hundred million people, and personally prayed and pleaded with seven hundred and fifty thousand sinners. All in all, it is very probably [true], as his admirers claim, that he reduced the population of hell by a million souls."[6]

In brief, Dwight L. Moody's name is synonymous with evangelism and revivalism. Any list of world-class people in this field of ministry, to be complete, must include this American whose life spanned almost two-thirds of the nineteenth century. Certainly such remembrance and legacy would please Moody, because he frequently said, "I would rather save one soul from death than have a monument of solid gold reaching from my grave to the heavens."[7]

MORE THAN AN EVANGELIST

The eminence of D. L. Moody as an evangelist is well established. Nevertheless, he should be remembered as much more than an evangelist. He led countless men and women into a personal relationship with the Savior, to be sure, but his range of influence reaches much farther. Any objective assessment of his impact shows that his contributions as encourager, educator, disciple-maker, and equipper of men and women—especially young people and the poor—set forces in motion that are still reverberating around the world.

If the numbers of converts to the Christian faith under Moody's ministry are impressive, even greater are the numbers affected in other ways. It is, of course, impossible to quantify the influence of religious leaders. Still, after sifting through approximately 1,800 letters to and from Mr. Moody, and after examining reams of other types of testimonial materials, the indelible impression I have is that many thousands of people were affected in substantial ways besides conversion. The testimonies, for instance, are legion from people who chose to enter Christian service after sitting under the preaching and teaching of Moody. Missionaries in Asia, Africa, Europe, the United Kingdom, and elsewhere testified that their calling came through his influence. American home missionaries to Native Americans, recently freed slaves, the urban and rural poor, and prison inmates claimed Moody nudged them toward lives of full-time service. Pastors of churches and Christian teachers offered identical stories. And equally important are the statements of thanksgiving from throngs of other Christians who said they returned to the faith through Mr. Moody's preaching, or they found the strength to maintain their Christian lifestyles because of his encouragement. Furthermore, a

D. L. Moody age 44

seemingly endless line of other people—some lay persons and others in career ministry—expressed gratitude to God for Moody's coming to their homes, churches, and communities to teach them to trust and use their Bibles, and also for teaching them how to pray and how to be empowered by the person of the Holy Spirit.

Throughout his life D. L. Moody emphasized "This one thing I do," referring to God's call on his life to work with souls.[8] It is apparent from his ministry, however, that he was referring to a call that encompassed the healing and nurture of souls as well as the rescue of souls, or evangelism. Moody always took the biblical view that the Great Commission (Matthew 28:18–20) calls us to make disciples, not mere converts. Consequently he labored incessantly to help people grow into strong, reproducing disciples, and he also strove to equip other men and women to become full-time workers in this broader disciple-making work of rescuing, healing, and nurturing souls.

Moody loved "the work," as he called his broader ministry. In one of his last letters, he made reference to both the formal and non-formal educational programs he founded, which he believed were among his most significant enterprises: "The work is sweeter now than ever, and I think I have some streams started that will flow on forever. What a joy to be in the harvest field and have a hand in God's work!"[9] He told his oldest son that his schools "are the best pieces of work I have ever done."[10]

THE NEED FOR THIS BOOK

A desire to paint a different portrait of Mr. Moody and his work is one reason I am adding another book to the list of approximately sixty biographies that already exist. Not that Moody's accomplishments besides evangelism have been overlooked by other writers—they have not. But most authors (both popularizers and scholars) have emphasized Moody's evangelistic efforts and knitted in his other enterprises as of secondary importance. This accent, for example, can be seen in the titles and contents of two of the most recent and best biographies: James F. Findlay, Jr.'s, well-written, exhaustively researched, and carefully documented book titled *Dwight L. Moody: American Evangelist, 1837–1899* (Chicago: Univ. of Chicago, 1969); and John C. Pollock's briefer but artfully written work for a more popular audience called *Moody: A Biographical Portrait of the Pacesetter in Modern Evangelism* (New York: Macmillan, 1963).

A celebration of some of the less prominent aspects of Moody's career could be accomplished in a long essay or small booklet, but a book-length study is required to probe more deeply some other issues. As D. L. Moody's son, Paul, so aptly phrased it in the preface to his biography of his father, "We can only write of another as he seems to us, and can never know the ultimate truth. Every biography is but partial. God alone knows all. Even the sum of our various knowledges is not the full truth."[11]

That every biography is only a partial portrait is true, in part, because every generation has its own questions to ask and its own issues with which to wrestle. Today's college-age students and young adults are asking probing questions about racial reconciliation, the value of denominationalism, evangelicals and Catholics working together, the role of women in ministry, and the proper place of careers and family in our lives. A generation of Christians coming of age at the dawn of the twenty-first century has a keen interest in the person and work of the Holy Spirit, divine healing, the deeper spiritual life, spiritual disciplines, and the process of spiritual development. As I join my students in grappling with these issues, I have looked at the issues in the context of D. L. Moody's life.

Beyond these emphases, this biography devotes much space to Mr. Moody's commitment to both formal and nonformal education. For instance, I have spent some time on the fourth school founded by Moody, the Northfield Bible Training School (similar to the Chicago Bible Institute, which would become Moody Bible Institute after his death, but distinct from the Northfield Seminary and Mount Hermon School). This institution has been ignored or given short shrift by most of Moody's biographers, despite Moody's belief that it was one of the most important works he ever undertook. Also, in the context of my emphases on education, the publishing ventures of Mr. Moody are given much more stress than typically found in other biographies.

This biography examines Moody's involvement in the American Civil War in more detail than earlier books because of my conviction of its importance to his spiritual development. Moody's wartime experiences were foundational to his understanding of personal work and the necessity of one-to-one care of souls.

AUTHOR BIASES

Many years ago when I was a graduate student, I read a splendid book by Eric Goldman entitled *Rendezvous with Destiny*. This history of modern American reform was well written, and the thesis persuasively presented. But what I found especially refreshing about the book was Goldman's forthrightness concerning his biases or point of view. Rather than shrouding himself in a phony cloak of objectivity, he said he hoped to be objective; yet he confessed that his New Deal-style liberalism no doubt informed his work. I admired that candor then, and I still do.

In this spirit let the reader be forewarned that I have a point of view. I like Dwight L. Moody. The more I have read his letters and probed his inner life, the greater my admiration has grown. This affection for my subject notwithstanding, I determined to reveal his considerable shortcomings. To make any attempt to cover them over is to distort the man and render him unbelievable.

Bias is also apparent in my attempt to examine the role of the Holy Spirit in Moody's life and labor. When I received training more than thirty years ago as a professional historian, naturalism reigned as the dominant philosophy of history. Serious scholars did not dare, even if so inclined, to include the supernatural in the schemata of cause and effect. Weaving in the supernatural was dismissed as subjectivism. Amazingly it did not occur to most professors who trained us that their Marxist, Freudian, or any one of a number of other trendy 1960s and 1970s presuppositions were equally subjective. On the contrary, there was celebration of a free trade of ideas—as long as the supernatural was not included.

For more than two decades now I have believed in Almighty God: Father, Son, and Holy Spirit. I am extremely grateful to those professors in the secular academy who helped me see the complexity of causes and effects in the historical process. But I also value some colleagues and students in the Christian academic community who have helped me see that ignoring the role of the supernatural in historical interpretation is at best limited and at worst a denial of the worldview I profess to believe. I agree with the late, eminent historian of American revivals, W. W. Sweet, that "the attempts of sociologists and psychologists to explain [Moody] seem trite and foolish."[12] Indeed, the great New Testament scholar and church historian, F. F. Bruce, said that Moody's tremendous power with all classes of people in Britain had nothing to do with his appearance, delivery, or education. The results "could not be put down to personal magnetism but must be ascribed to the power of God working through him."[13]

A major reason I have written this book is to encourage a new generation of young men and women. Researching D. L. Moody's life has reinforced my belief that God will use any man or woman to further His kingdom if this is truly the person's heart desire. It is my prayerful purpose that God will use this man's life story to assure people that our heavenly Father delights in employing people without regard to their cultural, social, educational, or personal disadvantages. Instead, His eyes search the world to strengthen those truly committed to Him (2 Chronicles 16:9). Likewise I pray that this book will encourage older Christian men and women to invest in children, youth, and young adults. Moody's boundless confidence in the younger generation, his outpouring of energy and time on those under twenty-five years old, was purposeful, brilliant, and extremely effective. His commitment to calling and equipping the younger generation should be an example and impetus to us.

Finally, looking back from the perspective of the late twentieth century, I hope that several aspects of Dwight L. Moody's life will be particularly instructive. For decades it has been fashionable in many American circles to deride the Victorians and their era for so-called quaint attitudes about hope, God, sexuality, and family. Moody was certainly a Victorian in his lifespan and standards. Granted the times are markedly different, but there is still something refreshing about a man of whom the following things can be said: His father died during his infancy, causing him to be raised in poverty; nevertheless, he insisted God allowed these difficulties as blessings rather than liabilities. Although he became famous and had opportunities to earn several fortunes, his life remained free from monetary scandal. He traveled incessantly, lived in hotels, suffered loneliness, and experienced the headiness of being idolized and sought out by millions; yet he stayed faithful to his wife and managed to help her raise three children who became admirable adults.

Surely Mr. Moody has something to teach us.

CHAPTER ONE

NORTHFIELD, MASSACHUSETTS
1837–1854

"I'm Tired of This—I'm Going to the City"

It was not easy to make a living in northwestern Massachusetts in the early and middle 1800s. Nevertheless, the people who settled the hilly and mountainous slopes along the Connecticut River Valley were strong and resilient. They possessed an inner strength equal to those stubborn gray stones that jutted out of the thin topsoil and made farming so difficult. Hardworking and frugal people—the offspring of families who knew hardship and deprivation—these descendants of early colonists could make a living in northern New England if anyone could.

This region's marginally productive soil provides a thin covering to some of the most beautiful land in North America. Northfield, Massachusetts, where Dwight Lyman Moody was born, is situated on a lovely mountain just south of the New Hampshire border. The Connecticut River separates Vermont from New Hampshire, allowing Northfield residents a panoramic view of the river with the Green Mountains of Vermont on one side and New Hampshire's White Mountains on the other.

The earth is richest and most profitable for cultivation along the riverbanks and floodplain. But the parents of Dwight L. Moody were not prosperous, even by the modest circumstances of most western Massachusetts farmers and small-town people. Consequently, they lived up the mountain on the eastern side of the river where land was rocky, poor, and least expensive.

The homestead of the Moody family was comprised of a white clapboard house with a gray slate roof, green shutters, and two red brick fireplaces. Built in 1823, the two-story building sat on firm stone slabs native to the local land. This typical New England farm-house was bordered on two sides by an unpaved road, and it was graced on the other two approaches by land that measured out to nearly two acres. The soil was reddish brown and rocky, but it was enough to support a large garden, two horses, a sturdy milk cow, and a few chickens.

DWIGHT LYMAN MOODY'S FAMILY

Edwin Moody, Dwight's father, was born on November 1, 1800. Like his father, he made a living as a brick and stone mason in the Northfield township of Franklin County, Massachusetts. Edwin's family had been in the region for several generations when he courted and married Betsy Holton. She descended from an old Massachusetts Bay Colony family that traced themselves back to the 1630s in the eastern coastal areas.[1]

The Holtons were a rung above the Moodys on the social ladder. Although the Moody clan could be traced to New England in the 1630s, the Holtons had a bit more schooling, more land, and a firmer foothold in the choicest Connecticut River Valley land. Nevertheless, Edwin and Betsy showed little concern for class consciousness. Their son Dwight grew up with such disdain for pedigrees that in later years, when asked about his family heritage, he always said, "Never mind the ancestry! A man I once heard of was ambitious to trace his family to the Mayflower, and he stumbled over a horse-thief. Never mind a man's ancestry!" Not all Americans would have agreed with Moody, especially those with colonial and revolutionary period ancestors. But years later Dwight Moody's son said his father was influenced by a "democratic spirit." He said Moody "disposed of the history of past generations, taking no credit to himself for their achievements, and feeling in no way responsible for their failings."[2]

Betsy Holton wed Edwin Moody on January 3, 1828, one month before her twenty-third birthday. Born February 5, 1805, she was five years younger than her husband. Silhouette portraits of the couple taken around the time of their wedding show Betsy to be fine-featured and petite next to Edwin, who was obviously large-boned, stocky, and more coarse-featured.[3]

Edwin maintained a reputation for being carefree and dashing. Some people said he was irresponsible and given to strong drink. Whatever the reason, he had little savings by the time of his marriage, so he was forced to borrow money to purchase a house and small parcel of land. During their first decade together, he went further into debt and was never able to stay more than a few steps away from his creditors.

Evidently the Moodys were more adept at raising a family than Edwin was at supporting one. By planting time in 1841, thirteen years after their wedding, there were seven children and Betsy was pregnant again. Among the children was Dwight Lyman, born on February 5 (his mother's birthdate), 1837. He was the sixth child from this reportedly happy union.

Family Tragedy

Tragedy struck the Moodys on Friday, May 28, 1841. While Edwin was out doing construction work, a severe pain in his side caused him to return home at midday. About one in the afternoon the pain grew worse. He moved toward the bed, collapsed on his knees, and fell dead before his wife sensed the seriousness of the illness.

Betsy Moody, eight months pregnant, immediately reacted with her motherly instinct to protect her economically vulnerable family. She sent her oldest son, Isaiah, to recover and hide his father's trunk-sized box of masonry tools while she hid their cow's young calf. Before anything else could be hidden, several creditors invaded the farm and took the horses, buggy, cow, and everything else of value, including a stack of firewood, and even the kindling in the shed.[4]

Fifty-nine years later William R. Moody said that his widowed grandmother lost everything except the children and the house. "The homestead itself was encumbered with a mortgage," according to Moody, "and but for the merciful provision of the law securing dower rights, the widow would have been left without even a shelter for the family." Although Betsy Moody was by law allowed to retain the property, she remained responsible for the mortgage payments agreed upon by her husband.[5]

A month after Edwin's death, Betsy gave birth to twins—a boy and a girl. She now had nine children (seven boys and two girls) under the age of thirteen. With regular mortgage payments due, no livestock, and no apparent source of income, she received counsel from family and friends to break up the family and place the older children with families or institutions that could properly care for them.

With Yankee ingenuity and uncommon determination, the widow Moody resolved to hold onto her family and homestead at any cost. A few neighbors came to her aid until the twins were born and weaned. Her brothers who lived in the vicinity were also quite helpful.

A generation after Edwin's death the family was still talking about their uncle's concern for their warmth the first morning after their father was buried. The children woke up to a cold house. Their mother told them to remain in bed and stay warm until it was time for school. There was no firewood in the shed. Although Dwight Moody had few memories of these very early years, many decades later he did recall: "I remember just as vividly as if it were yesterday, how I heard the sound of chips flying, and I knew some one was chopping wood in our wood-shed, and that we should soon have fire. I shall never forget Uncle Cyrus coming with what seemed to me the biggest pile of wood I ever saw in my life."[6]

Religious Interest

Besides her relatives, Betsy Moody was helped by the Reverend Oliver Everett, pastor of the Northfield Unitarian Church. According to W. H. Daniels, a Moody family friend, Pastor Everett was one of the few people who encouraged Betsy Moody "not to part with the children but keep them together as best she could[,] to trust in God, and to bring them up for Him." He also promised to help her with the children's educations and general necessities.[7] Years later the family looked back with gratitude to the generous pastor who helped them both by counsel and material assistance.[8]

The evidence is sketchy, but it appears that the Moody family had little interest in organized religion prior to Edwin's death. Once he was dead, however, Betsy found herself in a woefully precarious spot, so she accepted help from the only pastor who befriended her, and he pointed her to God. Soon after Edwin's burial the older children became members of the Sunday school. A few weeks later the entire family—mother and children—were baptized, according to William Moody, "in the name of the Father and of the Son and of the Holy Ghost." Then on January 1, 1843, a year and a half after her husband's passing and two days before what would have been her fifteenth wedding anniversary, Betsy Moody became a member of the Reverend Everett's Unitarian church.[9]

Both William Moody and the family friend, W. H. Daniels, suggest that the Reverend Everett was really a Christian even though he was a Unitarian. William cited the Trinitarian baptisms as proof, and Daniels argued, "It must be however born in mind that, in those days, the name [Unitarian] had not become associated with all sorts of heresies, as at present [1875]. His differences with his orthodox neighbors were mostly concerning certain points of speculative the-

Moody's birthplace at Northfield

Mrs. Moody with her children in 1862. D. L. Moody is directly behind his mother.

ology. He believed in the Bible as the inspired word of God, in Jesus Christ as the saviour. . . ."[10]

The truth is Mrs. Moody neither understood nor cared much about theology. What she found appealing about Pastor Everett was that he eschewed the predestinarian controversies which she found "peculiarly distasteful." According to Daniels, Dwight Moody's friend in Chicago from about 1868, Mrs. Moody found the strict Calvinism, especially the double predestinarianism that spread throughout much of their region, to be particularly odious. Pastor Everett, to her mind, whatever his theological shortcomings, did not embrace what had earlier driven her from the Christian community. Daniels says that when she made this move to institutional religion, "her Calvinistic friends reproved her for her rebellion against the divine decrees," but she paid them no mind. Indeed, the widow Moody became a loyal ally of the Good Samaritan pastor and his little village church.[11]

Dwight L. Moody maintained that he did not become a true Christian until he was nineteen years old. "I was born of the flesh in 1837. I was born of the Spirit in 1856," he emphasized on many occasions.[12] Nevertheless, Pastor Oliver Everett certainly had a profound impact on the boy in several marked ways. First of all, except for the Holton brothers, no one else seems to have supported the family materially and personally. Everett not only gave provisions from his meager larder, but he also offered invaluable personal support by encouraging the widow to stay the course and trust God to help her keep the family together. Over the years Dwight Moody celebrated his mother's faithfulness to the children, and he attributed many of his own achievements to her love, support, and prayerful reliance upon God. It is doubtful that she could have achieved her faith and maintained the support without the assistance of Pastor Everett.

The future preacher owed an enormous debt to the old Unitarian divine. Not only did he help keep the family intact, but he also pointed the mother and children to God, and he taught them that the heavenly Father's attributes include mercy, compassion, and love. Besides charity and these sound points of doctrine, the aged preacher gave little Dwight his first practical application of Luke 14:23, "Go out to the roads and country lanes and make them come in." Indeed, Pastor Everett taught his Sunday school flock to comb the neighborhood of East Northfield each Sunday morning for every child they could find for a time of teaching, fellowship, and praise.[13]

The Moody children were enthusiastic about their church until Reverend Everett was replaced by a younger man. The new pastor was "the worst of the rationalistic school," and when Moody became a preacher, he sometimes quoted "his sayings with horror."[14] Moody recalled that he began "to look upon Sunday with a kind of dread. Very few kind words were associated with that day. I don't know that the minister ever said a kind thing to me, or ever once put his hand on my head. I don't know that he ever noticed me. . . ."[15]

It is significant that decades later D. L. Moody still remembered the absence of kind words and affectionate touches. Moody had been an impoverished, love-starved little boy. To be sure, his mother loved him as dearly as she did his eight siblings. But how much time can a single parent of nine devote to each one? To make matters even more difficult, her oldest son, Isaiah—the one she depended upon most for help—deserted the family in 1843 when Dwight was seven. Isaiah, age fifteen, nearly devastated his poor mother. He never said good-bye or even hinted that he was preparing to leave. Her hair turned gray over a few weeks. Nothing was heard of him until he appeared at the door thirteen years later.[16]

D. L. MOODY'S CHILDHOOD MEMORIES

Dwight Moody passed on few childhood reminiscences, but those that have survived are revealing. He sometimes mentioned a childhood fear of death—not surprising, given what happened to his father and the subsequent mysterious disappearance of Isaiah. On the other hand, he never looked back with bitterness about their poverty. On the contrary, he frequently said he was glad he had had so little because it made him appreciative of what he did have, and the lack of resources made the family learn to depend on God. Moody never wallowed in self-pity over being fatherless, and he never mentioned that his mother's attentions were necessarily sparse. What he did do, however, was celebrate incidents of tenderness that he experienced during childhood that children from less deprived backgrounds take for granted. For example, a new teacher came to the one-room schoolhouse where the Moody children put in sporadic attendance. On her first day she did two things that astounded the pupils. First, she opened class with a prayer—an exercise that the man who preceded her had obviously ignored. Second, she announced that she was keen on discipline, but it would not be enforced by traditional whippings. Within a few days Dwight Moody had breached the rules. Years later in one of his sermons, he recalled the incident this way:

> I was told to stay after school. I told the boys if she tried the rattan on me there would be music. What do you think that teacher did? She sat down and told me that she loved every one of the boys, and that she wasn't going to use the rattan on any one of them. If she couldn't teach school without whipping the boys she would resign. She spoke most lovingly and wept while talking. That broke me all up. I would rather have had a rattan used on me than to see her cry. I said: "You will never have any more trouble with me, and the first boy that makes trouble, I will settle him." The woman won me by grace. The

next day one of the boys cut up, and I whacked him. I whacked him so much that the teacher told me that was not the way to win the boys.[17]

This brilliant woman won the fatherless boy's heart. He never forgot her compassion, and he told the story often.

Not long after his experience with the teacher, another encounter took place that marked little Moody for life. In later years, whenever Moody preached on the Good Samaritan, he told of this time from childhood:

> It brings the tears to my eyes every time I think of it. My father died before I can remember. There was a large family of us. The little twins came after his death,—nine of us in all. He died a bankrupt, and the creditors came in and took everything as far as the law allowed. We had a hard struggle. Thank God for my mother! She never lost hope. She told me some years after that she kept bright and sunny all through the day and cried herself to sleep at night. We didn't know that as it would have broken our hearts.[18]

Moody went on to say that his brother Luther,

> a year and a half older, had gone to Greenfield, and had done "chores," and he was so homesick that he was constantly writing for me to come. He wanted me so much that he wrote that he would come home for me. I said I wouldn't go. But one cold day in November,—I have never liked November, my brother came home, and said he had found a good place for me, and I must go down and spend the winter in Greenfield. I said I wouldn't go. But as my mother and I sat by the fire she said:
> "Dwight, I think you will have to go. I don't think I shall be able to keep the family together this winter."
> It was a dark night for me. But mother's wish was enough. If she said I ought to that settled it. I didn't sleep much that night. I cried a great deal. The next morning after breakfast I took my little bundle and started. I was about ten years old.[19]

Dwight Moody and his brother trudged thirteen miles over frozen ground to Greenfield, the county seat. When he met the childless husband and wife he was to live with all winter, he found them kind enough but not particularly understanding of children. After a week of milking their cows and doing their chores, the ten-year-old boy was overcome with homesickness. One afternoon he sought his brother at the home where Luther roomed, boarded, and did chores.

Moody recalled the afternoon this way:

"Brother, I'm going home."

"What are you going home for?"

"I'm homesick."

"You'll get over it if you stick it out."

"No, I won't. I don't want to get over it. I can't stand it. I don't like those people here, anyway."

"Dwight, come out and take a walk with me," my brother said.

He took me out near the courthouse square, led me to some shop windows, and showed me some jackknives. What's the use of looking at jackknives if a fellow hasn't any money to buy them with? My eyes were full of tears. I didn't care for these things.

"I'm going home," I said. . . .

All at once my brother, who was looking ahead, brightened up and said:

"There comes a man that will give you a cent."

"How do you know?"

"Why," he said, "he gives a brand-new cent to every new boy that comes to town, and he will give you one."

My tears went away as I saw the old man come tottering along the sidewalk, his face all lighted up. He reached me just in the nick of time and, looking down, he said: "Why this is a new boy, isn't it?" My brother straightened up and said: "Yes, sir, he is my brother, just come to town."

And the old man put his trembling hand on my head and looked down upon me. He got hold of my heart, and as he held my hand he told me that God had an only Son in Heaven, and that He loved this world so much He died for it. He went on talking about Heaven, and told how the Father loved me, and how my father on earth was lifted up, and how I had a Saviour up there, and he told me the story of the Cross in about five minutes. Then he put his hand in his pocket, and he gave me a brand-new cent. I had never seen such a bright and beautiful cent before, and I almost thought it was gold. He put it in my hand, and I never felt as I did then before or since. That act of kindness took the "homesickness" out of me. I felt that from that hour that I had a friend. I thought that man was God, almost.[20]

During the next seven years Dwight, like his brothers, spent most winters away, helping other families with chores. When they were close enough to Northfield, their mother liked to get them all together for Sundays. She took them to church and then put on the best meal she could afford for the entire family. These times together were precious and fondly remembered in the years ahead.[21]

In total Dwight Moody had, at the most, four years of formal schooling. Like the other boys, he went to the local school periodically from about age six to ten. From then on, he was considered old

D. L. Moody, age 17 (1854)

enough to work and help the family. In any case he had as much schooling as most people received in northern New England during the mid 1800s. The quality of his schooling, or at least his attentiveness to what was available, is open to question. The earliest of his letters that have survived date back to 1854 when he was seventeen. His spelling was phonetic. Punctuation was omitted from most early letters. (I have added periods in some places for clarity, but other punctuation and spelling retains the original errors.) Capitalization was randomly applied. If there were new paragraphs they must have been related to when he dipped his pen for more ink.[22] In brief, his spelling, grammar, and usage were surpassed in inferiority only by his penmanship. All of these skills improved over the years, but the crudeness of his early writing makes one certain that his formal schooling never totaled more than three or four years.

Unquestionably, young Dwight Moody could have mastered English if he had taken an interest in it. From his earliest years the boy demonstrated a clever mind and remarkable determination. His inclinations, in any case, flowed in other directions. Growing up in a house that boasted only three books—a cumbersome Bible that was used more for recording family marriages and births than for study, a catechism, and a small volume of personal devotions—his ambitions naturally turned to the practical rather than the academic. His father's tools were still on the premises, but none of the Moodys prospered in the stone and brick trade. Some of the Holtons, on the other hand, were doing quite well in retail business down in the thriving city of Boston.[23]

Betsy Moody told a friend in the 1870s that Dwight "used to think himself a man when he was only a boy."[24] Therefore, she was not surprised when he announced one evening in 1854, just a few weeks after his seventeenth birthday, while he was cutting and hauling logs on a neighbor's farm, "I'm tired of this! I'm not going to stay around here any longer. I'm going to the city."[25]

CHAPTER TWO

BOSTON
1854–1856

"I Have Always Been a Man of Impulse"

W hen Dwight Moody arrived in Boston, the hub city of the northeastern United States, none of his attributes suggested a destiny of worldwide fame. With the possible exception of his mother—she was told by a Gypsy woman that one of her boys would become internationally famous—no one would have believed that Dwight Moody would eventually lead revivals in the United States and Great Britain and that he would establish schools and programs to inspire and equip men and women to traverse the world planting churches and making disciples of the Lord Jesus Christ. And why should anyone expect exceptional accomplishments from Moody? After all, the seventeen year old who arrived in Boston in April 1854 came with few assets considered important for success. He had no father to teach him how to make the awkward transition from adolescence to manhood. His oldest brother, who could have been a father figure, disappeared. Although he had been blessed with a loving mother and siblings, he nevertheless had little education, was barely literate, and carried with him all the ignorance and narrowness of nineteenth-century people who lived in small, isolated communities. Added to these disadvantages was provincialism. Dwight Moody had seen nothing of the world except a few towns in the immediate vicinity of his birthplace.

Even if Moody had longed to travel, money was too scarce to allow such luxury. He seldom, if ever, saw Asians, African-Americans, or anyone from another race or culture, except some Irish émigrés who had come to the valley in the 1830s and 1840s. It is almost certain the young man never read books, discussed ideas, engaged in abstract thinking, or looked much beyond improving next year's crops or earning enough money for the next few meals.

If others failed to predict his future, Moody himself had no vision or ambition for anything related to the Christian faith and ministry. By his own admission, all his hopes and dreams centered on material success. Escaping the drudgery and poverty of northern New England farm life served as the major impetus for cutting home ties and moving to Boston. He had seen enough people die young with little to show for their backbreaking labors. Although he loved his family, restlessness and ambition prevented him from remaining in Northfield any longer.

During Dwight Moody's childhood, the population of the Northfield community had remained rather constant at about one thousand souls. The whole of Franklin County, by booming North American standards, was quite stagnant, only growing from 28,000 to 30,000 between 1840 and 1850.[1] Most of the excitement for young people in Franklin County was along the Connecticut River where boats moved from Vermont and New Hampshire down through Massachusetts, and then on to the Connecticut coast. Interesting people occasionally passed by Northfield, and swimming and rafting were always dangerous enough to provide summer thrills.

During Moody's youth, the Connecticut River, once the economic lifeline of the region, was rapidly being bypassed. Prior to the 1840s, the river carried most of the region's produce to markets and brought manufactured and processed goods back for local consumption. Soon after D. L. Moody's birth, this had all changed. The railroad relentlessly stretched forth in all directions, leaving river valleys important as fertile agricultural land, but increasingly obsolete as arteries of transportation. In 1830 there were only 39.8 miles of railroad track in the United States. In 1840, three years after Moody was born, the mileage had increased to nearly 2,800. By 1850, four years before he left home, track mileage was 8,571; and by 1860, the total would nearly quadruple to approximately 30,000 miles.[2] By the time the energetic Northfield lad reached his teens, the railroad was transforming America. As the rail network grew, cities mushroomed at terminuses and junctions along the way. The railroad stimulated industrial production, and immigrants poured into the United States to meet the new construction and industrial demands.

Even sleepy Northfield was aroused by the transportation revolution. In 1848 the Vermont and Massachusetts Railway connected Brattleboro, Vermont, with Boston. This event brought a minor revolution to southeastern Vermont, causing the little town of Brattle-boro, located on the Connecticut River just about fifteen miles from Northfield, to nearly double in population within a few years.[3] The new railroad went through Northfield and nearby South Vernon, with periodic stops at little stations in both towns. Although the so-called "fast trains" never stopped in Northfield, only at South Vernon, still Moody's part of the valley was directly connected with the enchanting city of Boston.[4]

DREAMS OF BOSTON

No doubt the youthful Dwight Moody dreamed of taking that train as he listened to stories of Boston and longed to see it for him-self. Indeed, in November 1853 he spent some time with two uncles, Samuel and Lemuel Holton. These brothers of Betsy Moody had left the Connecticut Valley a few years earlier and were prospering with two retail boot and shoe stores—one in Boston proper and the oth-er in a suburb a few miles away from the central city. Dwight heard his uncles talk. Their stories whetted his own appetite for adventure. He even asked the older uncle and leader of the shoe enterprises if he could join them in Boston. Uncle Samuel counseled Dwight to stay away from Boston. With rural New England directness, he sug-gested that Dwight's personality was too aggressive and he might get into trouble in the city. He also mentioned the loose living and a thou-sand-and-one temptations in Boston awaiting boys from the country. Too many immigrants from the farms, he revealed, were ruined by bad company before they could ever get a foothold in the competitive economy.[5]

Every attempt to discourage Dwight increased his desire. All winter he thought of little except the historic city. By the first of April he was on his way.

ARRIVING IN THE BIG CITY

Dwight Moody encountered a spectacularly booming city. A metropolis of more than 150,000 people by the time he arrived, it grew every few weeks by numbers that exceeded the total population of little Northfield. The streets in the core of the city were paved, markedly unlike the dirt roads back home. Boston streets were cov-ered with cobblestone, broken stone, and gravel; and there were hundreds of miles of lanes, streets, and avenues to explore. There were buildings two hundred years old and cemeteries with rows of slate markers that went back to the 1600s. Alongside everything old

were new graveyards, new houses, and modern shops. The noises of
the city were at first deafening to the young adventurer. He found
Boston at once attractive and frightful. Accustomed to the quiet of
nature, complemented only by the noise of birds, cattle, and wind;
the occasional clatter of a wagon or coach; or the sounds of no more
than one train a day, he now wandered a city where the continuous
roar of factories was only exceeded by the constant clatter of horse-
drawn commercial wagons, the rumble of numerous freight trains,
and the thunder of steam engines in the bay. Besides these incessant
new sounds were the voices of countless people—many of them talking in Swedish and German or with English accents he did not
know.[6]

A few days after Dwight arrived he wrote to his brothers that he
had seen "a steam hot gas ship come in and sutch a site I never seen
before. There was ship from liverpool loaded with emergrans. All the
Greeks in Boston was there. The sailors sung a song when they come
in site of their friends. Sutch meetings as there was there I never see."
The other remarkable attractions were "three great building full of
girls the handsomest there is in the city thuy all swor like parets. . . ."[7]

The first week of his high adventure was not all fascination and
thrills. By his own admission, he looked like "a tramp" when he arrived in the bustling port city. His brother George had handed him
five dollars when he left home, but he spent all that on the train ticket. Once on the streets and looking for work, he cut a singularly
unimpressive figure. His clothing and shoes were incredibly unfash-
ionable and rumpled, and a photograph made just before he left for
Boston shows him with a military-style cap that appeared at least
two sizes too small perched on his head.

Not only were the country boy's clothes rather seedy, but also
his conversation was "far more of the mountains than of the schools."
As he told a friend years later, his adversity was complicated by a big
boil on his neck, "which forced him to go about with head turned
down over one shoulder, in a way which did not improve his personal appearance or help his prospects for business."[8]

Finding a Job in Boston

When he first arrived in Boston he stopped at Uncle Samuel's
shop, no doubt hoping he would be offered a job and lodgings. But
his mother's brother only responded in surprise, having told Dwight
just four months earlier that he should not come to the city. When
the uncle met the young man with reserve rather than welcome,

Moody immediately put up an independent facade. When asked how he proposed to get a start, rather than humbly asking for help, he announced he could find something and soon went on his way.[9]

The stubborn teenager walked the streets for several days seeking work. In a sermon years later he described his sense of destitution. "I remember how I walked up and down the streets trying to find a situation and I recollect how, when they answered me roughly, their treatment would chill my soul. But when some one would say: 'I feel for you; I would like to help you, but I can't but you'll be all right soon!' I went away happy and light-hearted. That man's sympathy did me good." He mentioned how he felt all alone in the world. "For about two days I had the feeling that no one wanted me. I never have had it since, and I never want it again. It was an awful feeling."[10]

Moody remembered that he went to the post office two or three times a day to see if anyone from home had sent a letter. Although there was only one train a day from Northfield, he checked more often just in case. Finally a letter arrived from his twelve-year-old sister Lizzie. There was no money and not much news. Instead, Lizzie urged her big brother to be alert for pickpockets. She had heard they were always on the prowl in Boston. Even in his homesickness and confusion, the refugee from Massachusetts could smile as he thought about the slim pickings a pocket thief would find on him.[11]

Settling In

Homeless, unemployed, and utterly at the end of his self-reliance, Moody finally set aside his pride after a few days and asked Uncle Lemuel Holton, his mother's younger brother, if he could stay with him until he found a place. By the end of the week he still had no prospects, so he told Uncle Lemuel he was going down to New York to find work. Apparently he planned to walk. "Have you asked Uncle Samuel to help you to a situation?" inquired Lemuel.

"No," said Dwight. "He knows I am looking for a place, and he may help me or not, just as he pleases."

Lemuel assured him Uncle Samuel would be quite willing to get him started, if he would only show a bit of humility and a willingness "to be governed by people who were older and wiser than himself."[12]

He immediately followed the younger uncle's advice, went to Samuel, and asked for mercy. Moody remembered his uncle's words in the hat-in-hand meeting this way: "Dwight, I am afraid if you come in here you will want to run the store yourself. Now, my men here want to do their work as I want it done. If you want to come in here and do the best you can and do it right, and if you'll be willing to ask whenever you don't know, and if you promise to go to Church and Sunday School, and if you will not go anywhere that you wouldn't want your mother to know about, we'll see how we can get along. You can have till Monday to think it over."

The humbled nephew said he didn't need to think it over. "I promise now."[13]

Uncle Holton was good to his word. He hired Dwight as sales clerk, found him a room on the third floor of a house at 43 Court Street owned by Christians, and located a wholesome place for him to eat his meals. He also pointed his humbled nephew to the Mount Vernon Congregational Church, urging him to attend Sunday school and worship services there on a regular basis.[14]

Letters Home

The next two years brought profound changes in the life of the young man from the country. His letters reveal the beginnings of a first-rate general education. He was fascinated by the ethnic diversity of Boston, encountering southern Europeans and a black man—perhaps for the first time. He also displayed a keen interest in urban recreation, especially ball games and lectures. Indeed, Moody joined the Boston Young Men's Christian Association soon after he was settled, apparently not from religious motive or interest, but because of the inexpensive facilities and opportunities it offered. "I am going to join the Christian Satiation tomorrow night. Then I shall hav a place to go when I want to go away any where and I can have all the books I want to read free from expense only have to pay one dolar year they have a large Room and the smart men of Boston lecter to them for nothing and they get up a question. . . ."[15] The mention of a lending library and lectures at the two-year-old YMCA suggests an awakened interest in learning, as did a request that his brother "send me a Greenlief arithme etic for I get some time to study. . . ."[16]

Letters home in 1854 and 1855 suggest a continued interest in everything going on at home; especially important to him were conditions of corn and pea crops, or the price received for selling a good cow. There was also a residual interest in a young woman named Delia. Dwight hoped that her heart would not be stolen away by one of his brothers, and he frequently expressed plans to be up for a visit soon. The letters home were also replete with references to uncles, aunts, and cousins living in the Boston area, making clear that

Moody was not the typical refugee who went to the city from the farm and had no network of economic and moral support. He maintained continuous involvement with supportive relatives who not only got him started in work, church, and housing, but who also entertained him and kept him well connected with family and friends in Boston and back home.[17]

If Dwight Moody was no Horatio Alger-like poor boy who made it from rags to riches or from destitution to middle-class stability by his own efforts, he was, nevertheless, a hardworking young fellow who overcame many obstacles and did extremely well as a shoe and boot salesclerk. Within a few months he was able to purchase shoes for his mother, sisters, and brothers. "I will buy you shoes this fall and another year I will endeavor to help you more."[18] Obviously enjoying his role as a grown-up family provider, he postured as the helpful patriarch, urging one family member to tell Samuel, four years his junior, that "if he will take hold of the Books I will git him a place when he gits older." Actually, this image he paraded was not overly exaggerated. A bit of prosperity had come to the recently destitute greenhorn, he already knew his way around the city, and after three months he became the shop's leading salesman.[19]

He wrote a revealing letter to his mother, thanking her for her letter and urging her to write to him "every weak but you ned not think that I am home sick becaus I want to here from home for I am not. I would not go back a gain to liv for nothing. I nevr enjoyed my self so well be for in my life the time goes like a whirl wind." He was excited about "whare I bord thare is over 50 now and lot of them are bout my age." They were obviously having good fun together, especially since one of the young men had a horse and he allowed Moody to "hav a ride caisnely."[20]

MONEY, GOD, AND CHURCH

By his second year in Boston, Moody was learning about world markets, selling prices of grain in New York, and the impact of the Crimean War on agricultural prices. How accurate a prognosticator he was, it is difficult to tell, but he sent advice to his brothers about what to plant and sell if they wanted to turn the largest possible profit.[21]

If his letters home are an accurate index, earning money became the most important goal in Moody's life between 1854 and 1856. Delia ceased to be mentioned, and only rarely did he write about going to Sunday school or church. In one of his first letters to his mother he told her "I go to meating at Mount Vernon St. Othedx.

I don't know how it is spelt but you will know what I mean,"[22] but for at least another year, church merited no space in his letters.

Dwight Moody's apparent indifference to things of the Spirit notwithstanding, a true spiritual awakening came in spring 1855, even if it remained secondary to his desire to get ahead financially. Obviously Mount Vernon Church was Uncle Samuel's choice. In truth, Moody immensely disliked the place. Several years later he told the Reverend W. H. Daniels, a Chicago friend, that "the men and women were so rich and proper and pious, that they seemed to live in a world almost out of his sight." He was terribly insecure with these proper Bostonians because even "the young people wore good clothes and spent a good deal of money," but he could indulge in neither. By his own admission he was feeling sorry for himself, and his attitude was more at fault than the parishioners.[23]

Regardless of his feelings, he honored his promise to Uncle Samuel, and he trudged off each Sunday to the Mount Vernon Congregational Church. The pastor was a well-educated, orthodox, and widely respected man named Edward N. Kirk. Moody respected Dr. Kirk but found the messages impossible to understand. Years later he remembered sleeping during the sermons—somewhat out of boredom, but mostly due to exhaustion from six long days of work.[24]

Edward Kimball and Moody's Conversion

The man from Mount Vernon Church who wielded the greatest spiritual influence on Moody was Edward Kimball, a middle-aged lay Sunday school teacher. On the first Sunday Moody went to class, Kimball recalled that the eighteen-year-old shoe sales clerk came in and took a seat among the other young men. In Kimball's words, "I handed him a closed Bible and told him the lesson was in John. The boy took the book and began running over the leaves with his finger away in the first of the volume looking for John." Kimball said that the members of the class noticed Moody's fruitless effort to find the gospel, and they "glanced shyly and knowingly at one another, but not rudely." The teacher gave the young men "just one hasty glance of reproof. That was enough—their equanimity was restored immediately. I quietly handed Moody my own book, open at the right place, and took his." Kimball said he had no idea young Moody had sized up the entire scene until years later when he read some of Moody's remarks about being rescued from an embarrassing situation by a sensitive man.[25]

Edward Kimball possessed more than sensitivity; he displayed spiritual alertness and obedience to the Holy Spirit. On Saturday, April 21, 1855, he was bent over his Bible, preparing a lesson for the next day. Suddenly he felt constrained to go call on Dwight Moody and inquire about the condition of his soul. The Sunday school teacher immediately arose and obediently headed for the Holton Shoe Store. On the way he had second thoughts. Perhaps a foolish impulse rather than the Spirit had sent him on this errand. What if he disturbed the young worker during a busy time? What if the other workers overheard their conversation and would make fun of Moody because his teacher was trying to make "a good boy out of him"? Kimball was so absorbed with the pros and cons of the issue that he walked right past the store. "Then when I found I had gone by the door, I determined to make a dash for it and have it over at once." He found Moody in the back of the store wrapping and shelving shoes. "I went up to him and put my hand on his shoulder, and as I leaned over . . . I made my plea, and I feel that it was really a weak one. I don't know just what words I used. . . . I simply told him of Christ's love for him and the love Christ wanted in return."[26]

Kimball had no way of knowing how he had already won Moody's respect and devotion after covering for him in class that first Sunday. Kimball likewise could not see Moody's longing for the loving fatherly touch of an older man. In any case, the Sunday school teacher recalled that "the young man was just ready for the light that then broke upon him, for there at once in the back of that shoe store in Boston the future great evangelist gave himself and his life to Christ."

Moody's own recollection of this sacred event was similar, except for a difference on the timing of conversion:

> When I was in Boston I used to attend a Sunday school class, and one day I recollect my teacher came around behind the counter of the shop I was at work in, and put his hand upon my shoulder, and talked to me abut Christ and my soul. I had not felt that I had a soul till then. I said to myself: "this is a very strange thing. Here is a man who never saw me till lately, and he is weeping over my sins, and I never shed a tear about them." But I understand it now, and know what it is to have a passion for men's souls and weep over their sins. I don't remember what he said, but I can feel the power of that man's hand on my shoulder to-night. It was not long after that I was brought into the Kingdom of God.[27]

Kimball concluded that Moody "gave himself and his life to Christ" that afternoon in April 1855; Moody, on the other hand, although he frequently mentioned this encounter and credited Kimball as the witness God used to bring his conversion, nevertheless said "it was not long after that I was brought into the Kingdom of God." Likewise, because Moody often said "I was born of the flesh in 1837; I was born of the Spirit in 1856,"[28] he was either confused about the date of his conversion or he believed God worked on his soul in a more gradual way. Clearly the shoe-store encounter was the event God used to jolt Moody into an awareness of spiritual reality. "I had not felt I had a soul till then," Moody recalled. That Saturday brought the young clerk face-to-face with his spiritual side, and it brought home to him the love of Jesus Christ. In brief, the Holy Spirit ministered through Kimball's love even though Moody had no clear idea what inspired such tenderness.

Church Membership

If Moody was actually born of the Spirit during the sacred shoe-store meeting, the deacons at Mount Vernon Congregational Church did not believe it. Three and a half weeks later on a Wednesday night, Moody went before Dr. Kirk and a committee of deacons (including Kimball) to be questioned about his readiness for church membership. Langdon S. Ward, a deacon, recorded the May 16, 1855, interview this way:

> Dwight L. Moody. Boards 43 Court St. Has been baptized. First awakened on the 21st of April. Became anxious about himself . . . saw himself a sinner, and sin now seems hateful and holiness desirable. Thinks he has repented. Has proposed to give up sin and feels dependent on Christ for forgiveness . . . loves the Scriptures . . . prays once a day . . . desires to be useful . . . religiously educated . . . been in the city a year from Northfield in this state. Is not ashamed to be known as a Christian. 18 years old.[29]

These gleanings notwithstanding, the committee rejected the young man's request for membership on the grounds that there was, given their measuring stick, no solid evidence of conversion. When asked the question, "What has Christ done for you, and for us all, that especially entitles Him to our love and obedience?" he replied, "I think He had done a great deal for us all, but I don't know of anything He had done in particular."[30]

Moody failed their oral examination. Nevertheless, Kimball and two other men stayed close to Moody and encouraged him for several months. Then on March 12, 1856, at another Wednesday night prayer meeting, Dwight L. Moody once again sat before the deacons and pastor. The secretary recorded the milestone evening in these words:

> March 12, 1856. Mr. Moody thinks he has made some progress since he was here before—at least in knowledge. Has maintained his habits of prayer and reading the Bible. Is fully determined to adhere to the cause of Christ always. Feels that it would be very bad if he should join the church and then turn. Must repent and ask forgiveness, for Christ's sake. Will never give up his hope, or love Christ less, whether admitted to church or not. His prevailing intention is to give up his will to God.[31]

There was little in this interview, according to Kimball, to cause the committee to think the candidate had changed much over the last ten months. Certainly no one who interviewed Moody could have been persuaded that in the next score of years they would all humbly view him as their leader. Regardless, they voted to admit Moody to membership because he expressed a desire to repent, and because he was sincere, eager to learn, and cooperating fully with Kimball and the men who were serving as his mentors. Finally, on May 3, 1856, the clerk from Holton's store signed the church register. He was a member of the Mount Vernon Congregational Church.[32]

A Surrendered Will

No one, perhaps not even Dwight L. Moody himself, could be certain when the young man's new life began. What is evident, however, is that Moody was never the same person after he met Edward Kimball. This teacher's loving attentions from Moody's first day in class, through the ten months of nurture until the committee voted him to membership, were all used by God to bring Moody to repentance.

Moody noted years later that when Christ first beckoned him to repent and follow, there was "a conflict with my will." He said he resisted Christ's call for some time because "I had a terrible battle to surrender my will, and to take God's will."[33] When Moody finally surrendered to Christ, the inner conflicts and battles with his will subsided—at least for a season. "I remember the morning on which I came out of my room after I had first trusted Christ," Moody told a Boston congregation forty years later.

I thought the old sun shone a good deal brighter than it ever had before—I thought that it was just smiling upon me: and as I walked out upon Boston Common and heard the birds singing in the trees I thought they were all singing a song to me. Do you know, I fell in love with birds. I never cared for them before. It seemed to me that I was in love with all creation. I had not a bitter feeling against any man, and I was ready to take all men to my heart. If a man has not the love of God shed abroad in his heart, he has never been regenerated. If you hear a person get up in the prayer-meeting and begin to find fault with everybody, you may doubt whether his is a genuine conversion; it may be counterfeit. It has not the right ring, because the impulse of a converted soul is to love, and not to be getting up and complaining of everyone else and finding fault.[34]

Perhaps the new convert actually felt all this joy immediately upon repentance, but the mature Moody might have overstated the rapidity and depth of the transformation. Years later he apparently forgot how censorious and argumentative he became rather soon after joining Mount Vernon Church. During the spring and summer of 1856, Moody had a falling-out with Uncle Samuel. No one in the family could discern all the causes, and the few letters home give only clues that the nephew and uncle could not agree on some fundamental issues. Many years later, family lore glossed over the conflict and downplayed Dwight's own cantankerousness. His "position in his uncle's store seemed to offer little promise for the future; for, with extremely conservative methods, his uncle did not feel the same enthusiasm that fired the young man."[35]

MOVING OUT OF BOSTON

Whatever the issues, as early as October, 1855, Dwight Moody had fallen out of love with Boston and its sunshine, birds, and Commons. He was clearly restless, dissatisfied, and intrigued by a Holton cousin's plan to move west. "Frank is agoin west in the spring," he wrote home on October 11, and he noted he would be home next summer "if I do not go west."[36]

After a trip home for a few weeks in the early summer, Moody still could not reconcile differences with Uncle Samuel. Added to these woes were his problems with the Mount Vernon Church. Membership did not make the Northfield transplant feel that he really belonged among this congregation of relatively well-educated and affluent people. Furthermore, Moody's newfound faith increasingly manifested itself in outspokenness at prayer meetings, and he con-

Betsy Moody (D. L. Moody's mother) circa 1865

stantly searched for places to channel a growing evangelistic zeal.
The pastor and deacons were apparently unable to help Moody find
constructive ways to use his energy. Instead, they urged him to be
quiet in meetings and generally tried to bridle his enthusiasm. Several years later Moody confided to a friend that in both Boston and the
local church he "felt like a caged bird. The settled and finished condition of everything around him was a constant restraint. There
seemed to be no room for him anywhere."[37]

Betsy Moody promptly found a solution. She urged Dwight to
come back to Northfield and head up the family. She frequently
made clear that he should never have gone to Boston in the first
place. Out of loyalty to his mother, he tried to go home again. Indeed,
that is one reason he ventured back to the homestead in summer
1856. But Northfield was too confining for the young man who had
tasted the diversity and excitement of urban life. And while he might
have given in to his mother's pleas—especially because her oldest

son, Isaiah, had disappeared thirteen years earlier—this emotional appeal lost its effect when Isaiah unexpectedly returned home in July 1856.

Betsy Moody wrote a letter on July 5, 1856, explaining the grand reunion:

> I have some good news to tell you. . . . Last Thursday as I sat eating my dinner I looked at the east window and there stood a gentleman with his arms folded looking in at me. [I first thought he was a tramp but] . . . the next instant I went to him, said did you think I did not know you, said he, can you and will you forgive me and burst out crying. it was some time before he could speak again, then he said are all alive. I told him yes and tried to get him in the house but he said he could not come in until he had thanked God for preserving our lives until his return.[38]

"I have always been a man of impulse," Dwight Moody once told his son William. "Almost everything I ever did in my life that was a success was done on impulse. . . ."[39] On impulse he left Northfield and moved to Boston in 1854. Now in autumn 1856, just as New England's leaves were beginning to turn to glorious shades of auburn and gold, he acted impulsively again. The experience of early summer showed him he could not go home again—at least he would not be happy if he did. Boston, to be sure, was more to his liking than rural Massachusetts, but the contentment his Holton relatives found in that conservative, class-conscious city continued to elude him.

Early in September, without informing his mother, he packed his few belongings and boarded a westbound train. On September 11, he stepped out in Chicago, more than a thousand miles from his Massachusetts home.

CHAPTER THREE

CHICAGO
1856–1860

*"Your Son Here in the West [Is]
Surrounded by Temptations on All Sides"*

W hen Dwight L. Moody arrived in Chicago, two natures were
at war in his soul. One part of him burned with ambition to
acquire assets of $100,000, a fortune in an era when workers seldom
earned more than a dollar a day. Inside this same man was an equally powerful yearning to talk to people about the sickness of their
souls—a terminal illness that he was convinced could only be cured
by the Lord Jesus Christ.[1] The youthful, booming city of Chicago nurtured both of these drives.

Moody could not have picked a place to work and live where
expectations were higher for making fortunes. This young city located on the southwestern shore of Lake Michigan had only 350 people
in 1830. By 1850 the population had jumped to 29,963. The total had
exploded to approximately 84,000 by the time the New Englander
arrived in 1856, and that number would soar to more than 112,000
four years later in 1860. Americans, particularly from the northeastern states and Atlantic seaboard, were moving to Chicago by the
thousands, as were immigrants from Ireland, Great Britain, Scandinavia, Germany, and other parts of western Europe. Because of
Chicago's ideal location in the center of a rapidly growing middle
western grain belt, people thronged to the Windy City to take advantage of seemingly endless job opportunities.

Natural arteries of transportation connect Lake Michigan with
the Gulf of Mexico by way of the Chicago River, which flows to the
Des Plaines River and on to the Illinois River that merges into the
Mississippi. The natural waterway from the Great Lakes to the Gulf
was enhanced by the Illinois and Michigan Canal, an enormous

ditch started in 1836 and finished in 1848, which linked Lake Michigan and the Illinois River.[2]

Of much more importance, however, was the railroad network emanating from Chicago. Although Illinois rail lines were plotted on paper as early as 1836, the first functional line came in 1848. That year ten miles of track were opened westward from Chicago. By 1855, seven years later, three thousand miles of track (ten trunk lines and eleven branch lines) reached out in all directions from the city. Within two years a thousand more miles were laid. Three years later Chicago was the railroad center of Illinois, and Illinois led the Union in total rail miles.[3] A railroad map of 1860 made Chicago look like the body of a spider, with long legs reaching out in every direction except into the lake.

Chicago was not only the heart of America's vast rail network, but she was also the leader in grain shipping by 1858. Because the transportation network gave the growing metropolis access to an enormous agricultural hinterland as far north as Wisconsin and Michigan, west to Minnesota and Iowa, and southward into the heart of Dixie, the Windy City became a livestock market as well as a grain storage center; and quickly it became a leader in food processing and distribution. Farm equipment manufacturers relocated to this commercial hub, as did manufacturers and wholesalers of dry goods, shoes, boots, hardware, and groceries.

Along with this industrial, transportational, and commercial boom came thousands of unskilled and skilled job openings, plus employment opportunities in services and sales. Likewise there was a real-estate boom of unprecedented proportions, and hefty profits were being made in every legal and illegal enterprise imaginable. In brief, Chicago was the dominant regional metropolis when Moody arrived, and it quickly outdistanced its rivals to become one of the major cities in America. It was the Queen City of a New West where men and women from the East, South, and Europe were flocking to find opportunities to earn a living wage and buy a piece of land they could call their own.[4]

Chicago's atmosphere was exhilarating for an ambitious young man like D. L. Moody. Within two days another Holton relative, Uncle Calvin, who owned a farm less than thirty miles northwest of the city in Des Plaines, helped his nephew find employment with two Massachusetts friends, Charles and Augustus Wiswall. The Wiswalls were proprietors of a thriving boot and shoe store on Lake Street in the city.[5] One of the Wiswalls said that when the young man from Boston arrived, "His ambition made him anxious to lay up money. His personal habits were exact and economical. As a salesman he was . . . [a] zealous and tireless worker." A fellow clerk recalled that from the outset "Moody was a first-rate salesman. It was his particular pride to make his column foot up the largest of any on the book, not only in the way of sales, but also of profits."[6]

A sample of D. L. Moody's handwriting (October 7, 1858)

D. L.'S AMBITION

Letters sent by the young salesman to his family in Northfield were full of boasting about material success in this western haven of opportunity. He noted that he had an excellent position with a personable and astute entrepreneur. He was making more in a week ($30) than he had made in Boston in a month. Not only was the retail boot and shoe trade paying him well; real estate and money lending were affording ways to earn still more on the side. For one piece of land that he purchased, he was offered a fifty-dollar profit before he had put a penny down. Likewise, he was lending money to a man for nearly 20 percent per day, and he was quickly doubling his investment on land near Uncle Calvin's farm.[7]

Despite his ambition to stockpile a small fortune, Moody was generous with his money. He sent more than two months' wages by New England standards to his sister Lizzie, who was teaching school in New Hampshire. He also sent money to remodel and expand his mother's cramped living quarters on the Northfield homestead—a place that doubled as a dormitory for any or all of the nine children who happened to be there. Moody also loaned money at no interest to a relative down on his luck.[8]

Moody's material goals, achievements, and boastings were in tension with a young but vibrant spirituality. After his conversion back in Boston, he felt a need to speak up during church meetings and become more active in church-related work. A strong impetus to his spiritual growth also came as he rode across the country on the train from Boston to Chicago. Ironically, as the steam engine pulled him to the city of economic opportunity, two women passengers who engaged him in conversation apparently drew him into deep and lengthy spiritual conversations, causing him to think more about the Lord Jesus Christ than the rival god Mammon that was drawing him to Illinois.[9] In the same vein, he had a memorable encounter with a Chicago woman who learned that he was rooming and boarding above Wiswall's shoestore. She offered him free lodging and meals at her house if he would give up the shoe trade and go into full-time Christian service. He eventually boarded with the Christian woman as a paying customer, but the very suggestion that he turn his back on business and pour all of his energy into "Christian work" became an irritant causing constant distress.[10]

If Chicago of the late 1850s rewarded people who were economically ambitious, it also provided stimulation and encouragement for men and women who were spiritually hungry and alert. Churches grew fast—almost keeping pace with the population. Roman Catholic churches and most Protestant denominations experienced prodigious growth, and the number and size of new worship facilities flourished as well. By the time Dwight Moody arrived, churches were already beginning to segregate along ethnic and economic class lines. Several major denominations had started outreach missions to the poor, and both Catholics and Protestants were planting churches among the major non-English-speaking peoples. Bessie L. Pierce, one of Chicago's ablest historians, revealed that in the mid-nineteenth century

> The churches . . . faced the problem of keeping pace not only with the physical expansion of the city, but also with the adjustment necessary to the unprecedented conditions created by an urban civilization and by a rapidly increasing wealth. The physical manifestations of church growth paralleled other aspects of development. From the South Side religious bodies spread into the North and West divisions as these sections were built up. Within sixteen years [1848] after Chicago was incorporated as a town, her citizens proudly acclaimed her "the city of churches," the place of a "congregation of spires."[11]

D. L.'S CHRISTIAN FAITH

Nineteen-year-old Dwight Moody quickly discovered that the religious life of Chicago was more than buildings and congregations. People were friendlier as a whole than they were in Boston. The new West had more of a leveling effect on society than historic Boston had, with its two centuries of tradition. He wrote to his mother that less than a week after his arrival "I went into a prayer-meeting" and within a few minutes "I had friends enough." He was heartily welcomed and treated as though he were a flesh-and-blood relative. Boston at its best was never so warm.[12]

Moody's letters to his family reveal that his interest in Christian spirituality began to rival his joy in making money. Indeed, for two years he celebrated his pursuit of money in the same letters that he enthusiastically wrote about things of the soul. For example, in early 1857 he bragged to his brother George about quickly earning 25 percent on a $100 land investment. He rejoiced that he "lent 100 dollars the other day for 17 per sent a day. I tell you hear is the place to make money." A few sentences after unabashedly revealing his sin of usury, he urged George to study "the promises in the Bible," maintaining "I find the better I live the more enjoyment I have and the mor I think of God and his love the less I think of this worlds troubles. George don't let any thing keep you from the full enjoyment of Gods love." He concluded by saying "I think it become Christians to pray for each other. I have brout you be for God in my prayers and I hope you have don the same. Yours in Christ."[13]

There is no evidence of Moody's being troubled by the wide gap between his lifestyle and biblical teaching, but this is certainly un- derstandable. For a man who was just becoming acquainted with the Bible, it probably never occurred to him that his interest rates were usurious. Instead he merely went with the flow of the culture, charg- ing all that the borrower would pay.

TEMPTATIONS FOR A YOUNG BELIEVER

Young Dwight Moody brings to mind Dr. Samuel Johnson's adage about a dancing dog: What is remarkable is not that the dog dances awkwardly but that he dances at all. Remembering that Moody had been a Christian for less than a year before he moved to Chicago, it is astounding that he was in a prayer meeting six nights after arriving in the city, that he found a church to join, and that he avoided the powerful temptations to frequent saloons, gambling dens, and houses of prostitution. Such entertainment establishments were more ubiquitous than churches and prayer meetings. In fact, the so-called "City of Churches" was even more famous for its wide- open vice and crime. By the time Moody stepped off the train, Chicago had more than one hundred houses of prostitution beckon- ing the wide-eyed young men from farms who had never seen such seductively clad women. The police, according to a March 1858 Chicago newspaper report, could easily arrest a thousand prostitutes on any given morning. Gambling, brawling, and drunken orgies were so commonplace that the local press was calling for an all-out effort of moral reform.[14]

In the midst of these temptations, D. L. Moody remained chaste, sober, and frugal, but he admitted he struggled. He wrote to his mother and begged her to pray because "your son here in the West [is] surrounded by temptations on all sides." Nevertheless, he remained faithful, worked hard, and earned the respect of his em- ployers. Soon he was sent on business trips, traveling the length and breadth of the state. He pushed himself to a point that would have broken most men, and he always determined to be back in Chicago by Saturday night so that he could be in Sunday school and church.[15]

D. L.'S CHURCH WORK

Typically Moody devoted six days a week to business, with Sundays given solely to God's work. Soon after arrival in the Windy City, he transferred his membership from Boston's Mount Vernon Church to Chicago's Plymouth Congregational Church. He followed Dr. Kirk's advice to stay in the same Calvinistic tradition. In his typically impetuous style, he immediately determined to be more than a passive worshiper. Years later his son William said that he turned to what was probably the only hands-on church experience he ever had before moving to Boston—that of being a recruiter for the Northfield Unitarian Sunday school—and he remembered he handled his job rather well. Consequently he "at once hired a pew, which he undertook to fill every Sunday." He hailed idle young men off street corners, he beckoned early risers from rooming houses, and he even went into saloons and called forth young inebriates who were getting drunk in the ubiquitous watering holes that were open on Sundays. "Whether the novelty of the invitation or the irresistible earnestness and cordiality of the young man [was the reason, he] induced a large number to attend." William Moody pointed out that "the object was at any rate attained, and before long he was renting four pews, which he filled every Sunday with his strangely assorted guests."[16]

Despite quantifiable success in footwear sales and Sunday school recruiting, Moody displayed a general sense of restlessness. Soon after he moved to Illinois, he grew a beard that not only made him look less boyish, but also placed him in step with a fashion sweeping the land. But a series of photographs taken during the 1850s and 1860s show that he was not sure what image to portray. He had both partial and full beards in 1858 and 1859; mutton chops in 1862; long chin whiskers in 1864, and a full beard again in 1865. But dissatisfaction with personal appearance only manifested a deeper unrest that erupted in many ways. First of all, he changed employers with almost as much regularity as he changed facial hair. By 1857 he left Wiswalls and joined the ranks of C. H. Henderson and Company. Within twenty-four months he was on the staff of Buel, Hill and Granger. For each employer he sold footwear and collected accounts owed his employers, but all in all he worked for three firms in less than four years and he engaged at least three different places of lodging.[17]

There was also a restlessness in Moody's church affiliation. He joined and attended the Plymouth Church regularly, but within a few months he also was going to an early Sunday school class at the First Methodist Episcopal Church. If the mixing of Plymouth's Calvinism with First M.E.'s Wesleyanism would have perturbed some men with theological pretensions, Moody seemed unbothered by such doctrinal and denominational differences. It is doubtful that he even understood them at this time. Consequently, Moody attended both churches and recruited nonchurched young men for each place. Likewise, he frequently went to prayer meetings at a third institution—the First Baptist Church—where he became well acquainted with "Mother" H. Phillips—a woman who became a spiritual mentor to him and several other young men. At First Baptist he also met Emma Revell, his future wife; they would be married in that church in 1862.[18]

CHICAGO WINDS

Two mighty winds—one economic and the other religious—were blowing through Chicago in the late 1850s, and Moody felt the effects of both. The first—a surging economy—put lots of money in his pockets and the pockets of others. The nationwide Panic of 1857—a financial and commercial panic precipitated by the August 1857 failure of the New York City branch of the Ohio Life Insurance and Trust Company—had little lasting effect on Chicago. Although there was a shortage of money during the winter of 1857–1858, there were still brisk land sales, and livestock and grain inundated Chicago markets. For D. L. Moody it was mostly business as usual. He was lending money, purchasing land, and building up a substantial savings account. In a letter to his brother in February 1858, he complained that money was scarce so collections were more difficult than usual. He noted that collectors from other states were finding times tough as well. Consequently grain, and even building and land mortgages, were taken on account in place of cash. But for Moody, business was so brisk that he continued to travel throughout Illinois, and he could not find time to visit his mother. His personal financial situation was so strong by 1859 that he made plans to wipe out his mother's indebtedness.[19]

Between 1856 and 1860 more than a million acres of land for farming was carved up and sold along the railroad routes. These parcels were laid out from Chicago in the north to the tip of southern Illinois, and westward and northward into Minnesota and Iowa. Hundreds of thousands of tons of grain were stored in hastily constructed elevators along rail lines at river junctions in the upper

Midwest, and farmers sometimes waited for hours or even days to have their wagonloads of wheat, corn, rye, and oats weighed and sold to agents who shipped them on to Chicago for processing and distribution. During these years millionaires were made in Chicago, as men like Philip Armour built an empire in meatpacking; Marshall Field took advantage of the need for dry goods; and Cyrus Mc-Cormick made a fortune manufacturing new types of harvesting equipment that enabled farmers to cultivate vast acreages of the rich lands of Illinois, Iowa, Minnesota, and Wisconsin.

Moody himself was amassing a substantial nest egg. By 1860 he had somewhere between $7,000 and $12,000 stashed away. He was debt free, and his income was increasing annually.[20]

As the economic wind carried D. L. Moody and others to prosperity, a religious gale hit the Chicago area as well. This wind was so powerful that it altered the course of many lives, including D. L. Moody's. Although several prominent historians have argued that the so-called Revival of 1858 was a rather minor awakening that can be explained as a response to the financial panic that began in August 1857, the evidence is strong that it was much more.[21] Many Chicago newspapers reported signs of revival already in 1856, and Moody wrote to his mother on January 6, 1857, that "there is a great revival of religion in this city." He had been too busy to "leave business" and visit Uncle Calvin (only twenty-five miles away) for either Christmas or New Year's, but he did find time to "go to meeting every night."[22]

Revival in the City—and in the Shoe Salesman

In the last weeks of 1856 there was an unusual excitement about prayer, the Holy Spirit, and walking more faithfully with the Lord. Moody himself began attending numerous meetings in late 1856 and on into 1857. Unless he was out of town on business—and this was often the case by 1857—he was in a prayer meeting every evening. Mrs. H. Phillips, or "Mother" Phillips as she was known at First Baptist Church, spent much time nurturing this new convert from Massachusetts. She taught him to be more faithful in prayer, and she also passed on to him her enthusiasm for lost souls. Mother Phillips actively participated in the great revival, and she is probably the person responsible for the rhetorical changes in Moody's letters home. After he fell under her spiritual care, his letters stressed the importance of prayer—especially for the need that we have for one another's prayers. He also revealed concerns about the spiritual well-being of his brothers, and he urged his sister Lizzie to use her influence as a teacher to introduce the students to prayer and memorization of Scripture—in particular Psalm 23.[23]

Mother Phillips

Because Moody began rooming and taking meals at Mother Phillips's house in 1857, she had ample opportunities to encourage him and help him grow in the faith. From her he learned not only the importance of prayer, Bible study, and Scripture memorization, but she also stressed the importance of child evangelism and disciplemaking. These were new concepts to the enthusiastic but untrained shoe dealer. Most of his service to the Lord had consisted of direct, cold evangelism, followed by bringing as many men to church services as would follow his lead. He mentioned in one of his anecdote-laden sermons many years later that when he first moved to Chicago, he would fill several pews at his church with men he had rounded up, but he never talked to them about their souls or made any attempt to do follow-up work. He assumed a good sermon in an orthodox church was what they needed. It never occurred to him to do more.[24]

During the revival, many Chicago churches started rescue missions to reach men and women who were broken by the harsh realities of urban life. Alcoholics, opium addicts, prostitutes, and many others who were destitute because of illness, injury, and other varieties of sin and bad luck were given meals, clothing, counsel, and temporary shelter. Gospel services were also held in those missions where city missionaries attempted to minister to lost and sick souls. Besides rescue missions, the revival inspired churches and individuals to reach out to the thousands of poor children who roamed the streets and alleys of the lowest social and economic class neighborhoods. Mother Phillips was deeply involved in Sunday-school work among impoverished street children. She seems to be the first person to urge Moody to work in this unglamorous yet fruitful vineyard.

J. B. Stillson

Mother Phillips was not the only person who offered spiritual encouragement to Dwight Moody. J. B. Stillson, a man perhaps twice Moody's age, frequently engaged in evangelistic work among sailors who lived in ships or lodging houses along the Chicago River. A Presbyterian elder and a recent transplant from New York, Stillson often handed out New Testaments and tracts and did street preaching among seamen who were not likely to frequent a church.

One spring day in 1857, Stillson encountered a "stout, hearty-looking" twenty year old who was walking the riverway "doing the same thing." The two evangelists immediately teamed up. Moody was attracted to Stillson's "fatherly ways," and he asked the New Yorker to take him along when he did outreach ministry. Moody confessed that he wanted to work for the Lord Jesus Christ, but he "did not very well know how." Stillson took the eager young Christian under his care, showing him how to be a soul physician to the poor people in the shipping industry, as well as those in hospitals and jails. Together Stillson and Moody recruited children for at least twenty different mission Sunday schools, feeling more comfortable in bringing youngsters to other teachers than in doing instructional work themselves.[25]

Clearly Stillson was sent from God to Dwight Moody. He served as a surrogate father, and he helped Moody study the Bible in a careful and systematic fashion. Stillson recalled that when the two first met, Moody had no idea of how to study. Indeed, "his method of reading the Bible had been to open the book at random, and begin with the first chapter that caught his eye." Stillson taught him how to study each book of the Bible as a whole, and he introduced him to aids such as a Bible dictionary and a concordance. Just as important as teaching the neophyte to get more out of Scripture, the older man met with his wide-eyed disciple once a week before they went out to witness. During those times he taught Moody the importance of seeking the Lord's blessing in the work they were undertaking that night. Only after a "season of prayer for God's blessing upon the work they were about to do" did the two men venture forth to visit the sick, read the Bible to shut-ins, or encourage, sing, and pray with those whom the Lord led them to see. A book Stillson loaned to Moody—George Mueller's *A Life of Trust*—proved also to have a powerful impact.[26]

Room to Grow

If Moody was learning to pray, study Scripture, and witness in a more effective manner, he still bore the marks of an immature Christian. Rather than lead men and women into the presence of Christ so that He could convict them of sin, Moody felt a need to tell everyone in his range of influence what they needed to do to live holier lives. Some of Moody's associates from the late 1850s in Chicago paid him no compliment when they said "Moody was a Puritan. He hated theaters, billiards, cards, and all such pastimes," and he never failed to make his point of view known. In later years he mentioned with sadness that he had had a horrid temper for several years after his conversion—a confession that can be corroborated by his Chicago associates. A fellow clerk remembered that their zealous friend came "into the store one night from some religious meetings" to discover some of his friends involved in a friendly game of checkers. "In an instant he seized the board, dashed it to pieces, and before a word could be spoken, dropped upon his knees and began to pray." Presumably the prayer was for the souls of his co-workers, not a confession of his own fiery, self-righteous temper.[27]

Moody had plenty of room left for spiritual maturity, but his desire to serve the Lord and work for souls was extraordinary. His sincerity, guilelessness, and seemingly boundless energy for kingdom work transformed most of his critics and detractors into admirers. Although he had learned much from others—and his desire to learn was quite humble and purposeful—he went about his avocation of ministry with an originality and effectiveness that could only be supernatural in origin.

A NEW SUNDAY SCHOOL

For a few months Moody tried working with new mission schools that were multiplying during the revival. Soon, however, he set out on his own and organized a new school. It was not that Moody was a lone ranger. On the contrary, he knew his limitations and sought help from others with more experience. Nevertheless, he detected that most mission schools were not reaching the lowest social and economic levels of society. Well-intentioned teachers and superintendents of these mission Sunday schools seldom attracted and almost never kept the poorest of the poor. Moody was discouraged when he led little flocks to these schools, only to see them flee the next week. The problem was that the schools were designed for children who understood discipline and orderliness. In brief, the most deprived children were being forced into a middle-class mold that would not contain them. The typical mission Sunday school was organized by people who simply did not understand these children's types of homes and families or lack of families.

Moody found himself increasingly attracted to children forced to live in the most degrading conditions imaginable. Most city missionaries avoided going to the neighborhoods and dwelling places of those on the lowest rung of society's ladder. Moody was one of the few who had the audacity and courage to go into the worst district of Chicago, "the Sands." Sometimes labeled "Little Hell," this is where Moody went to rescue souls. The Sands, located just north of the Chicago River on Lake Michigan's shore, was a place where children usually had only one parent—and that one was typically an alcoholic or drug addict. Children in Little Hell were usually illiterate. They never attended school because no parent made them go; and in any case, the impoverished family needed them to find ways to help buy food, clothing, and fuel for heat and cooking. These children were emotionally and physically wounded. Often beaten,

An artist's illustration of "Crazy" Moody with the children of "the Sands" in the 1860's

sexually abused, malnourished, and exposed to drinking, gambling, fighting, and prostitution, these youngsters were discarded and treated like the rats and other vermin that roamed their wooden shanties and tenement hovels.

Chicagoans were warned to stay away from the Sands. Foolhardy people who drifted there, especially after dark, usually experienced a mugging or worse; and if they survived their exploration, they never went back. Even the police gave Little Hell no more than a cursory glance, allowing the place, as one contemporary phrased it, to attract "bad women and worse men, who had fallen too low to feel at home anywhere else."[28]

Young, trim, strong, and fast, Dwight Moody entered the Sands armed with a God-given confidence that he was to rescue the children. With only about three years of formal schooling, a reality that put him at a disadvantage in polite company, he found in Little Hell a place where his meager learning would not be noticed. Furthermore, Moody knew what it was like to live with only one parent, and he had experienced loneliness and poverty, if not the exposure to crime, physical abuse, and sexual degradation.

In 1858 Moody rented a vacant, decrepit wooden saloon. He cleaned it up as well as he could and turned it into "Sabbath School" for the urchins of the Sands. In those early days he had no chairs or tables, so he had the children sit on the floor—a posture they both liked and were used to. An old barrel served as a stand for the Bible and kerosene lamp. Superintendent Moody recruited teachers from the business class—usually churchgoing men stirred up by the revival to do more than attend worship services and prayer meetings. With the help of his mentor Stillson (who helped until business required him to go back to New York in June 1859) and an amateur musician named Trudeau, they enticed scores of girls and boys to leave Little Hell for a couple of hours on Sunday night.

A Unique Style

A man from Peoria, Illinois, told a Canadian Sunday school convention in the mid-1870s that he visited Moody's school in the late 1850s. He described the scene in this manner:

> The first meeting I ever saw him at was in a little old shanty that had been abandoned by a saloonkeeper. Mr. Moody had got the place to hold a meeting in at night. I went there a little late; and the first thing I saw was a man standing up, with a few tallow candles around him,

holding a negro boy, and trying to read to him the story of the Prodigal Son; and a great many of the words he could not make out, and had to skip. I thought, if the Lord can ever use such an instrument as that for His honour and glory, it will astonish me. After that meeting was over Mr. Moody said to me, "Reynolds, I have got only one talent: I have no education, but I love the Lord Jesus Christ, and I want to do something for Him; and I want you to pray for me."[29]

Because the little "street Arabs," as they were derisively dubbed in those days, had no interest in interrupting their Sunday evenings to attend a meeting where singing, prayer, and Bible readings were a three-part venue, Moody had to pull out all of his entrepreneurial skills to draw them in. No doubt remembering the old man in Greenfield who gave him a penny, Moody offered pennies or pieces of maple-sugar candy to any youngster who would accompany him to meetings. A few cynics said it was unbiblical to bribe souls to hear about Jesus, but one of Moody's defenders noted that "Moody's missionary sugar" was no different except in kind from the enticements "offered to more elegant sinners by the ministers and managers of fashionable congregations." Moody's friend argued that "fine architecture, fresco and gilding; inlaid pulpits, and upholstered pews; three-bank organs; quartette choirs, whose music costs a dollar a stave; chimes of bells; elaborate vestments; rhetoric, poetry, and all manner of literary and social attractions, as used in the higher circles of society,—are so many arguments in favor of that missionary sugar."[30]

A Growing School

The Sunday evening meetings in the renovated saloon became popular. Soon Moody's fame spread among the children in the Sands. Every Sunday session had prayer, singing, Bible readings, and stories, and each part of the class was punctuated by fights, screams, scuffles, and laughter. Moody's gatherings were much noisier than the typical Sunday school or mission school, and no doubt the odor of unwashed bodies and filthy clothes made "Mr. Moody's School" unusual by any standards. Nevertheless, the children thronged to the place in ever-increasing numbers. Outsiders began to refer to Moody as "Crazy Moody"—after all, who in his right mind would go into the Sands at night, let alone try to civilize those monsters? But Moody was driven forward by a deep sense of God's calling and a growing love for his rowdies. "One important qualification for his work," wrote his Chicago friend W. H. Daniels, "was an intense and almost womanly love for children. He never seemed happier than when in the midst of a crowd of boys and girls, with whom he romped in the wildest fashion, beating them at their own sports and games, until he won their fullest confidence. . . ."[31]

About this time a marvelous photograph was taken of Moody with fourteen boys from the Sands. Dubbed his "Body Guard," these street-hardened lads took a liking to Moody. They spent much time in his presence and promised to protect him from anyone who disapproved of religion or his school. Some of their names, carefully preserved and recorded by William Moody, were splendidly descriptive and indicative of their rough-and-tumble lives: Red Eye, Smikes, Madden the Butcher, Jackey Candles, Giberick, Billy Bluecannon, Darby the Cobbler, Butcher Lilray, Greenhorn, Indian, Black Stove Pipe, Old Man, and Rag-Breeches Cadet. (One boy is unnamed.) The well-preserved photograph shows, as do the names, that there was an African-American and a Native American among the group. The "Body Guard" was a remarkably diverse clan for pre-Civil War America. It was a singular fraternity that offered a preview of what Moody would promote in his schools several decades later.[32]

Relocating the School

By autumn 1859 "Crazy Moody" had outgrown the saloon-turned-school. With growing confidence in God's provision for the work, he went to the mayor of Chicago and received permission to use a large hall over the city's North Market. The facility was frequently used for dances on Saturday nights, so Moody and some of his boys spent Sunday afternoons removing empty beer barrels, sweeping out cigar butts and sawdust, and giving the spacious place some fresh air.

By the time Moody moved his Sunday school into the North Market Hall, he was attracting more than three hundred students. He, Stillson, and Trudeau had been doing most of the work with a few other volunteers from First Baptist, First Methodist, and Plymouth Congregational churches, but they desperately needed more help. As soon as he moved into the larger facility, he recruited two volunteers who proved to be more than longtime and faithful assistants; they became confidants and lifelong companions. Each left profound marks on Moody's character and work.

Two Valuable Workers: Revell and Farwell

The first and more important was Emma Charlotte Revell. Born in London, England, July 5, 1843, she was six and a half years younger than Dwight. In 1849 her parents, Fleming Hewitt and Emma Manning Revell, relocated the family to Chicago. Raised in relatively comfortable circumstances—her father was a skilled ship construction worker—Emma was the third of seven children. In many ways she and her future husband were polar opposites. Dwight Moody was 5'9" tall with large bones, a muscular body, and pronounced features. She was several inches shorter, small-boned, petite, and fine-featured. Emma Revell was by far the better educated of the two; and she had the benefit of a stabler and more cultured family life. Both of her parents lived until she was a young woman, nurturing and encouraging her while she grew up. They also possessed the good fortune to shield her from the grinding poverty that stalked the Northfield Moodys.

Apparently the Revell family was only nominally Christian in the 1850s. Emma committed her life to the Lord Jesus Christ in late 1856 or early 1857 during the revival. At that time she joined the First Baptist Church, and her first contact with D. L. Moody was when he was asked to tell her church's Sunday-school assembly about his ministry among the poor. In 1858 they became well acquainted when she agreed to take a Sunday evening class for his mission school. Emma occasionally helped Dwight when his school was still in the old saloon building, and she pledged regular teaching support once he moved to North Market Hall and issued a call for help.[33]

John V. Farwell was the second significant person to respond to Moody's plea for aid. Born in rural western New York in 1825, he moved with his family to Ogle County, Illinois, approximately one hundred miles west of Chicago in 1838. Living and laboring on the family's little farm on the Rock River for the next few years, he learned to read and write well enough to attend the Mount Morris Seminary during the winter terms between 1841 and 1844. Then in autumn 1844, after the crops were in, nineteen-year-old John Farwell hitched a ride on a wheat wagon bound for Chicago. With $3.45 in his pocket, some formal education in his head, and a zeal to make a fortune, Farwell responded to the lure of urban America. Like thousands of other young men in the mid-nineteenth century, he said good-bye to the back-breaking drudgery of farm life and set his eyes on the city, where he hoped to make an easier living in business. Starting out as a bookkeeper for a Chicago firm, he quickly moved into dry goods sales. He worked for other men for four years, but in 1849 he joined another firm where he soon became a partner. This rural raised and educated young man, who had earned only $96 his

John V. Farwell

first year in Chicago, made $600 in 1849. Two years later the firm bore only his name, J. V. Farwell & Company, and annual sales were more than $100,000 and growing.[34]

It was probably in 1858, at Chicago's First Methodist Episcopal Church, that Farwell and Moody first met. Farwell was a devout Methodist who had converted at an Illinois camp meeting when he was fifteen. Radically committed to Christ from then on, he gave $50 of his first year's earnings ($96) in Chicago to the First Methodist Episcopal Church. The devout businessman recalled that his earliest recollections of Moody were of "a late attendant of a nine o'clock morning class meeting in the old Clark Street M.[ethodist] E.[piscopal] Church—coming in a little before ten o'clock." Farwell, an ambitious, punctual, and well-organized man, initially took Moody for a buffoonish, lazy Christian who never bothered to come to class on time. Many years later he recalled that his hasty judgment of Moody "haunts me still" because "I ascertained afterwards, that he came in after spending all the morning in getting poor children into a Mission Sunday School, while I was only attending because it was one of the rules of the church, and not to get spiritual motive power for Mission work for Christ as he did."[35]

Moody's example shook the prosperous entrepreneur to the core of his being. He confessed his self-centered, judgmental nature and immediately repented by getting acquainted with this man, thirteen years his junior, whose ambition for souls was putting him to shame. Farwell began to accompany the young shoe salesman-evangelist once in a while as he went into alleys and tenements to ferret out students for the first Sands mission school. When Moody won access to North Market Hall, he took advantage of Farwell's offer of any financial assistance he needed for the children's ministry. The big hall had no benches or chairs. Although this arrangement had worked in the old building, it seemed the right time to develop a more formal and reverent atmosphere.

Farwell picked up the tab for benches and chairs, and Moody promptly rewarded this generosity with an invitation to deliver one of several five-minute addresses to be given to the noisy crowd from Little Hell the following week.

When Farwell arrived he discovered that the seats had not been delivered and the "rabble of ragged children" were lined up along the walls and sprawled all over the floor. "Gathered by Mr. Moody" this throng "were repeatedly only . . . quieted to listen, by gentle music, always needed at the end of the five minute talks, to quiet the boisterous ways of this gentile sea of juvenile humanity."[36] Another Chicago man observed that for anyone who had never been to Mr. Moody's mission school, the scene before them "was a new one. All . . . previous Sunday School notions were put to flight." The obstreperous urchins were "jumping, turning somersaults, sparring, whistling, talking out loud, crying, 'Papers!' 'Black your boots!' 'Have a shine mister?'—from which state of confusion they were occasionally rescued by a Scripture reading . . . a song . . . or a speech from Mr. Moody."[37]

It was in this environment that a well-dressed and dignified John V. Farwell stepped up to speak. When he took center stage, his piercing eyes, strong face, and heavy black beard gave him an aura of authority. Likewise, his towering height for those days—about 6'4"—caused even the children from the Sands to take notice and be quiet for this thirty-four-year-old man. Farwell "ventured a few words, and only a few, lest he should weary the patience of his audience." At the close of his remarks, to his horror, he heard "himself

John Farwell and D. L. Moody with Moody's "Body Guard"—a group of his Sunday school boys from the Sands

nominated by Moody as superintendent of the North Market Mission Sunday School! Before he had time to object, the school had elected him with a deafening hurrah."[38]

That Sunday evening in 1859 solemnized a partnership and friendship that grew and lasted until Moody's death forty years later. Farwell learned from Moody the importance of putting feet to one's faith and pouring one's whole heart before Christ and "the least of these" He calls us to love. He also learned from Moody that a busy and dedicated businessman could make a difference for the kingdom of God.

On the other hand, Moody learned and gained much from Farwell. This older brother in Christ offered financial support for his mission work, and he introduced Moody to other prosperous business people who were willing to help. Farwell not only gave Moody access to an upper echelon of Chicago society, but he also taught the culturally deprived young man how to dress in more polite company, as well as how to conduct himself at meetings and meals with Chicago's social elite.[39]

The School's Method

Dwight L. Moody's boyish innocence, utter originality, and unconscious transparency and sincerity drew both Emma Revell and John V. Farwell into an ever-widening circle of admirers. Although Moody observed many Sunday school missions and sat at the feet of numerous city missionaries to learn all he could, he embarked on a markedly different path. His Sunday school was organized in a unique way. Because his children were unruly—to the point of being incorrigible, some said—they disrupted and ruined every class that they attended. Whereas other schools gave up on them—refusing to recruit or even allow their riotous presence—Moody thoughtfully and prayerfully came up with an ingenious program. He herded the "Little Hellions" into a mass meeting where they were gradually broken in like horses are broken for riding. He kept them enticed with sugar treats, pennies, or clothes, and gradually got them accustomed to sitting still and listening to a speaker. He believed that music would calm their spirits, so he had five-minute talks punctuated by a minute of freetime (rowdiness) and then songs. This rhythm was employed for approximately two hours each Sunday. Then after about three months of being gradually exposed to the disciplines of silence, listening, and sitting, he promoted them to smaller classes where there were fewer breaks and where sustained periods of singing were followed by instruction from the Bible.[40]

This singular approach was so successful that Moody became the talk of Chicago. His fame spread outside too, because whatever and whoever became important in the great metropolis became sought after in the rest of the state as well. By summer 1860 Moody wrote to his brother, informing him that his school is "on the incres all of the time." He also mentioned being invited to speak to children in another part of the state.[41]

A Famous Visitor to the School

By 1860 attendance at the North Market Hall Mission consistently ranged between 1,000 and 1,200, reaching about 1,500 by the end of the year. The program's fame was so great that President-elect Abraham Lincoln visited the school in mid-November on his first visit to Chicago after the election. He sent word that he wanted to visit this model program but he would only come on the condition that he not be asked to speak. John Farwell said that Lincoln left a dinner party early so he could see the Sunday school while it was still in session.

The president-elect looked in for a while, and "as he was about to leave Mr. Moody remarked to the school, 'If Mr. Lincoln desires to say a word, as he goes out, of course all ears will be open.'" Farwell remembered that Lincoln walked to the center of the hall in a manner that suggested he would not speak. But "he suddenly stopped, and made a most appropriate Sunday School address, in which he referred to his own humble origin." His closing words were: "With close attention to your teachers, and hard work to put into practice what you learn from them, some one of you may also become president of the United States in due time like myself, as you have had better opportunities than I had." Farwell noted that when President Lincoln issued his call for 75,000 soldier volunteers a few months later, seventy-five students and teachers who heard him that night were among the first to enlist.[42]

President Lincoln's visit to the mission school gave "Crazy Moody" some respectability among the status conscious, but what attracted quality people like Emma Revell and John Farwell to Moody was his tenderness and love for souls. One of Moody's contemporaries said, "His heart had always been sensitive and tender. He loved all the little things. He also had the instinct of helpfulness to a high degree. It [seemed] natural for him to run to the assistance of any one in trouble. . . ."[43] Moody showed a particular love for people who were the least advantaged—people hardly anyone else in Chicago was willing to touch, let alone love. The untouchables of the Windy City grew to love Mr. Moody too, and he gradually gave away treats only as favors, because he no longer needed bribes. Indeed, by 1860 Moody did not have to recruit as hard as he used to because the children were coming to him. When he came into the Sands on his pony, they ran out to greet him and asked for a ride. He not only obliged these simple requests, but he also responded when the calls were more demanding and time consuming. Because the flotsam and jetsam of Chicago did not belong to churches, there was no church home for them to turn to when the worst troubles came. Moody said "when sickness or death came into their families they used to send for me." He was sometimes involved in three or four funerals a day.[44]

The work of unofficial pastor of the Sands added pressures to the already busy schedule of Moody the businessman and overseer of the mission school. And if all of this were not enough, he became increasingly involved in the Young Men's Christian Association, an organization taking on new life as a result of the 1857–58 revival. Working alongside John Farwell, who helped organize the Chicago YMCA in the late 1850s, Moody took an active part in the YMCA's daily noontime prayer meetings when he was in town, but his travel for business frequently took him away.

D. L.'S SOUL STRUGGLE

Moody's letters reveal that he enjoyed traveling, but his deep commitment to ministry made it increasingly burdensome. Consequently, by early 1860, a struggle troubled his soul. Years later he said in a sermon that "whenever God has been calling me to higher service, there has always been a conflict with my will. I have fought against it, but God's will has been done instead of mine." Moody said that in 1860 God was calling him to give up business and go into ministry full-time. The initial skirmish of this war came several years earlier when Mother Phillips had urged him to quit business and take up "the call." Moody put this thought as far away from his mind as he could, yet it persistently returned. "When I came to Jesus Christ, I had a terrible battle to surrender my will . . . [and then in 1860] I had another battle for three months."[45]

As time passed the struggle grew fiercer because Moody earned so much money. He had at least $7,000 in the bank by 1860, and his earnings were topping $5,000 annually. Added to this sense of fulfillment was the realization that he was good at what he was doing commercially, and others were taking notice.

An especially flattering appeal came to him from the widow of his recently deceased employer, C. H. Henderson. It seems Mrs. Henderson was disappointed with the administration of her husband's estate. She was also convinced that only Dwight Moody was capable of handling outstanding collections of $150,000, and only he could be trusted to sell some valuable business property. In a letter to his mother on February 10, 1860, he admitted, "I feel honored for they had a great many friends here. [Also] two nephews who are good business men" are in the family, but Mrs. Henderson "said I must take it. I have never been put in such responsible situation in my life and my prayer is that I may do myself credit." This assignment "will take me three years to close it up at least."[46]

If all of this was not enough to cause Moody agony and sleepless nights, he had the added pressure of being in love. To his mind no woman in the world could suit him but Emma C. Revell. He loved her and he wanted her for his wife. To be sure she was only seven-teen. Even if she said yes, the wedding would have to wait for a year or two. But would she agree to marry a man who walked away from a lucrative career to enter ministry with no assurance of a steady in-come? And what would her parents say?

Emma Revell, the Henderson offer, and appearances notwith-standing, the call to full-time service was still there. "I fought against it. It was a terrible battle."[47]

The Girls' Sunday School Class

In the midst of this spiritual war, a series of events unfolded that helped bring an end to Moody's great inner conflict. He had a Sun-day school class of unruly girls that no one could effectively handle. He finally turned them over to a teacher who was at least keeping the noisy group quiet. One Sunday the teacher was sick, so Moody him-self took the class. "They laughed in my face," said Moody, "and I had a great mind to open the door and order them out."

Later that next week the teacher went to Moody's store, an-nouncing he must say good-bye. "I have had a hemorrhage of the lungs and the doctor tells me I can't live here; I am going home to my widowed mother to die." As Moody tried to assure him he need not fear death, the sick man said he was not fearful of death, but he grieved over the souls of the girls in his Sunday school class. Moody suggested that together they call on each of the girls "and tell them just how you feel."

Not certain he had the strength to make the calls, the teacher nevertheless agreed to Moody's suggestion. Moody ordered a car-riage and they set off to make the calls. Later Moody said, "I don't believe I should be here [in ministry] now if it had not been for that day's experience; God gave me a revelation that day." They arrived at the first house where the pale and weakened teacher said, "Mary, I must leave Chicago; I can't stay here any longer; but before I leave I want you to become a Christian." They talked awhile and then he prayed. Then Moody prayed, and the girl became a Christian.

Over the next ten days as the teacher found his strength, Moody helped him make calls on the other girls. Several days later the teacher came to Moody with good news—the last girl had yielded her heart to Christ. "I'm going home tomorrow. I have come to bid you good-bye." Moody asked him to come to one last meeting of the class that night. The weak but joyous teacher agreed to a farewell time of prayer. Moody got a message to all of the girls. "That night," he said,

"God kindled a fire in my soul that has never gone out. I can't tell you what a night it was!" The dying teacher testified about how God had given him strength to visit each of them. Then he read some Scripture and prayed. Moody said,

> He prayed for me as superintendent of the school; after he prayed I prayed; and when I was about to rise, to my surprise one of those scholars began to pray, and she, too, prayed for the superintendent. Before we rose from our knees every one had prayed. It seemed as if heaven and earth came together in that room.
>
> The next day I went back to the store, but, to my great amazement, I had lost all ambition for business.[48]

Entering Full-Time Ministry

If Moody was usually a man of impulse, the decision to renounce his treasured ambition of fortune and influence was not made impulsively. This choice to surrender his will came slowly and agonizingly over nearly four years—culminating in a powerful spiritual struggle that lasted three months. Once the decision was made, however, it was typical of Moody to move forward without looking back. Immediately he gave notice to his employers and informed close friends of his vow to the Lord. He also inauspiciously took steps to save money for the lean times ahead. Without informing anyone but his landlady, he gave up his Michigan Avenue room and board accommodations. He kept his whereabouts and lifestyle secretive because he wanted no one to know or feel pity for him. He apparently dined on cheese and crackers and took an occasional meal in a cheap restaurant. He also slept on benches in various hideaways, eventually taking a small room in a makeshift YMCA facility where he did some janitorial work and slept on chairs lined up under the staircase.[49]

Inasmuch as most people—even sincere Christians—have difficulties understanding radical obedience that leads to a life of sacrifice, it is not surprising that most of Moody's friends counseled against this "wild undertaking" of full-time ministry. Soon after he resigned his job, his old employer saw him and asked, "What are you doing now, Moody?"

"I am working for Jesus Christ" was his joyful response. To those who chided his lack of wisdom, he merely smiled and answered, "I am working for God and he is rich."[50]

Only two of Moody's closest companions—John V. Farwell and Emma Revell—refused to join the chorus of worldly wisdom urging

Moody to stay in business. For a time both of these friends remained silent and watched. However, when John Farwell saw Moody's sleeping quarters and learned that his savings were being spent for living expenses and given away to the poor, his admiration for the missionary soared. Farwell vowed that Moody would never want for the necessities of life as long as he could personally do anything about it.[51]

Farwell's support warmed Moody's heart. But Emma's response brought even more joy. Rather than flee from this "thoroughly unconventional" man, she decided she had found precisely the kind of mate she wanted to spend her life with. Only seventeen years old, but with unusual spiritual alertness, she "promised to cast her lot with his."[52]

CHAPTER FOUR

A SCHOOL OF PRACTICAL THEOLOGY
Chicago and the Civil War

1861–1865

"I Am [Driven] More Now Than Ever in My Life."

On February 5, 1861, Dwight L. Moody celebrated his twenty-fourth birthday. He could have looked back on nearly a quarter century of life and licked his wounds of hardship and deprivation. But when he found time to reflect, he refused the temptation of self-pity. His letters home are replete with a genuine spirit of gratitude for good health and good fortune. Most of all he exuded joy over his growing relationship with Jesus Christ and Emma Revell.[1]

In a paradoxical sort of way, Moody's disadvantages became his strengths. Increasingly humbled by his lack of education, the "city missionary," as he was labeled in the city directories of the early 1860s, sought out anyone who would teach him how to become a better Christian worker and disciple of the Lord Jesus Christ. God had not opened the way for formal theological education, but in the 1850s Moody was given tutors as he needed them along the way. Soon after the transplanted New Englander arrived in Chicago, Mother Phillips and the deacons at First Baptist Church taught him the foundational principles of a daily devotional life. These unheralded saints taught him that there must be spiritual depth in his personal life before God would use him for the wider work of ministry to others.

J. B. Stillson also came along and taught Moody how to study the Bible and teach its precious truths to others. John V. Farwell encouraged Moody and provided for many of his temporal and spiritual needs.

If Phillips, Stillson, and Farwell were Moody's earliest teachers, his preparatory school was the Sands. Because the rural New Englander lacked the sophistication to minister in the local churches, he went to those whose backgrounds and disadvantages matched his own. Moody suffered from no illusions about his own importance. It was not that he lacked self-esteem; rather, he had no higher educational training in theology, and at least an unspoken part of the curriculum of most theological training conveyed the wisdom that those men—and they were almost always men—who graduated were rewarded with a couple of rungs up on the ladder of social and religious mobility. They assumed they were too well educated to serve in lowly places like the Sands. It was a common pattern in the nineteenth century for the better educated clergy to minister in the wealthier, established churches of the cosmopolitan and more comfortable communities. This left the frontier and rural work, as well as ministry among the urban poor, to be undertaken by relatively less educated men and by women.[2]

D. L. Moody seemed ambitious for nothing but the rescue and nurture of souls. He had no plan to use his ministry to children and youth, his Sunday schools, or his pastoral care to the poorest of Chicago's poor as stepping-stones to loftier pulpits. To Moody, his work among the poor *was* his calling—and it was a high one indeed. He never applied for or longed for more prestigious callings, in part because he never felt educationally qualified, and also because he truly believed the work he was already doing was pregnant with eternal possibilities.

OPPORTUNITIES OF INFLUENCE

When opportunities did come to widen Moody's sphere of influence, he had not initiated them. For example, as early as 1861 he was invited to address the third annual Illinois State Sunday School Convention. The invitation came because men and women were intrigued at the scope and success of his work among poor children. Many people in urban America were trying to minister to these so-called "dangerous classes," but with little measurable success. Moody, however, was doing the work and he was doing it well. To his utter astonishment, people wanted to meet him and have him pass on to them the lessons he had learned in his school of practical theology.[3]

As Moody faithfully shared the lessons he was learning from ministering to the urban poor, he in turn discovered new sources of education for himself. In 1861, when he was invited to Peoria, Illinois, to lecture on urban Sunday schools, several pastors and lay leaders in this thriving little city gathered at the home of a local layman for dinner. One of those present, D. W. McWilliams, remembered the event this way:

> On being introduced to those present Mr. Moody soon turned to one of the ministers and said, "How do you explain this verse in the Bible?" giving the verse in full. Soon after he turned to another minister, quoted a verse, and asked, "What does that mean?" The entire conversation that day was exposition of Scripture in reply to Mr. Moody's rapid questions, and a stirring of hearts in the direction of personal work for the salvation of others. The impression made upon the guests that day was of Mr. Moody's love for the souls of others and his intense desire for Bible knowledge.[4]

The YMCA

Besides these informal seminars that Moody pursued with tireless regularity, he found the Young Men's Christian Association to be an important school of practical theology. Over the years he often repeated these or similar words: "I believe in the Young Men's Christian Association with all my heart. It has, under God, done more in developing me for Christian work than any other agency." He also praised the YMCA because it provided an avenue for him to do evangelistic ministry when no church or other organization believed he was qualified.[5]

Moody's involvement with the YMCA dates back to the Revival of 1857–1858. During that time the original association, moribund from a lack of leaders, experienced revitalization when a group of young Christian businessmen were inspired to get their eyes off themselves and start looking for ways to glorify God. In hopes of reaching some of the burgeoning population of young men who had come to Chicago searching for work, they started holding noontime prayer meetings. Headed by Benjamin F. Jacobs, John V. Farwell, Cyrus Bentley, and a half dozen others, these meetings were held daily, Monday through Friday. The gatherings were focused on prayer, praise, and worship, but a few words of challenge to non-Christians were usually spoken. When Moody was not away on business trips, he was a regular participant in the YMCA noon prayer meetings. His love for evangelism, coupled with a desire to learn from others, made him a natural for such occasions. He could regularly be found standing in front of Metropolitan Hall, hailing men and women on their way to lunch, urging them to come in for a few minutes of hymn singing and prayer.[6]

Moody made no effort to elbow his way into the little power structure that oversaw the YMCA or its daily services. What he did, however, was humbly serve wherever needs were not being met. For instance, Chicago's reorganized YMCA was decidedly evangelistic, declaring as its goal "The improvement of the spiritual, intellectual, and social condition of young men." In Chicago, at least, evangelism and spiritual nurture were highest priorities for the association until the late 1880s. Consequently, Mr. Moody's desire to rescue souls fit perfectly into the program.

Always willing to serve in lowly places, the Sunday school teacher-evangelist could be found making himself useful in more ways than ushering lost souls to meetings. For instance, after 1859, when the association rented its own facility on the First Methodist Episcopal Church block at Washington and Clark streets, Moody would get a fire started on cold days before the prayer meetings or evening lectures. He shoveled coal, carried out cinders, and voluntarily performed most of the janitorial duties for the unendowed organization.

In 1860, when Moody turned from business to pursue full-time ministry, he devoted even more time to the YMCA. The organization recognized him as their "city missionary and librarian," and he also served as unofficial janitor and superintendent. He refused compensation from the association, maintaining that the God who owned the cattle on a thousand hills would provide for his needs. Besides, he wanted to be free to come and go as God led him, without being tied to a schedule set by those who paid his salary. But even if he had wanted a salary, it is doubtful if one of any magnitude would have been forthcoming. In 1862, for example, total income to the Chicago YMCA was only $445.70. Most of this money came from membership dues, and all of it went to pay rent, utilities, and incidental expenses. In brief, there was not any money for Moody, despite John Farwell's 1861–1862 annual report that praised "Brother D. L. Moody" who "has given his entire time and energies in executing the several plans of doing good [charitable distributions of donated food, fuel and clothing] referred to herein, and to his efforts mainly are we indebted for their practical execution. Not having raised any funds outside of membership dues, we have not been able, as an Association, to make him any remuneration." Farwell went on to "recommend his continued employment as city missionary, for which service he is eminently qualified. . . ."[7]

Benefits to Moody

Moody was neither destitute nor without compensations. First of all, he had his savings, which he willingly drew upon for the necessities of life. Likewise, the association allowed him to sleep in the hall, thereby saving the cost of rent. Moody received compensation, too, from the credibility that his official appointment with the YMCA provided.

In 1861 the Chicago association assumed formal sponsorship of Moody's North Market Hall Mission and Sunday School. This provided him with respectability, contacts for teachers and donors, and a group of men to hold him accountable. Being employed by the association gave Moody access to letterhead that provided at least an element of formality to a very informal man. Finally, Moody and his ministry benefited from having loyal friends such as Farwell, the dry goods merchant, and Benjamin F. Jacobs, the successful real estate

D. L. Moody, age 25 (1862)

agent, both of whom held Moody in high esteem. No one, Moody said on countless occasions, ever counted him worthy of doing ministry until these men with the Chicago YMCA took him in, gave him an official title as city missionary and librarian, and made him believe he was valuable, if not indispensable.

Moody would weep in later years when he looked back on Chicago in the 1860s. These association men "gave me a chance when no one else had any use for me." It is significant to remember that prior to his formal ties to the YMCA, Moody was known as "Crazy Moody" by the Chicago religious community. Some of the leaders shunned him, and at least one ordained minister even berated him from a public platform. Moody had given a talk at a gathering of Sunday school workers. When he finished, the pastor took the podium and during his own speech criticized Moody, saying his address was poorly organized and made up of newspaper clippings and other ephemera. Moody's son-in-law wrote that when the pastor sat down, Dwight Moody "stepped to the front again, and said he recognized his want of learning and his inability to make a fine address; he thanked the minister for pointing out his shortcomings, and asked him to lead in prayer that God would help him to do better."[8]

Moody's humility notwithstanding, only the most insensitive observer would fail to see that such a public humiliation would cut even the most confident of men to the core. Therefore, it must have been a soothing balm when the association directors honored him with title, approval, and applause, even if there was no monetary remuneration. It also could not have been lost on Moody that these eminently successful men of high repute were publicly referring to him as "Brother Moody," thereby quietly burying the hurtful title "Crazy Moody."[9]

Benefits to the YMCA

Brother Moody became an incalculable blessing to the YMCA. The directors and officers were all businessmen. They were needed to bring credibility, stability, and funds to the work, but they were too busy to devote the time and energy necessary to keep the association going on a daily basis. Moody, on the other hand, with the energy of two or three normal men and a vision for the rescue and nurture of souls unmatched by anyone in the Windy City, lived in the headquarters and gave fifteen to twenty hours a day to the work. He continued to oversee the mission Sunday school where he did the lion's share of the teaching in the large lecture. He also started a Sunday afternoon program for young men who were eager to grow in their faith.

Along with these Sunday obligations, the city missionary constantly called on families in the Sands and other areas inhabited by the destitute and extremely poor people who had never found the promise of riches in the bustling Lake Michigan city. To these people Moody was an angel sent from above. With the help of his "Body Guard" and other young men who wanted to serve, he delivered buckets of coal, baskets of food, and bundles of clothing—most of it provided by men in the YMCA. Moody prayed for those he called upon, and he read Scriptures if they would permit it. Many of these people became Christians as a result of this ministry.

A glimpse of his work as part of the YMCA's "Visiting Committee" is revealed in a letter he wrote to one of his brothers in January, 1862:

> I am very sorry I have not answered you 3 last letters but I have had so much to do I could not find time you seam to be very anxious to know what I am doing this winter wall I will tell you. . . . I take care of the poore of the city. I have some 500 hundred or 800 people that are dependent on me for their daily food & new ones coming all of the time. I keep a sadall horse to ride around with to hunt up the poore people with & then keepe a nother horse & man to carry around the things with & then I have a man to waite on the folks as they come to my office. I make my headquarters at the rooms of the Young Mens Christian Association & [I have three meetings to attend each day] besides calling on the sick & that is not all [I] have to go into the countrey about every week to buy wood and provisions for poore also coal wheet meal & corn then I have to go to hold meetings.[10]

The treasurer of the YMCA remembered that when the YMCA was started in Chicago it was "quiet and conservative." Then Moody got involved and his presence "was like a stiff northwest breeze. His zeal and devotion were the life and hope of the Association." Some people were "shocked" by Moody's lack of a "nice sense of propriety," especially as he pointed the association away from its exclusive focus on the middle class and onto the wretched poor. As S. A. Kean saw it, under Moody's influence the YMCA "became, like the North Market Mission, a free and popular institution—extending its influence to all classes of society, and bringing the cultured and wealthy to the assistance of the ignorant and poor."

Kean also noted that Moody worked hard for long hours, yet re-

fused any salary, "saying it would embarrass him, and limit his freedom to go out at a moment's notice wherever the Lord might call
him." Kean, who was treasurer all the years Moody was involved,
said they never him paid him one dollar for his services or the money he spent for assistance to the poor.[11] The Reverend W. H. Daniels,
who knew Moody well, confirmed Kean's observations, showing
that one year during the early 1860s Moody visited 554 families and
bestowed more than $2,300 worth of charity on them. This he did
without asking the association for a dollar. To be sure, his own savings dwindled quite soon; but Moody had read George Mueller's *Life
of Trust*. If God could help Mueller feed, clothe, and house thousands of England's street urchins, Moody believed He could
certainly help ease the burdens of hundreds of bruised and broken
unfortunates in Chicago. With confidence in God, Moody stepped
out in faith—and he was not abandoned by the One he trusted.[12]

Moody became much more than the dispenser of charity for the
YMCA. He assumed leadership of the organization's evangelistic
outreaches. With him at the helm of all practical work, Chicago's association became known by the local press as the "evangelizing
organization."[13] He pulled everyone he could into the noontime
meetings, and he organized and found speakers for evening prayer
and evangelistic programs during the week. Under his influence the
Chicago association opened its doors wide for women, not just inviting them to prayer and evangelism meetings, but encouraging them
to use the reading room with its small library.[14] Moody also encouraged women to join the association as auxiliary members as early as
May 1861. In fact, the Chicago association became remarkable for
its openness to women during the years of Moody's involvement. But
women were marginalized late in the century when Moody left the
scene.[15]

Ministering to Women

Moody seems to have been freer from bias against women in
ministry than many men of his era. His Sunday school always recruited women teachers and his YMCA endeavors reflected a similar
inclusiveness. No doubt Mother Phillips's influence on him, plus the
work of women teachers in the Sands, served to show Moody the
ministerial effectiveness of women. Beyond these examples, however, Moody was profoundly affected by his own love for souls—souls
of women as well as men. In this field male or female was no issue.
To Moody's mind, Jesus had died for women as surely as He had died

for men. Therefore, women could lead souls to Christ as well as or better than men. Consequently, they should be deeply involved in kingdom work.

Without question D. L. Moody's relationship with Emma Revell reinforced his admiration for women in ministry. To Moody she was the loftiest of all people he had ever known, and time only strengthened his attitude. She was not a public speaker. In fact, she was uncomfortable opening herself up to crowds. What she could do, on the other hand, was effectively minister to souls on a one-to-one basis. Moody always said to his closest friends that Emma could get through the hard shells of souls that he could not penetrate. Whenever they ministered together he relied upon her, frequently turning over the most troubled souls to her care.

THE CIVIL WAR

All the diplomatic tact on the continent could not assuage the demons of war in the United States. Not long after Abraham Lincoln visited Moody's mission school, he was faced with a crisis of unprecedented proportions in the United States. Because Lincoln had campaigned on a platform that promised to prohibit the extension of slavery into the territories—thereby blocking the addition of more slave states to the Union—South Carolina voted to secede from the Union in December 1860. This explosive action ignited a fire that spread throughout the slave states. A month before Lincoln took office, seven states had seceded. Four more states would follow shortly after his inauguration, forming the Confederate States of America in 1861.

Few people in the Union or Confederacy had any idea of the magnitude of the impending crisis. Talk filled the air for a time about negotiating a settlement, but this illusion vanished when secessionists opened fire on Fort Sumter on April 12, 1861. Lincoln's response to this "insurrection" came three days later with a call for 75,000 three-month volunteers. His purpose was to protect Federal properties throughout the rebellious states. President Lincoln and most loyal citizens north of the Mason-Dixon line believed that a "short war, fought quickly" would once and for all time put an end to this secessionist nonsense. Southerners did not agree. The four states that had wavered on secession immediately withdrew, the Confederacy was established, and the South predicted quick and easy repulsion of any Yankee aggressors who entered their sovereign states. The Confederacy began raising and arming troops and building fortifications.

Lincoln's call for 75,000 volunteers drew an overwhelmingly supportive response. Many states, among them Illinois, immediately formed so many companies of volunteer soldiers that state quotas were filled and hundreds—even thousands—of would-be fighting men were turned away. At the outset Dwight Moody and the Chicago YMCA were involved in the mobilization effort. Many association members answered Lincoln's call, and the association held mass meetings and rallies to raise money to buy horses, food, and equipment for the hastily organized companies. Five companies of approximately 150 men each were raised by the Chicago YMCA. These were joined with the companies of the Board of Trade and Mercantile Association to form the 72nd Illinois Volunteer Regiment.[16] In response to the rapid mobilization of fighting units, a "Committee on Devotional Meetings" was also formed by the YMCA with the purpose of ministering to the spiritual needs of the local soldiers. D. L. Moody was elected chairman of the committee; serving alongside him were B. F. Jacobs and John V. Farwell.

Moody's sentiments about the national crisis had been formed years before in Massachusetts. He had relatives who had fought in the Revolutionary War and the War of 1812, making him staunchly loyal to the federal government. Furthermore, his two years in Boston had a profound impact on his love for the Union and his loathing of slavery. Emma Moody wrote in her journal that when hostilities erupted in 1861, he was deeply concerned. "To one who had always taken an intense interest in the questions of the day, and especially those which concerned his own country, it stirred his whole soul. He had lived in Boston, and had heard stirring speeches in Faneuil Hall, had imbibed much of the [anti-slavery] spirit of those times. Many of his friends enlisted, and more and more of his heart went out to the front with them."[17]

Moody Volunteering for the 72nd

As soon as the 72nd Illinois Volunteer Regiment was organized, Moody, as a friend of many but also as a representative of the YMCA, went to them, read Scripture, preached, and prayed. For a few weeks, the 72nd remained at Camp Douglas, a makeshift rendezvous camp three miles south of Chicago's city limits. This flat piece of land was transformed into a combination recruit depot, basic training center, and equipping and processing stage for Union regiments being hastily mobilized and assigned to various armies to the west and south.

The men of the 72nd loved Moody and he reciprocated their affection. The city missionary spent several hours each day and evening with these men who were enthusiastically preparing for what most of them thought was at best a summer lark or at worst a few skirmishes to bring the South back into line. Moody, like his friends, showed little awareness of the ominous war clouds that hovered over the nation. He wrote to the folks at home in early 1861 that "I do not know what is goin to become of us out here if the strife goes on South but I suppose it will come out all rite."[18]

The jubilant men of the 72nd Illinois implored Moody to join the army as their chaplain. He was almost persuaded until numerous other regiments began to descend upon Camp Douglas, turning it into a massive white-tent city that suddenly became one of the largest little cities in Illinois. When Moody saw thousands of men huddled together, playing cards, drinking whiskey, and being solicited by prostitutes who were already moving in and encircling the all-male city, he concluded, in Emma's words, "that he could do more for the soldiers by being free rather than confine himself to one regiment."[19]

Moody's decision was prescient. Within a few weeks he had overseen the printing and distribution of 3,500 Sunday School Union hymnals, complete with an American flag emblazoned on each cover. Thousands of Bibles were distributed too, as were sundry forms of gospel booklets and tracts. He held between eight and ten gospel meetings every twenty-four hours at Camp Douglas. One local observer recalled that when the flood of soldiers began inundating Camp Douglas, "Mr. Moody instantly saw and grasped the opportunity." When the first regiments arrived, Moody boldly determined to have a Christian Association Tent for each regiment. Tents were hastily pitched, and inside each one "were placed all kinds of religious literature and long tables with abundant writing material, in order to remind the soldiers of the duty of writing home."[20]

Practical Aspects of the Vision

The vision of a tent for each regiment was one thing—but practically working it out was another. Moody, however, showed some administrative brilliance. He recruited 150 clergy and lay people to manage tents, distribute literature, and serve as speakers and song leaders for the meetings. These men and women served faithfully and well. Consequently, hundreds of soldiers were converted and countless men rededicated their lives to Jesus Christ. Before the war ended 1,500 gospel services had been held at Camp Douglas. B. F. Jacobs

recalled that "in these meetings Mr. Moody seemed almost ubiquitous. He would hasten from one barrack and camp to another, day
and night, week-days and Sundays, praying, exhorting, conversing
personally with men about their souls, and reveling in the abundant
work and swift success which the war had brought within his
reach."21

During the first months of the Civil War the focus of the Chicago association's work remained on evangelism, spiritual nurture, and
encouragement to lead moral lives. This ministry was directed toward young men who were overall happy, optimistic, and afraid of
only one thing—that the secession controversy might end before
they left Camp Douglas and had an opportunity to fire a shot toward
the gray-clad Confederates. But after the force of 30,000 Union
troops advanced from its position below Washington, D.C., and
headed toward the Confederate capital at Richmond, Virginia, in
July 1861, the mood of both North and South changed dramatically.

First Bull Run

The quickly mobilized, poorly drilled, and scarcely trained
Union troops under General Irvin McDowell fought well at first.
They seemed to be on the verge of victory over the rebel defense
forces that stood between the Yankees and Richmond at Manassas
Junction. Several hours into the battle, however, General Thomas J.
Jackson moved his troops up to reinforce the beleaguered Confederate commander, General P. G. T. Beauregard. General Jackson's
timely and courageous stand halted the Union advance. Observers
noted that Jackson's troops stood like a stonewall, earning the general the sobriquet of "Stonewall." Within a few hours the Union
forces were not only blocked, but their lines broke, retreat was signaled, and the undisciplined men in blue became confused. An
orderly retreat became a rout back toward Washington. As a result
the Southerners were more convinced than ever that the Union had
neither the skill nor the will to put down the secession and reclaim
confiscated federal properties. The Union effort, on the other hand,
convinced President Lincoln and the Unionists that they needed
more troops—thoroughly trained troops—before they could go forth
to end a rebellion they had no intention of tolerating.

In the wake of this humiliating Northern defeat called the Battle
of First Bull Run, the YMCAs across the northern states determined to
form a Christian Commission. The goal was to minister to Union
troops at the growing number of camps and forts where they were be-

ing assembled and trained. A national convention was held with fifty delegates representing fifteen different YMCAs. A national YMCA headquarters was established in New York, where plans were made for every city to appoint "delegates" to go to military installations and minister to the troops. During the course of the Civil War (1861–1865), five thousand delegates were sent by the Christian Commission from the northern states to the armies. Dwight L. Moody earned the distinction of being the first official delegate sent to the Union troops. He had been working as a Chicago association representative for several months without benefit of the nationally approved title. Nevertheless, when he was dispatched to Kentucky to serve Union soldiers in October 1861, he was the first of thousands of delegates.[22]

A Civil War Chapel

Because all signs pointed to a longer war than originally expected, Moody decided a more permanent place of worship and outreach needed to be established among the soldiers at Camp Douglas. Using his contacts with many of Chicago's businessmen, he raised funds in late 1861 to build a wooden frame chapel. He wrote to his brother Samuel, "I have just raised money enough to erect a chapell for the soldiers at the camp 3 miles from the city. I hold a meeting down thar evry day & 2 in the city. . . ."[23]

In spring 1862 the tempo of the war radically changed and, along with it, the ministry of Moody and the Christian association. Lincoln discovered Ulysses S. Grant in 1862. This Ohio born, West Point-trained veteran of the Mexican War had left the regular army in the 1850s. Married to the daughter of a Missouri slaveholder, Grant moved his family to Galena, Illinois, in 1860. This quiet, unassuming man took an Illinois Volunteer Regiment at the outset of the war. He did well with his Illinois volunteers, pushing rebels all over Missouri. President Lincoln liked him and promoted him to the rank of general in the regular army. General U. S. Grant soon assembled a great fighting force at Cairo, Illinois, a strategic location at the junction of the Ohio and Mississippi rivers.[24]

Cairo

Grant's plan was to take command of Cairo—protecting it from a Confederate assault. After securing and fortifying this transportation center on the Illinois Central rail line, he planned to move bluecoats southward to gain control of the Mississippi River, thereby cutting the South in two. In one swoop Grant would truncate the Confederacy and take away a major supply line. It required many months—into 1863—to accomplish these objectives. In the meantime Cairo, Illinois, became a vital center for the Union war effort. Thousands of men and incalculable tons of supplies came into this city by rail and river. From there they were disseminated to various southwestern armies.

Dwight Moody and the Chicago Christian Commission recognized the importance of Cairo early in the war. Consequently, the YMCA established its own command post at that river city. From there they held gospel services and gave Bibles and hymnbooks to even more men than they were helping in Chicago.

It is no wonder Moody had little time to write to his mother. Indeed, it is amazing that he had time to court Emma. Between the work at Camp Douglas, raising funds for its chapel, continuing the mission Sunday school, and making numerous trips to Cairo to establish Christian association work there, Moody seldom had time to eat or sleep. His schedule was incredibly packed, but it would soon grow more crowded. In February 1862 Union land and naval forces under General Grant and Commander A. H. Foote moved like lightning against Confederate forces on the Mississippi, Tennessee, and Cumberland Rivers. Fort Henry on the Tennessee was taken on February 6 and Fort Donelson surrendered on February 16, after a four-day siege. Nine days later, February 25, Nashville fell to the Union forces.

CHANGING MINISTRY

Two big changes came to Moody's ministry in the wake of this Union advance. First, nine thousand rebel prisoners taken at Fort Donelson were placed at Camp Douglas under a Union guard regiment. At first many Chicagoans were alarmed, fearing these captured soldiers would escape and terrorize the city. Moody, on the other hand, saw this as an opportunity rather than a potential disaster. Within a few days he had organized some helpers, obtained passes, and began a preaching and one-to-one prayer and counseling ministry to these despondent prisoners of war. Ultimately thousands of Confederates heard the gospel and experienced love and pastoral care from some evangelical Yankees.

The second big change, coming with the Union thrust in the Southwest, was the condition of the soldiers. Prior to February 1862, Moody and his compatriots ministered to relatively healthy and happy would-be warriors. Now they not only had freshly mobilized troops but thousands of sick, wounded, and dying men who were

D. L. Moody, age 25

laid out in makeshift hospitals at every battle site of the war.

After the siege of Fort Donelson, Moody penned a glimpse of the multifaceted new ministry that engaged him and many others:

Cairo, March 4, 1862

Dear Mother

I have thought I would write for a long time but I have put it off un-till now. I am at Cairo with things to relieve the wants of the sick & wounded soldiers. I was sent to Fort Donelson Tenn—last week & as soon as I got hom they sent me back with 7 or 8 hundred dollars worth of things for the wounded. One hospital has about 1400 hundred an-other 800. . . . I tell you mother as I was goin through the Hospitals to day I . . . asked to a ladie that was with me if I was goin to be sick I would want to be to home for thare is nothing like home who could take so good care of me as you could. The symithy goes a grate ways to I tell you you do not know how roughly the poor fellows are treat-ed. Our army are very healthy as a general thing some sickness among them not much. I was on the battle field be fore they buried the dead it was awful to see the dead laying around without being any one to burry them. They all are burried now the prisoners are up to Chicago a good many of them we have meetings with them daily—[25]

Moody became personally linked to General Grant's forces throughout much of the war, going to the front nine times to minis-ter to the wounded and dying. All the while he tried to oversee the continuation of his Chicago Sunday school, outreach to Chicago's poor, and ministry to Union enlistees and Confederate prisoners at Camp Douglas. Perhaps the most physically draining, emotionally stressful, and spiritually demanding time for him came in April 1862. The Union forces had been moving rapidly and successfully against the rebels all winter, and in the process Union casualties were mini-mal. Then on April 6 and 7 the rebels, who had been continuously defensive, struck an early morning surprise attack at Shiloh, moving with frightening speed to Pittsburgh Landing. It was a staggering blow to General Grant and other Union commanders who had as-sumed the Confederates were on the run and likely to be subdued in a few months without heavy fighting or substantial losses. Surprised and humiliated but by no means devastated, the Union armies num-bering 63,000 in the Shiloh area sustained 13,000 casualties in two days. They regrouped and counterattacked, killing one of the Con-federate generals and inflicting 11,000 casualties on the stubborn rebel forces of 40,000.

Shiloh was a traumatic, sobering battle. The North had lost more men in two days than anyone dreamed would have been sacrificed in the entire war. "The Sesesh," as the Confederates were labeled, were not afraid to engage the Yankees. The men in gray fought and they fought well. Apparently it was going to be a long war—an incredibly costly war.

God's Faithfulness

As the war increased in fierceness by spring 1862, the carnage reached proportions that had hitherto been unimaginable. During this trying time, Moody's faith in God's greatness reached mountain-like heights. The crises of war showed him that the God he served was the same One who had parted the Red Sea, fed thousands on hillsides with a few loaves and fishes, and raised Jesus Christ from the tomb. His postwar sermons were rich in stories of God's glory in the midst of hellish wartime conditions. One instance took place late at night on a field after a raging battle. The armies had withdrawn, and a party of Christian association workers were left behind to walk the shell-pocked, body-strewn fields in search of survivors. The hundreds of wounded men were bleeding and suffering from dehydration. A nearby creek became the source of fresh water, but there was no store of rations to feed those who desperately needed nourishment. After searching the haversacks of the dead and wounded, they had hardly gathered enough rations to feed a dozen men. With no one to turn to but God, the little band of missionaries stormed heaven and asked for bread for the weak and hungry wounded. Later some workers admitted that they were doubtful God would respond.

As the sun was casting the first light of dawn on the battle-torn field and the lines of dew-covered wounded, a large wagon appeared on the horizon and rumbled toward the battlefield shepherds and their wounded sheep. It was a spacious farm wagon, piled to capacity with loaves of bread. The driver approached the wide-eyed camp and related this story in answer to questions of why he came:

> When I went to bed last night I knew the army was gone and I could not sleep for thinking of the poor fellows who were wounded and would have to stay behind. Something seemed to whisper in my ear, "What will those poor fellows do for something to eat?" I could not get rid of this voice.

Consequently he got up, awakened his wife, and asked her to bake as much bread as she could. While she set to work in the kitchen, he hitched his team to the wagon and called on all of their neighbors, beseeching them to give him all the bread they had in their houses. "Some hours later when I reached home my wagon was full, but my wife succeeded in piling her baking on top, and I then hastened to bring the bread to the boys, feeling just as if I was being sent by our Lord Himself."[26]

Experiences such as this gave Moody even more purpose and urgency than before. A medical student in Chicago, who was not a Christian during the Civil War, drew a fascinating portrait of Dwight Moody that was etched on his memory after the battles of Shiloh and Pittsburgh Landing in April 1862. The enormity of the list of wounded overwhelmed the surgical and nursing staffs that followed the armies. Consequently, a call went throughout Chicago, via the YMCA, for nurses and doctors to go and help tend the wounded. The battle had ended on Monday, news arrived on Tuesday, and the call went forth early Wednesday.

That evening a special train was made up by the Illinois Central Railroad. This medical student was part of the party of sixty to seventy-five physicians and three hundred nurses. "I had a seat in the centre of [our] car, which was comfortably full." When they had traveled about three hours out of Chicago, and everyone was getting settled to fall asleep, he was "aroused by a gentle tap on the shoulder and asked if 'I would not attend Mr. Moody's prayer-meeting, which was then to be held in the front of the car.'" Because he was not a Christian he declined the invitation. Nevertheless "my conscience gave me a stinging rebuke and I was set to thinking." At the front of the car was Moody holding a prayer meeting. Simultaneously, at the rear of the car, there "was a company of men playing a game of cards. I couldn't help realizing the wonderful zeal of the man in his great work, and how earnest and how careful he was that no duty be neglected, no opportunity lost."[27]

Controversy

Moody's zeal for souls was not always appreciated during those turbulent years. On another trip men and women war missionaries had taken the train from Chicago to Cairo, and then took a steamer up the Ohio and Tennessee Rivers to get access to another battle-torn group of soldiers. On board the steamer a discussion arose as to how they should conduct their ministry to the sick, wounded, and dying.

One of the ministers with Moody and the others remembered a

rather spirited debate. "Mr. Moody, full of the idea of saving souls, urged that the very first business in every case was to find out whether the sick or dying man were a child of God." If he is a believer, said Moody, don't linger too long in his company. He is "safe enough already. If not, he was to be pointed at once to the Saviour."

A Unitarian, Robert Collyer, begged to differ. He said that "the first comforts to be administered to these men who were ready to perish were whiskey, brandy, milk-punch, and the like." He urged that they calm the nerves of the dying "and help keep them alive, rather than begin by trying to prepare them for death."

A Congregationalist, the Reverend Dr. Patton, agreed with both men. Favoring a double treatment, he advocated bracing up the suffering and encouraging them to hold on. But if a man was clearly at death's door, "the thing to be done was to offer him a short and swift salvation, by telling him the story of the thief on the cross."

The Unitarian rose to his feet and exclaimed: "What! Are we to tell our dying heroes, who have gone forth to fight our battles and save our flag, while we stay comfortably at home,—are we to talk to them about thieves?"

The crowd on deck applauded the patriotic speaker, according to one witness, because they neither understood nor cared about orthodox Christian theology. Instead, they "were full of that strange belief common to both armies in all battles, that patriotism is one form of piety, and that, somehow or other, though in a way not laid down in the Bible, to die for one's country is a quick way of getting to heaven."[28]

Moody neither argued with his opponents nor was swayed from his purpose. On the contrary, as soon as he entered a tent or building converted to a hospital, he set out to talk to the bedridden one by one. He bent over each soldier and inquired about his soul. Many men were unconscious or too wounded to speak. In those cases he offered a whispered prayer near their ears in hopes they could hear. Some men contritely confessed their sins and eagerly heard the good news of God's mercy to all who would lean upon Christ Jesus. Many other men, of course, rejected the gospel, choosing to enter eternity on their own merits or in the confidence that there was only nothingness on the other side. In any case, Moody's work, to him, was purposeful and urgent.

Frontline Ministry

On his nine trips to the front lines, he labored for souls around the clock until his mind and body were so exhausted that he was

compelled to sleep. In one of his sermons delivered years later, he recalled a time that he was at a Murfreesboro, Tennessee, hospital in
1862 near the battlefield of Pittsburgh Landing. He had fallen asleep
only to be aroused in the middle of the night and informed that a
man in one of the wards was calling out for him.

> I went to him and he called me "chaplain"—I was not the chap-
> lain—and said he wanted me to help him die. And I said, "I would take
> you right up in my arms and carry you into the Kingdom of God, if I
> could; but I cannot do it. I cannot help you die!" And he said, "Who
> can?" I said, "The Lord Jesus Christ can—He came for that purpose."
> He shook his head, and said: "He cannot save me; I have sinned all
> my life." And I said, "But He came to save sinners." I thought of his
> mother in the north and I was sure that she was anxious that he
> should die in peace; so I resolved I would stay with him. I prayed two
> or three times, and repeated all the promises I could; for it was evi-
> dent that in a few hours he would be gone.
> I said I wanted to read him a conversation that Christ had with a
> man who was anxious about his soul. I turned to the third chapter of
> John. His eyes were rivited on me; and when I came to the fourteenth
> and fifteenth verses. . . he caught up with the words, "As Moses lifted
> up the serpent in the wilderness, even so must the Son of Man be lift-
> ed up; that whosoever believeth in Him should not perish, but have
> eternal life." He stopped. He asked me to read it again, and I did so.
> He leaned his elbows on the cot and clasping his hands together, said:
> "That's good; won't you read it again?" I read it the third time; and
> then went on with the rest of the chapter. When I had finished, his
> eyes were closed, his hands were folded, and there was a smile on his
> face. Oh, how it was lit up! What a change had come over it! I saw his
> lips quivering, and, leaning over him, I heard in a faint whisper, "As
> Moses lifted up the serpent in the wilderness, even so must the Son of
> Man be lifted up: that whosoever believeth in Him should not perish,
> but have eternal life." He opened his eyes and said: "that's enough;
> don't read any more." He lingered a few hours, pillowing his head on
> those two verses; and then went up in one of Christ's chariots, to take
> his seat in the kingdom of God.[29]

MOODY'S CARE FOR NORTHFIELD

Dwight L. Moody was blessed with an unusually strong body.
He frequently ministered around the clock, week after week, in late
1861 and early 1862. Finally in June 1862, he pulled himself away
from Chicago and the front lines of war work and made that long-
promised trip to Northfield to visit his mother. Perhaps the tireless
lover of souls got some rest and sleep on the eastern bound train, but

the trip was hardly a vacation. He arrived in Boston on June 11 and went directly to the YMCA to exchange war ministry insights with the leaders of the Massachusetts Christian Association. When he reached Northfield on June 21, he immediately poured himself into an outreach to the spiritually indolent community. He described the working vacation to Farwell:

> The Lord blessed me in my native town—25 or 30 cases came out, besides some children, and when I came to Boston I got them so interested in it that they sent a man up there to preach for them. When I came away they came to the depot to inquire what they should do to be saved. God the Lord never blessed me as He did there. I was there eleven days and held a meeting from 6 until 9:30 and then again from 3 until 12 at night some nights, and most of them are Unitarians at that. I wish you could have been with me you would have enjoyed it.[30]

It made no difference where D. L. Moody happened to be; he was always on the alert for souls. When he was on vacation in New England, the rescue of souls was foremost in his thoughts as he started and finished each day with meetings designed to diagnose and heal sin-sick souls. Even after he boarded the Boston-bound train in early July, the spiritual welfare of Northfield dominated his agenda. Once he arrived in Boston he wrote to Northfield that he was enclosing fifty dollars for his mother and he had a favor to ask of his brothers George and Edwin. "The good folks of Boston have raised money to send a man of God to Northfield. He will be there tomorrow." In a manner typical of Moody, he urged others to join into the work with the same hope and fervor he expressed. "I am very anxious to have a good House"—a large crowd out to hear the man—"for he is one of the greatest preachers in the *State* and I am very anxious he should have a good House." Consequently, "I want to have Geo and Edwin stir up the folks and get them out and if you get word to John Fisher and the folks up in that district I would like it."

He urged them to reap while they could because "I do not know as you could . . . ever be able to get such a good man into the town again for years." He implored his mother and brothers to "get Uncle Cyrus and Alvin Long out to hear him" and "put forth every effort you can. . . ." Pouring out his heart for his native community, the ardent missioner concluded with these words: "How often I have thought of Northfield since I left there several years ago. [I] have been praying to God to raise up some one to preach the gospel to them! I think he had heard my prayer and I am confident you all will like this man."[31] It never occurred to Moody that he had been an answer to that prayer as well.

With a strong preacher secured for Northfield from among the Boston community of disciples, Moody took the train down to New York and put the finishing touches on his working holiday. He wrote to John V. Farwell on July 11, saying he was yearning to get back to Chicago "and cast my lot with the little praying band of the Noon Union Meetings, and also that blessed band on the corner of Michigan and Dearborn streets. I think of them daily. My prayer is that they may be kept from the world." He went on to explain that he had stopped off in New York to persuade the American Tract Society "to give us 5000 Messengers and 15,000 tracts a month for one year . . . so you can see I am working all the time with my eye, not only on my Savior's interests here, but in Chicago also, and Jesus has helped me so far."[32]

Once Moody returned to Chicago, he was back on the whirlwind schedule that included the Christian association, Sunday school mission, prayer meetings, Camp Douglas, and points south. Soon after unpacking from the eastern trip he wrote to Samuel, "I am home but for several days," and then expressed concern about their brother Luther's soul.[33]

MARRIAGE AND MINISTRY

Despite his near obsession with Christian ministry, Moody—now twenty-five—was devoted to Emma. To Moody, marriage was a part of God's call on his life, the same as full-time missionary service. To him the two callings were complementary and one did not compete with the other. On August 23, five days before they exchanged vows, Dwight wrote to Samuel, "By the time you get this I shall be married and away on my wedding tower." The wedding notwithstanding, he implored Samuel to come to Chicago and stay with them. Moody was confident he could find employment for his brother, despite problems in Chicago's wartime economy.[34]

Emma Revell and Dwight Moody

From the time of their engagement in 1860, Emma and Dwight ministered together as much as possible. She taught in the Chicago public schools after her high school graduation in 1860, so this confined her availability to evenings, weekends, and summer vacations. Nevertheless, Emma Revell became Dwight's right arm in the mission Sunday school, and she frequently worked alongside him in other YMCA work that focused on outreach to the poor. She felt particularly inclined to the distribution of food and clothing, and she experienced fulfillment working with the sick and bereaved. Because Emma and Dwight were so obviously devoted to each other and already working together quite well as a team, no one near them seemed surprised when they married in 1862.

The wedding was a simple affair. It took place on Thursday, August 28, in the First Baptist Church. The Chicago economy had been dreadful during 1861 and 1862, marked by high unemployment and

Mr. and Mrs. D. L. Moody in 1864 and in 1869

business failures. The coming of the Civil War complicated all aspects of life even more, and Emma's own family had suffered severe economic reversals due in part to an injury her father received at work. A wedding and reception with anything but the basic necessities would have been in poor taste if not impossible. And the slightest hint of display would have been contrary to the religious convictions of the bride and groom.[35]

If there was a honeymoon, it too must have been unpretentious. No mention of a trip or newlyweds' hideaway was ever mentioned by anyone. Most likely the couple slipped off quietly to their new home—a very small, plain single-family dwelling located downtown on Chicago's north side.[36]

Betsy Moody's Opposition

Emma and Dwight Moody's courtship and marriage seem to have been celebrated with enthusiasm by all of the important people in their lives except one—Betsy Holton Moody. This hardworking, independent mother of nine children was rather cold to the relationship from the beginning. It is doubtful that Mrs. Moody had any problem with Emma Revell; she had never met her. But from the time Edwin Moody died, Betsy fought relentlessly to keep all of her brood nearby. It was no secret that she opposed Dwight's move to Boston. Then when he moved still farther away to Chicago, she made known her deep hurt. He informed her of the move after he reached Chicago because he dreaded her attempts to change his mind.

By 1859 or 1860 there were clear signs that she was more mellow about her son's lifestyle, especially since he was making plenty of money and being generous with the family. Nevertheless, some strains appeared in their correspondence. Although it is difficult to imagine a more thoughtful son who dutifully wrote to and financially supported his family, he did not write as frequently in 1860 and 1861 as he had in earlier years. He begged forgiveness for the length of time between letters, explaining the tremendous pressures from ministry and work. He argued that the demands on his time were so great that he could not promise when he would make a visit home to Massachusetts, but he would do all in his power to be there soon.

Betsy Moody was a clever woman. She probably discerned that Emma Revell, as well as work and ministry, was responsible for Dwight's inattention to family at Northfield. She perhaps even wondered if this young woman had caused him to leave business for ministry in 1860. Whatever her thoughts, a letter that the lovestruck son wrote to his mother on June 5, 1861, is rather revealing:

> I have been very busy this winter and spring. I have so much to do I
> hardly find time to do it. I shall send this by Mr. Young who is goin to
> Northfield. I shall also send the dagurotype of myself and Miss Emma
> Revell who I shall bring down home with me the next time I come.
> When that shall be I do not know. I should have come this summer if
> our money had not all become bad but all our banks are failing. . . .
> Miss Revell I have known ever since I com west. . . . I think dear
> Mother you would love her if you could get acquainted with her. I do
> not know of anyone that knows her but that likes her. She is a good
> Christian girl. I would not tell anyone of it [except] the family. I mean
> I suppose you will now say that is why I have not written to you
> offtener but dear Mother it is not for I have been to prayer meetings
> every night but 2 for 8 mos. So you can see I am all taken up with this.
> Oh no Mother I think of you as often as I ever did but if I could see
> you and Tell you how the Lord is blessing me in my labors I think you
> would say God Bless you, go forward. . . . I am drov more now than
> ever in my life. I have crowed houses where I go. Last week where I
> was the house was full and the sidewalk outside so they had to open
> another church and I had to speak in two houses and the Lord blessed
> me very much. . . . Oh Mother if you could be out here you never
> would be sorry I gave up my business. . . .[37]

Four months later Emma also attempted to bridge the widening
gulf.

> Dear Mrs. Moody:
>   Your last letter was received by Mr. Moody about 3 weeks ago as
> he was then sick and at our house. He requested me to read it to him,
> which I am glad I did as by it I learned the false impression you had
> in regard to me because of our different views on religion.
>   I thought by what you wrote that you had the idea that because I
> was a baptist and you was a different sect, that I would not esteem you
> as much, but please do not think so a moment longer for I assure you
> that it makes no difference in regard to my feelings.
>   I think that it makes very little difference to what sect we belong to
> here on earth, as long as our hearts are right in the sight of God. I
> thought also that you might have thought that because Mr. Moody
> was of a different denomination to what he had been trained in youth,
> that his love & respect for his mother had abated, but I know that
> such is not the case. Besides some of Mr. Moody's warmest friends are
> unitarians.
>   It seemed strange to me when I first thought of writing to one
> whom I had never seen (as it is something I have never done before)
> but have heard Mr. Moody speak of you so often, that it seemed as

though I too know you & felt that I loved you.

When your letter was received Mr. M. was quite unwell, but do not be alarmed about him now as he has entirely recovered & is now enjoying very good health. While he was sick, he was at our house & though I did what I could for him, I know it was very little compared to a mother's tender care. I think he must have missed you very much as he spoke of you often then.

When I first spoke of writing to you Mr. M. said we could send our letter together, but as he is now out of town for a few days, I thought I would not wait & he said he would write to you from where he now is. I have heard Mr. M. speak often of his sister Lizzie. Will you please remember me to her in much love.

Yours in much esteem & love,

Emma C. Revell[38]

Emma had a gift of diplomacy, which her husband at this point in his life did not. On September 13, 1862, more than a fortnight after the ceremony, the new groom wrote a long letter to his mother, expressing concern about his brother Warren who had just joined the Union army. Tucked in the middle of this lengthy epistle was the jarring phrase, "I went married on the 28 of last month my wife will write to Warren today."[39]

Through patience, tact, and sincere devotion, Emma was eventually able to win Betsy Moody's unguarded approval. Smooth sailing for mother and daughter-in-law was not easily accomplished, but by December 1862 a favorable wind was blowing. Emma wrote to Mrs. Moody, "I thank you very much for your kind letter. . . . I have thought often of you and though I have never seen you I feel quite well acquainted, I hope we will become still better acquainted. Pray for us. Your affec' daughter, Emma."[40]

Emma's Ministry

Precisely how Emma felt about D. L.'s work and their new life together is unknown, but it does appear that she had many of the same passions that fired her husband. A journal written by Emma several years later contained these words in her handwriting: "D. L. Moody and Emma C. Revell married on August 28, 1862. D. L. busy with his work among the soldiers."[41]

It was compatible with Emma's genuinely humble character that she did not note her own work among the soldiers either in this journal or in her succinct Civil War journal. But the truth is that Mrs. D. L. Moody had a remarkable ministry to the Union army. She did not travel away from Chicago as much as Mr. Moody, to be sure. Nevertheless, she was one of the official Christian association delegates. Among the five thousand active delegates across the nation, only a small minority were women—10 percent at most. In any case the petite, youthful-looking newlywed joined this noble but unheralded throng. Along with her husband, she made two trips to the front herself, the first in 1863, visiting troops in Kentucky, Tennessee, Mississippi, and Alabama. Then in 1864 she again went with him to minister to General Grant's winning but battered troops as they engaged in the bloody "sledgehammer campaign" to Richmond.[42]

When Emma Moody was not on extended Christian association trips to the South, she was busy on the home front of the war. She ministered often at the Camp Douglas chapel. She also helped keep the Sunday school mission vital and growing, and she made countless calls on the poor in the city. Besides these activities Emma Moody cooked, kept house, and entertained Samuel during his extended stay. She wrote Mrs. Moody about three months after the wedding: "My dear husband arrived safely home last Tuesday. It was the first time we had been separated since our marriage and I was very glad to see him again." It was a pleasurable time having Samuel with them. He was "in the kitchen with me a great deal of the time and I think it afforded him some sport as I could sometimes see a smile on his face."[43]

Samuel Moody's Visit

It was important for the family to see Samuel smile. When Samuel responded to the invitation to come to Chicago, Dwight and Emma discovered something that Betsy Moody had managed to hide for many years. Samuel, everyone knew, was rather weak—even sickly. Samuel, four years younger than Dwight, was one of the twins born a month after their father died. What Dwight and Emma discovered during the visit was that, among other ailments, Samuel suffered from epilepsy. Little was known about this disease in the middle 1800s, but a man or woman with this condition was usually misunderstood and often assumed to be demon-possessed or mentally incompetent and, therefore, unemployable. To Emma and Dwight this younger brother became even more of a treasured loved one, and they finally understood the shadows of despondency that frequently accompanied his presence. They were sad when he returned to Northfield to live in the Moody family house, near the protective care of his mother.[44]

Despite his poor health, Samuel had a splendid time in Chicago, even though he decided not to stay. "I like the city very much," he reported, especially with all the excitement over the war. His brother's energy amazed him, and he wrote that "Dwight is run from morning to night. He hardly gets time to eat. Camp Douglas is situated here (there is about 17,000) he holds meetings down there most every night. It is a treat to go down there and hear the soldiers sing which is about 300 or 400 gathered as they come from most every state." He was particularly fascinated with "the Rebels" who are among them.[45]

A NEW COMPANION: DEATH

Perhaps Dwight Moody's grueling pace in ministry was fueled in part by a foreboding sense of death. He was, after all, continually hearing the last words of dying soldiers. He too was shelled on the front lines. No doubt seeing thousands of men dead and thousands more writhing in agony made this life seem fragile and fleeting at best. And now there was Samuel's condition that brought concerns of life and death even more to the fore for him and Emma. Samuel would die early, but he would not die yet. But then the Moodys could not be sure. In a note to his mother in 1862, Dwight penned these words: "I am drove from piler to post. I wish I had time to write you my feeling but I must go to Camp Douglas now but dear Mother if we do not get time to talk here on earth about these things we must try to get to heaven and then we can talk them all over."[46]

As the war raged on it became increasingly ghastly. In September 1862 Union and Confederate forces relentlessly smashed each other in a one-day battle at Antietam. In what became one of the bloodiest single days of the war, more than 2,000 Union soldiers died and almost 9,600 were wounded; Confederates buried 2,700 men and carried away more than 9,000 wounded.

Autumn 1862, and then spring and summer of 1863, brought more battles and more carnage. By now the hope of a short and glorious war was dashed for both belligerents in this humanly devastating conflict. Moody himself continued to minister, but he spent an equal amount of time identifying, equipping, and sending out others to meet the seemingly endless calls for chaplains, nurses, and supplies. In February 1863, for example, he wrote a quick note to his mother, explaining that he had sent "one man to look after the sick and wounded soldiers of [General William S.] Rosecrans army," at Nashville, and another was on his way to Louisiana. Besides the cry for spiritual and medical personnel, there was an urgent call for material for the wounded and dying. The armies could not keep up with the demand for mattresses, cots, bandages, whiskey for anesthesia, and special food for the unique dietary needs of the wounded. Increasingly Moody and his Christian Commission colleagues found themselves involved in more than the cure of souls; they were dietitians, support staff recruiters, and quartermasters who oversaw the collection and dispersal of vast tons of food and medical supplies.

The war, from the outset, had been a school of practical theology for D. L. Moody. It presented him with endless opportunities to preach, and in those dirty, fly-infested, impersonal field hospitals he learned the delicate art of one-to-one personal counseling—and he learned to do it with urgency and compassion. But the Civil War was also a leadership and administration training program where this unschooled young man learned how to administer programs, delegate responsibilities, find a wide range of talent, train missionaries, locate and disperse resources, and raise the funds to cover the entire operation.

Undergirding all of this, Moody learned to rely upon God. There is no way by experience, age, or education that Dwight L. Moody was capable of handling the responsibilities that fell on his shoulders between 1861 and 1865. His correspondence demonstrated that he neither sought these tasks nor assumed he was, on his own, able to carry them through. What his letters showed and his friends observed, however, was that he was willing to persevere and tackle the next problem once he was certain it was a call from God. With that confidence he engaged in prayer and unabashedly solicited the prayers of others. Perhaps the greatest education Moody received during the awful Civil War was learning with certainty that those whom God calls, He also instructs and supports.[47]

Moody learned these lessons while stepping out in faith. These were neither devotional notions nor textbook theories. The learning came over time—a demanding and harrowing time. His education was a difficult process. Once in a while he grew discouraged and wondered if God had really called him. For example, the newlyweds lost their first house to a fire in 1863. This was a frightful event for a couple just getting started. Also, during the year Moody's savings had vanished. At least once he grew discouraged, crying out to his wife, "I have no money and the house is without supplies. It looks as tho the Lord had had enough of me in this mission work and is going to send me back to selling boots and shoes." Soon, however, the money came in. Moody felt wind at his back once again and he went on to the next task. Years later he would say they never were without necessities. "The Lord has taken care of me."[48]

D. W. WHITTLE

Not only did God teach Moody about faith and trust, but Moody recognized that the Almighty maneuvered him into situations where he met men who were destined to be colleagues with him in future ministries that God had already prepared in advance for them to do. One of these providential wartime encounters was with Daniel Webster Whittle, a Massachusetts-born man who had moved to Chicago in 1857. Whittle, three years younger than Moody, was working as a cashier for Wells, Fargo and Company when the Civil War began. Converted during the revival at the First Congregational Church in 1857, he joined an Illinois infantry unit in 1861, receiving a direct commission. Serving throughout the war and climbing the ranks from lieutenant to major, Whittle served most of the time with General William T. Sherman. He was seriously wounded at Vicksburg in 1863, but he recovered and was part of Sherman's famous March to the Sea.[49]

Moody and Whittle first met in Chicago in autumn 1863, where Lieutenant Whittle was recuperating. When Whittle was barely on his feet and still weak, being only partially recovered, a group of prominent Chicagoans persuaded him to sit on the platform at a patriotic rally. During the meeting Whittle was asked to speak. He recalled that when he stood up, he felt faint and foolish, wondering why he had agreed to this public appearance. Just when he thought he could not go on, "directly in front of me, in the centre of the hall, a sturdy young man jumped to his feet and cried: 'Give him three cheers!'" He recognized the cheerleader as D. L. Moody. "This manifestation of sympathy nerved me for the few words that followed, and I have often thought it was a specimen of what his courage, faith, and example have been to me all through my life."

The two men talked about that rally several years later. Whittle thanked Moody for coming to his aid; Moody responded, "I took you into my heart that night and you have been there ever since!"[50]

The evening they met in 1863 was a portent of a close and abiding friendship. They stayed in contact throughout the war and became prayer partners after 1865. Whittle returned to Chicago in 1865 and accepted a $5,000-per-year position with the Elgin Watch Company. A dedicated Christian businessman, he helped Moody

Major D. W. Whittle

with Bible studies and occasionally accepted speaking and preaching engagements arranged by his Civil War-era friend. In 1873, largely because of Moody's influence, Major Whittle gave up business and set forth on a life of preaching and Bible teaching. Like Moody he gave up wealth to become a preacher. And like his spiritual mentor, he never regretted his decision. He died in 1901 at age sixty-one. He and his wife had led a happily married life and raised a family, and he preached all over the United States and the United Kingdom. He wrote four books, and his daughter, Mary, married Moody's older son, William R. Moody.

O. O. HOWARD

The Civil War also brought Moody into a lifelong friendship and ministry relationship with General Oliver Otis Howard. Seven years older than Moody, Howard was born in Leeds, Maine, to a well-to-do farm family. His father died when he was nine, and he was sent off to live with an uncle who gave him a good home. By middle nine-teenth-century standards Howard acquired a first-rate education. He attended Monmouth Academy at North Yarmouth, Maine. Before his twentieth birthday in 1850, he graduated from Maine's Bowdoin College, having supported himself by teaching during vacations. The next autumn he entered West Point. In 1854 he graduated fourth in his class. A year later he married and embarked upon a lifelong military career.[51]

Howard's life was significantly changed in spring 1857 while he served as a green second lieutenant in Florida. Still on what he de-scribed as the "outskirts" of Christianity, he was invited to attend a Methodist revival meeting by his commanding officer, Colonel L. L. Loomis. Out of a sense of duty, he went along. At the close of the ser-mon, the preacher called upon those in the congregation who had never surrendered their lives to Christ to come forward. The gather-ing was full of army enlisted men. Quite a few of them began to snicker and make fun of the evangelist. Feeling nothing but a desire to support the preacher, Lieutenant Howard got up and walked to the front. The young officer's action quelled the critics, but he ad-mitted he sensed nothing in his own soul. Nevertheless, later that night Howard felt overwhelmed by a sense of his own sinfulness and lostness. By himself he got on his knees, cried out for mercy, and sur-rendered his life to Jesus Christ. From that night forward he had new purposes for living.

Within a year he was promoted to first lieutenant and sent to his alma mater, West Point, as a mathematics instructor. While there he became a devout Methodist and sensed a calling to go into full-time ministry. His wife, Lizzie, on the other hand, felt absolutely no desire to become a pastor's wife. Because of her reluctance, Howard held on to his commission, continued teaching at West Point, and be-gan studying theology and Hebrew on the side, just in case she changed her mind.

Fortunes changed markedly for Howard in 1861. When the Civil War began he resigned from the Military Academy to become Colonel of the 3rd Maine Regiment. By September 1861 he was brigadier general of volunteers, and he became major general in 1862. In 1864 he was made a brigadier general in the regular army.

A Controversial Christian Soldier

General Howard saw much action. He fought valiantly at First Bull Run and in the Peninsula campaign under General McClellan. During the later offensive he lost his right arm leading a charge at Fair Oaks. After surgery he was quickly back in action. Some years later he was awarded the Congressional Medal of Honor for his bravery at Fair Oaks. Early in the war, under McClellan, Howard was a controversial corps commander. No one ever considered him cowardly, but his judgment and aptitude were sometimes questioned. Some of the criticism was no doubt warranted, but a good part of it probably stemmed from disdain for his Christian faith. Christians who served with him sang his praises, but those who had no use for the Christian faith maligned him and labeled him the "Praying General" or "Biblical Soldier." General Howard's faith caused him great concern and compassion for blacks who were running from bondage and seeking solace with Union forces. This courageous stand engendered still more criticism.

If praying, Bible reading, and concern for ex-slaves was not enough to inspire pockets of opposition, General O. O. Howard became the brunt of criticism for his compassionate concern for the noncombatant Southerners. As his men swept through occupied parts of the South, the devout Methodist commander treated the vanquished civilians with kindness, and he consistently and vigorously punished any of his men who were discovered harming civilians or looting and destroying civilian property. As his biographer John A. Carpenter noted, his vital Christian faith influenced his soldiering.[52] Not everyone found that appealing.

Meeting D. L. Moody

General Howard and Dwight L. Moody met for the first time in April 1864, at Cleveland, in east Tennessee, where Howard, battling with only one arm, was beginning to truly distinguish himself. Soon he would be the commander of the right wing of General Sherman's army. Providence had kept the 5'9", 160-pound military leader alive and out of the ordained ministry, so he felt his God-given task in this conflict was to be a good soldier, follow orders, and lead as many of his men as possible into a vital relationship with Christ. When Moody, under the banner of the Christian Commission, arrived at Howard's Fourth Army Corps camp, he was warmly received. The general remembered their meeting this way:

It was about the middle of April, 1864. I was bringing together my Fourth Army Corps. Two divisions had already arrived, and were encamped in and near the village. Moody was then fresh and hearty, full of enthusiasm for the Master's work. Our soldiers were just about to set out on what we all felt promised a hard and bloody campaign, and I think were especially desirous of strong preaching. Crowds and crowds turned out to hear the glad tidings from Moody's lips. He showed them how a soldier would give his heart to God. His preaching was direct and effective, and multitudes responded with a confession and promise to follow Christ.[53]

An ordained minister who accompanied Moody and three other Illinois Christian Commission delegates recalled that General O. O. Howard gave them a cordial welcome, and he ordered "the churches in the town cleansed and opened for divine service." Services were held in camp with the regiments during the day. And then at night soldiers were invited to meetings in the Cleveland churches. Howard joined Moody and took an active part. The trim, uniformed general not only spoke to his men, but he also "took a class of little girls in our Sabbath-school, and an active part in our night meetings—praying for penitents, and sometimes addressing the congregation with great power." The last address he gave before the offensive was on May 1. "The corps was under marching orders, and the General spoke out of a full heart, familiar with the experience just before every man in that congregation." At the general's closing invitation "eighty-three came forward, desiring prayers, and a goodly number, before the meeting closed, entered into a covenant with their Heavenly Father."[54]

One Christian Commission delegate reported that "a marvelous revival began" at Cleveland, Tennessee, just before Howard's army set out for what would be a four-month campaign for the siege and capture of Atlanta. If the commissioner's observations are accurate, the revival began the first night they arrived. At the initial meeting, an invitation was given for all to stand who were desirous of becoming better Christians. Howard was the first on his feet. Next some of his staff rose, and soon the Holy Spirit was "pouring forth."[55]

Howard, who already had a reputation as one who "never drank and never swore, and on Sundays liked to visit hospitals and distribute religious tracts and baskets of fruit,"[56] delighted in the company of Moody and his men. After all, they came bearing "potatoes and other vegetables" which were "difficult if not impossible, to obtain,"[57] and best of all they came proclaiming the Good News of Jesus Christ. As General Howard put it, these agents came "encouraging chaplains and aiding them with books, Bibles, Testaments, and with themselves, ready to speak of Christ crucified . . . bringing to us, professing Christians, cheerful faces and warm pressure of the hand, with a 'God bless you and protect you,' and following us [to] hospital and battlefield, to point to the only Name whereby a soldier can be saved."[58]

His Ministry After the War

General Howard made a powerful impression on D. L. Moody. Few senior officers exuded this man's warm heart and sincere faith.

General O. O. Howard

Furthermore, Howard was a good preacher—and Moody always had an eye open for men who were zealous and willing to preach. Consequently, the Chicago-based missionary kept in contact with the general throughout the war, and afterward they became close friends. Although O. O. Howard remained a career soldier until his retirement in 1894 (his wife never felt supportive of his pastoral calling), Moody gave him many opportunities to speak and preach. Over the years Moody brought him to speak at the schools he would start in Chicago and Northfield. He also called on him for Sunday school and YMCA conferences, and the two men providentially ministered together in 1892 on an ocean liner that nearly sank. In fact, Moody's encouragement of General Howard as a lay preacher and Bible teacher encouraged the general to retire to Vermont, not far by train from the Moody family home and Northfield conference center in Massachusetts.

Before the war ended, President Lincoln selected General Howard, because of his devotion to black men and women, to lead the Bureau of Refugees, Freedmen, and Abandoned Lands. After Lincoln's death and the South's surrender, President Andrew Johnson made Howard the military chieftain of that organization commonly known as the Freedman's Bureau. General Howard saw the Bureau as a way to educate ex-slaves for freedom, and at the same time he encouraged them to become ardent disciples of Christ. To this end the middle-aged soldier continually recruited teachers to go into the South and make at least a three-year commitment to his teaching ministry.

Moody's Recruitment of Others

Wherever a door opened to fresh fields of harvestable souls, Moody showed keen interest. Although he would not officially involve himself in the Bureau's work, he did much to find workers for this worthy cause of helping thousands upon thousands of refugees. Among the people Moody recruited for General Howard was Josephine Barbour of Romeo, Michigan. In her diary she described meeting Mr. Moody during the war. As soon as hostilities ended, he urged her to go to Tennessee and become a teacher and missionary to freed men and women. Her initial hesitancy suggested to Moody that she was short of funds for the trip. Typical of his zeal, he sent her another letter, encouraged her to get moving, and enclosed money to cover her expenses to the South. Over the years Miss Barbour praised God that she listened to Moody. She remained in touch with the evangelist, and when she concluded her three-year commitment to

General Howard's work, she wrote to Moody, who urged her to visit him and his family in Chicago on her return to the North. During that visit in 1869, she met Emma Moody's brother, twenty-year-old Fleming Hewitt Revell, who worked—also at Moody's inspiration—editing a Christian monthly entitled *Everybody's Paper.* The two were immediately attracted to each other. In 1872 they were married in Romeo, Michigan, but lived in Chicago where Fleming H. Revell was building a major Christian publishing company.[59]

The Howard-Moody relationship produced an almost endless line of reciprocal encouragements. Moody, for example, watched with interest as the decorated Civil War hero founded and became president of a university for black men and women. Eventually named Howard University, this institution provided a place for the educationally disadvantaged people of color to get a start—a start they were not getting in white-dominated institutions. General Howard, on the other hand, watched the progress of Moody's Sunday school mission that became a Chicago church. From Moody's church General Howard found inspiration to start a similar program that became a Congregational Church in Washington, D.C. Howard also caught his friend's enthusiasm for the YMCA. By the 1880s, despite being the superintendent of West Point, among other things, he traveled to Europe as a delegate to the International YMCA in Berlin.

General O. O. Howard, for his part, taught Moody much about leading educational institutions. He also instructed Moody about the complicated and delicate issues of race in America. In the years ahead he would be one of Moody's invaluable confidants, counselors, and supporters.

WHAT D. L. GAINED FROM THE WAR

If the Civil War had given Mr. Moody nothing but experience in practical theology, training in administration and recruiting, plus friends like D. W. Whittle and O. O. Howard, it would have been an astoundingly rich period in his life. The Civil War truly became a time for Moody when circumstances meant for evil could be redeemed for good by remaining faithful and leaving the results to God.

The Civil War also provided Moody with a powerful lesson about ecumenism. The Revival of 1857–1858 in Chicago did much to bring competitive, if not conflicting, denominations together. An outcome of this was the renewed YMCA and its "Union" (interde-

nominational) prayer meetings. The war brought various sects together in a stronger bond because needs were so great that no one
group could go it alone. For Moody, this need to band together in a
time of crisis provided a glimpse of a larger, if seldom seen, reality.
There was a worldwide war going on for souls. The Civil War in
America gave him a taste of what it was like when men and women
from every sect and denomination, pulled together to take on the
common foe. Never again in the thirty-four years he had left to do
kingdom work would he be a party to divisive sectarianism. Men like
Moody, Farwell, Whittle, and Howard would spend their careers calling for "union work."

The Civil War showed Moody that Christians could work together, and it also showed him that professional clergy were not the
only ones who could get kingdom work done. He never complained,
but still it must have pained him the way many ordained clergy attempted to marginalize or outright oppose his efforts in Chicago
prior to the war. After the war, however, the professionals were
forced to acknowledge that God could use a man with no education,
let alone formal theological training.[60] Whether divine guidance or a
tinge of reverse snobbery became the cause, Moody refused formal
ordination opportunities and insisted on being called "Mr." Moody
rather than "Reverend" Moody. The impetus aside, the YMCA, a lay
organization, gave him his start. Through the YMCA, he gave other
untrained people opportunities to serve as missionaries during the
war. The overall effectiveness of lay people in ministry that he observed in the 1860s caused him to keep pushing this line throughout
his life.

Moody never opposed the professional clergy. On the contrary,
he became one of their greatest boosters. What he did urge, however, was that ordained and lay persons work together—and do so
without regard to sectarian labels whenever possible. Using military
metaphors, he said an army at war should never fight one another.
There is an enemy to defeat.

The Civil War produced still more effects on D. L. Moody. It
helped make Chicago a religious center of America, and it vaulted
Moody into the forefront of the city's Christian leadership. Being
elected president of Chicago's YMCA (Chicago was one of the most
famous of the YMCAs) in 1865 was only the first of many signs that
Moody was going to be a leader in postwar Christian circles. Under
his leadership Chicago would become the Christian capital of America during a brief but dynamic "Golden Age of Religion" in Chicago.[61]

THE MOODY FAMILY

No doubt Dwight Moody would have counted his and the city's growing fame as so much rubbish compared to what those years produced in the way of family. On October 24, 1864, their first child and only daughter, whom they named Emma for the mother and grandmother, was born. The proud father wrote to his mother that "I have named the child after Emma." He also boasted, "Both of her little fingers are crooked as mine. They all say she looks like me but I must say I can't see any resemblance."[62]

Moody would have agreed with his wife's assessment of their accomplishments during that time. Only the enterprises bearing eternal fruit, such as having a family and reaching lost souls, were important. Looking back on those turbulent and terrible times, she felt satisfaction in later years when Mr. Moody "went about holding meetings in different cities . . . [and then experienced the] joy to find those who date their conversion to some time when they attended some service conducted by him during the war."[63]

Mrs. D. L. Moody and little Emma (circa 1866)

CHAPTER FIVE

A WIDER CIRCLE
At Home and Abroad
1865–1870

"I Love the Dear Friends in London."

By 1865 two people were instrumental in keeping Moody's Chicago mission school alive while he traveled and recruited for the battlefield missionary effort. Although he delegated responsibilities to many people, John V. Farwell and Emma Moody did the bulk of the work required to keep this enterprise going. Because Mr. Farwell and Mrs. Moody were unusually gifted teachers and administrators, the mission school not only survived, but it prospered. Farwell had money and he used it generously. He also had a knack for finding helpers, and he was a brilliant administrator. Emma had all of Farwell's assets, except money. She also brought her teaching talent to the school, and she had a lot of time to contribute, which the dry goods merchant did not. Farwell was extremely important to the work, but Emma was invaluable.

The extent of Emma Moody's impact on her husband and the ministry can scarcely be exaggerated. When the war ended he was twenty-eight and she was only twenty-two. Her youthfulness notwithstanding, she had social and educational advantages well beyond those of her husband; but even more important, she possessed unusual wisdom, discernment, and tact. Even before their marriage she helped answer some of his letters, but after their marriage she handled an increasing portion of his mail. Thanks to Emma's tutorial skills, Dwight's spelling and grammar gradually improved, as did his unintentionally but frequently abrasive and abrupt comments to co-workers. In this vein Emma's hand can be seen in the style and content of a letter he wrote to a young Chicago woman who had been helping out as a teacher: "I cannot tell you how bad it makes me feel to think I hurt your feelings. I can see, though, I gave you good reason to feel hurt, but I did not intend to injure your feelings, and I hope you will forgive me."[1]

Emma Moody did more than polish her blundering husband's social skills and letters; she went to work on his personal appearance as well. After their wedding his beard remained consistently well trimmed and of medium length; his clothes likewise took on a more tailored appearance and were kept mended and clean. Near the end of the war Dwight sent some shirts to his brother Samuel—prized garments on which he bragged "I can wear them weeks and they will not have to be washed" when traveling with the troops. He confessed

Mrs. D. L. (Emma) Moody, circa 1870

Emma's extreme embarrassment that shirts in such condition were in use. He noted that her distress peaked upon learning the shirts were bundled and sent to Samuel without her attention.[2]

Besides personal appearances and social skills, Emma became a charitable yet honest critic of her husband's speeches and sermons. Pleased that he had numerous opportunities to speak in Chicago after the war, she went along as often as possible. Out of concern for his effectiveness, she provided honest critiques of each message. He told a friend that Mrs. Moody always tried to hear him speak on Sunday nights. To be ready for these meetings, he recalled, "I prepare each week giving all the time I can. My wife tells me each Sunday evening how I have succeeded for she knows better than I do. During the week I accept invitations to speak in other places and there I use what she says have been the best of my talks here."[3]

Bright, cheerful, and energetic, Emma Moody assisted her sometimes boorish man in scores of ministerial as well as personal ways. Perhaps her greatest missionary contributions came to the mission Sunday school during the Civil War. Her tireless work as an administrator and teacher, plus her personal ministry to indigent children and parents, was a major cause of the need to plant what was destined to become one of Chicago's—indeed, one of the nation's—most dynamic and influential churches.

THE MISSION SUNDAY SCHOOL

The mission Sunday school was doing well when the Civil War began, but attendance declined once Moody diverted attention to war efforts. After the wedding and once Emma stopped teaching school, she rounded up helpers and poured herself into this ministry that was genuinely dear to the hearts of both Moodys. By spring 1863 Dwight proclaimed that the "Sunday School is now larger than it has been for months," and soon attendance was greater than ever.[4]

The crowds were coming in ever greater numbers because Emma Moody and a host of her recruits were giving careful personal care to the children. When one little chap was asked why he trudged three miles to the mission school every Sunday, even though there were schools near his home, his answer was quick and to the point: "They love a fellow over there."[5] Others like him testified that besides being loved, they were fascinated by the Sunday school. Children had a good time with teachers and fellow students. And no wonder. It had always been Dwight Moody's assumption that "if we make Bible truths interesting—break them up in some shape so that children can get at them, they will begin to enjoy them."[6]

Enjoy them they did. Children, teenagers, and an increasing coterie of adults began to crowd into the North Market Hall, filling it to capacity. D. L. Moody, the favorite speaker at the school; Farwell, the superintendent; as well as Emma Moody and a few friends from the YMCA board, all prayed and sought guidance for the solution to the space problem. Finally it was agreed in mid-1863 that $20,000 should be raised to purchase a lot on the corner of Illinois and Wells Streets in the heart of Chicago's impoverished North Side. Unlike the fashionable South Side where many of the more affluent Chicagoans lived, land was cheap there and the facility would be handy to the dwellings of the mission's primary clientele—the poor, the unschooled, and the abused.

Within a few months Moody and his friends had purchased the lot and raised all of the $20,000, thanks in large measure to Farwell, who kicked off the fund-raising drive with a contribution of $10,000. By February 1864 a large brick structure was completed that included a 1,500 seat auditorium, several spacious classrooms, and a small office and library. The building looked much better than the old facility, but with plain houses crowded along both sides. A contemporary observer said, "It looks almost as if pains had been taken to make it as plain as possible so that no one, however poor, might be driven away by any outward display."[7] In short, they built a splendid structure. Nowhere in the nation did such a Sunday school facility exist—let alone one dedicated for ministry to the poor.

A CHURCH

The new building solved the space problem for the mission, but it did not solve the need for a church. By 1864 approximately one thousand children and teens thronged the Illinois Street hall on Sundays, and along with them came nearly three hundred adults. Of the latter group many were parents, but increasingly adults were coming just to hear the Bible taught with such unusual clarity and clear personal application. The number of adult attendees also grew because some of those who had been attending the school since the late 1850s were now young adults.[8]

To Moody's credit he had always tried to get along with all the pastors in the city. From his earliest days in Chicago he had involved himself personally in programs and services with at least three denominations—Methodist-Episcopal, Baptist, and Congregationalist. This predisposition toward sectarian harmony became a matter of principle to him once he became active in the nonsectarian YMCA and attended its famous noontime interdenominational union prayer meetings.

In this spirit Dwight Moody always urged his Sunday school pupils to attend a church of their choice in the city. If the youngsters had a denominational affiliation, he would recommend a Bible-teaching church of that sect to them. If they had no preference, he would point them to a theologically conservative church near their homes. From the outset, however, this attempt to avoid building one more competing church in Chicago failed. Almost invariably the young people tried churches and felt uncomfortable. For the most part they reacted toward middle-class worship services the same way they had reacted to middle-class Sunday schools—they simply did not feel comfortable among people who lived, talked, and dressed in ways so foreign to them.

Consequently, by late 1864 the Moodys and their associates called upon pastors from several denominations and asked them to consider pooling resources to start a union church. Everyone eventually agreed that only a new church could meet the particular requirements of the folks who attended the Illinois Street mission Sunday school. What they could not do was find a way to have one church be faithful to the distinctives of each denomination, when distinctives essential to one tradition are in some instances incompatible with essentials of another one. In the end the pastors were charitable and encouraging but unable to lay out common ground for a union church in the way they all supported union prayer meetings. Therefore, Moody either must see the little flock absorbed into one of the existing denominations, or he could go forth on his own and start a new church that would be comfortable for himself and his followers. The latter course proved to be the only practical one.[9]

The Illinois Street Church was formally dedicated December 30, 1864. Although the Congregational denomination proved extremely helpful in getting the new venture launched, Moody respectfully declined its offer to ordain him. Consequently, although the church adopted a congregational government, from the start it stood as an independent evangelical church with the most aggressive evangelism program in Chicago. A friend of Moody in those years said that the church could not have been started in any other way because the worshipers "had come up together out of poverty and ignorance; they had learned their duty in the same school, and under the same teacher; and thus their fellowship of suffering, as well as their fellowship of faith, was something with which no stranger might inter-meddle."[10] In an age of rented and purchased pews and high-fashion dress for churchgoers on Sundays, a large sign next to the front door said it all: "Ever welcome to this house of God are strangers and the poor." A separate sign noted "The seats are free."[11]

In early 1865 Dwight L. Moody served as pastor of a large and growing church. Despite his refusal to be called "Reverend," and even though his ministry went forth without benefit of ordination, he held the position of senior pastor. As an ordained minister friend of Moody's, W. H. Daniels, put it, "The Illinois Street Church . . . was a company of saved sinners with Mr. Moody for their pastor and Jesus Christ as the Head over all." Daniels went on to say that "as a pastor Moody was a success. He was acquainted with all his people, and all his people felt acquainted with him. All the poor and unfortunates who lived in his vicinity were quite familiar with the number on the door of his modest little house." Daniels observed that "the congre-gation is not all made up of the humble classes of society. . . . Wealthy and cultivated ladies and gentlemen, though not all of them belong-ing to his communion, are among the teachers and workers."[12]

THE YMCA PRESIDENCY

Soon after the Illinois Street Church began holding regular Sunday morning services, the Chicago YMCA voted to ask Moody to be its president. In the eyes of these men Moody seemed an ideal choice because he had demonstrated that he could quickly raise funds for buildings used for religious purposes. Such talent, they knew, was crucial for the YMCA because it desperately needed a new facility. Furthermore, the need for a large building was the di-rect result of Moody's effective ministry during the four years of war. Added to these qualifications were Moody's enthusiasm for evange-lism, his often-proclaimed love for the YMCA, and his overall skill at recruiting and employing volunteers.

This was a flattering offer to the man who only four years earlier had been sleeping on chairs in the YMCA; and if he was known at all in those days, it was as "Crazy" Moody. Consequently, Brother Moody, perhaps partly from the spiritual immaturity that assumes every need is a call from God, and partly from the pride that was creeping into his soul, accepted the honor and served from 1865 to 1870.

It is not known what Emma Moody thought of this added re-sponsibility. After all, they now had a church to oversee. Moody did a masterful job for the YMCA on the one hand; but on the other, his own personal life began to unravel and he developed some rather serious problems.

Moody's Influence

There is no way to measure Moody's prodigious influence on the YMCA during these immediate postwar years. As the official historian of the Chicago YMCA phrased it nearly a century later, Moody "left so strong an imprint on the Chicago Association that his ideas continued to dominate its program even after his departure."[13] He kept evangelism as the primary mission of the association, with Bible teaching to nurture Christians as a strong secondary purpose. Fund-raising for facility construction took much of his time, but he did this in conjunction with the other programs, which never stopped.

Along with keeping an evangelical focus and constructing buildings, there were, for that time in history, some rather forward-looking social programs. For example, in the wake of the war came serious economic dislocation as troops returned home and the economy had to be reconverted to a peacetime footing. Under Moody's leadership the Chicago YMCA in 1867 alone disbursed $24,325.38 in material relief of bread, clothing, and coal. More than 3,800 families were assisted, including 2,300 immigrants. Moody also saw to it that English classes were provided for the newcomers, and his people distributed more than 42,000 copies of foreign-language religious newspapers to immigrants. Not surprisingly, the Chicago association led many of the immigrant poor to a relationship with Christ.[14]

Besides reaching out with a helping hand and the Good News to the immigrants and the poor, the YMCA during the Moody era provided housing for young women. Inasmuch as many teenage girls came to Chicago in search of employment, and because many of them were taken advantage of and forced into prostitution, the YMCA tried to stand in the gap. In 1866 it established a boarding house for working girls so that at least a wholesome place to live and eat would be available for some women. Thirty-five young women were taken in before the facility had to close for lack of funds and workers.

The association also joined hands with the Chicago Theological Seminary and Hahnemann Medical College in recruiting volunteers to help those who were stricken in the postwar cholera epidemic. The water system proved inadequate for the quickly growing city, and in 1866 a bout of the dreadful disease hit the community. Patients infected with cholera were considered "untouchables," but volunteers from these three organizations nursed the sick, offered prayers, performed last rites, and helped bury the dead.[15]

Major D. W. Whittle volunteered some of his time to help the YMCA in the late 1860s. He particularly wanted to help Moody fulfill his vision to carry the gospel of Jesus Christ to hitherto unreached people in the city. Not only were immigrants from abroad searched out, served, and witnessed to, but so were the thousands of people who were moving to Chicago every year from the farms and rural villages of America. Moody, of course, had always gone after these men—he was one of them. But thanks to the Civil War and the interaction with freed slaves, Moody and Whittle, with the encouraging example of General O. O. Howard, teamed up to reach the blacks who had come to Chicago in greater numbers right after the war. The Chicago association did not advocate complete integration of the races. Indeed, General Howard attempted integration with a church in Washington, D.C., with a resultant disruption that destroyed the church and ultimately disappointed both races.[16] But Moody and Whittle did accomplish the formation of "an auxiliary association of colored men," and the promise that "the Association is open to them and that we will do all that we can for them."[17]

In the midst of all of these activities, the YMCA started publication of a four-page religious periodical. Entitled *Heavenly Tidings,* it contained inspirational stories from other religious papers and it sold in bulk quantities to associations in other cities across America. Moody became the driving force behind *Heavenly Tidings* because he had a vision for religious publications produced in bulk quantities. The Civil War had shown him the usefulness of such materials, and he had been in New York near the end of the conflict to learn as much as he could from the American Tract Society on how to produce and distribute such items in large quantities.[18]

Beyond keeping a hand in all of these YMCA activities, Moody managed to raise funds for a magnificent multipurpose building. The largest and most impressive association building in the nation, it was five stories tall, fronted with marble, and designed by the city's leading architect. The structure included a 3,500 seat auditorium, library, reading room, lecture hall, gymnasium, and space to rent out for offices as a source of ongoing revenue. The construction was finished in summer 1867 with a grand dedication held in September. Although some people proposed to name the building for Moody, he immediately declined the honor and insisted the name should be Farwell Hall. This certainly was more appropriate because John Farwell had served the association longer and he had personally put up a substantial portion of the $199,000 investment.[19]

Difficulties

While Moody helped transform the YMCA into a powerful instrument for the spread of Christianity and at the same time pastored a new and growing church, distressing personal signs appeared in both Dwight and Emma Moody. Each in his or her own way began unraveling emotionally, and both seemed on the verge of serious breakdowns. Emma drove herself—or allowed Dwight to drive her—at the same grueling pace he had kept up for several years. Within five months after the birth of their first child, she accompanied Dwight as they represented the Chicago association among the Union forces in Virginia. Writing to Samuel from Fort Monroe on the Atlantic coast, Moody informed his brother that they were on their way to General Grant's army and planned to stay for a month. "My wife is with me but she will not be able to go East" with him if he tried to come and visit the family. "She will have to hurry back home as soon as she possibly can for the child is not with us and it is a long time to leave her." Both Emma and Dwight were with the army in those last weeks, and they were among the first who entered Richmond when it fell to the Union.[20]

This trip to Virginia had to be difficult for Emma. First of all, she had been quite ill after the baby was born in October 1864. Her lack of strength and ability to snap back was mentioned by Dwight as late as January 1865, three months after the baby's arrival.[21] Second, she undoubtedly grieved her absence from little Emma. Added to these considerations was the heavy stress of those horrid last weeks of the war when thousands of men were slaughtered in both armies.

Even back in Chicago they maintained a relentless pace. There was the mission school, the church, and the YMCA. Then in early June 1866, Dwight decided a trip to Massachusetts would be good for Emma's health; besides, he felt pressure to see his mother. They all arrived in Massachusetts on schedule, but while they were there, Emma's father became critically ill. They fled by train back to Chicago, but were too late. "I suppose Mr. M has written to you of father's death," she wrote to Mrs. Moody. "I had hoped so much that I might see him living and it was so hard when coming to the house to see the [black] crepe on the door." This blow staggered Emma because she and her father were quite close and she had no inkling of his impending death.[22]

After the burial, Emma took the baby and got away from the pressures and choleric climate of Chicago. She visited relatives in Hyde Park, eight miles below the city. Dwight came by train and spent the nights. Then in August she spent a month with Dwight's brother Warren and his wife on a farm in Woodstock, Illinois, near the Wisconsin line. In September she visited other relatives in Milwaukee, Wisconsin, and Elgin, Illinois, returning home in early October.[23]

Emma gained strength by pulling out of their grinding schedule, whereas her husband became busier than ever and soon paid the price. Telltale signs of his own imminent collapse were numerous and ominous. His problems included increasing forgetfulness, a condition that typically accompanies impending emotional collapse. Unable to keep his dozens of affairs in order, he could not even remember to pick up food for his wife and baby. Dashing hither and yonder for the YMCA, or making speaking engagements all over the Midwest, he so overbooked himself in 1866 that he did not even get home for Christmas. It is not at all surprising that in the midst of his duties he increasingly lost his temper. One night when a heckler rankled him rather abusively, the usually controlled evangelist grabbed the offender and pushed him down a short flight of steps. The repentant preacher confessed his sin to the congregation, and he asked them and the man he shoved for forgiveness. Nevertheless, the damage was done. There was a rage inside that cried to be quelled.[24] Moody's trusted friend, D. W. Whittle, noted this in his diary:

> He had become mixed up with building Farwell Hall and was on committees for every kind of work and in his ambition to make his enterprises succeed because they were his, had taken his eyes off the Lord and had been burdened in Soul and unfruitful in his work for months. He longed for deliverance.[25]

Full deliverance did not immediately come. Moody, however, tried to help it along through a trip to England. Emma's health had taken a turn for the worse during Christmas 1866 while he was away at a conference in Pennsylvania. A cough in late autumn worsened as the months rolled by. Emma's physician recommended a trip abroad, maintaining that sea air on both legs of the journey would be just the tonic to promote healing.

SAILING FOR ENGLAND

During the time between raising the funds for the YMCA's Farwell Hall in early 1867 and the dedication in September, the Moodys left baby Emma with Mrs. Revell and set sail for England. The trip's goals were respiratory healing for Emma and an opportunity to visit friends and relatives she had not seen since her family emigrated to America eighteen years earlier.

The trip became more than a health cruise for Emma; it evolved into a way for Dwight to assuage his guilt of neglect. Furthermore, he had always wanted to meet George Mueller, whose autobiography, *A Life of Trust,* had unleashed such a profound effect upon his soul. Moody also longed to hear London's Charles H. Spurgeon preach. Moody had read many of his sermons with profit. He had heard, too, that Spurgeon, much like himself, had little formal education and no theological training, yet was called and led by God to preach. In case these incentives were not enough to justify the long voyage, there was an important Sunday school convention in London. Furthermore it would be useful for the Chicago YMCA president to go to London and meet George Williams, the founder of the YMCA.[26]

The Moodys boarded the train for New York on February 12. Ten days later they sailed for England. Where Moody found the money for such an expensive trip is uncertain, but all the evidence points to John V. Farwell. In any case, the voyage across the Atlantic made Mr. Moody seasick but Emma's cough and general health improved for a few weeks.[27]

Early in the trip both Emma and Dwight expressed homesickness for family and friends in America—especially their baby who was not yet three years old. They also found England archaic, crowded, and dirty. Dwight wrote, "I do not like the old country as well as our own"; and Emma implored her sister to "write me often, dear Anna, for I do enjoy a letter so much from home. It is real hard work for me to keep from being homesick sometimes, and especially when I do not feel well. There is no place like home." Emma admitted that the sea voyage had been a boon to her health for a time, but a relapse set in. Nevertheless "[I] hope to show you by the time I return that I have improved. . . . I am thinking now my own little girl would do me as much good as a doctor at present. I do so long to see her."[28]

Unhappy beginnings were soon forgotten. Mr. and Mrs. Moody were extended warm hospitality in England, Scotland, and Ireland. The gracious receptions from people in Great Britain began when D.

L. Moody attended the Sunday school convention in London. Early in the conference he was asked to bring greetings from America and report on the status of the Sunday school movement there. America's Dr. Henry Clay Trumbull was there and he related this account of Moody's first speech in the United Kingdom:

> The vice-chairman announced that they were glad to welcome their "American cousin, the Rev. Moody, of Chicago," who would now "move a vote of thanks to the noble Earl" who had presided on this occasion. With refreshing frankness and an utter disregard for conventionalities and mere compliments, Mr. Moody burst upon the audience with the bold announcement:
>
> "The chairman has made two mistakes. To begin with, I'm not the 'Reverend' Mr. Moody at all. I'm plain Dwight L. Moody, a Sabbath-school worker. And then I'm not your 'American cousin'! By the grace of God I'm your brother, who is interested with you in our Father's work for His children.
>
> "And now about this vote of thanks to 'the noble Earl' for being our chairman this evening. I don't see why we should thank him, any more than he should thank us. When at one time they offered to thank our Mr. Lincoln for presiding over a meeting in Illinois, he stopped it. He said he'd tried to do his duty, and they'd tried to do theirs. He thought it was an even thing all around."[29]

This opening made the audience gasp. They had never heard such a man. As Trumbull viewed it, "such talk could not be gauged by any standard." Nevertheless "its novelty was delightful." From that moment on, "Mr. Moody carried his English hearers."[30]

In the wake of this novel yet inspirational talk came invitations to speak in more places than their schedule allowed. Likewise people from all levels of society sought to shake Moody's hand and offer hospitality to this brother and sister from across the Atlantic. Emma wrote home of their invitations to teas, dinners, and weekend visits—invitations that came from a member of Parliament and an arsenal employee, as well as people associated with a bank and Newgate Prison. "We have invitations nearly two weeks ahead to take teas, dinners, etc.," she informed Anna. Similar delightful occasions transpired in Scotland, and "we have had a very pleasant time."[31]

The Moodys visited YMCA facilities, Sunday schools, prayer meetings, and worship services in England, Scotland, and Ireland. At almost every stop Mr. Moody gave sermons or lectures that stirred people, and he encouraged them to pursue kingdom work with more vigor. Near the end of their trip they made a quick visit across the En-

D. L. Moody (1867)

glish Channel to France where they took in the World's Fair, or Paris Exposition, that was inaugurated by Napoleon III.

There is no way to measure Moody's impact on the British Isles during this four-and-a-half month trip, but his influence, if not wide, was profound. A sixteen-year-old lad named John Kenneth MacKenzie, who eventually became a well-known medical missionary to China, dated his spiritual transformation to hearing Moody speak in Bristol, England, on May 10, 1867. Fourteen other young men sought Moody's counsel and prayer at the same session. Moody's ministry in Liverpool caused the Reverend Charles Garrett to open cheap restaurants in that city for the working-class people, as an alternative to the many public houses and other drinking establishments. A pastor and editor took Moody's suggestion and started a union prayer meeting (along the lines of Chicago's model) at a YMCA in London. This man personally directed it for the next forty-one years.[32]

At a July 1, 1867, farewell reception given for the Moodys at London's Aldersgate YMCA, it was apparent that one of their most enduring influences was touching the hearts of their new friends. One of the speakers at the farewell gathering put it this way:

Few men who have visited a foreign shore have endeared themselves to so many hearts in so short a time, or with an unknown name and without letters of commendation won their way so deeply into the affections of a multitude of Christian brothers as had Mr. Moody. Few had even heard of him before, but having talked with him or heard him speak of Jesus, asked for no other warrant to yield him a large measure of their love.[33]

Moody's impact on Britain in 1867 was profound, but Britain's influence on Moody was even greater. He wrote to his mother on March 19, "I do not expect to visit this country again. One trip across the water is enough for me." But then he wrote to the Rev. R. C. Morgan as soon as he got home in July: "I want to tell you how thankful I am for ever going to London; it seems to me that I was almost in darkness until I went over there. I have enjoyed myself much more in Christ since I got back. I would not take anything for what I have learnt while in your city. I love the dear friends in London more than I can express with this pen, and my heart goes out to you all very much."[34]

Spurgeon and Mueller

Among those who held a part of his heart—who had left an indelible mark on him—was London's most famous preacher, the bearded, round-faced, and rather rotund Charles Haddon Spurgeon. At a London celebration in 1884, Moody looked back on his first personal encounter with Spurgeon in 1867. He said that soon after he was converted he began to read about "a young man preaching in London with great power." He related that "everything I could get hold of in print that he ever said, I read," even though "never expecting that, some day, I should myself be a preacher."

Moody noted that when he made his way to England in 1867 "the first place to which I came was this building [Spurgeon's church]. I was told that I could not get in without a ticket, but I made up my mind to get in somehow, and I succeeded." Moody remembered that he sat in the gallery and feasted on the words sent forth from his hero. It happened to be the year Spurgeon preached a series at the Agricultural Hall, so Moody followed him there. He imbibed several more of Spurgeon's messages, "and he sent me back to America a better man."[35] Over the years Spurgeon's sermons markedly influenced the American preacher. He owned a set of Spurgeon's published sermons and liberally quoted from them during three decades of preaching.

Moody informed John V. Farwell that he had met Spurgeon and was in high hopes of getting him to America to preach. "The churches [in England] are dead and [Spurgeon] is trying to bring them to life. I think he will do it." Moody continued, noting that the great En-

The Rev. Charles H. Spurgeon

glish preacher has trained "130 men for the ministry and had 80 men in his school [for pastors]." It amazed Moody that Spurgeon "speaks five nights out of the week and preaches three sermons that are published every week. . . . I suppose I have not learned half yet that he is doing. But he does not give much attention to Sunday Schools and they are fifty years behind us."[36] As much as Moody admired Spurgeon, he did not grovel to him or fail to look at things with a discerning eye. To Moody's mind, not giving proper attention to children's ministry was a serious shortcoming.

Next to Spurgeon, the man Moody most longed to meet was George Mueller, a German-born, university-trained expatriate to England. Mueller had made quite a stir in evangelical Christian circles with the publication of his autobiography, *A Life of Trust*. Mueller did not want to write his life story, but the pressure of friends caused him to produce a volume that he subtitled *The Lord's Dealings with George Mueller*. The autobiography no doubt found even a wider readership than the publications of Spurgeon's powerful, biblical sermons. J. B. Stillson had given *A Life of Trust* to Moody in the late 1850s. Certainly it was one factor in Moody's decision to give up business and go into full-time ministry, expect great things from God, and never ask anyone for money for himself.

Mueller's autobiography graphically shows what God can do through an ordinary person completely surrendered and full of faith in a great God. Mueller became a Christian in his native Germany in the midst of a somewhat dissolute life as a hard-drinking, big-spending, lazy university student. During his riotous student career he had several encounters with devout Christians who led him into a relationship with Jesus Christ. Much to his father's chagrin and dismay, Mueller became a radical disciple of Christ. He turned his back on a law career and decided to become a missionary to European Jews. Eventually God pointed him to England, and after a series of obedient steps he went (with a wife and daughter) where God was leading, although he could not fully see what God would have him do.

Finally Mueller arrived at Bristol, a thriving seaport city on England's west coast. Bristol had a large harbor and a busy area of docks, warehouses, and factories. Heavy traffic in goods and people brought trade and profits, as well as an equal measure of poverty and human degradation. In Bristol the Muellers were appalled at the exploitation of the poor—especially children. Bristol was teeming with indigent children—among them thousands of orphans—who were forced to work long hours for extremely low wages. These youngsters were malnourished, dressed in filthy rags, and forced to live in housing that made Chicago's "Sands" look upscale. The Muellers started a school—complete with room and board—for children no one seemed to care for. Over the years the Muellers and their co-workers housed, fed, clothed, and taught thousands of children. Many of the little wretches they fished from the filthy streets of Bristol became Christians and went on to live lives that brought great glory to God.

Perhaps the most remarkable aspect of Mueller's life was not that he followed God's leading to England—a country whose language he did not know; nor was it so astounding that he and his wife opened a Christian orphanage and school. Indeed, other people had ministries to poor children. What was so phenomenal about the Muellers was that they never asked anyone for money to do their work. They prayed for God to help them provide for these little children—and God did provide. Money, food, clothing—everything that was needed—always came in. *A Life of Trust* told the ongoing story in numerous British and American editions.

The Moodys went to Bristol, met George Mueller, saw the orphanage and school buildings, and learned that the program was spreading to other cities. Dwight Moody was enthralled. He wrote to Farwell, "I was at Bristol the other day. . . . Bristol is where the great orphan school of George Mueller is." At the present time "he has 1150 children in his house but never asks a man for a sent of money to support them he calls on God and God sends the money to him. It is wonderful to see what God can do with a man of prayer." Moody made clear that he was going to get stories together on Mueller's work and see to their publication in *Heavenly Tidings* and various Sunday school publications.[37]

Moody always assumed the role of student around people who knew more about God and ministry than he did. Consequently, when he was with the venerable Mueller he soaked up stories about how God had led him and his wife, met their needs, and touched the lives of children. Moody also plied Mueller with questions about how he gleaned so much nourishment out of the Bible, and how he became such an effective Bible teacher. Moody granted that "there are different ways of studying the Bible," but he said, "I received from George Mueller the idea of taking one book of the Bible at a time . . . and reading it at one sitting. . . . If I am in a hurry on a given day," Moody said, then I "take a short Epistle, or one of the minor prophets." In any case, from his time with Mueller, Moody avoided chopping up texts. He said if Emma sent him an eight-page letter he would not read a page a day. If he did, he would forget from day to day what he had already read. And besides, he might miss the major point of the whole letter.[38]

The Plymouth Brethren

Among the many things Moody received from his visit with Mueller was an introduction to a fairly young sect of evangelical Christianity called the Plymouth Brethren. Mueller was a member of the Brethren movement, whose roots went back to the 1820s. Beginning as a protest against some doctrines of the Church of England, it eventually, under the zealous leadership of John Nelson Darby, seceded from the Anglican denomination and became a separate sect. The Brethren were unswervingly committed to Scripture as the inspired revelation of God. They stressed conversion as a dynamic and life-changing experience, and they were noted for their evangelistic and missionary zeal. They also had an uncompromising belief in the imminent, bodily, and premillennial return of the Lord Jesus Christ.

Moody found these doctrines markedly attractive, and many Brethren friends he met encouraged him to cling to these positions with all his strength. Just how far along Moody was in his own theological thinking by 1867 is hard to say, but at the least the faithful Brethren encouraged him in these doctrines.

No doubt the Moodys found certain other trappings of the Brethren movement rather affirming of their own position. For example, the Brethren frowned on the ordination of ministers and relied instead on their understanding of the primitive Christian church. To this end, they set aside laymen as elders to preach, teach, and lead in the weekly worship and breaking of bread. Faithful to the simplicity of the first-century church as they interpreted it, Darby's followers likewise eschewed prayer books, liturgy, clerical vestments, stained glass, crosses, and every other vestige of "formalism" and "popery" that they found offensive in the Anglican Church.

Moody's initial love affair with the Brethren movement was inspired by their love for the Bible and their purposeful focus on reaching the lost for Christ. Therefore, Moody spent much time in Brethren assemblies on his trip, and he would invite many, including John Nelson Darby, to come to America and preach at the Illinois Street Church.

Within a few years, however, Moody became uncomfortable with the Brethren. Not that he eventually swayed from his commitment to Scripture, premillennialism, missions, and evangelism, but he did find the increasingly separatistic views of the movement to be personally distressing and ultimately harmful to Christian unity. For instance, Darby was a staunch Calvinist who held unyieldingly to predestination and a doctrine of the elect. Increasingly, Darby unleashed verbal warfare against anyone who gave quarter to the Arminian and Wesleyan view that Christ died for all men and women. Moody was never a predestinarian, and as the years went by, his proclamation theology was like that of John Wesley rather than the one embraced by John Calvin (and Darby). Furthermore, while Darby wanted less and less to do with Christians who advocated clergy ordination, liturgy, and using women in ministry, Moody was seeking ways to unify all of the denominations.

Finally, Darby personally launched an ugly, verbal attack on Moody's "Arminian" views, arguing that he and most Americans, except for a few Presbyterians, did not know "the first principles of grace." Indeed, one day while doing a Bible reading time at Farwell Hall in Chicago, he and Moody had a verbal exchange on free will. The session ended when Darby, in disgust with Moody's emphasis on "whosoever will may come," closed his Bible and walked out; and he never returned.[39]

Fortunately in 1867 these battle lines were not yet drawn; Moody could revel in the presence of the Plymouth brothers and learn all he could from Mueller and some other men God placed in his path. One of these was a West Londoner named Henry Varley. A butcher by trade and a devout prayer warrior and evangelist by calling, Varley took a liking to Moody and managed to open the doors of many Brethren halls so that the American could preach. Thanks to Varley's good offices, the Moodys were invited to Dublin, Ireland, where Mr. Moody spoke.

Henry Moorhouse

In the wake of Moody's message, an encounter took place that, at the time, seemed inconsequential to the Americans. A Lancashire-born lad who stood no taller than Moody's shoulders had crossed the Irish Sea from England to hear the singular American preach. After the meeting this Plymouth brother, known among the Brethren as the "Boy Preacher" (he was actually twenty-seven years old), came up to Moody, introduced himself, and said, "I'll preach for you in America." Moody recalled that he scarcely took Henry "Harry" Moorhouse seriously. He was short, with a boyish-looking face. He did not appear to be a day older than seventeen. Furthermore, Moody was certain he could not preach, because to his mind he did not look like a preacher. But Harry showed determination. He inquired when and on what ship the Moodys were going home to America. Moody was glad he could not, at that moment, remember the details of their departure, for he had no intention of taking this stripling back with them to Chicago.[40]

God had other plans for Moody and Moorhouse. Several weeks after the Moodys were back home in Chicago, a letter arrived from Harry Moorhouse saying he was in America and would be pleased to come out to Chicago and preach. Moody sent him a less than cordial letter: "If you come West, call on me." He assumed he would

Henry Moorhouse about 1870

never hear from Moorhouse again. A letter came by return mail, once again offering to preach at Moody's church. Moody responded again, only slightly more invitingly: "If you happen to come West, drop in on me." Moody recalled that in few days a third letter came "stating that on a certain Thursday he would be in Chicago and preach for me. Then what to do with him I didn't know. I made up my mind that he couldn't preach. I was going out of town on Thursday and Friday, and I told some of the officers of the church 'to let him preach on Thursday night.'"

Moody recalled that the officers demurred. "They said we are beginning to get a strong interest in our evening services and we don't need a stranger who 'might do more harm than good.'" On some impulse he did not understand at the time, Moody said, "You might try him" on Thursday. The regular prayer meeting was Friday. "After hearing him you can either announce that he will speak again the next night or you can have your usual prayer-meeting. If he speaks well both nights you will know whether to announce him or me for the Sunday meetings. I will be back Saturday."[41]

The Response to Moorhouse

Moody took his trip and left Moorhouse to Emma and the church officers. As soon as he returned to Chicago, Moody went home and asked Emma how Moorhouse had gone over with the congregation. He recalled their conversation this way:

> "They like him very much."
> "Did you hear him?"
> "Yes."
> "Well, did you like him?"
> "Yes, I liked him very much. He has preached two sermons from that verse of John, 'For God so loved the world, that He gave His only begotten Son, that whosoever believeth in Him should not perish, but have everlasting life,' and I think you will like him, although he preaches a little differently from you."
> "How's that?"
> "Well, he tells the worst sinners that God loves them."
> "Then," said I, "he is wrong."
> "I think you will agree with him if you hear him . . . because he backs up everything from the Bible."

Moody said when he went into church on Sunday morning everyone had their Bibles. Once again the former pickpocket and rowdy-turned-evangelist preached from John 3:16, and he did so for seven meetings in a row. "I had never heard anything quite like it," said Moody. He preached "the most extraordinary" sermons from that one verse. "He just took the whole verse, and then went through the Bible from Genesis to Revelation to prove that in all ages God loved the world. God had sent prophets and patriarchs and holy men to warn us, and then He sent His Son, and after they killed Him, He sent the Holy Ghost."

Moody declared in all sincerity, "I never knew up to that time that God loved us so much. This heart of mine began to thaw out; I could not keep back the tears. It was like news from a far country: I just drank it in. So did the congregation."[42]

Transformation of D. L. Moody

Moorhouse's visit to Chicago had an utterly transforming effect on D. L. Moody. He was never the same man. Nothing prior to this time, except his conversion, had such a profound impact on his soul.

The Holy Spirit used Moorhouse to show Moody that God is love and that Christ came to save sinners—that salvation is unearned, undeserved, and unrepayable. It is all grace. Perhaps Moody knew this in his head prior to 1867, but he did not see it with the eyes of his heart. Likewise, until Moorhouse's visit he had not preached this kind of grace. Heretofore he essentially proclaimed only that a just and holy God is going to judge sinners, so non-Christians should flee from the wrath to come. This was true, but as Henry showed him, "your sword is only partially out of the scabbard." The just and holy God loves sinners. If they will only respond, He will bring them to Himself and make them His children. "Come unto me," cried Jesus. As William Moody summed it up, "Mr. Moorehouse taught Moody to draw his sword full length, to fling the scabbard away, and enter the battle with the naked blade."[43]

Moorhouse pointed Moody to this biblical and transformational proclamation theology of "Love them into the Kingdom";[44] and he also helped Moody change his whole approach to preaching. Moorhouse prophetically told Moody that he needed to become a better student of the English Bible. Indeed, he "told him frankly that he needed a better knowledge of that Bible to enable him to win souls." He suggested that Moody get a concordance and use it to trace themes throughout the entire Bible. Although some wise people cautioned Moody that this method can be a rather imperfect way of interpreting Scripture (certainly Mueller's way of reading is more helpful), Moody managed to adopt this reading approach with profit. He did not limit himself to this method; rather, he used it as a way to see a text, a theme, or a key word in a wider biblical context.[45]

F. C. Bland

Another British encounter in 1867 had long-lasting effects on D. L. Moody. F. C. Bland, the High Sheriff of Kerry County, Ireland, was an influential worldling who became a Christian in the 1861 Kerry Revival. Bright, articulate, and well educated, he quickly became a deep and perceptive student of the Bible. J. Edwin Orr wrote that Bland "drank deeply of Brethren teaching, without ever joining their ranks," presumably remaining a communicating member of the Church of Ireland. After Moody and Bland met in 1867, Moody was markedly impressed by the layman's biblical knowledge and teaching skill. The two became friends, and, as Orr phrased it, the result was "Bland becoming Bible consultant of Dwight L. Moody."[46]

Moody certainly needed a Bible consultant, but he and Emma

left England with much more than that. Besides someone to write to when he had interpretive questions about Scripture, Moody was immeasurably enriched by meetings with Spurgeon, Mueller, Varley, and a host of others. At a farewell dinner in London before the Moodys left for America, new friends gathered and gave testimonies of their appreciation for their visit. They gave Mrs. Moody a gold watch, and they handed her husband an envelope with a large honorarium. Both gifts were offered "as a token of . . . affection and esteem." Several people also commented on the solidarity now being formed between evangelicals on both sides of the Atlantic.[47]

Among the other treasures and memories the Moodys took home was the knowledge that God had His hand on them, that He would provide for their needs, and that Mr. Moody could preach with effectiveness in a land that still viewed Americans as colonists and therefore a bit inferior to the citizens of the mother land. The Moodys likewise went home with sincere friends—among these some of the most influential members of British evangelicalism's inner circle. As they sailed they certainly pondered the wonder of their bonds with the Spurgeons, the Muellers, Lord and Lady Kinnaird, and R. C. Morgan. Likewise, Henry Varley's parting words to Dwight Moody, "The world has yet to see what God will do with and for and through and in and by the man who is fully and wholly consecrated to him," pierced the American's heart.[48]

Moody determined to be that man.

CHAPTER SIX

TRIAL BY FIRE
A City and a Soul Aflame
1868–1871

"It Is Almost Too Sacred an Experience to Name."

Emma and Dwight Moody returned to Chicago in late July 1867. Emma's health showed marked improvement, and they were both inspired and encouraged by their trip. Dwight was not at all rested by the whirlwind tour of Britain, but the people he had met and the insights he had gained provided temporary rejuvenation.

No sooner did they get home than Mr. Moody started a series of speaking engagements that took him away from Chicago three to four days a week. He evidently tried to match Spurgeon's ambitious schedule—making certain he was home to preach at his own church on Sundays but delivering messages almost nightly in other places during the week. Determined now to devote most of his energy to preaching and lecturing, he accepted a wide range of speaking opportunities from YMCA associations, Sunday school conferences, and local churches. When these were added to his responsibilities at the Illinois Street Church and the Chicago YMCA, his schedule soon became more demanding than the one he had left. He wrote to his mother after being home from England for a month, informing her that he was traveling so much that she now would see him more "often than you did when I lived in Boston. . . ." He also mentioned an invitation to speak in Vermont in September, "so you will see me sooner than you expected."[1]

As far as appearances went, everything seemed to be going well for Dwight Moody. Farwell Hall, the first large, multipurpose YMCA building in America, received its finishing touches in late summer. On Sunday, September 29, the YMCA leadership held a grand opening and dedication, with an over-capacity crowd in attendance.

Visitors and dignitaries from several states came for the celebration. During the course of the afternoon John V. Farwell was honored, as were several Chicago philanthropists, including farm equipment magnate Cyrus H. McCormick. Front and center in all of this stood D. L. Moody. No longer viewed as a slightly deranged buffoon, Moody reigned as president of this august YMCA with its magnificent building. A proven fund-raiser and widely sought-after speaker, he now behaved quite comfortably on platforms with business, philanthropic, and religious leaders from either side of the Atlantic Ocean.

Moody's speech for this gala celebration reflected his newfound international vision. The forces of evil had been on the offensive long enough. The "strongholds of sin" needed to be aggressively attacked. Let us call upon the Lord to use this Chicago Association, he urged, to unleash a Christian influence that "should extend to every county in the State, to every State in the Union, and finally crossing the waters, should help to bring the whole world to God."[2] Moody's address had all the ring of the Union army's 1861 cry, "On to Richmond."

SUNDAY SCHOOL WORK

Besides YMCA work, Moody had other offensive weapons to use against the forces of darkness. One of his most potent turned out to be the renewed Sunday school. After the Civil War, Moody became vice president of the Chicago Sunday School Union. Soon thereafter he was also elected to the State Sunday-School Executive Committee. From these vantage points he encouraged the publication of a periodical, *The Chicago Sunday-School Teacher,* designed to give teaching hints and inspirational stories to Illinois teachers. With this journal, as well as the YMCA's *Heavenly Tidings,* now under his influence, he launched a major assault on disorganized, unbiblical, and uninteresting Sunday schools.

Moody did much more than criticize ineffective ministry—he offered a solution. Along with a Peoria friend, William Reynolds, and his Chicago colleague, B. F. Jacobs, he unveiled a plan to publish Bible lessons to be used each week in every school. They tried this idea of unified lesson plans first with several Chicago Sunday schools. The effects were excellent. Consequently, the lessons were published weekly, and the experiment caught on and spread. By 1868 unified lessons were in use among many evangelical churches in Illinois, Michigan, Iowa, Wisconsin, and Minnesota. In 1869 the National Sunday-School Convention in Newark, New Jersey, adopted the idea, appointing a committee to encourage the spread of unified lessons across the nation and into several foreign countries.[3]

A NEW HOME

In the midst of Sunday-school lesson promotions and YMCA functions, John V. Farwell and some of his friends decided to thank the Moodys for all they were doing for the advancement of Christ's kingdom. Moody had honored Farwell by insisting that the YMCA building be named Farwell Hall, and now Farwell honored his dear friend with a different building. On January 1, 1868, Emma and Dwight were given the keys to a new house, fully furnished, on State Street about three blocks from where they were living. Farwell, who continually developed land and built houses on it, decided the Moodys should live in one of his houses—rent free. The house and lot were provided by the Farwells, and all the furnishings were donated by several other Moody admirers. Among these interior gifts were two large portraits—one of Emma and one of Dwight. These were donated by the artist, G. P. A. Healy, a prominent portrait painter and well-known Roman Catholic.[4]

THE YMCA FIRE

The Moodys enjoyed their new home in solitude for only a few days. The peace and quiet of the New Year ended abruptly on Tuesday, January 7. That morning a fire broke out in downtown Chicago. Within a few hours most of Farwell Hall was destroyed by flames, as were a number of other buildings adjacent to the three-month-old structure. The secretary to the Chicago YMCA's Board of Managers wrote a terse description of what happened:

We were called upon in the Providence which God permitted to visit us to "pass under the rod" and literally to obey the voice of the prophet, "Glorify ye the Lord in the fires." At a quarter past nine the cry of fire in Farwell Hall rang sharply through the office, seeming at first as the cry of one who mocketh, but soon realizing as true in the awful conflagration which swept in an hour to the object of our prayers and labors for years. But in the hour of the fierce, fiery elements, God's hand was manifest in kindness, for no flame kindled upon the person of our young men in the work and no life was lost. Many friends came to the rescue of such effects as could be saved and we succeeded in securing all the Association records, part of the library and rooms furniture, with nearly eight hundred volumes of the most valuable works in our library. When the flames were fiercest, a call for prayer was sounded and a daily prayer meeting, which has never been suspended for one day since its organization, gathered in the lecture room of the Methodist Church at the usual hour for prayer and praise. Most earnestly and humbly we bowed before the great and all-wise Giver, blessing the hand which took as well as gave. The test of our faith was also a test of our friends, and until the flames had wrapped our buildings as a winding sheet, we had never known how many and how true were those who loved our Association. Scores wept as though their own homes were burned.[5]

Mr. & Mrs. Cyrus H. McCormick

Before the embers cooled, Moody and many friends of the YMCA began knocking on the doors of businessmen, seeking funds to rebuild the partially insured structure. People responded with extraordinary generosity. By April $85,000 of the $135,000 needed beyond insurance money was subscribed through tax-exempt stock sales. Moody asked Cyrus McCormick, the farm equipment manufacturer, if he could guarantee the $50,000 balance so that work could commence. McCormick, a generous man who seldom turned a deaf ear to Moody's pleas, covered much of the need.[6]

On January 19, 1869, doors opened on Farwell Hall number two. A structure considerably more modest than its predecessor, the new YMCA facility included neither a gymnasium nor dormitory space, and the auditorium and library were considerably reduced in size. Nevertheless, Farwell Hall became a monument of civic pride. There were two hundred gas jets to illumine the 2,500-seat auditorium, and the walls were decorated with biblical frescoes. A local newspaper editor called it a "modern Pantheon" where "Arminianism and Calvinism sit side by side."[7]

TRIALS AND DIFFICULTIES

The years 1868 and 1869 were trying and exhausting ones for the Moodys. Raising funds again, as well as carrying on YMCA, Sunday-school association, and church activities, added enormous pressures to the young family. Moody still preached at his own church on Sundays, and he went to speak at other places too numerous to count during the week. And if all of this did not generate enough pressure, he started a young men's group in the YMCA called Yokefellows. They prayed together two nights a week and then made commitments to canvass rooming houses, saloons, and corner hangouts within a mile radius of Farwell Hall. Yokefellows knocked on doors and gave people a piece of evangelistic literature. Those who showed interest were brought to Farwell Hall for evangelistic services. If the recruits had no church home, they were made welcome at Illinois Street Church.[8]

In the midst of this flurry of activity, back in Massachusetts brother Samuel Moody fell on hard times. He wrote to Dwight and Emma and asked for a loan. It hurt Dwight deeply to have to say no, for the time being, because he and Emma were temporarily without funds themselves. In fact, they were searching the mail daily for the return of a $300 loan they had made to a St. Louis man who promised to repay them eight weeks earlier, but they did assure

Samuel they would send $300 as soon as it came.[9]

To complicate matters even more, Emma was pregnant with their second child. On March 25, 1869, William Revell Moody was born. His health was excellent, but Emma did not have an easy time with the pregnancy and delivery. Certainly Emma's condition was complicated by the pressures of their busy life, being short on money, and watching her husband burn himself out. In any case, three months after delivering William, Emma wrote to Mrs. Moody that "I do not feel strong yet as I was sick a long time after the baby was born." Somewhere Dwight found the money to employ a nurse for a few weeks, as well as "two very good Norwegian girls" to help with little Emma and the household chores.[10]

Not having money to help his brother, and being frequently out of town and away from his wife, left Dwight Moody feeling overwhelmed with guilt. Already burdened with a sense of inadequacy, he experienced more agony when his mother chastised him for not visiting Northfield. On December 21, 1869, trying to finish his work in Davenport, Iowa, so he could be home with Emma and the children by Christmas, Dwight Moody wrote an apologetic letter to the family in Massachusetts. Hoping to reassure Samuel and his mother of his intention to help alleviate their hardships, he said he was sorry to learn that Samuel had lost his broom corn crop. "I do hope he will not get discouraged. I think of him so often and . . . I cant tell you how much I love him. . . . I will soon be in condition so [I] may help him more than I have. I hope you will not think I am forgetful of you but my thought has been to give him a start and then he will be able to see your wants." He finally assured his mother, "You must never think you will ever come to want. God will help us provide for you."[11]

THE NEED FOR DELIVERANCE

Signs appeared showing that Dwight Moody was on a guilt-ridden and work-laden pathway toward emotional and spiritual collapse. Exhausted, yet plagued by a constant feeling of never doing enough for Emma, the children, his mother, and Sam, he was even more burdened by a sense of never pleasing God because he could not meet the massive needs he observed everywhere he turned. Looking back on this time, Moody admitted that "in my work I was quite discouraged, and I was ready to hang my harp on the willow." Sometimes he would find temporary solace in a Bible story—Noah, after all, did not get discouraged and quit. But guilt and anxiety inevitably reappeared. They were constant companions he could not elude. Moody did not see it at the time, but later he knew that "pride and selfishness and ambition and self-seeking, and everything that is contrary to God's law" were the root cause of the malady. He was close to finding the cure, but it was not quick or easy in coming.[12] "O, it [my deliverance] was preceded by a wrestling and a hard struggle. I think I had never got out of this miserable selfishness. There was a time when I wanted to see my little vineyard blessed and I could not get out of it."[13]

Glimpses of Deliverance

The first glimpse of liberation came as Moody kept recalling a strange encounter he had had one night years earlier after addressing a Sabbath school. "There seemed to be a great deal of interest and quite a number rose for prayer, and I remember I went out quite rejoiced." Then, Moody recalled, "an old man followed me out—I have never seen him since. I had never seen him before, and don't even know his name." This stranger "caught hold of my hand and gave me a little bit of advice. I don't know what he meant at the time, but he said, 'Young man, when you speak again, honor the Holy Ghost.'" When the old man departed Moody went on to speak at another meeting. But those words never went away: "Honor the Holy Ghost." Moody pondered the strange evening.[14]

Cooke and Hawxhurst

In 1868 Sarah Cooke, a woman who would help clarify the question and become an instrument for Moody's deliverance, moved to Chicago with her husband. From the window of their apartment on Wabash Avenue, she recalled looking out as multitudes hurried by. Somewhat overwhelmed by the size of Chicago—the population was nearly 300,000 by 1870—she wondered where she could find a place to serve God. A quarter century later she wrote: "The first place I found was the YMCA. . . . Mr. Moody was an active worker there—'A diamond in the rough'—most truly, with the desire to do good burning through everything, his very earnestness moving people, but withal such a lack in his teachings of the divine unction and power." His shortcomings notwithstanding, "he was always kind and friendly and anxious to enlist in any way the help of Christians. He always encouraged me to take part in his meetings."[15]

For two years Sarah Cooke ministered at the YMCA. She attended meetings and took an active part in prayer time and follow-up with new Christians. In 1870 she befriended Mrs. W. R. Hawxhurst, a new convert who surrendered her life to Christ at the

YMCA. Hawxhurst, a young widow with a little girl to raise, welcomed the friendship offered by Sarah Cooke, and soon the two women became close friends. Cooke became a mentor to Hawxhurst, and one of the things she did was take her along as she prayed and ministered with others. In summer 1871, Cooke and Hawxhurst attended a Free Methodist camp meeting about thirty-five miles west of Chicago in a rural town called St. Charles. While there, Cooke explained, "a burden came upon me for Mr. Moody, that the Lord would give him the Baptism of the Holy Ghost and of fire. No opportunity after that was lost in urging upon him his great need and encouraging him to speak with the certainty that it was for him."[16]

Mrs. Cooke and Mrs. Hawxhurst began to attend all of Moody's preaching sessions at the YMCA. At the close of the meetings they always told him, "We are praying for you."

One night when his temper was threadbare, he looked at them and said: "Why are you praying for me? Why don't you pray for the unsaved?"

As Moody told the story to R. A. Torrey, the women replied, "We are praying that you may get the power." Sarah Cooke did not sense any antagonism from Moody, but he demonstrated absolutely no "conviction of his need of any further work." Nevertheless, Moody told Torrey several years later that he was irritated by these two well-meaning but presumptuous Christian workers.[17]

Urgent Prayer Meetings

As Moody grew wearier on his ministry treadmill, he cried out to God for help. In the wake of his prayers, his attitude toward Hawxhurst and Cooke gradually softened. Could their comments, he wondered, be related to the words from the old man who had confronted him several years before? With nothing to lose but his pride, in early autumn 1871 Moody called these prayer warriors aside after a meeting. "I wish you would tell me what you mean" about this power, he exclaimed. According to Torrey, "They told him about the Holy Ghost. Then he asked that he might pray with them and not they merely pray for him."[18] Cooke said Moody "asked us to meet with him in Farwell Hall every Friday afternoon for prayer."

For the next several weeks they met as often as Moody found the time to attend. "As we met there from time to time, he would get increasingly in earnest," and on Friday, October 6, "he was intensely so." Sarah Cooke published her account several years before Moody died, so it is unlikely that she exaggerated the event, especially since

Moody himself spoke of both of them with thanksgiving and fondness until his death. Cooke said, "At every meeting each of us prayed aloud in turn, but at this meeting Mr. Moody's agony was so great that he rolled on the floor and in the midst of many tears and groans cried to God to be baptized with the Holy Ghost and fire."[19]

Moody left this prayer meeting unchanged—he experienced no freedom from the mental and spiritual agony that bound his soul. He wondered if he could carry this burden much longer.

THE CHICAGO FIRE

Deliverance was near, but Moody still faced a trial by fire. On Sunday night, October 8, he found the strength to preach at Farwell Hall. Emma was not there; she was home tending the children. Sarah Cooke and her husband were there, and no doubt one of them, at least, was praying for the liberation of Moody's imprisoned soul.

At the close of the service the city fire bell sounded. This alarm caused no particular concern inasmuch as Chicagoans, living in a hastily constructed city of tarpaper and soft wood, were continually plagued by fires. On this night, however, the alarms continued to sound. Rapidly the city was engulfed in what federal officials would describe as "the most destructive fire of modern times." Several factors conspired to make this fire unusually devastating. The Chicago area was experiencing severe, almost drought-like conditions. Added to this was "a violent southwest wind." These conditions, according to a local observer, when added to a city "rapidly built, and, to a very large extent, of pine lumber, so that there were miles of buildings and sidewalks of thoroughly seasoned pine, . . . conditions existed as favorable as can be conceived for a conflagration."[20]

The Devastation

Chicagoans were used to fires, but this was an inferno. No one could have predicted the extent of the devastation. The holocaust consumed nearly four square miles. According to federal investigators, "the fire laid in utter ruin the entire business center and a very large proportion of all the residences of the city." Over 18,000 buildings were destroyed and more than 100,000 people were left homeless. "All the principal hotels, and all the public buildings, national, state, city, and county, were consumed. The vast warehouses, grain-elevators, steamboats, vessels in the river, bridges, railway stations, etc. were burnt. The total loss [was] carefully estimated at $200,000,000"—a staggering fortune by 1871 dollars—which left fifty-seven insurance companies insolvent and bankrupted countless businesses and people. It was estimated that more than one thousand people perished. No one could certify the number of deaths because many bodies were totally consumed and the city was full of uncounted and unknown newcomers and drifters.[21]

The firestorm was no respecter of persons or religions. Christians, Jews, and nonbelievers alike were wiped out by this torrent of flames that raged "all Sunday night, and Monday and Monday night," and did not burn out until Tuesday afternoon, October 10. Most of the damage was north of the South Branch of the Chicago River, spreading north and eastward from there to Lake Michigan. The North Side of Chicago was leveled—only one house eerily remained standing in a three-and-a-half-square-mile part of the city.[22]

Moody's Losses

Much of the physical kingdom Dwight Moody had labored to build lay in ruins. The Illinois Street Church, the second Farwell Hall, and their gift house on State Street were gone. At first Moody did not give a thought to the buildings; it was his family he feared for. His recollection of the early part of the night appeared in many sermons over the years. He especially remembered that at the end of his message he had not asked people to surrender to Christ. As a result the inquiry room was sparsely filled. After he had prayed with the few who lingered, the city bell rang out again. But to Moody "that was nothing in those days, and I paid no attention to it." He said that

> after the inquiry-meeting we started for home. As soon as I started I found the city was doomed; even the clapboards of the building we were in were falling; and the burning shingles were dropping down. The fire was breaking out all around me. It was a very serious question whether I could get home to my wife and children and get them to a place of safety. When I got them out of the bed, flames thirty feet high were following me, and before midnight the hall where I preached that sermon was in ashes; before two o'clock the church where I worshipped was in ashes; before three o'clock the house that I lived in was in ashes. . . . It seemed to me that I had a glimpse in that fire of what the Day of Judgment will be, when I saw the flames rolling down the streets, twenty and thirty feet high, consuming everything in its march that did not flee. I saw there the millionaire and the beggar fleeing alike. There was no difference. That night great men, learned men, wise men, all fled alike. There was no difference. And when God comes to judge the world there will be no difference.[23]

Portrait of D. L. Moody painted by G. P. A. Healy (1867)

When Moody finally arrived home and roused his wife, she went to little Emma's bed and awakened her. "If you will not scream or cry, I will show you a sight you will never forget." She then took the girl and her baby brother and quickly put two layers of clothing on each of them, assuming it would be a long time before they had access to a change of clothes. Then Emma took the children to a large window and showed them a quick glimpse of Chicago aflame. Immediately the children were crowded into the carriage of a neighbor, who generously took little Emma and William to Moody family friends in a far northwestern suburb. Dwight and Emma remained behind as long as possible to assist other North Side refugees.[24]

The Children's Memories

William Moody could not remember the ordeal of the great fire. He was only two years old. But his parents often recalled the events of that dreadful night. Almost nothing from the house could be saved. The fire was progressing northward too quickly. Only a few personal items were thrown into a baby cart and sent along with the children. Emma Moody decided to save Healy's portrait of Dwight. William wrote:

> This portrait Mrs. Moody prized above anything the house contained.
>
> A stranger who had entered the room assisted in taking it from the wall. Calling Mr. Moody, his wife urged him to save it for her. The ludicrous side of the situation at once appealed to him, notwithstanding the terror of that awful night.
>
> "Take my own picture!" he said. "Well that would be amusing! Suppose I am met on the street by friends in the same plight as ourselves, and they say:
>
> "Hello, Moody, glad you have escaped; what's that you have saved and cling to so affectionately?"–wouldn't it sound well to reply:
>
> "Oh, I've got my own portrait?"[25]

Mr. Moody would not lift a hand for his portrait, so Mrs. Moody knocked the canvas out of its heavy frame. She personally carried it off. Over the years the portrait was cherished because it was one of the few relics rescued from their home.[26] Dwight Moody did salvage his favorite Bible, and two weeks later he drove the family back to the ashes of their house. Little Emma remembered that "father got down in the ruins, going over everything with a cane. The only thing of value that he found was a little toy iron stove of mine, in perfect condition."[27]

The Aftermath

After the fire the Moodys stayed for a time with Emma's sister, who had a house on the city's far west side, upwind and beyond the fire's range. There they stayed until they could make a decision about the location of a new home.

Immediately money, clothing, and medical supplies poured in from all over the United States, Great Britain, and Europe for emergency relief. And once again, Dwight Moody became a fund-raiser and dispenser of relief. A YMCA relief committee, comprised of John V. Farwell, B. F. Jacobs, Major Whittle, Moody, and two pastors (C. E. Cheney and Robert Patterson) by mid-December oversaw distribution of nearly a thousand large packages of clothing and supplies. They likewise collected more than $16,500 in cash earmarked for emergency relief work.[28]

More Fund-Raising

Less than a month after the fire Moody went to New York, Philadelphia, and several other east coast cities, trying to raise funds to rebuild Chicago's churches and missions. A form letter he sent to religious and business leaders summed up the need and the call:

New York, Nov. 24, 1871

My dear Sir:

You know some thing of the sad state of things in Chicago as far as the Spiritual work is concerned. Fifty churches & missions are in ashes, and the thousands of men, women & children are without any Sabbath home. The temporal wants of the people are well supplied but there is no money to rebuild the Churches and Missions. The churches in the part of the city that was spared, can do nothing. Their moneyed men are either bankrupt or so badly crippled as to prevent them from helping outside enterprises.

My Mission School & Free Church on the North side, went with the rest. One thousand children and their parents are looking to me for another building. I have no earthly possessions & apply to those in sympathy with God's work, who have the means of helping. My plan is to raise $50,000 & put up a Tabernacle to accommodate seven or eight burnt out missions. It is for this purpose I have come to New York on a hurried visit. In a very short time there will be 50,000 mechanics and others back to the north side.

The grog shops are already rebuilding & some are doing business. The Theaters are helping the theaters. The infidel Turner Hall which desecrated the Sabbath so many years is to be promptly rebuilt. Will you help us? I enclose a subscription paper. Remittances can be made to Geo. H. Stuart, 13 Bank St., Phila., or to John V. Farwell, Chicago.

I will thank you to return the subscription paper to me as soon as possible.

Yours respectfully,

D. L. Moody

P.S. I enclose a circular that my friends are sending out to S. Schools.[29]

In a matter of days Moody was given $3,000 from Philadelphia philanthropists, including banker George Stuart and department store magnate John Wanamaker. With this money Moody was able to put up a temporary building, seventy-five by one hundred feet, on a lot near the ruins of the Illinois Street Church. On December 24, 1871, just two and a half months after the fire, the doors opened on a plain wooden structure with the new name of North Side Tabernacle. Compared to the Illinois Street Church, the tabernacle was neither attractive nor spacious, but it served the North Side well for the next three years, until funds for a new building could be secured.[30]

SOUL TORMENT AND BLESSING

As Dwight Moody walked the streets of New York seeking funds for rebuilding the religious facilities of Chicago, he admitted, "My heart was not in the work of begging. I could not appeal. I was crying all the time that God would fill me with His Spirit."[31] Moody was so burned out that nothing else really mattered. He said that "it did not seem as if there were any unction resting on my ministry." He had endured almost four months of intense spiritual agony. "God seemed to be just showing me myself. I found I was ambitious; I was not preaching for Christ; I was preaching for ambition. I found everything in my heart that ought not to be there. For four months a wrestling went on in me. I was a miserable man."

But suddenly, "after four months the anointing came. It came upon me as I was walking in the streets of New York."[32] The Holy Spirit came upon Moody in great force while he was walking down Wall Street. All of a sudden nothing was important except to be alone with the Lord. He went as fast as he could to the residence of a New York friend and asked for a room to pray in.

"Ah, what a day!—I cannot describe it, I seldom refer to it, it is almost too sacred an experience to name—Paul had an experience of which he never spoke for fourteen years—I can only say God revealed Himself to me, and I had such an experience of His love that I had to ask Him to stay His hand."[33]

He explained this profoundly sacred experience to his friend D. W. Whittle, who noted it in his diary: "God blessed him with the *conscious* incoming to his Soul of a presence and power of His Spirit such as he had never known before. His heart was broken by it. He spent much time in just weeping before God so overpowering was the sense of His goodness and love." Moody, Whittle wrote, "lost interest in everything except the preaching of Christ and working for souls. He determined to go to England that he might be free from all entanglements in the rebuilding of his Church and the [Farwell] Hall."[34]

GUIDANCE FOR THE NEXT STEP

While Moody tarried in New York in late 1871, M. K. Jessup, a member of the city's religious power elite, approached him to consider relocating to their city. Perhaps God was closing Moody's work in Chicago, given the fact that he had lost every facility he had labored so hard to build. Jessup wrote to Farwell to inform him that "Moody and I had quite a talk about getting hold of the masses in this city . . . and my mind has rather been led to the fact that Moody is the man to come here and enter upon this work. . . . We must do something in a large way for the masses in this city." He told Farwell they all needed to pray for guidance. New York did not want to take Moody "from Chicago unless it is the Lord's will." But should Moody decide to move, Jessup promised, "I should be willing to take the expense on my shoulders of caring for Moody's needs, in the same way Farwell cared for him in Chicago."[35]

A larger city, a greater challenge, a new harvest field to reap—here was bait that the old D. L. Moody would have found difficult to refuse. But Moody's recent experience with the Holy Spirit set him free—free from the mania that sees every great need as a call.

Time would reveal a liberated Moody. Every need could not be a call. Never again would he go off on his own to do kingdom work and ask God to support it. Instead, he would listen for the Lord's call to him personally, and then he would go forth and obey those marching orders. In the past Moody had fallen into the habit of making decisions about kingdom work, and then in prayer asking God to back these plans. As an experienced Civil War missionary he had seen enough of war to know better. Soldiers do not arise in the morning, make plans, and then call upon their commanding general to provide supplies. On the contrary, loyal troops get up, receive the orders of the day, and then go out in obedience, assuming their needs will be amply supplied to accomplish the objective.

In early December Moody thanked Jessup for his confidence and flattering offer. But no promises were made. Moody said he must return to Chicago, gather Emma and the children, and travel to Northfield. They needed distance from Chicago, New York, and Philadelphia. They needed the springtime to rest in the hills of western Massachusetts. And most of all they needed to prayerfully seek the counsel of the Holy Spirit.

CHAPTER SEVEN

A CALL TO THE UNKNOWN
England and Chicago
1872–1873

"Good Bye, from Your Old Friend."

One night in Brooklyn, New York, Moody introduced the congregation of Central Presbyterian Church to G. Campbell Morgan, a speaker from Great Britain. Moody fascinated listeners with the story of how Morgan was filled with the Holy Spirit after he struggled five hours in prayer over God's call to ministry. Moody then said that "at the end of those five blessed hours he was filled with the Spirit and decided to be a messenger of the Lord." Moody, who increasingly stressed the need for a filling with the Holy Ghost for anyone who hoped to lead a truly productive life for Christ, celebrated the special blessing given to Morgan. He went on to say that "in like manner the disciples were all dead failures until they became filled with the Spirit of God. They all bungled until Pentecost. Rest assured, no man is fit for God's service, until he is filled with the Holy Spirit."[1]

Moody could be given to overstatement. Indeed, people could infer that he personally had been unfit "for God's service" until his penetrating experience with the Holy Spirit in New York in autumn 1871. This, of course, was untrue. Moody had been used mightily by God for several years. Nevertheless, the quality of his relationship with God and his discernment of the difference between God's call and man's was so sharpened, and his power in ministry so enlarged, that it sometimes seemed to him as if he had scarcely been alive—let alone useful—until that blessed time.

THE STUDY TRIP

After Moody's personal "Pentecost" he displayed more openness to the leading of the Holy Spirit. Consequently, he was set free to pursue a path that initially appeared as absurd as his move from business to full-time ministry had looked a decade earlier. In early 1872, he felt a pull to Britain that was too strong to ignore. He maintained that he had only one purpose—he wanted to sit at the feet of some of the brilliant English Bible teachers whom he had met in 1867, in order to gain a deeper knowledge of the sacred Scriptures. Ambition to go abroad and become one of those men who boasted of ministry in foreign countries apparently played no role in Moody's desire to go to England. Ambition of this sort actually wearied him. In 1867 he had been asked to come back and do an extended preaching tour, but he declined. Instead, for this trip he wanted to study, listen, and spend time seeking the Lord's guidance about the future.

It was a rather long way to go for Bible study and a retreat, but Moody could get no rest from this desire. Therefore, in June 1872 he set sail for England. This time he traveled alone. For a brief trip Emma and the children could stay behind. In any case there was no money for the entire family to travel, even for a short time.

THE BEGINNING OF REVIVAL

When Moody got to England he slipped into meetings, took notes, and began some serious study. One night after a London prayer meeting at the Old Bailey, a North London pastor, the Reverend Mr. John Lessey, spotted Moody and implored him to preach for him the next Sunday. Moody, at first reluctant, finally agreed. He preached the morning service and people seemed indifferent to his words. But the evening service was quite a different story. He told his son William some years later that when he preached to the same congregation, on the same Sunday, in the same New Court Congregational Church "at half-past six in the evening, it seemed, while he was preaching, as if the very atmosphere was charged with the Spirit of God. There came a hush upon all people, and a quick response to his words, though he had not been much in prayer that day, and could not understand it."[2]

After his sermon Moody asked for people who desired to become Christians to please stand. All over the church, people were standing. Assuming his call was misunderstood, he followed this with "all of you who want to be Christians just step into the inquiry-room." So many people crowded into the room that extra chairs had to be pulled in. Moody and Pastor Lessey were amazed. Neither one of them had expected such a response. So again, in the inquiry room

Moody asked those who wanted to become Christians to stand. "The whole audience got up." Moody, still doubtful about the seriousness of these people, prayed for them and asked those "who were really in earnest to meet the pastor there the next night."[3]

The following day Moody sailed across the Irish Sea, expecting to visit some Irish Bible teachers, among them most certainly Brother F. C. Bland. But Moody had no sooner reached Dublin than John Lessey sent an urgent dispatch imploring him to return because more inquirers came on Monday night than had been present Sunday. Moody took the next ferry back to England. When he made it to North London, he preached and ministered for ten days. Four hundred people made professions of faith and joined Lessey's church during this local revival.

A Praying Girl

This outpouring of the Holy Spirit astounded Moody. Sensing that prayer must be somewhere underneath the community's response to his preaching, he said, "I wanted to know what this meant. I began making inquiries and never rested until I found a bedridden girl praying that God would bring me to that church. He had heard her, and brought me over four thousand miles of land and sea in answer to her request."[4]

Moody's remarkable discovery centers on an incident that defies all probability for coincidence and can best be attributed to the promptings of the Holy Spirit. In 1872 there was a bedridden young woman named Marianne Adlard who was "twisted and distorted by suffering." Despite her painfully infirm condition, she spent many hours daily in prayer. An intercessor for her New Court Congregational Church, she had been asking God to send revival to this congregation "of which she was a member, and yet into which even then she never came." On one occasion while reading an issue of R. C. Morgan's periodical *Revival* (later titled *The Christian*), she read a story of a man named D. L. Moody who was doing a significant work among Chicago's poorest children. She saved the article, kept it under her pillow, and began to pray, "O Lord, send this man to our church."

G. Campbell Morgan, who years later became pastor of Lessey's church, knew Marianne Adlard well. Once on a pastoral visit he elicited her side of this remarkable story:

> When in 1901 I was leaving England for America I went to see her. She said to me, "I want you to reach that birthday book." I did so and

turning to February 5 I saw in the handwriting I knew so well, "D. L. Moody, Psalm xci." Then Marianne Adlard said to me, "He wrote that for me when he came to see me in 1872, and I prayed for him every day till he went home to God." Continuing, she said, "Now, will you write your name on your birthday page, and let me pray for you until either you or I go home." I shall never forget writing my name in that book. To me the room was full of the Presence. I have often thought of that hour in the rush of my busy life, in the place of toil and strain, and even yet by God's good grace I know that Marianne Adlard is praying for me, and it is for this reason that to her in sincere love and admiration I have dedicated this book [*The Practice of Prayer*]. These are the labourers of force in the fields of God. It is the heroes and heroines who are out of sight, and who labour in prayer, who make it possible for those who are in sight to do their work and win. The force of it to such as are called upon to exercise the ministry can never be measured.[5]

Moody, like G. Campbell Morgan, never doubted the efficacy of Marianne Adlard's prayers. Until his death he believed his 1872 visit to Britain was prompted by the Holy Spirit through a faithful young woman's prayers.

A Preaching Tour

Adlard's prayers nudged Moody to England for what he assumed would be merely a study trip, yet the outbreak of revival at New Court Congregational Church provided a keen sense of new direction on how God wanted to use him. Given the unexpected flow of God's grace at those meetings, Moody began to sense God's leading for him to preach, so he began to take seriously all the invitations to preach.[6]

After the North London meeting an Anglican priest asked Moody to speak at Chelsea Chapel. Moody went, and he spoke with power. A few days later he visited an American Presbyterian on holiday. Moody confided in this fellow countryman that after speaking at New Court Church and Chelsea Chapel, "they wish me to come over here and preach in England." Dr. Theodore Cuyler responded, "Do. These English people are the best to preach to in all the world." Moody said, "I will go home, secure somebody to sing and come over and make the experiment."[7]

Before Moody returned home, several other people confirmed this call for an extended series of meetings in Great Britain. Henry Bewley at Dublin wanted Moody and promised money for traveling expenses. Cuthbert Bainbridge, a wealthy Methodist layman from

Newcastle-upon-Tyne, offered to pay expenses as well.[8]

William Pennefather

No doubt D. L. Moody had already been persuaded to hurry home, get Emma and the children, recruit a song leader, and return to Britain as soon as possible. But if he needed any more signs to confirm this plan, he found a strong one in the persuasiveness of the Reverend William Pennefather, an Evangelical Anglican who pastored the parish of St. Jude's, Mildmay Park, in the north of London. Moody attended a conference sponsored by Pennefather because it was billed as a series of meetings with an emphasis on the very issues so important to Moody. A precursor to the Keswick Conventions, the Mildmay conferences (which dated back to the 1850s) were distinctive in their stress on holiness, home and foreign missions, and the imminent return of the Lord Jesus Christ. Although Mildmay was spearheaded by Anglicans, Pennefather, like Moody and Farwell, was decidedly undenominational. He stressed the spiritual unity of all Christians regardless of their traditional affiliation.

All of this had immense appeal to Moody, but particularly attractive to him in 1872 was Pennefather's stress on the work of the Holy Spirit. David Bebbington, the foremost historian on evangelicalism in Britain, wrote that "the distinctive note in [Pennefather's] instruction was the stress on the work of the Holy Spirit. The Saviour had promised to send the Comforter. 'Are we not then to look for the power of the Holy Ghost?'" Evidently Pennefather characteristically opened these conferences "with an exhortation to seek the Holy Spirit."[9]

Such a focus thrilled D. L. Moody. He could not return to America until he had imbibed all the refreshment the Mildmay deeper-life people could serve. The speaker for the opening session was Pennefather. The Mildmay founder left an indelible mark on Moody's soul. As Moody reminisced in later years,

> I well remember sitting in yonder seat looking up at this platform and seeing the beloved Mr. Pennefather's face illuminated as it were with Heaven's light. I don't think I can recall a word that he said, but the whole atmosphere of the man breathed holiness, and I got then a lift and impetus in the Christian life that I have never lost, and I believe the impression will remain with me to my dying day. I thank God that I saw and spoke with that holy man; no one could see him without consciousness that he lived in the presence of God.[10]

Moody met Pennefather and heard him preach. Then the well-known English leader insisted that Moody address the gathering of more than one thousand British Christians comprised of clergy and laity from many denominations. Moody spoke and his reception was overwhelming. At the close of his message the large crowd of British evangelicals gave him a hearty ovation. Moody spoke to them with a new voice. His language was plain, yet full of vivid illustrations. He spoke passionately without theatrics. God used him to open hearts of men and women from England, Wales, Scotland, and Ireland.

The Reverend Pennefather made clear to Britain's evangelical community that "Mr. Moody was one for whom God has prepared a great work." These prophetic words were spoken publicly—in Moody's hearing—before Moody returned to the United States. Later, Pennefather followed up his remarks in a letter written to Moody in late August from Germany's Black Forest region. The Englishman urged Moody to come back to Britain with all expenses paid. Although only fifty-seven years old, the Anglican was not well. The conference had worn him down, and he retreated to the healing springs and balmy air of southwestern Germany in hopes of rejuvenation.[11]

R. C. Morgan

R. C. Morgan was especially keen on Moody's spirit and message, and he made his feeling clear in two issues of *The Christian*. He reported on Moody at length, finishing his endorsement with a plea for British Christians to pray that Moody "may soon be led to recross the Atlantic, and pay us another visit. We think that if the way were made plain for him to come here for a year or more, accompanied by Mrs. Moody and their two children . . . that he would gladly respond to such an invitation, soon as he could effect the necessary arrangements at home."[12]

TWO MINISTRY PROJECTS

By the time Moody returned to Chicago in September 1872 he exuded enthusiasm for the future. He immediately put two projects to work that he had learned about during this visit abroad. First, he made a deal to buy Christian tracts, small booklets, and papers in Dublin, Ireland, for paper cost alone. He ordered thousands of these and then set the Chicago Yokefellows to putting up racks in hotels and passenger depots, offering tracts free to people who would take one. He also sent letters to forty businessmen, asking them to help the Association buy a year's supply of materials from Dublin. He had arranged free transportation all the way to Chicago, making these pieces of literary evangelism "six times as cheap as the American tracts." He needed $1,000 for the project, so he asked forty men to give $25 each. The Yokefellows would place this evangelistic literature in the racks and keep the locations serviced three times a week.[13]

Missionary Women

Moody's second project was more ambitious. He had been markedly impressed by William Pennefather's pioneer program of establishing an order of deaconesses in the Church of England. These women were ordained to the deaconal ministry—a ministry of service to the community under the protection and authority of the church. Pennefather's deaconesses focused on helping the poor, overseeing an orphanage, helping women, and conducting Bible studies. Most of their work was conducting home missions work among lower economic class women and children. The deaconesses had their own house, which not only gave lodging to them, but also served as a training center for women who volunteered for full-time home and foreign mission work.[14]

Emma Dryer

To Moody, this idea of training women for full-time home missionary work was rich with promise for reaching lost souls, nurturing new believers, and reproducing future workers. Consequently, he called upon a woman he and his wife had met two years earlier, Emeline Dryer, to begin a work that would have far-flung consequences. Emeline Dryer, or Emma, as she was known to her friends, radiated talent and intelligence. Born in Massachusetts in 1835, she was two years Dwight Moody's senior. While Emma was still a child, her parents died, causing her to be sent to New York to be raised by an aunt. Not a typical orphan, Emma found educational opportunities beyond those of most people in rural New York, and she took full advantage of her good fortune. An excellent student from the elementary grades forward, she went on to graduate from LeRoy Female Seminary with highest honors. After graduation she joined the faculty of Knoxville Female College, but left there during the Civil War. After some elementary school teaching she joined the faculty of Illinois State Normal University in 1864. Throughout her teaching career she displayed a deep Christian commitment, and she frequently spent her summers and holidays doing Christian work such as teaching, evangelizing, disciple-making, and relief work.

Emma Dryer's Faith

In 1870 Emma Dryer fell victim to typhoid fever and no one, including her doctors and Emma herself, expected her to live. But the Lord provided complete healing, she believed, in order for her to meditate on "the needs of the dying world, as never before. . . . And in my earnest, prayerful meditation, God gave me new light from the Scriptures, and taught me the coming of Christ." From this experience Emma Dryer decided to commit her life to Christian service rather than secular teaching, and she also became an early Chicago proponent of premillennialism.[15]

Becoming a full-time Christian worker was not an easy choice for Miss Dryer. Serving as the head of the women's faculty at Illinois State Normal University, she received good pay and much respect. Moving to Chicago in 1870, she gave up salary, security, and a fair amount of prestige for a position that offered no salary (she lived by faith) and no worldly acclaim. She immediately became a friend of the Moodys as well as the W. H. Daniels family. They all admired the faith of a thirty-five-year-old woman who would set out on a pilgrimage for which only the Lord knew the pathway.

What Moody Liked About Dryer

Dryer and Moody became fast friends. He delighted in her courageous move—it reminded him of his own agonizing choice back in 1860. But Moody saw more in Emma Dryer than robust faith; he saw a brilliant woman—one with extraordinary high intelligence. Whatever Dryer set her mind to, she did and did well. A superb teacher with a deep and practical knowledge of Scripture, she also became a first-rate administrator, and she likewise developed the sensitivity and insight required for one-to-one ministry. Time proved her to be dependable, energetic, and motivated to keep work going forward.

Moody saw even more in Emma Dryer. She possessed a contagious view of the Holy Spirit. Like Moody, she had experienced the Spirit's presence in a profound way on two occasions: First, when she was healed from typhoid and called to ministry, and then on a subsequent occasion when the Reverend W. H. Daniels, suffering from double vision, asked her to take over his weekly Bible teaching program. Dryer had a keen sense that God wanted her to do the work, but she, too, suffered from an eye disorder and believed the reading would be impossible to manage. One night, after retiring to her living quarters, she got on her knees and asked the Lord to heal her. She experienced instantaneous healing with perfect vision.

From that day on, Emma Dryer taught about the Comforter—the Counselor—the One called alongside to assist the sincere disciple. She also taught divine healing as one of the ways Christ ministers through His Spirit. Moody agreed that the Holy Spirit anoints, empowers, teaches, and guides, but he had to pray about this doctrine of healing. Moody agreed that God occasionally heals people, but he sensed no leading to stress this doctrine in his teaching and preaching. Dryer, never afraid to push her beliefs, urged Moody to take the larger view of the Spirit's work, but she had only modest results. In a long letter to Charles Blanchard written years after Moody died, she said this regarding her differences with Moody on the doctrine of healing:

Emma Dryer

I favored it, as I understand it. I knew that our Lord had mercifully healed me for His service, answering prayer, and adding remarkable experiences of his guidance into Christian service, even when I had no understanding of the doctrine of Divine Healing. I could not neglect that experience! And similar healings were repeated. Mr. Moody's views of this subject changed somewhat, before he died.[16]

Unlike her doctrine of healing, Emma Dryer's position on premillennialism utterly inspired Moody. He grew confident that this doctrine of the Second Coming helped explain much of the Bible. The Brethren in Britain had urged him along this pathway in 1867, and in Emma Dryer he finally found an ally in Chicago who understood and agreed. What fascinated Moody, too, was that Dryer did not come to this position through Brethren teaching—she claimed the Lord revealed it to her in prayer.[17]

The Women's Work in Chicago

With encouragement and prompting from Moody, Dryer worked as the head of Chicago's Women's Aid Society and as superintendent of the Women's Auxiliary of the YMCA (later the YWCA). Then in early 1873, a few months before the Moodys were to go back to Britain for what D. L. predicted would be an eight- to ten-month campaign, Moody persuaded Dryer to launch a school similar to Pennefather's deaconess work in London. It was to be a training program, first for women, but eventually to include men, who wanted to enter home or foreign missions or evangelistic work but needed systematic training in Bible, theology, and practical ministry.

Already in 1877 W. H. Daniels labeled this deaconess-inspired effort as "Mr. Moody's Theological Seminary, if in its small beginnings it will bear so large a name, proposed to dispense with homiletics, dialectics, and other traditional forms of theologic lore, and to replace them by the eternal word of God." Daniels pointed out that within three years of starting the work, Dryer had overseen an impressive program. In one year alone, she and her "Bible readers have held 673 cottage prayer-meetings, 78 mothers' meetings, 165 school prayer-meetings; have directed 502 sessions of sewing-schools, made 2,820 calls for Bible reading; 479 visits to the sick, and distributed 10,628 tracts and religious papers; this in addition to their own regular hours for daily Bible study."[18]

Earlier Moody had expressed weariness with begging. But for this work he readily made exceptions. He found funds to support Dryer while the Reverend Daniels provided her housing. Moody also solicited funds for deaconesses in training. He wrote to C. H. Mc-Cormick and asked for a contribution "to pay the salary of a lady missionary for one month among the poor and destitute on the North side; it would cost you ($50). . . I want to get Bible readers to work," he continued, "ladies who will go and carry the Gospel into dark homes where Jesus and His word are not known." Moody went on to say that "I am convinced that there is no better way of reaching the masses than this," and, by the way, "$600 will keep a good intelligent Godly woman in the work 365 days in the year."[19]

McCormick helped support deaconesses, and so did other people who loved evangelism and felt compassion for Chicago's underclass. As a result Dryer received support and so did many other women home missionaries. None of them realized that this humble beginning in 1873, inspired in part by Pennefather's deaconess movement, and at least indirectly by Spurgeon's little college of Christian workers, would be the genesis of the Chicago Bible Institute (later Moody Bible Institute).

THE RETURN TO BRITAIN

By early 1873 optimism and enthusiasm so dominated Moody's thoughts about ministerial opportunities in Chicago that he turned down the New York City offer. For a few weeks he toyed with remaining in Chicago, but finally the call to return to Great Britain became too strong. The thought of leaving Chicago for another extended period saddened him, but he had trained up a first-rate corps of workers to keep everything moving forward in the great Midwestern metropolis.

Charles Morton

Among the ablest of those men Moody personally reached out to and trained for ministry stands Charles M. Morton. His story is a fascinating one. He said that he grew up with no knowledge of God. When the Civil War broke out, he signed up, shouldered a rifle, and went to the front. "Our lives then were wicked. I was a ring leader in drinking and gambling, and it used to be my boast that I could blaspheme the name of God in more ways than any other man about."

Before the war ended Morton lost his right arm, so he made his way to Chicago to recuperate and spend what was left of his pay on drinking and carousing. After wasting every dollar on fast living, Morton walked into the YMCA's Employment Bureau, but he discovered it was difficult to place a rough, uneducated man in anything but a position of common labor. Having only one arm, Morton suffered rejection each time he sought unskilled work. Therefore, one of the men at the mission gave him a job with the YMCA "as a man-of-all-work about the Association rooms." Another YMCA worker, Frank Rockwell, who had been given a room by Moody a year or two earlier, agreed to share his place at the YMCA with Morton. Rockwell remembered their first evening together:

> When Morton came to be my room-mate, he brought, along with his other small properties, a pouch of tobacco and a pipe, and when I came home that evening I found him sitting with his chair tipped back, his heels on the window-sill, his hat stuck on the back of his head, smoking til all was blue. Taking up the Bible, I mentioned that I was in the habit of reading a chapter and offering prayer before I went to bed, and asked him if had any objections.
>
> "Objections! no; none at all. You can pray as much as you like without disturbing me."

For several nights Rockwell read and prayed while Morton smoked. Rockwell gradually took an interest in his roommate and began bringing up his name for prayer at the noontime union meetings. For twenty-one days Morton's name was lifted up in prayer by the group. At night during those three weeks, Morton stopped smoking during Rockwell's Bible reading and prayer time, and he even took his feet down from the window sill. Eventually Morton even bent down and silently joined in Rockwell's prayers. After twenty-one days Rockwell attended an evening prayer meeting at a Baptist church and offered up fervent prayer for Charley Morton. When Rockwell got home it was late and he found Morton in bed. Rockwell then sat down beside him and said:

> "Charley, we have been praying for you to-night."
>
> "Have you? I thank you, Frank," said he, his voice choking with emotion; and then he turned away and buried his face in the pillow. About midnight he arose, and went into the prayer-room adjoining, where, after an hour of mighty wrestling with God, he felt his sins forgiven; and, when he came back, his infidelity had vanished and he was a saved and happy man.

Dwight Moody immediately took a liking to Morton, seeing promise in the man with the empty sleeve and Union army cap. Moody nurtured and groomed him to be an evangelist and personal worker and finally to be assistant pastor of the Illinois Street Church.[20]

D. W. Whittle

Besides Charley Morton, Moody concentrated efforts on training Major D. W. Whittle. After 1865, Moody showered attention on this Civil War veteran, using him part-time yet keenly sensing that he was called to full-time ministry. Whittle, thanks to Moody's unyielding encouragement and powerful example, took a leap of faith after eight years of prodding. Early in 1873, Whittle surrendered all and declared himself available for full-time ministry.

Moody put Whittle and Morton, as well as one or two others, into prominent ministry roles at the church. He also passed on to them evangelistic preaching invitations that he was too busy to take. Consequently, by summer 1873 there were able men ready and willing to oversee the Sunday school and the church.

If Moody had any doubts about the experience and dependability of these men, he knew that his faithful friend John Farwell stood in the wings to encourage them. Farwell had become one of Moody's closest friends, serving as a partner in every Christian endeavor. The dry goods merchant remained dependable and certain of his calling. Farwell would stand by his post in Chicago, help rebuild the charred city, resurrect his dry goods business, and get the third YMCA building in place. Moody also knew Farwell could be counted on to help keep the Sunday school and church on course during his absence.

THE END OF AN ERA

Despite the fact that Moody assigned able men to cover all the posts at the church, the mission school, and the YMCA, and even though Emma Dryer had launched her exciting new work, John V. Farwell did not want Moody to leave Chicago in 1873. "I did all I could to persuade him to stay in Chicago and help build up from the ruins of the fire along religious lines, but to no effect. . . . With his own home, that of the YMCA and of his Sunday School and the Union Church all in ashes, all barriers were burned away which stood in the way of an invitation to come to England to take up evangelistic work, which had been given to him [in 1872] while on a visit there."[21]

Farwell had great affection for Moody. The two men had worked closely for well over a decade, through good times and tragic circumstances. He had a premonition that the Moodys would never return. They might return to Chicago for a visit, but if they left

Mrs. D. L. (Emma) Moody, circa 1873

this time, he felt certain they would never live in the Windy City again. Nevertheless, Farwell would not stand in their way. He went to the railroad station in early June to see them off to New York, the port city from which they were scheduled to take a ship for England.

Moody evidently sensed the end of an era as well. He embraced his friend and made him a present of a treasured personal Bible. Farwell slipped Moody an envelope with $500, a sum equal to a worker's annual wages. Neither man realized at that moment how essential the money would be in New York. None of the promised funds for transportation awaited them on the East Coast, because all three men who had guaranteed travel support—Pennefather, Bewley, and Bainbridge—died after Moody's departure nine months earlier. No word of their deaths had reached Chicago.

When Emma, Dwight, little Emma, and William reached New York, Dwight sent a letter to Farwell:

> I want to thank you for the $500. I can't tell you how I appreciate it, and all your acts of love and kindness. It is a wonder to me at times, and I do not see why you do not get sick of me and cast me off. The more I know of myself, the less I think of myself.
> Good bye, from your old friend.

D. L. Moody [22]

CHAPTER EIGHT

THE SPREADING FLAME
Britain Ablaze

1873–1875

"I Would Like to Go Round the World and Tell the Perishing Millions of a Saviour's Love."

D. L. Moody's experience with the Holy Spirit in 1871 left him profoundly changed. Inner peace, disappearance of spiritual depression, focused goals, a calmer demeanor, and preaching with new power now characterized the man. If the changes were not as apparent to Moody himself and to friends and family closest to him on a daily basis, people who saw him after lengthy separations noticed appreciable differences. Henry Varley had met Moody in Dublin, Ireland, in 1867, again in 1872, and in 1874. He observed great changes. Even between 1872 and 1874 he witnessed a marked increase of "Divine energy." A self-generated energy manifested in hustling to and fro had disappeared. In its place Varley noticed a Spirit-led, purposeful march along a pathway that was soon crowded with changed lives. Moody himself sensed some of this metamorphosis; he lost all ambition to erect buildings that were tangible monuments to his labor in Chicago, and he embraced a new desire that he clearly expressed: "I would like to go round the world and tell the perishing millions of a Saviour's love."[1]

Dwight and Emma Moody, plus both of their children, sailed from New York to Liverpool on June 7, 1873, with several invitations and an increasing sense of purpose and destiny. Accompanying the Moodys were Ira Sankey and his wife of ten years, Fanny. Leaving their children behind with grandparents, the Sankeys, both in their early thirties, were making this trip strictly as a favor to Mr. Moody.

Ira Sankey was born in 1840 in Pennsylvania. He grew up in a prosperous family, and his father served as president of a bank in Newcastle. The family attended a Methodist Episcopal Church, where Ira was baptized and confirmed. At an early age he learned to read music and sing; he also received an excellent education in the public schools of Pennsylvania. After graduating from high school he took a clerking position in his father's bank, the church elected him superintendent of the Sunday school, and he assumed direction of the church choir. A few years later he married Fanny Edwards, a choir member, and he served one period of enlistment with the Union army during the Civil War.[2]

After the war, Sankey began a career with the federal government, but singing church music became his avocation. He not only served as choirmaster of his local church, but he also performed concerts throughout Pennsylvania and did occasional solo singing performances at Sunday school and YMCA conferences. When the International YMCA convention met in Indianapolis in 1870, Sankey and Moody had their first personal contact. Both attended as delegates.

MOODY AND IRA SANKEY

For several years Moody had been learning the importance of music to successful ministry. No musician himself, Moody nevertheless had learned as early as the late 1850s that music will soften the hearts and calm the souls of some of the most hardened and unruly children. He took his first cues from Bible stories, especially David's musical ministry to bedeviled King Saul. Later Moody observed the effects of good singing on the spiritual lives of those to whom he ministered. For several years Moody had been on the alert for good soloists. He had encouraged the extremely popular P. P. Bliss, who frequently teamed up with him and evangelist D. W. Whittle in joint efforts of evangelism through song and sermon. Moody also spurred on singer Philip Phillips. Both Bliss and Phillips worked with Moody in his Chicago church, and they each accompanied him from time to time as he traveled and preached.

Moody knew from experience that good singers were more difficult to find than good preachers. And even when talented vocalists were discovered, they too often were halfhearted Christians or unwilling to give up secure employment to travel around doing ministry and living by faith.

Meeting Ira Sankey

When Moody met Sankey he knew he had found an unusually gifted man, so he moved quickly with all of his power of persuasion to recruit the unsuspecting singer. Sankey had gone to a 6:00 A.M. prayer meeting at the Indianapolis conference because it was conducted by Moody. The Chicagoan was already well known, and Sankey got up early in order to meet him. Arriving a little late, Sankey was quietly pulled aside by a member of his own Pennsylvania Country delegation who whispered, "Sankey, the singing here has been abominable; I wish you would start up something." Rather quickly Sankey stepped to the front and drew the congregation into a spirited rendition of "There Is a Fountain Filled with Blood." As soon as the meeting ended, Moody introduced himself. The portly two-hundred-and-twenty-pound singer made a comical first impression: balding and sporting an unusual crop of facial hair—sort of a cross between a beard and mutton chops with winglike projections sweeping upward from the cheeks. Sankey shook hands with the evangelist, who nearly swept him over with a barrage of questions. Sankey remembered it this way:

> "Where are you from? Are you married? What is your business?" Upon telling him that I lived in Pennsylvania, was married, had two children, and was in government employ, he said abruptly, "You will have to give that up."
>
> I stood amazed, at a loss to understand why the man told me that I would have to give up what I considered a good position. "What for?" I exclaimed.
>
> "To come to Chicago and help me in my work," was the answer.
>
> When I told him that I could not leave my business, he retorted, "You must; I have been looking for you for the last eight years."[3]

Sankey Joins Moody

Moody asked Sankey to go off with him and pray over the matter. They prayed together and Sankey was "much impressed by Mr. Moody's prayer, but still undecided." Sankey returned to Pennsylvania and promised to ponder the matter further. For six months he eluded Moody's snare, but in early 1871 he agreed to go to Chicago, see the church, and get a glimpse of the work. This visit destroyed Sankey's defenses. After a week with Emma and Dwight, and in the wake of some encouraging ministry in Chicago with Moody, he went home, resigned his secure and well-paying position with the U.S.

Ira D. Sankey

Treasury Department, and moved his family to Chicago.[4]

By 1873 Sankey supervised the music ministry of Moody's church. In fact, he and Whittle teamed up to handle all the regular worship services whenever Moody was away. Once Moody decided to go back to England, he asked Philip Phillips to come along and do the music, but prior commitments in California forced him to say no. Moody approached P. P. Bliss next, but he, too, had to turn down the opportunity. Sankey was Moody's third choice—not for lack of talent, but because Moody did not want to tear the gifted man from the ministry of the church. Finally, with no other options, Moody reluctantly pulled Sankey from Chicago with a promise of all expenses paid for him and his wife and a stipend of $500 for eight to ten months of work.

Trial of Faith and Finances

When the Sankeys and Moodys docked at Liverpool on June 17, they stepped out on a journey that immediately tried their faith. To their utter dismay they learned of the deaths of Pennefather, the Anglican of Mildmay, London; Bewley, a member of the Brethren in Dublin; and Bainbridge, a Wesleyan of Newcastle-on-Tyne, who had all died since Moody shook their hands in 1872 and accepted pledges of paid expenses.[5]

The dismayed American couples prayed and parted, awaiting guidance from the Holy Spirit. The Sankeys went to Henry Moorhouse's home at Manchester, and the Moodys went to Emma's sister's house in London. A short time later Moody reached Sankey and mentioned an invitation to York from George Bennett, a chemist by profession and the organizer of that cathedral city's YMCA. He told Sankey, "Here is a door which is partly open, and we will go there and begin our work." Three days later, leaving their wives behind, Moody and Sankey went to York to see if the door would open wide.[6]

The English-speaking world that the Moodys and Sankeys visited was as diverse and challenging as the American nation that they left behind. In some ways the nations on opposite sides of the Atlantic were quite similar. The common language, common ancestry, commitment to liberty, and a heritage of Christianity had traditionally provided a set of guidelines for human conduct that, if not always embraced, at least provided generally accepted boundaries that prevented social and moral chaos.

GREAT BRITAIN IN 1873

Great Britain, like the United States, was in the throes of an urban-industrial revolution that was transforming the nation, for better and worse. In England and Wales, as in America, there was rapid population expansion and a mass movement from rural areas to cities. The population soared from just under 9 million at the turn of the 19th century to over 20 million by the 1870s. Where there had been only fifteen cities with more than twenty thousand population in 1801, the number of such cities had quadrupled by 1851, and more were mushrooming so fast that there would be nearly 190 forty years later. Trends were similar in Scotland but not as pronounced. Ireland, on the other hand, had actually lost population since the 1840s. The potato famine of the 1840s took 700,000 lives, and this disaster, plus a lack of resources for industry, conspired to drive millions of people to England, Wales, Australia, and North America by the late 1860s. Overall, the United Kingdom experienced a population growth during the nineteenth century, but there was a mass exodus abroad at the same time. Indeed, more than 5 million people left Ireland, England, and Wales alone between 1820 and 1891.[7]

These mass population shifts were caused in large part by the rapid rise of industry and the railroad network that crisscrossed the United Kingdom. With factories, railroads, commerce, and cities came unprecedented economic opportunities and equally unprecedented poverty and human suffering.

In the midst of the changes and problems was the dominant religion of the United Kingdom—Christianity. Christians varied in their response to the urban-industrial revolution. On one level the church had accommodated the drives for money, status, and power in the new order. Secularism had infiltrated the church on a grand scale; at first as a sincere way to attract worldly people, but gradually secularism became dominant and transformed the church. The pulpit had been evolving into a podium for lectures, until sermons sounded more like learned addresses than biblical proclamations. The ministry of music also gave way to the upwardly mobile tastes of a growing middle class. Classical music was exalted more than the Holy Trinity, until orthodox hymnody was gradually replaced by mere displays of artistic talent.

Rather quickly the urban poor were alienated from traditional Christianity. Displays of wealth, manifested by the way worshipers dressed, when added to the services that were fashioned to meet the tastes of Victorian aesthetes, combined to build enormous barriers between the classes. Even Great Britain's Methodism—a movement that for a century had built bridges from traditional Christianity to the poor—was becoming secularized and set apart from the masses.

But there was much more to Christianity in the United Kingdom than accommodation to secularism and middle-class values. A modest but genuine revival of the evangelical faith had spread throughout the land since 1859, and its force was still present on the eve of D. L. Moody and Ira D. Sankey's visitation. Men and women were being convicted of sin, and they were hungering for biblical teaching, banding together for prayer, and reaching out to the wretched and poor. The Booths had seceded from Methodism to start the Salvation Army, which marched to an Arminian tune in its war against the forces of darkness; the Brethren were spreading a Calvinistic evangelistic zeal. Evangelicalism invaded established church circles too, as leaders of Pennefather's stripe were calling men and women to repentance, as well as to lives of holiness and service to the poor and lost both at home and abroad.

REVIVAL AND EVANGELISM

It is sometimes said that Moody and Sankey brought revival to the United Kingdom. It is more accurate to say that they were mightily instrumental in helping turn an already existing small flame into a raging fire.[8]

Before William Pennefather died, he predicted that the United Kingdom was a parched land waiting to be ignited. He also prophesied that Mr. Dwight L. Moody was the man who would set the fire. Few evangelicals held such high expectations. Except for Marianne Adlard and the two men who had recently died, one of the few other optimists was George Bennett, secretary of York's YMCA. When Moody and Sankey went to York without any forewarning, he told Moody that he had not expected them so soon, and furthermore their timing was poor inasmuch "as all the people are away at the seaside." Moody was nevertheless confident. He laughed off the cool reception, he asked Bennett to do them the favor of securing a facility, and they went forward with a few placements of this notice:

EVANGELISTIC SERVICES
D. L. Moody of Chicago will preach, and
Ira D. Sankey of Chicago will sing, at 7 o'clock P.M.
tomorrow, Thursday, and each succeeding evening for a week,
in the Independent Chapel. All are welcome. No Collection.[9]

The beginning of Moody's ministry in the conservative, relatively quiet, nonindustrial cathedral city of York was inconspicuous. Fifty people came the first night and sat as far away from the pulpit as possible. Once seated they looked over the thirty-six-year-old Moody, who was slightly rotund and beginning to show signs of premature gray in his beard and along his receding scalp line. Sankey was much less impressive. Unlike Moody, who was stout but solid and commanding, Sankey, though three years younger, was much balder and looked rather phlegmatic. In brief, his appearance was not fetching.

Sankey recalled that on the first night, "I sang several solos before Mr. Moody's address, and that was my first service of song in England. It was with some difficulty that I could get the people to sing, as they had not been accustomed to the kind of songs that I was using."[10]

The meeting was not well received, but Moody announced the noontime prayer meetings, as well as the Bible readings that would be an hour later each afternoon. Although only six people came to the YMCA room for the next day's prayer meeting, Moody carried on with a conviction that they were precisely where they should be and in the center of God's will.

F. B. Meyer

But on the fourth day things changed. The atmosphere of these tepidly received and sparsely attended meetings came to life. A twenty-six-year-old Baptist pastor named Frederick B. Meyer, a new man to ministry who had been at the York Baptist chapel only a year, stood up in the prayer meeting attended by a few pastors and warmly endorsed Moody's comments on ministers' need for empowerment by the Holy Spirit. The ice was broken. Several pastors opened their chapels and churches to the Americans and began promoting the work among their people.[11]

Meyer's endorsement of Moody (he was not as keen on Sankey) was remarkable, considering the differences between the two men. Much more than the North Atlantic separated them. The Englishman was born into a comfortable London merchant family. He was loved at home and well cared for, and he received a first-rate university education. Ten years younger than Moody, the Baptist minister was thin, well groomed, and fastidious about his appear-

The Rev. F. B. Meyer at Northfield

ance. He carried himself with dignity and looked and acted almost unctuous with his neatly combed hair, clerical collar, long Roman nose, and pursed lips. His biographer pointed out that "in spite of the differences between Moody and himself, he felt drawn to the stranger. He recognized beneath his rugged utterance a spiritual power which he himself longed to possess."12

The meeting was providential for both men. For Meyer it was, as he phrased it, "the birthday of new conceptions of ministry, new methods of work, new inspirations and hopes. . . . I had been brought up in a holy home. I had been in business for a little while, then took my degree at college, but I didn't know anything about conversion, or about the gathering of sinners around Christ, and I owe everything, everything in my life, I think, to that parlor room [with Moody leading two sinners to Christ] where [for] the first time I found people brokenhearted about sin. I learned the psychology of the soul. I learned how to point men to God."13

Meyer went on to become a close personal friend of D. L. Moody, always saying that Moody helped him discover his gift of evangelism. With Moody's encouragement, he developed that gift and used it in America as well as in England. Over the years Meyer wrote more than seventy books, and Moody celebrated the man and his writings throughout the United States. In truth, Moody played a large role in helping Meyer realize sales of more than 5 million copies of his books and pamphlets in his lifetime.14

Meyer, for his part, provided tremendous encouragement to Moody. Despite his inexperience and rather recent tenure at York, Meyer gave Moody respectability in a community that was unsure about Moody. The youthful Meyer opened the way for several more days of meetings in York, which went increasingly well each night; so well in fact that Emma and the children came to stay for a few days, arriving in time to celebrate her thirtieth birthday.15

Moody and Sankey had been relatively successful at York. There was no united meeting called by all of the churches; instead, Moody preached in a city hall, Wesleyan chapels, a Congregational church, and a Baptist and an independent chapel. But the turnouts were quite good, and many men and women sought prayer for salvation or more surrendered lives.

Arthur A. Rees

Because of these victories at York, an invitation came to go up to the northern English shipbuilding town of Sunderland. The request came from a Baptist minister—a hardfisted, no-nonsense, ex-sailor named Arthur A. Rees. He wanted Moody by July 20, but he did not express an interest in the American vocalist. Sankey went to Sunderland early to do reconnaissance work and make certain no collections would be taken. When he arrived Pastor Rees plied him with numerous questions about Moody, and then asked if D. L. Moody was the man named Moody who had been in Ireland a year or so before. Rees had stayed at the late Mr. Brewley's home and shared a bedroom with an American named Moody. "Before retiring," Rees recalled, "Moody suggested that they have evening devotions, and [he said] that he had never heard anything that equaled Mr. Moody's prayer and burning desire for a greater knowledge of God's Word and power to preach it." Sankey assured him it was the same Moody, so Rees was delighted and insisted they should come.[16]

After their conversation Rees took Sankey to the home of their chapel treasurer, a wealthy ship merchant named William Longstaff. In the corner of their host's parlor stood an American organ, and Sankey was informed that it had been played by Philip Phillips, who had done a recital in Sunderland. Sankey had no idea that Rees "was strongly opposed, not only to solo singing, but to organs and choirs as well, never allowing anything of the kind in his church." In blissful ignorance of Rees's bias, Sankey obliged Longstaff's request to play. Among the songs he played and sang were "Come Home, O Prodigal" and "Free from the Law." Rees sat in silence but seemed moved by the singing.

Singing the Gospel

A few days later, when Sankey and Moody arrived in Sunderland, they were greeted by large posters on many billboards and walkways with this notice: "D. L. Moody of Chicago will preach the gospel, and Ira D. Sankey of Chicago will sing the gospel in Bethesda Chapel every afternoon and evening this week, except Saturday, at 3 and 7 o'clock. All are welcome." Ironically, the phrase that became famous, "Sankey will sing the gospel," was coined by "one of the most conservative ministers in England"; and later Longstaff would write the words to one of the most famous hymns of the last century, "Take Time to Be Holy."[17]

Moody and Sankey ministered in Sunderland for more than a month. Emma wrote in her journal that "after a stay of 5 weeks and 2 days [they left] with a feeling that one minister had done much to hinder more blessing among others."[18] No doubt there were hindrances, but the work was extremely successful. The attendance grew so large that the meetings were held in Victoria Hall rather than Rees's Bethesda Chapel. Capacity crowds of more than three thousand were on hand, and the inquiry meetings after the main services were held at Bethesda Chapel. One night a stirring incident occurred at the Bethesda Chapel. A young man, who had long been living a sinful life, came up the aisle to where his parents were seated. "He first put his arms around his father's neck, and kissed him, asking his forgiveness with many tears; then kissing his mother, and asking her forgiveness; afterwards kissing his younger brother." This open display of a prodigal's return inspired many to repent that night and in nights to come.[19]

Sankey's First Songbook

It was during the Sunderland campaign (*campaign* was Moody's word—he typically used words and metaphors from the American Civil War to illustrate spiritual warfare) that Sankey's first songbook, *Sacred Songs and Solos,* was published. This little hymnal that God used to open the hearts of countless masses had a singular beginning. Sankey usually sang solos before Moody preached, and he usually asked the congregation to join him on the choruses. Because many of his songs were new to the British congregations, they began to clamor for copies of the words. Sankey used songs from Philip Phillips's *Hallowed Songs,* but he introduced many newer songs as well. So he sent a letter to Phillips's publisher and asked them to bring out a new edition with a few of these newer, popular pieces bound in the back. The publisher refused. Sankey asked two or three British publishers to produce a booklet of a few pieces, and they likewise refused to risk their capital. When he mentioned this to R. C. Morgan, the editor of *The Christian,* who had come to Sunderland to write articles on the campaign, he volunteered to put his own firm, Morgan and Scott, behind the venture.

Ira D. Sankey promptly pulled out his worn little scrapbook of songs and removed "twenty-three pieces, rolled them up, and wrote on them the words, 'Sacred Songs and Solos, sung by Ira D. Sankey at the Meetings of Mr. Moody of Chicago.'" Morgan took the bundle to London the next day. Within a fortnight he sent five hundred folios containing sixteen pages each. Sankey put them out at a Sunderland meeting and immediately sold every copy at six pence per volume. This launched a British series of *Sacred Songs and So-*

los that eventually sold more than 8 million copies in several editions all over the world.[20]

More Hymnals

Two years later, after Sankey returned to America, he approached P. P. Bliss, who had teamed up with D. W. Whittle in a song-sermon team identical to Moody and Sankey. Whittle and Bliss had produced a little volume called *Gospel Songs* to sell at their meetings. Sankey and Bliss agreed to combine their small books into one corroborative work entitled *Gospel Hymns and Sacred Songs.* In one year this 1875 publication sold more than 1 million copies at crusades in Philadelphia and Brooklyn alone, and it rather soon became a multimillion-copy best-seller.[21]

Sankey's hymnbooks sold well for several reasons. This British revival of 1859-1860 had stimulated prayer meetings and Sunday school work, but there were no inexpensive paperbound hymnbooks available. Also, people were deeply moved by the new tunes and lyrics introduced by Sankey. They wanted copies to take home for personal use and to share with others. Britain, like America, was ripe for new soul-stirring music that spoke to the hearts of that generation, yet also remained faithful to biblical doctrine. And also, Sankey made the hymns come alive. This is quite amazing considering that he had little voice training and his baritone voice was not particularly exceptional. But as one of his biographers phrased it, "he could move vast audiences profoundly. Generally accompanying himself on a small reed organ, he sang simply but with careful enunciation and much feeling and expression. He had a dramatic sense that enabled him to choose the song best fitted to the occasion, and frequently he prefaced it with words that added to its effect." In brief, he had special ability to relate the gospel message with verse and song in an engaging and unforgettable manner.[22]

MOODY'S STYLE OF PREACHING

Moody's preaching, like Sankey's music, struck the British people as both unusual and enthralling. One woman who heard Moody preach many times noted that he had the good judgment to cut his sermons to twenty-five or thirty minutes if the crowd was large and the meeting long. This succinctness refreshed people who often endured doctrinal sermons that lasted an hour to an hour and a half. She also observed that

He is a master in his work: he aims at one thing, viz.; getting people to consider their state before God, and he brings everything to bear on the one object—to accept Jesus, as offered to us in the Gospel. From this aim he is never for a moment diverted. His simplest illustrations, his most touching stories, his most pathetic appeals, his gentlest persuasiveness, his most passionate declamation, his most direct home thrusts, his (almost unfair) reference to people and places, all are used, and unsparingly, unfearingly, used, for the one purpose of touching the heart, that Jesus and Father may come in and abide there.[23]

This astute observer recalled that Moody loved to tell stories to illustrate his biblical points, and "he never seemed to grudge the time spent on the simplest story." Once during his later Dublin campaign she asked him why some people criticized his telling of stories during a message. He replied that some well-meaning people don't "seem to understand why I use these stories, it is to touch the heart and while it is soft, send right in the arrow of truth."[24]

One minister who often heard Moody preach summed up his popular acclaim this way:

He had learned to preach simply,—let us rather say he had not learned to preach otherwise; and in the unaffected language of nature, uncorrupted by the fastidious culture of the schools, he spoke face to face with men; and they heard him. Sprightly and vivacious, with a touch of humor as well as pathos, direct and pointed in his appeals, urging to an immediate decision, and feeling his dependence of the Spirit of God, he compelled all classes to acknowledge that he was a man of power. And yet God gave him the grace to be humble; not to think of himself more highly than he ought to think, but to feel that he was himself nothing and that God was all.[25]

This striking criticism of the way men with theological education were being taught to preach was not offered by an insecure, ignorant bumpkin. On the contrary, A. T. Pierson had two degrees, one from Union Theological Seminary in New York. What he rightly observed was that ministers on both sides of the Atlantic were increasingly being trained to deliver critical discourses from the pulpit rather than biblical proclamations prayerfully designed to cause people to confess, repent, serve, and grow in Christlikeness. Although Pierson did not make the connection, it is supportive of his point that Britain's most popular preacher in the late 1850s was Charles Spurgeon, who had no formal homiletic or theological training. Moody, tremendously influenced by Spurgeon, was equally untrained. In the same vein, G. Campbell Morgan, who was markedly affected by both Spurgeon and Moody, had no college or theological training, and he became one of the most influential preachers in Britain in the next generation.

Whatever the precise reasons, two untrained and relatively obscure Americans ministered in northern England until late November, 1873. After Sunderland they went to several other English communities in Yorkshire and Northumberland, culminating their work at the English city of Carlisle on the Scottish border. There they spent the week of November 15. A man from Carlisle reported what he experienced and saw:

> This is the Lord's doing: it is marvelous in our eyes. As in other places, the meetings have been crowded to excess; the United Presbyterian Church, of which Mr. Christi is the pastor, proved altogether inadequate to accommodate the throngs, and the large Wesleyan Chapel close at hand was also thrown open, both buildings being completely filled. The power of God was present in a most marked degree; the solemn and magnificent songs, seeming now to bring Jesus of Nazareth right down into the streets of our own city, or, again, to take us right up to the gates of heaven, prepared the way for the word of life from the lips of Mr. Moody; that word was with power, and many were the anxious souls pressing forward to know the way of life. Jesus has become precious to many; souls have been born of God, and tears of contrition have given place to tears of joy.
>
> This much as to the blessing bestowed on the unconverted; but what shall be said as to that which has rested upon the Christians? It has been a time of drawing together such as we have not known anything of before. Ministers of the different denominations have thrown themselves heart and soul into the work, and the close of the week finds us recognizing, not in theory but in fact, that we are all one in Christ Jesus, and banded together, that by our union in Him we may honor His blessed name.[26]

THE SCOTLAND MEETINGS

News of this revival spread across the border into Scotland. Unbelievers were being converted, backsliders were returning to the fold, Christians were revitalized and witnessing, and both joy and unity were evident among previously competing and warring ministers and laity of many sects. Many people said this had to be the work of the Holy Spirit. No men—and certainly no Americans—could effect such extraordinary circumstances on their own. This was a bright shaft of light, a strong ray of hope, to Scottish Christians who had been at war with one another for over a generation, ever since the Free and Established Churches split apart in 1843 and subsequently spent many years condemning one another.

Several Scotsmen recalled that only a few months earlier a venerated old saint, R. S. Candlish, had prophesied just before his death that "a great blessing" was about to fall upon Scotland. He added that this blessing would be from God and that the people should receive it "though it will come in a strange fashion."[27]

Prophecy and good news from the south intrigued the Reverend John Kelman of Free St. John's Church at Leith, Scotland. He went to England to observe things for himself. What he found was electrifying. On his return he corroborated the rumors. The witness of Kelman and a few others led to an invitation for Moody and Sankey to come to Edinburgh and Leith with the promise of support from most, if not all, Free and Established Church of Scotland pastors.

This was a large step for the Americans to take. It was one thing ministering to the ordinary people of northern England; it was quite different going into Edinburgh, a cultural, educational, and theological center of nearly a quarter million souls. Neither Moody nor Sankey felt equal to the task by education or experience. But John Kelman insisted they must come because when the revival set Edinburgh aflame, the fire would spread across the whole of Scotland. There would be no way to stop it. Edinburgh's range of influence was powerful and extensive.[28]

Moody and Sankey humbly prayed. They were led to go forward, and they promised to arrive on the night of November 22.

Meetings in Edinburgh

The door to the heart of Edinburgh was opened before they arrived. Once Kelman received Moody's promise, prayer meetings for revival were held by leading ministers and lay people daily at 3:00 P.M. A contemporary reported that "these meetings were characterized by . . . remarkable fervor, unction, and faith. . . . Supplications poured forth from hearts intensely earnest for the bestowal of the desired blessing." These prayer meetings were characterized as "hallowed seasons," and flowing forth from them was a powerful sense "that a great blessing was about to descend upon Edinburgh."[29]

The opening meeting on November 23 got off to an awkward start. A capacity crowd of more than two thousand people quickly filled Music Hall. A thousand were turned away. Several ministers and laymen took part in the service, and Sankey pleased everyone with his sacred songs; Mr. Moody, however, had such a sore throat that he could not even come, let alone preach. Moody's absence, notwithstanding, there was so "much unction and power," according to one observer, that people were mightily blessed by several brief messages and many songs.[30]

Thanks to the prayers of the faithful and the aid of Professor (Sir) Alexander Simpson (a physician who had treated the ailing evangelist with a new throat spray), Moody rose from his bed to speak on November 24.[31] From that night on there was constantly growing support. Reliable witnesses talked about the power of Moody's preaching: "There is nothing of novelty in the doctrine which Mr. Moody proclaims. It is the old gospel—old, yet always fresh and young too, as the living fountain or the morning sun—in which the substitution of Christ is placed in the center, and presented with admirable distinctiveness and decision."[32]

One witness noticed the amazing variety among those who attended meetings and went into inquiry meetings afterward. The age span was "from the old man of seventy-five to the youth of eleven," and there were "soldiers from the Castle, students from the University, the backsliding, the intemperate, the skeptical, the rich and the poor, the educated and the uneducated."[33]

The System of Meetings

The pattern and rhythm of meetings varied slightly from week to week depending upon what Moody and a diverse group of sponsoring pastors discerned would be helpful. But a general system was developed in northern England, fine-tuned in Edinburgh, and generally employed throughout the United Kingdom and Ireland. First there was a noontime meeting that usually began with a hymn or two, followed by a brief (five- to seven-minute maximum—Moody bluntly cut these off if they went overtime) meditation on a portion of Scripture. Then people took turns praying as the Spirit led. If Moody felt people took advantage of their prayer time, he would interrupt and call for the singing of a hymn. His sometimes ungracious interruptions of people whom he discerned were self-serving no doubt rankled the offenders, but the large congregation applauded his courage, if only in private.[34]

Following the hour of prayer came a second meeting referred to as the question-drawer. Here Moody employed a technique he first observed at YMCA meetings in Boston when he lived there in the

D. L. Moody (1882)

1850s.[35] The effectiveness of this time for audience interaction so impressed him in those days that he employed it whenever he had the opportunity. These meetings began with prayer, and then all attendees were encouraged to write one question on a sheet of paper. A box was passed around to gather the questions, and then Moody (always with the assistance of one or two pastors) would draw out a question and he and the pastors would take turns answering. These meetings lasted exactly one hour. Like the prayer meetings, they started and ended on time. The businessman in Moody loathed inefficiency.

These sessions served several important functions. First, the people had some input in the campaign. If they had serious questions they received honest and thoughtful answers. Second, Moody learned about issues on the minds of particular communities of people, and thus he was able to select more appropriate sermon topics and illustrations to meet the local needs. Third, many ministers were directly involved in the campaigns this way. Moody had the opportunity to know them better, and their presence and direct participation made them a genuine and useful part of the overall work. And finally, Moody furthered his theological education when the pastors responded to questions first.

These question-drawer meetings also afforded opportunities for more than one denomination and theological persuasion to be represented on the platform. This gave Moody an opportunity to encourage unity among pastors, and it let the congregations know that all of them were brothers and sisters in Christ—that their differences were not on the fundamentals of the faith—and that the enemy to Christ and His kingdom was much greater than the differences between traditions.

If there were more questions than could be answered in the hour-long sessions, Moody typically called for a follow-up session the next morning or later in the afternoon. Likewise, if questions were being raised that could not be edifyingly discussed in gender-mixed gatherings, he would call a special "men's meeting" or "women's meeting" for an afternoon or early morning. Invariably Moody and two or three carefully selected pastors took the men's meetings, and he turned the women's meetings over to women whom the pastors had identified as articulate and sensitive, as well as biblically and theologically informed.

These sessions were extremely popular, as were the mid-afternoon Bible reading hours, which usually occurred after an hour or two break for lunch and rest. Sometimes several of these were scheduled at one time in the larger cities, with Moody and Sankey, as well as several pastors or lay leaders, each leading a meeting. At these gatherings a portion of Scripture was read and then an informative and applicable exposition of the Scripture was set forth. Often in the larger communities Moody placed other men in charge, and then he moved from gathering to gathering just to make an appearance, encourage speakers and listeners, and keep everything moving along. These meetings were extremely popular everywhere. Jane MacKinnon wrote that "for my own personal feelings, I enjoyed the afternoon

Meetings most. . . . I never experienced more intense enjoyment in anything that I can remember, than I did these afternoon Bible Readings." She observed that "all around one, people were intensely interested. The Ministers especially seemed to enjoy the Readings— I suppose they could best appreciate the difficulties and therefore knew best the success."[36]

MOODY'S STRENGTHS AND WEAKNESSES ON DISPLAY

Moody's humility and genuine spirit of nonsectarianism was evident in the way he arranged these Bible readings and question-drawer sessions. He had no desire to be the star of the show. He sincerely wanted to share the leadership with pastors and lay leaders because he knew they had much to teach the people. Indeed, sometimes individually, and always en masse, they had more to offer than he did. The effect was a community effort to reach a community. This was Moody's desire, the pastors sensed it, the community knew it, and the people reaped the reward.[37]

Moody, of course, knew there were things he did well, and he was not hesitant to do them. He oversaw and orchestrated the campaign as a whole. He was not about to turn that over to committees, who usually ended up bickering over small issues, thereby paralyzing the work.

Moody also took charge of meetings designed to encourage young men and women who felt called to full-time work. For years Moody had a keen sense that he was called to challenge and encourage people to go into ministry. D. W. Whittle, Charley Morton, J. H. Cole, Emma Dryer, and Ira Sankey were just a few who gave testimony to the fruit of this special calling. In the continued pursuit of this unique work, Moody always tried to hold one or two sessions devoted to men and women exploring a call. To those privileged gatherings he spoke words of exhortation and encouragement. He also entertained questions. He prayed for the people, and he frequently offered one-to-one counsel.

Moody also liked to have at least one session especially for children in every community. Often he took these sessions, but he sometimes delegated them to people known to be effective with youngsters.[38]

At the evening meeting, Sankey sang solos and pulled in the congregation on the choruses. Once the little hymnbooks were available, there was usually a time of congregational singing, and in some places a choir sang a few numbers. Moody himself did the nightly message—one always tailored to call non-Christians to repentance and believers to a more radical commitment to Christ.

His Central Theme

Moody's messages came from many texts in both testaments, and illustrations were designed to illumine the text rather than serve as decoration. Overall, however, he had one central message to share with the people: Men and women are all created to be friends and lovers of God. We are made for no other end. Until we realize this we will live lives of turmoil, confusion, and even desperation. Our heavenly Father has wooed us to be His lovers since the Garden of Eden and the time of the Fall. First He walked the garden and cried out, "Adam, where are you?" Then He sent prophets to call the unfaithful back to Him, and then His only begotten Son—the Lord Jesus Christ—was sent on the ultimate wooing mission. The Lord Jesus Christ comes to tell us we were made for God, that He is our purpose, and that we are designed to be one with Him. Because we do not realize this truth, we fail to understand that all of our strivings, dreams, hungers, and ambitions are really for Him.

Moody preached "Whosoever will may come." He told the gathered throng passionately, often with tears, that the Holy Spirit is here now, walking the streets just as Jesus walked the roads of Galilee nineteen hundred years before; the Lord is walking the aisles of the church right now, and pleading, "Come unto me all you that labor and are heavy laden and I will give you rest." Moody not only preached the love of God; he promised to take people by the hand and introduce them to the One who would be their groom if they would assent to be His bride. It is not that Moody ignored the judgment and the ultimate separation of believers from unbelievers—the first to eternal happiness in the presence of God and the latter to eternal punishment in hell. But Moody emphasized God's love rather than judgment. He stressed that there is still time to find peace, joy, fulfillment here on earth and in the life of the world to come. To this end Moody urged all who would like to inquire more about this deeply personal, intimate relationship that God calls us to share to adjourn to an inquiry room (sometimes in another building nearby) at the close of the meeting and after a closing hymn and prayer.[39]

The Inquiry Meetings

It was in these inquiry meetings that some of the campaign's most important work went on. Mere numbers never interested

Moody. Of course he was elated when the halls and churches were filled. People needed to hear the gospel. But to him the significant work was what he called "personal work"—that one-to-one listening, counseling, and praying that God gave him experience in and a love for during his home visitation days in the Sands in the late 1850s and also as he went from bed to bed ministering to wounded and dying soldiers during the Civil War.

That Moody put utmost priority on inquiry meetings is evident by the care he took to train workers. There is no way that he and Sankey alone could handle all the "anxious" people, as they had been commonly labeled since the days of Charles Finney's revival meetings and the era of frontier itinerant evangelism in America. Typically in the United Kingdom (and later in the United States) Moody's messages drew anywhere from forty to seventy people to the inquiry room.[40] In cities such as London or New York, the inquirers numbered in the hundreds. Therefore, pastors and devout lay men and women were needed to assist in this work. Without them it could not be done. To make certain that it was done properly, Moody conducted training sessions for workers in every new community where he worked.

In these training sessions Moody first instructed the workers to take each person seriously. "Don't hurry from one to another, don't grudge the time spent on one person," he insisted. Even if many were waiting for counsel, and the counselor was tempted to move quickly so that everyone would be helped, he should take time. The others would wait. If they left, so be it. "Remember the value of one soul," he stressed. "The other night," he mentioned in one training session, "I saw people [workers] waiting a minute or two with one, and then going on to another—wait patiently, and ply them with God's word, and think, oh! think, *what* it is to win a soul for Christ, and don't grudge the time [given to] one person."[41]

Right after an evening preaching service, as ushers were helping inquirers find their way to the appropriate room or hall, Moody would assemble the "personal workers" for prayer and a brief reiteration of instructions. He always stressed prayer with the person one had counseled, and he urged the workers to ask, "Are you a Christian?" Listen to the "anxious one," and listen also to the Holy Spirit's nudgings for questions one should ask or Scripture to read. And if the worker had a problem he could not handle, he should call for Mr. Moody or one of the pastors. Moody then offered up "a very short prayer, earnest and pointed. I remember it distinctly," wrote a campaign worker. "'O God, we thank Thee that so many have gone to the Inquire room. Send many more,' and then he said to the Christian [workers] 'Oh! do speak to those about you, people are just waiting to be asked, I have spoken to quite a number, and they are all gone into the Inquiry room.'" Then he urged the workers to "go and speak to them, and don't let them go without accepting Christ."[42]

THE IMPACT ON SCOTLAND

The impact of the personal work was wide-ranging and profound. The numbers of souls transformed is incalculable, and the chain reaction was astounding. The Reverend Dr. William Blaikie, a professor at the Free Church College in Edinburgh, gave public testimony to the depth and breadth of this amazing work:

A working man of fifty years of age, for example, is impressed and brought to peace in believing, and immediately he comes to the minister and cries out, with streaming eyes, "Oh! pray for my two sons!" A father and his son are seen at another meeting with arms around each other's neck. In many cases the work of conversion seems to go through whole families. That peculiar joyfulness and expectation which masks young converts, is often the means of leading others to the fountain, and two, three, four, and even more members of the same family share the blessing.

Blaikie went on, in the wake of the Edinburgh meetings, to say he saw "some very remarkable conversions of skeptics." The Edinburgh *Daily Review* reported, "Never probably, was Scotland so stirred." Dr. Charles Brown, one of the most respected and most senior of august Edinburgh's ministers, said he had "watched all the religious movements of the last forty years, and I have never seen anything that, in extent and depth of interest, approached to the present movement." He said he had prayed for and longed for such a visitation from God for decades. It was many years in coming, but now "I am so enriched with gladness at the sights around me, that I could say with Simeon, 'Now, Lord, lettest Thou Thy servant depart in peace, according to Thy word, for mine eyes have seen Thy salvation, which Thou has prepared before the face of all people.'"[43]

Emma Moody revealed in her dairy that "D. L." often was in meetings from nine in the morning until eleven or later at night. His schedule was fatiguing, but both she and Mr. Moody were exhilarated and grateful. Both her diary and Jane MacKinnon's journal make clear that she was almost as busy as her husband. She went to most of the evening meetings but stayed with the children during the day. She also answered most of his correspondence, which was growing so overwhelming that the Blaikie family, where the Moodys stayed over Christmas 1873, gave them "a present of a writing desk."[44] This "desk" was an especially handsome black leather-covered box with brass handles and trim, measuring about 12" by 7" by 4"; the versatile case contained his pens, ink, paper, envelopes, blotters, stamps, and a folding board to write on. Probably no gift ever received more effective use, and always afterward he traveled with it. Nothing could have been more useful, because several months later Moody wrote to Farwell that he feared "you will think I have forgotten you, but I am so driven I do not get time to read all my letters. The work goes on well, interest increases every month."[45]

Moody and Sankey soon realized that John Kelman had been correct. Edinburgh welcomed them, the city was ripe for harvest, and the news spread across the length and breadth of Scotland, across the sea to Ireland, and back down into the major cities and small hamlets of England. Requests inundated Moody and Sankey from hundreds of communities throughout the United Kingdom and Ireland: Would they please come for a month, or at least a fortnight, a week, or even a day or two? There was enough work available to last them a lifetime.

MOODY'S FAMILY

Fortunately for D. L. Moody and his family, ever since his sacred anointing in New York in 1871, he did not feel that every need was God's call. He and Sankey talked and prayed and made their choices. In the face of growing clamor for their personal appearances, they declared sacred time for the Lord, their families, and themselves. Saturday became a day of rest. And although Moody preached several times on Sundays, they did no inquiry meetings on the Lord's Day because these consumed too much time and would take workers from their own parish churches.[46]

Moody and Sankey spent time apart from each other so they could be alone with their families. Moody took time on Saturdays or on free days between cities to go with Emma and the children on outings to castles, on picnics, and for short boating trips on some of Scotland's beautiful lochs. They often stayed in hotels rather than with families who begged to offer hospitality, thereby protecting their private space and time. Midway in their British campaigns they did live for a time with Peter and Jane MacKinnon because this Scottish

Emma Moody in her forties

couple owned an isolated estate and promised to protect the Moodys from all unannounced reporters, zealous well-wishers, and well-meaning but energy-draining spiritually needy souls.

The protective MacKinnons marveled that the Moody children were so well-behaved, that their father was so natural and playful with them, and that he enjoyed romping and stomping outdoors. Moody also amazed people when he went out of his way to find a challenging game of croquet or agreed to an extended stay somewhere in exchange for a scenic tour of the Highlands.[47]

That the Moody children all turned out so well as teenagers and adults can be attributed in large part to Mr. Moody's obvious love and attention to them, even in the midst of an arduous schedule. Even more important, however, was Mrs. Moody's unselfish devotion to Willie and Emma's well being. She refused to have a servant or a nurse care for the little ones, even when such help would have been abundantly available. Jane MacKinnon astutely observed that "her constant attendance on them consequent on having no servant, prevented her from being present at many a meeting where her heart was. But she took these things so quietly that people thought she did not care about them. Man sees but a little way."[48]

Emma Moody's tireless and unselfish servanthood not only bore fruit in well-adjusted, disciplined, and secure children, but it also made her husband's work much more productive. A woman who became one of her closest friends as a consequence of the British campaign of 1873 to 1875 said that even one day with both Emma and Dwight demonstrated "what a source of strength and comfort she was to her husband." She observed that the more she saw of Emma Moody over the months, "the more convinced I was that a great deal of his usefulness was owing to her, not only in the work she did for him, relieving him of all correspondence, but also from her character. Her independence of thought, not a mere unthinking echo of a master mind and will" were particularly impressive. Likewise, "her calmness, meeting so quietly his impulsiveness, her humility, her great nobility of character, and her sincerity, her crystal-like purity and transparency, could not *but* make her an unspeakable help to him in his arduous and trying work."[49]

However one looked at Emma and Dwight Moody during this extended trip abroad, they appeared to make an increasingly complementary team. He turned thirty-seven in 1874 while they were in Scotland, and his thirty-one-year-old wife put on a party in Dundee. Despite sick children now and then, as well as Dwight and Emma's both taking ill one time each, there seemed to be no tensions between them, and they managed to enjoy the adventure and gracefully absorb the pressure.

THE SCOTLAND STRATEGY

At the outset of the ministry in 1873, Moody and Sankey moved to the only places where doors were open. Once the revival fire spread, they had before them the difficult decisions of which invitations to accept. As soon as news of the successes of Edinburgh and Glasgow reached England's large cities, pastors began clamoring for Moody to turn from the smaller cities of the north and come down to the heavily populated urban centers of central and southern England, where they could reach more people and establish their credibility in the most prestigious locations.

Moody and Sankey were led otherwise. After long intervals of prayer and discussion, they elected to stay in Scotland, gradually traveling up into the sparsely populated Highlands after their great successes in Scotland's largest cities. They ministered in such out-of-the-way places as Huntly, Strathpeffer, Wick, John o' Groats, and Campbell. After Scotland they went over to Ireland, despite the pressures to come down south to the urban centers of England. In Ireland they followed a more Pauline strategy of focusing only on the major cities, and this they did at Belfast, Londonderry, and Dublin, until they finally moved down to England late in 1874.

The overall campaign strategy in England was almost identical to what they had developed in Scotland and Ireland. Union prayer meetings were held for several weeks in each city prior to Moody and Sankey's arrival. As ministers and laity from many denominations congregated to ask the Holy Spirit to visit their cities, the hard ground of churchism and denominational worlds was broken up as hundreds and even thousands gathered daily in a plea for lost souls and revitalized life for believers.

Not only were prayer meetings and at least a strong showing of sectarian unity laid out as prerequisites before the Americans would go, but there had to be promises of adequate facilities and pledging of funds to cover estimated expenses. The expenses factored into the total never included honoraria for Moody, Sankey, or other ministerial workers. Anything offered to them was unsolicited and given (if at all) on a strictly voluntary basis. Increasingly, large halls that held six to fifteen thousand people were required if the anticipated crowds were to be accommodated, and in Liverpool, with no functional facility available, a ten-thousand-seat wooden auditorium was hastily constructed and named Victoria Hall in honor of the long-reigning queen.[50]

GLASGOW

From Dundee they moved on in late February, moving westward in Scotland to Glasgow. In Scotland's largest city, with a population of more than half a million, they were in a place over twice as large as Edinburgh. They ministered in industrial Glasgow until late May of 1874. There the meetings attracted so many people that tickets were needed to provide equal access to churches and halls and to keep people from feeling cheated. Moody sometimes spoke out-of-doors to people who tried to get into churches or thronged parks and quadrangles just to see his face. And once he even conducted an outdoor meeting where it was estimated that 10,000 heard him preach.[51]

Everything was going well with the family, and the interest in the gospel surpassed anything the Moodys or anyone else had ever seen. "We got to Aberdeen to hear Mr. Moody's . . . address on Monday night," wrote a witness in August 1874. "It was the old thing over again,—crowded cabs, hurried walking in the unheeded drenching showers, unwearied sitting long before, to secure a place [even with tickets], unwearied standing or taking the corner of a step to sit on. The address was powerful as usual . . . the rapt faces of the thousands listening for the last time to the earnest pathetic pleading of the preacher, to take the water of life freely, and not die."[52]

DIFFICULTIES TO BE FACED

These joys and triumphs notwithstanding, not all was tranquil and quiet for the Moodys in the United Kingdom. Despite the distance of thousands of miles, Moody could not escape the problems in the United States. In Chicago there were still insufficient funds to put up a permanent structure in place of the temporary frame tabernacle. This continued to concern Moody, and he kept seeking solutions. Also, three of the best men he had discipled and encouraged to enter full-time ministry were having financial problems. Then came the inevitable temptations for these men to give up ministry and go back into business. P. P. Bliss, D. W. Whittle, and Charley Morton were needed more than ever to oversee the church and keep the Sunday-school mission alive. Besides, there was much evangelism to do because Chicago was growing faster than almost any city in North America. To stop the possible attrition of first-rate workers, Moody urged the board at the church to get more money to Whittle, Bliss, and Morton. He also pledged $500 of personal funds to aid these key men. In late 1874 he sent funds (possibly from gifts people gave him in Britain) to Whittle and Morton, and he sent $2,000 to Bliss. Along with stipends for three men, Moody took time out of his draining schedule to send encouraging words to these friends who meant so much to him—men he was certain should be completely "out now from business," as he phrased it for Whittle.[53]

A financial panic hit the United States in September 1873, and this caused some of the fiscal problems. Stock prices soon fell, and widespread economic dislocation lasted until well into 1874. Moody's support for his friends served as a timely buffer. Not one of these men was left destitute, and all three spent the remainder of their lives in full-time ministry.

Attacks on the Campaign

The threat of losing valiant warriors on the western front consumed precious time and energy, but it was a simple problem to solve compared to some of the thunderous attacks that Moody began to receive at home and abroad. The shells of destruction were launched in Moody's direction from several sources. First, there were some militant predestinarians in Scotland who were determined to drive Moody from the land. Quite simply, his preaching that Christ Jesus died for all men and women (although he maintained that not all would appropriate this gift) drove some of the separatists to the point of fury. They first refused to join the union efforts; then they did all in their strength to disrupt the cordial relationships that were being built in the midst of the British campaign.

A Highland preacher from Dingwall, the Reverend John Kennedy, circulated a pamphlet throughout northern and western Scotland entitled *Hyper-Evangelism: "Another Gospel" Through a Mighty Power*. In this venomous piece Kennedy argued that "the present movement ignores the sovereignty and power of God." Furthermore, Moody and his followers deny "the utter spiritual impotence of souls 'dead in trespasses and sins.'" The well-known and influential John Kennedy further attacked the inquiry room and singing "human" hymns; he also maintained that organ music is "unscriptural, and therefore all who have subscribed the Confession of Faith are under solemn vow against it." Finally, Kennedy argued that those prayer meetings have become "factories of sensation."[54]

Even more, the Reverend Kennedy loathed talk of reunion. A Free Church pastor, he saw all discussion about reuniting the major factions of the Scottish Presbyterians as a betrayal of Calvinism. And talk of union beyond the boundaries of Presbyterianism was, to his mind, no better than forming an alliance with the devil.

The Letter

Kennedy was widely read, well educated, and well traveled. In fact, just before Moody and Sankey came to Britain, he had been to

America. Kennedy received a letter from Chicago in early 1874, although precisely how the contact was made and who caused a letter to be written is unclear. Regarding whether or not the Scottish divine asked for it, history is silent. What is known is that this pastor, who seemed to be a sincere Christian, circulated copies of an unverified and libelous letter to many men in the United Kingdom. The letter in essence said that Moody was a heretical teacher who "wishes to get the people of Scotland drifted quietly from their moorings." No one could argue that the author, John Mackay, a Chicagoan who had emigrated to America from Scotland, had no right to take different theological positions than Moody. The remainder of the letter, on the other hand, was full of outright lies about Moody's past and his character. Moody was charged with dishonest dealings with one of his Chicago employees. Moody's old boss had reportedly found him out and forced him to resign in disgrace. In the wake of this revelation and the resultant unemployment, Moody, Mackay reported, decided to go into full-time ministry.[55]

Kennedy was obviously willing to destroy Moody's reputation, if necessary, to block a movement toward uniting the churches of Scotland. Without talking to the unsuspecting American or his friends, the irate Dingwall pastor circulated the letter among clergy in Scotland and other parts of the United Kingdom. Moody himself did not see the letter until it had been in circulation for two or three months. When he eventually saw a copy, he was heartsick. On May 7, 1874, he wrote a letter from Glasgow to John Farwell, informing him about the letter and its slanderous contents: "Who the man is I do not know but I cannot tell you how much it has grieved me to think anyone in our city would do such a thing." Moody implored Farwell, not for his personal sake but the sake of the ministry in Britain, to get a letter signed by pastors and lay leaders in Chicago to vouch for his character. "What you can do in this matter do because the Edinburgh committee have asked you to do for I do not want to ask anyone to defend me, but," he continued, "I wish you would do what you can at once for it would be a pity to have this work stopped."[56]

Moody's Character Witnesses

Moody told Farwell he would soon receive this request in a letter from the Reverend John Kelman, the man who had invited him to Scotland. He requested that "if you will give some time to this at once you will do me a great favor for no one knows me here and if my friends in Chicago do not stand by me who will, for every one in the country who is opposed to lay preaching and revivals are doing all they can to break me down."[57]

In a matter of days Farwell had mobilized his troops and charged into the gap. Within two weeks from the date of Moody's letter, a notarized document signed by thirty-six men was sent off to Kelman, commending Moody "as an earnest Christian worker, worthy of the confidence of our Scotch and English brethren, with who he is now laboring; believing that the Master will be honored by them in so receiving him among them as a co-laborer in the vineyard of the Lord." The signatures were mostly from pastors (Congregational, Baptist, Methodist-Episcopal, Presbyterian, and Independent), plus seminary professors, a university president, an editor, a public relief administrator, and several other men highly respected in Chicago's Christian community.[58]

Other pockets of opposition appeared simultaneously. Noises came from some of the highly educated people and the professional clergy who believed a layman should not preach. Then there was a volley of fire from people who thought Moody had a heretical view of the Holy Spirit. On this latter point the Reverend R. Lowe of Newcastle, who did Bible readings with Moody on John 14, publicly came to the American's rescue and effectively stilled the accusations of heresy.[59]

"Enthusiasm" Charges

It was not so easy to combat charges that there was too much "enthusiasm" and too many unwarranted manifestations of the Spirit in some of the prayer and inquiry meetings. Compared to rural American revival meetings of this era, Moody's campaigns in Britain were models of quietude and order. Compared to Scotland's "staid and orderly religious assemblies to which [most Scots] had been accustomed," there certainly were displays of emotion. Occasionally, display came from overzealous and disruptive people, but most of the complaints were lodged against men and women who showed understandable emotion when they repented of sins they had been carrying for years. In brief, there was no way to defend the ministry from people who were offended if others wept for joy when they finally surrendered to Christ; there was no way to prohibit people from crying noisily when there was reconciliation between individuals who had hated each other for years. Those who felt that such displays were a diabolical "spasmodic convulsion" most likely would have been offended when people shouted praises for joy when Jesus entered Jerusalem.[60]

Except for his one appeal to Farwell, Moody ignored his Scottish critics; he preferred to move ahead and minister to souls as long as the door to Britain was open. Some of his newfound friends, however, rallied to his defense. Kelman circulated the Chicago letter; Lowe testified about Moody's view of the third person of the Trinity; and Dr. Horatius Bonar, a brilliant, influential, and greatly respected pastor of a large Free Presbyterian Church in Edinburgh, came to Moody's defense. Bonar, the older brother of author A. A. Bonar, was sixty-six when Moody arrived in Scotland. A graduate of the University of Edinburgh who also had an earned doctorate in theology, he wrote a devastating critique of the published charge that Moody was bringing darkness to Britain with "Man-made revivals," "Arminianism," "sensational shocks," "unscriptural inventions," and the like. Bonar's tract took on the criticisms one by one. He used Scripture and church history (both Scotland's and world history) to prove that this revival was in the mainstream of all revivals from Pentecost to the nineteenth century.[61]

Moody's defenders—especially prestigious ones like Bonar—helped undercut the opposition's force. But it was the continual witness of the Holy Spirit through Moody and Sankey to the souls of the truly prayerful Christians and to the sincere seekers that made the final judgment. Detractors could say whatever they would, but the crowds kept coming (10,000 came out one night in Glasgow), the invitations to preach piled embarrassingly high, lives were being changed, and the campaign in Scotland alone was extended to nine months.[62]

The Catholic Issue

As in northern England and Scotland, opposition was strong in Ireland. In Dublin, for example, the total population was 250,000—with only 40,000 Protestants. When Moody and Sankey arrived, there was so much interest, and so much interaction between Catholics and Protestants, that Cardinal Cullen published an interdict forbidding Catholics from attending these "heretical" meetings. Some of the Protestants took special delight when it was learned that Catholics were coming anyway.[63]

Moody did not like the spirit of these brothers on this issue. He never appreciated sectarianism of any variety. One of the lessons he had learned in the YMCA circles was that Christians can unite and do many things together. Although he saw no virtue in abolishing de-nominational distinctives, he carried an abiding aversion to focusing on what he considered nonessentials. He particularly disliked label-ing, criticizing, and then breaking fellowship with brothers and sisters of different traditions. Scotland's sectarian warfare, and the vile fruit he tasted from this conflict, made him all the more vehe-ment in his union position. He applauded Farwell who maintained that "Union work and Lay Preaching have taken root too deeply now to be rooted out by sectarian swine."[64]

In this spirit, if not with the same rhetoric, Moody insisted that workers in his meetings drop all mention of Catholics who were en-tering into new or deeper relationships with Christ. "Why should we distinguish between different kinds of converts?" he exclaimed. "Are we not all one in Christ?"

Moody's friend W. H. Daniels, a Methodist Episcopal pastor in Chicago, noted that Moody "was a good Protestant, of course; but still more was he a Christian."[65] This sensitive and nonsectarian spir-it no doubt served as an antidote to some Roman Catholic venom. Several Catholic papers criticized Moody and Sankey, echoing the Cardinal's concerns, as well as reservations relating to worship style and music; but at least one major Catholic paper came out in praise of Moody's refusal to win proselytes. The editor implored Catholics to stop anything they were doing "to excite the hostility of our Catholic population against the religious services" conducted by the American missionaries.[66]

Moody's determination to avoid all sectarian labeling in Ireland was a bold one. To many Catholics, Moody's stand seemed a show of goodwill; to others it was viewed as a veiled tactic to entice Catholics to the meetings. Some of the separatistic Protestants were won to Moody's viewpoint; others began to question the discernment and ultimate value of this man to world missions and evangelism.

LESSONS FOR D. L.

Dwight L. Moody learned some important lessons in the midst of his Scottish campaign. Just because God led and blessed, and be-cause there was a precious abundance of the sacred anointing, there was no guarantee that everything would go smoothly. On the con-trary, Moody discovered only too vividly that in the midst of important victories are times of dreadful opposition. He learned that great spiritual leaders, like great political leaders, do not please everyone. They are at once loved and loathed. Moody and Sankey were now household names in Great Britain. While this was gratifying, even heady, it was also a woefully lonely place to be.

Virulent opposition did not destroy Moody's powerful sense of mission any more than fame compromised his humility. He went forward all the more confident that God had led them to Britain and He would part the Irish Sea if necessary to get them to the next place where they were called to minister. The next place, he felt quite certain, was Ireland—the heart of Roman Catholic country.

Not surprisingly, Moody was given much gratuitous advice about the invitations to go to Dublin. Many conservative evangelicals urged him to ignore this center of papacy; others goaded him to go there with guns blazing against the Catholic Church. Moody listened to neither side. He boldly announced at a noon prayer meeting in Scotland that God was leading them to Belfast, Londonderry, and Dublin. He would be grateful for prayer.

The campaign in Ireland was conducted similarly to the ones in England and Scotland. The same types of daytime and evening meetings produced similar effects. People in Ireland, like in Scotland, traveled long distances (sometimes a hundred or more miles) to get to one of the cities where Sankey and Moody were scheduled to be. Tickets were issued and thousands were turned away. Prayer meetings preceded the arrival of the Americans, and once again thousands flocked the halls, and hundreds huddled in the inquiry rooms and prayer meetings. Bible readings were also well attended, and thousands repented for the first time, while believers who had fallen away came back to the Lord, and many young people committed to full-time service.[67]

IRISH RESULTS

In Ireland—whether in Protestant Belfast or Catholic Dublin—naysayers were once more marginalized and ignored. They could inflict wounds, but the blows were not mortal. Emma Moody exuded joy in her Ireland entries to the diary: "The meetings in Belfast have been wonderful." In Dublin she celebrated "an immense crowd present [in Exhibition Hall]. Numbers estimated at from 10 to 15,000." And just before leaving Ireland, after nearly four months of campaigning, she rejoiced that "the meetings have all been crowded & many have we hope been blessed." Dwight Moody was especially pleased that in Ireland "the active cooperation of the Episcopals and the respect and tacit sympathy manifested by some of the Roman Catholics" were present.[68]

BACK IN ENGLAND

On November 29, 1874, the Sankeys and Moodys left Ireland and returned to England, the country where this lengthy campaign began. They traveled first to Manchester, an industrial city of almost 360,000 people. They were in Manchester for a month, moving from there to Sheffield in time for New Year's Eve. In this industrial metropolis of nearly a quarter of a million people they ministered for just over two weeks. Then on January 16, 1875, they went to the massive steel manufacturing center, Birmingham, population 350,000. They only stayed in Birmingham for nine days, going on to Liverpool, a port city of approximately one-half million people, on February 7. After Sankey and Moody ministered in Liverpool for one month, they moved up to the great city of London for a United Kingdom finale of more than seventeen weeks. London, the largest and most cosmopolitan city in the world at that time, boasting a population of nearly 4 million, was the place Moody and Sankey chose to conclude their campaign that altogether lasted just over two years.

Across Class Lines

Like elsewhere, the crowds grew large and tickets were used (more or less successfully) to make access equitable. In London Moody even insisted on holding meetings consecutively in four separate portions of the massive city so that the working-class people in London's poor East End could get to a hall as conveniently as the upper crust in the exclusive West End, and that the middling folks could get with ease to two other centrally located facilities. It is doubtful that these locations made an appreciable difference in which classes attended in any one place, because people traveled by train, by horseback, and on foot from great distances to hear the famous Yankees. Nevertheless, the fact that Moody expressed a desire to accommodate all classes made a lasting impression on many people, convincing the poor that perhaps God didn't care about class lines. A few outspoken aristocrats and members of the educational and professional elite, on the other hand, saw this attempt at class leveling to be still more evidence of foreign vulgarity.[69]

That all classes of Britain's structured society took part in the Moody-Sankey meetings is beyond dispute. Secular and Christian newspaper reporters and religious observers from both sides of the Atlantic testified to the fact that class lines as well as denominational ones were constantly crossed during this revival. But although a mixture of social and economic classes was observed in the large preaching and singing sessions, the inquiry rooms showed a progressive but unplanned division. Jane MacKinnon, who worked in inquiry rooms in Scotland, Ireland, and England said that "the longer they stayed in a place, [the more] the numbers coming to the Inquiry Room kept increasing, and always in the same order: first the middle class, then the lower, and last the higher. We knew some [upper class] wished to come who did not muster courage enough."[70]

The YMCA

Throughout the English industrial cities Moody urged support for the YMCA—asking people to serve in the associations and also to give money to build attractive and functional facilities. In Liverpool he helped spearhead a successful building-fund drive. A splendid building was erected and Moody himself laid a memorial stone on the spot where the building was to be; he also signed hundreds of fund-raising letters that went to wealthy Christian business leaders in England.[71]

This drive to encourage YMCA work culminated in a grand plea for this ministry in London. To make the case as strong as possible, Moody managed to entice three busy Americans—the presidents of the three largest and most aggressive YMCAs in the world—to come and speak in summer 1875. Those who came and gave talks were John V. Farwell, Moody's close friend from Chicago who succeeded him as president; William E. Dodge of New York; and John Wanamaker from Philadelphia. They each spoke several times, and they were all present at the closing London meeting, which was a large assembly of Moody's new friends and ministers held on July 12.

Wanamaker, Farwell, and Dodge spoke at the closing meeting. So did Dr. Andrew A. Bonar, author of numerous books, including *Memoir and Remains of Robert Murray McCheyne, A Commentary on Leviticus, Christ and His Church in the Book of Psalms,* as well as several minor-figure Christian biographies. At this meeting held at Mildmay Conference Hall, where Moody had spoken at the Reverend Pennefather's invitation three years earlier, gathered an attentive throng that included a rich union of more than seven hundred ordained ministers. Among them were "188 Church of England, 154 Congregationalists, 85 Baptists, 81 Wesleyan Methodists, 39 Presbyterians, 8 foreign pastors, 8 United Methodists, 7 Primitive Methodists, 3 Plymouth Brethren, 2 Countess of Huntingdon's Connection, 2 Society of Friends, 3 Free Church of England, 1 Bible

Christian," and more than twenty more whose denominations were not identified.[72]

THE CLOSING SERVICE IN LONDON

Moody refused to allow this closing London assembly at Mildmay to become a sentimental affair designed to honor him or Sankey. He refused the offer of a memorial. Instead, he insisted that God be glorified, the Lord Jesus Christ be lifted high, and challenges be set forth to keep the work alive. His closing remarks, which he had to interrupt once because he was overcome with emotion, were the final words at the assembly before the closing hymn, "Safe in the Arms of Jesus":

> For two years and three weeks we have been trying to labor for Christ among you, and now it is time to close. This is the last time I shall have the privilege of preaching the Gospel in this country at this time. I want to say that these have been the best years of my life. I have sought to bring Christ before you and to tell you of His beauty. It is true I have done it with stammering tongue. I have never spoken of Him as I would like to. I have done the best I could, and at this closing hour I want once more to press Him upon your acceptance. I do not want to close this meeting until I see you all in the ark of refuge. How many are willing to stand up before God to-night and say by that act that they will join us in our journey to Heaven?

In characteristic Moody fashion—so there could be no opportunity for applause that might take the focus from Christ and interrupt a divine encounter with a soul—he issued an invitation: "You that are willing to take Christ now, will you not rise?"

Many did rise. Mr. Moody prayed. Workers went to those standing, and the Moody and Sankey families with their American friends slipped away for a three-week rest at a Liverpool man's country estate at Bala, Wales. But even at Bala, Moody could not elude the public. While in Wales he gave three gospel addresses and did several Bible readings. He also conducted two more services in Liverpool as they prepared to sail home. On August 3, 1875, the exhausted but joyful preacher spoke at an afternoon session of a Christian conference, and that night he gave a farewell message at Victoria Hall.[73]

Emma recorded in her diary, "We feel there is fervor in the meeting and hope for much blessing. . . . Sailed from Liverpool for New York Aug. 4th 1875."[74]

CHAPTER NINE

A GREAT HARVEST
Abroad and at Home
1875–1877

*"It Was a Grand Reaping Season
and the Gleaning Time Has Lasted Long."*

Sunrise on Saturday, August 14, 1875, revealed an end of an era for the Moodys. No longer could they live as ordinary people either at home or abroad. As the steamship *Spain* came into New York Harbor and slowly made its way up the North River toward its pier, an agile barge moved into position alongside the massive vessel. In the dawn's first light the little vessel looked like an escort or a tug. By 6:30 A.M. the passengers on the *Spain,* who had crowded the deck to get a good look at New York, saw that the barge carried a throng of religious leaders from New York, Philadelphia, and Chicago, who entered the harbor to welcome home the Moodys and Sankeys.

Another crowd awaited the sea-weary celebrities as they put their feet on American soil for the first time in more than two years. Mr. Moody charitably offered a few words of thanks, then he informed the welcoming crowd of their plans to go to his mother's house in Northfield for several weeks of rest. Quickly the Moodys were whisked away in a horse-drawn carriage and taken to Manhattan's Grand Union Hotel. There they hid out and rested until they caught the evening train for Hartford, Connecticut. That night they traveled westward, making their way through familiar country. When the train stopped at Springfield, Massachusetts, the Moodys slipped off. Always refusing to travel on Sundays, the four Moodys stayed twenty-four hours at Springfield. Then on Monday morning, August 16, they climbed aboard a northbound train, reaching Northfield by midday.[1]

It was far too early for Emma and Dwight to understand what had transpired in the past twenty-five months. They sensed that the mission had been extremely successful, but just how that success would be manifested remained unclear. In the wake of their trip were profound effects on Great Britain and Ireland. Some of the impact of their ministry could be traced and even quantified. But much of it could not possibly be seen by them or their contemporaries; and it cannot be fully discerned by historians more than a century later.

It is well documented that millions of people heard the Good News. During Moody and Sankey's last seven months in England alone, more than 2,530,000 people attended nearly three hundred meetings. Hundreds of thousands more had listened to Moody and Sankey during the previous year and a half, and somewhere between 150,000 and 250,000 people were personally counseled and prayed for in inquiry rooms in England, Scotland, Ireland, and Wales.[2]

Dwight Moody himself was never impressed by statistics. He knew that head counting revealed only a vague indication of what the Holy Spirit was doing. One night when he and a Scottish friend chatted about the crowds in a particular meeting, Moody emphatically said, "We must not expect *every* impression to result in conversion; nor every impression on people already converted, to result in a higher life and walk. It is still as it was before, when Christ spoke; there are four different kinds of hearers and the corresponding amount of fruit bearing."[3]

It befit Moody's character that his assessments of his own ministry were modest. Others, however, have been freer to pass judgment. A late twentieth-century writer argues that because a British supporter of Moody's ministry paid R. C. Morgan for the cost of giving away 30,000 subscriptions of *The Christian* to pastors during the first few weeks of the campaign, and since that paper praised Moody and touted his accomplishments, then it was no wonder large crowds came out. It was a revival promoted by a well-financed media campaign, pure and simple.[4] This type of analysis, of course, is grossly oversimplified. All the time that *The Christian* encouraged people to hear Moody and Sankey, the Archbishop of Canterbury and the Anglican establishment as a whole refused to endorse the two Americans, as did large numbers of ordained clergy in the established Church of Scotland.[5] Likewise, papers with much larger circulations than *The Christian,* such as the London *Times* and several ultra-Calvinistic publications, were decidedly cool to Moody and Sankey, and sometimes they were blatantly hostile.[6]

PETER AND JANE MACKINNON

Two people who became friends and co-workers with Moody while he was in Britain, Peter and Jane MacKinnon, were wealthy, comfortable, and influential people. They initially went to hear Moody out of curiosity, after reading a few issues of *The Christian* that reported on his work at Newcastle. What they observed and what they personally experienced is rather revealing. At first they were merely curious, if not actually skeptical. But the well-educated, intelligent, and reflective couple quickly responded to the magnetism of the Americans. Gradually convinced that God ordained the work, they assisted Moody for nearly two years.

While keeping a journal of this extraordinary time, Jane Mac-Kinnon said she could write detailed accounts "*about* the work and about the Worker, and so little of *The Work* itself" because "it is so great, so solemn, and it is so delicate a thing to represent in my poor words—we see a face touched, we see another illumined, but how," she reflected, "can I put in words the feelings that fill my mind as *I know* the Spirit of God is working there, and how can I tell, I cannot even guess—the commerce of these souls with the unseen realities—with God himself? That is the Work." She finally retreated to one of Mr. Moody's sermons from John 3: "How plain he seemed to make it!—We cannot *see* the wind, but we *know* it is working; we cannot *see* the new life, but we *know* it has begun." MacKinnon's most striking comments came with the perspective of a later time: "It was a grand reaping season [when Moody and Sankey were here] and the gleaning time has lasted long."[7]

CHILDREN'S MINISTRY

A rich harvest and long gleaning season were evidences of supernatural work, but so were the seeds left behind that reproduced and yielded future crops. For instance, Moody unleashed a work among Britain's children that was a small revival all on its own. After the first few weeks in Britain, Moody called special meetings for children in every community. When the American twosome remained in a city for several weeks or more, weekly meetings were offered for the youngsters, usually one afternoon a week. Heroic efforts were made to go into the poorest working-class districts and bring the little ones to meetings. Building on what he had done in Chicago's Sands district, Moody encouraged workers in many cities to turn these Saturday campaign programs into permanent church school classes. In many cities the challenge was taken up. Schools were started that were going strong years after the 1873–1875 awakening.[8]

The Wordless Book

Moody frequently talked to the children himself, and in one city he unveiled a large booklet with four leaves—black, red, white, and gold. Holding this wordless book up in front of the children, he engaged them in an interchange of questions and answers that he drew from the colors. With simple visual aids and verbal responses, he led them into dialogue that eventually pointed to their need for a Savior. This booklet caught on in the United Kingdom. Eventually it was used as he used it or in a modified form on both sides of the Atlantic by people involved in child evangelism.[9]

Maggie's Home

Moody's long-term impact on children's ministry can be demonstrated in numerous ways. One illustration comes from a letter William Moody received in 1919 from the son-in-law of a man in Glasgow, who was inspired by D. L. Moody. In 1874 Dwight Moody wrote a letter to a large urban newspaper, *The North British Daily Mail*. The editor of the paper published Moody's letter, complete with a touching story about "Little Maggie," a ragged child who sold newspapers on the streets of Glasgow. Moody wrote that many people view her and her ilk as "ragged pests," but in truth "it is just the old, sad story of every city street. Not for itself has that life lived. These rags were the emblem of the drunkard's child. The little fingers are the feeders of a drunkard's home. And as you drop the copper into the tiny palm, you know that wasted form is but the channel through which the drops are trickling to hollow the drunkard's grave." Moody said many people tell him that there "are already a hundred charities which touch the question on every side." He argued that this response reveals a problem. "A hundred touch it but none meet it." What is needed is a safe home for these abused and exploited children. Cannot the Christian people of Glasgow see this need and do something "before the cold winds of the coming winter thin the little ranks" of these ragged ones who often cannot go home to the drunken father? "Let it be called 'Maggie's Home.'"

As D. J. Findlay wrote to William Moody years later, this letter to the editor became a major factor in causing William Qarrier to begin "the City Orphan Home for working boys and girls which has been in existence ever since [your father was here]. Your honored father had also some interest in the inauguration of the Orphan Home at Bridge-of-Weir. . . . Today [1919] the Homes embrace three departments . . . about 350,000 pounds has been expended in houses, land, and daily bread costs now about 100 pounds a day. All these great sums of money come in just as required in answer to prayer. No personal appeals are ever made, and not one penny is expended in advertising for funds."[10]

SINGLE YOUNG MEN

Moody's work did more than stimulate interest in ministry to children. One theme that was not present at the outset of the campaign, but that grew to become a standard part of the regimen during the last nine months in England, was a concerted effort to reach single young men who were moving to England's industrial cities from the villages and farms of Britain. Moody, as he had done in America, showed his heart for such men who arrived in the big city with all of their support and accountability left behind. Like them, he had been a refugee from the farm, and he knew their loneliness and even despair.

He knew the hearts of young men in these cities, and he recognized their need for companionship and a place to belong. The lure of the drinking establishments, dance halls, gambling dens, and houses of prostitution—the latter complete with drinks, dancing, and companionable young women in gaily decorated parlors—were not only welcoming the lonely men, but they recruited them. Moody cried out to Christians in these industrial cities full of such men, asking them to pursue these men as energetically as the recruiters of darkness did. That Moody understood the social and economic changes manifested in modern cities was abundantly clear. In Liverpool he urged Christians to enter into this war for souls:

Fifty or one hundred years ago young men lived at home. They lived in a country home, and did not come to these large cities and centres of commerce as they do now. If they did come, their employers took a personal interest in them. I contend that they do not do so now! Since I have come to Liverpool there is hardly a night in walking from this hall to my hotel I do not meet a number of young men reeling through the streets. They may not be your sons, but bear in mind, my friend, they are somebody's sons. They are worth saving. These young men who come to large cities want somebody to take an interest in them. I contend that no one can do this so well as the Christian Association [YMCA]. Some ministers claim that Associations are doing the church harm—they draw young men away from the church. That is a mistake. They feed the church; they are the handmaids of the church. They are not tearing down the church; they are drawing men into it. I know no institution which helps to draw churches so much together as these Young Men's Christian Associations.[11]

At most cities he held prayer meetings in YMCA facilities, and he openly solicited workers and financial support for associational activities. Moody led a fund-raising drive to build a first-rate building in Liverpool, and he brought three Americans to London to trumpet the YMCA cause. It was estimated that he helped raise more than a million dollars for YMCA permanent properties, and he personally donated several thousand dollars a year from 1875 until his death to the YMCA International Committee.[12]

INCLUSION OF WOMEN

According to Moody's oldest son, he also "was strongly opposed to the exclusion of women from the Sunday gospel meetings of the Association." His position met marked opposition in Great Britain, making some men believe "that Mr. Moody was disloyal to the organization." His advocacy of women having access to association meetings, plus his constant emphasis on the primacy of the religious side of the YMCA, engendered criticism, but his towering reputation by the 1870s enabled him to leave a mark in these areas that could not be erased for another quarter century.[13]

MOODY'S DEVELOPMENT OF CHRISTIAN LEADERS

Moody's interest in young men and women was directed to more than those who were lost in sin. He also had a keen eye open for those people he felt should be encouraged to develop as Christian workers. Moody was constantly on the alert for more Christian workers. Certainly one of the most effective contributions he made during the 1870s trip to Britain was the training of a new generation of workers.

Miss Cotton and Moody's Ministry

One young woman's story sheds light on Moody's method and its effect. A Christian newspaper sent a young woman, identified only as Miss Cotton, to cover the Moody-Sankey meetings in Scotland. Moody observed that she attended most meetings, so he asked an acquaintance about her. Once he discovered her commitment to Christ and her willingness to do personal work, he had her in inquiry rooms where he could supervise her and some others he had put to work.

In one Scottish town it became obvious that there was more work to be done among women than men. Consequently, he asked Miss Cotton to speak at a small, special meeting for women. Because she was an able speaker who made a strong impression on the women, he gradually gave her more responsibilities. Within a few days she became a dependable and valued co-worker; so effective, in fact, that when Moody and Sankey had to move on to another community, he called upon Miss Cotton to stay behind and do several days of follow-up work with women who were just awakening to the reality of the Lord Jesus Christ and what He wanted to do in their lives.[14]

The Cotton story is no isolated example. Indeed, Moody did the same thing with Jane MacKinnon, among others. The truth is that wherever Moody went he was looking for Timothys or Marys who were willing and eager to learn.

Encouragement of Henry Drummond

Of the many young men he met and encouraged in Britain, the one whom Moody loved the most was a young man named Henry Drummond. Born in Stirling, Scotland, in 1851, Drummond became a highly celebrated natural scientist, author, and promoter of university students in foreign missions. Drummond was fourteen years younger than Moody. He grew up in an evangelical Scottish family where a deep commitment to orthodox Christianity of the Calvinistic variety was combined with a growing sense of human responsibility in the process of personal conversion and salvation. Drummond matured in the Free Church of Scotland. He studied at the University of Edinburgh, New College Edinburgh, and he spent one summer reading and attending lectures at Germany's famous Tübingen University.

When he met Moody he was preparing for ministry, a calling that was more his family's desire than his own. Drummond eventually received ordination in the Free Church of Scotland, but he made his career as a lecturer and finally professor in natural science at his alma mater, New College. In later years the young Scotsman became rather controversial in Christian circles with the publication and wide dissemination of *Natural Law in the Spiritual World* (1883) and *The Ascent of Man* (1897). Drummond, a man who loved Jesus Christ and grew deeply committed to foreign missions, was also a popularizer of theistic evolution. One of his goals was to reconcile

Henry Drummond (1893)

biblical doctrines with the theory of evolution.[15]

The most careful and thorough modern study of Drummond makes clear that Moody had a profound impact on Drummond that lasted throughout Drummond's life.[16] The Moodys lived in the house of Professor and Mrs. William G. Blaikie during the Edinburgh campaign. Blaikie, who had met the Moodys on a trip to Chicago several years earlier, received hospitality from the Moodys when he preached in Moody's church, so he happily returned the favor. Blaikie was professor of pastoral theology and Christian apologetics at New College. When Moody asked for some dedicated university men to assist him in ministry to teenagers and college men, Blaikie recruited Henry Drummond and a few other students from New College. Moody put Drummond and his friends through the brief inquiry-room training program, then employed them in this personal work every night during the Edinburgh campaign.

First Impressions

Immediately Drummond attracted Moody's attention. He stood out from the others. The young Scotsman was a charming fellow who possessed the rare combination of a brilliant mind, a warm heart, and genuine compassion for souls. Within a few weeks Moody persuaded Drummond to take a leave from his studies and join the team as it expanded the crusade northward through Scotland.[17]

For two years Henry Drummond worked with D. L. Moody. Historian Mark Toone maintains that Drummond's experience in inquiry rooms, the one-to-one personal work, and the follow-up meetings after the campaign moved to the next city "had the most significant impact of any in preparing him for the work he would later do."[18] Drummond, with twenty years hindsight, recalled that "it was the writer's privilege as a humble camp-follower to follow the fortunes of this campaign personally from town to town, and from city to city, throughout the three kingdoms."[19]

Drummond was every inch as humble as Moody, and he did not tell how much Moody needed a man of his ability and character to minister to the young men in Scotland, Ireland, and England. Nevertheless, Moody did help shape his thinking. He also gave Drummond an unusually rich training program in preaching, teaching, and practical theology. The timing of their meeting was not coincidental. Indeed, both of them insisted their relationship was providentially arranged. Only a few days before Moody and Sankey commenced work in Edinburgh, Drummond read a paper to New College's Theological Society entitled "Spiritual Diagnosis." His thesis maintained that preaching is not the most important work ministers do with souls. Far better, he argued, is personal work, for it is only at this level that a pastor detects diseases of the soul related to sin, anxiety, and so forth.[20]

Interest in Inquiry Rooms

Drummond was hoping to pursue this "spiritual diagnosis" in a "scientific" manner when D. L. Moody arrived. Although the American preacher would never use the rhetoric or scientific methodology of a natural scientist, he had come to a similar conclusion through his personal ministry with soldiers and Chicago's lower classes. To Drummond, Moody was not only an effective preacher and a sincere man, but this American evangelist employed inquiry meetings as a method to get inside the minds and souls of individuals. It was precisely this focus on the individual that Drummond in his paper had argued was missing in traditional church methods. To the Scottish student's utter astonishment, here was an unlettered American who embraced the identical assumption and was doing something about it. To Drummond, "the inquiry meetings bridged the gap between the preacher and the hearer, and brought them together, man to man, before God."[21]

Inquiry rooms excited Drummond. There he applied his theory and developed it. Moody gave him opportunities to speak at young men's meetings, and he gave him preaching assignments in places where follow-up work was needed after a campaign's conclusion. In the gleaning time at Sunderland, for instance, Drummond and two young ministers (James Stalker and John F. Ewing) preached in the wake of Moody-Sankey, and the records show that one thousand more young men committed themselves for the first time as disciples of Jesus Christ.

In places like Sunderland, Drummond practiced the rhythm of preaching and personal work he had seen Moody perform so admirably. According to one of Drummond's friends, Sunderland made him "a man." From this work "he won . . . not only the power of organizing and leading his fellow men, but that insight into character and knowledge of life, on its lowest, as on its highest, levels, that power of interest in every individual he met, which so brilliantly distinguished him and in later years made us who were his friends feel as if his experiences and sympathies were exhaustless." To put a fine point on it, Drummond's time of being mentored by Moody "was the infirmary in which he learned spiritual diagnosis."[22]

Drummond not only found a teacher who could give him more than the professors and clergy had provided, but Moody found, according to a British observer, "his best instrument" to work with young men, and "it had almost magical results. From the very first, Drummond attracted and deeply moved crowds, and the issue was that for two years he gave himself to this work of evangelism in England, in Scotland, and Ireland. During this period he came to know the life histories of young men in all classes." He also became "a great speaker; he knew how to seize the critical moment; and his modesty, his refinement, his gentle and generous nature, his manliness, and, above all, his profound conviction, won for him disciples in every place he visited."[23]

Drummond's Life and Work

Perhaps because of such an atmosphere of encouragement, after Moody returned home Henry Drummond went forward with what he had learned. During the next two decades he spoke to hundreds of gatherings of college and university people, urging them to follow Christ and consider careers in full-time ministry or foreign missions. Moody would bring him to America where his winning manner and effective speech nudged many an American onto a pathway of service. Despite the furor that surrounded Drummond when his theistic evolution writings were published, Moody refused to repudiate him. He stood by his friend and urged him to help recruit workers.

Perhaps the most important book Drummond published—one that has stayed in print for more than a century, long after his natural science writings have been superseded—is a slender little devotional volume entitled *The Greatest Thing in the World*. Published as a small book in 1894, this is still a timely and readable devotion on 1 Corinthians 13. Drummond, a slightly balding, mustached man with a high forehead, strong eyebrows, and piercing eyes, wrote this widely read and influential classic in part because of his relationship with Moody. *The Greatest Thing in the World* carries the rich aroma of Moody's "love story" approach to Scripture, as well as his "love them in" proclamation theology, and his union emphasis in ministry. Finally, it resonates with Moody's charitable approach to life that constrained him to love Drummond and stand with him when others parted ways with him and even openly reviled the modest Scotsman. Whatever Moody's influence was on content, "The Greatest Thing in the World" was a lecture Drummond gave at a Northfield conference arranged by Moody in the summer of 1887. Moody heard the address, was powerfully affected by it, and promptly urged its publication. Although Drummond published the talk in a little book in 1894, Moody put the lecture version into print in late 1887 in a volume titled *A College of Colleges* (Revell, 1887).

Mobilization of Others

Moody played a significant part in mobilizing unnamed thousands in the United Kingdom, besides people like Drummond, to do personal work. Countless Christian men and women learned, once they were drafted and trained for inquiry-room work, that God wanted to use them to work with souls. Without question one of the most enduring effects of Moody's campaign was the enormous army of people who had been awakened to how they could be used for the rescue, healing, and nurture of souls. Moody had said in Sheffield that "the

Master's heart [is pierced] with unutterable grief, . . . not [over] the world's iniquity, but the Church's indifference." To this task he urged the mobilization of "every Christian man and woman."[24]

In this same vein many ministers who came alongside Mr. Moody were taken into the inquiry meetings and shown how to diagnose soul sickness, and then how to prescribe, through counseling and prayer, the love and presence of the Holy Spirit in life-giving ways. One man with his finger on the spiritual pulse of Manchester, England, wrote,

> If one class has been blessed more than another during those past weeks, it has been the regular Christian ministers. . . we have received nothing less than a fresh baptism of the Holy Ghost. Our souls have been quickened; our faith in the adaption of the glorious Gospel of the blessed God to the wants and longings of the human spirit has been deepened; our sense of the magnitude and responsibility of our offices as Heaven's ambassadors, charged with a message of reconciliation and love for the guiltiest of the guilty and vilest of the vile, has been greatly increased.

He concluded by saying, "Mr. Moody has demonstrated to us in a way at once startling and delightful that, after all, the grand levers for raising souls out of the fearful pit and the miry clay are just the doctrines which our so-called advanced thinkers" are telling us to "discard as antiquated and impotent."[25]

OTHER MEN AFFECTED BY MOODY'S CARE FOR SOULS

The long arm of D. L. Moody's influence touched some special men who in their turn went on to reach countless more. Duncan Macrae was converted when Moody preached in Scotland in 1874, and he became a pastor of a Presbyterian church, where he touched souls from 1878 until his death in 1906.[26] Another 1874 convert, this one in a meeting in England, was Edward Studd. Although he never became a pastor or evangelist, he became greatly concerned about the spiritual welfare of his three sons. He told them stories of Moody, who led him to Christ, and as a result these lads were instrumental in bringing Moody to Cambridge in the 1880s. One of these sons, C. T. Studd, was greatly affected by D. L. Moody. He eventually went to Africa and became one of Britain's foremost missionaries and the founder of Worldwide Evangelization Crusade. He also recruited innumerable college men to go into missions upon graduation.[27]

On the other end of the social scale was Thomas Champness,

an uneducated poor man from London's East End. He had felt a call to preach the gospel for several years. Discouraged because he had hardly any formal schooling and because he was far from being a polished man in his use of English grammar, he went one night in the 1870s to hear Dwight Moody. He ran home after the meeting with his soul on fire and full of hope. He told his wife, "Lass, I can do as well as yon man." And he did. He went forth to take the gospel to England's poorest people. Like Moody, he prayed for more workers to reach the large harvest. He too, as a historian who knew him well phrased it, instinctively understood that "the masses would be reached most easily and quickly by an order of evangelists raised from among themselves, an order of godly men able to speak their plain, straightforward, simple language, able to sympathize and fraternize with the common people, and win them for Christ." Out of Champness's vision came Cliff College, a modest little Methodist training school. Cliff College prepared uneducated men and women for the work of home missions and evangelism. Moody befriended this remarkably effective man and encouraged him in a work similar to what Spurgeon was doing from a Baptist perspective.[28]

Charles Spurgeon, himself a man who had earlier influenced Moody, fell under the spell of his American friend. In the 1860s Spurgeon had tried something similar to the inquiry room, but he abandoned it due to his ambivalence about its ultimate effectiveness. During the 1870s, though, he observed Moody's obvious success. Consequently, Spurgeon adopted the practice in his church, passed it on to his disciples, and helped hundreds of young pastors employ the same strategy.[29]

Another well established and widely admired man whom Moody marked for life was William Hay M. H. Aiken, an ordained Anglican priest six years older than Moody. Converted during the 1859-1860 Revival in Britain, he soon thereafter committed his life to ministry. In 1870 he was installed in the parish of Christ Church, Everton, Liverpool. Aiken was tremendously successful in reaching nonbelievers and unchurched people. He built an eight-hundred-seat mission hall, and he had Sunday schools for seven to eight hundred poor children. Moody discovered him in 1875 while conducting the Liverpool campaign. The men became friends, and Moody's magnetism attracted Aiken. According to J. Edwin Orr in *The Second Evangelical Awakening*, "The keen eye of Dwight L. Moody alighted upon him, and the American persuaded the Englishman to relinquish his parochial duties in order to devote himself wholly to evangelism."

Aiken began in itinerant evangelistic ministry under the umbrella of the Church of England and the auspices of the Aiken Memorial Mission Fund (honoring his clergyman father). The Church Parochial Mission Society evolved from this fund, and eventually one thousand missions were held with a reported 100,000 converts to Christ over the next four decades. Aiken gained such admiration among evangelical Anglicans that in 1898 he was honored and given a canonry at Norwich. Until his death at age eighty-six he helped make evangelism and evangelistic meetings fashionable among many Anglicans who had not been predisposed to such work.[30]

Several other men in Liverpool were deeply affected by Moody in 1875. One, Charles Garrett, oversaw the Wesleyan Methodist Liverpool Mission, and he counted D. L. Moody as one who encouraged and helped in significant ways. As a result Garrett's mission became a principal source for his denomination's "Forward Movement," which promoted practical Christian outreach. Moody, the grandfather of nineteenth-century practical outreach, spurred on Charles Garrett; and Garrett, in turn, passed the flame to William Taylor, who did so much to set Australia ablaze in the coming years.[31]

Another spark set off by Moody—one that helped set a fire that has never died out—ignited in Aberdeen, Scotland. In 1874 the Reverend Clarence Chambers, a Baptist, went to observe Moody and Sankey. He testified to being deeply moved and personally affected by what he observed and experienced. This in itself was hardly an unusual phenomenon. On the other hand, the child that this father touched with some of the 1874 fire was a most unusual lad. His name was Oswald Chambers. He grew up to become an exceptionally anointed man who understood the diagnosis, healing, and nurture of souls as well as anyone in the English-speaking world. He ministered in America as well as Britain, and he founded a vibrant Bible training college. He died in Egypt during World War I, but his wife had taken copious notes of his lectures and sermons, resulting in the publication of books such as *My Utmost for His Highest, Devotions for the Deeper Life,* and *Biblical Psychology.* These inspired works and many others still feed souls of people all over the globe.[32]

DEVELOPING OTHERS TO WIN SOULS

A lesser man than Moody might have been intimidated by well-educated people like Miss Cotton or Mr. Drummond, but he celebrated their talents and urged them to the front. It was souls Moody wanted to see transformed; he was not interested in his own glory.

This singleness of purpose freed him to select, encourage, and develop others. R. A. Torrey, another man Moody helped become an extremely influential Bible teacher, preacher, and educator, recalled:

> Oh, how he loved to put himself in the background and put other men in the foreground. How often he would stand on a platform with some of us little fellows seated behind him and as he spoke he would say: "There are better men coming after me." As he said it, he would point back over his shoulder with his thumb to the "little fellows." I do not know how he could believe it, but he really did believe that the others that were coming after him were really better than he was. He made no pretense to humility he did not possess. . . . He really believed that God would use other men in a larger measure than he had been used.[33]

PERSONAL WORK WITH SOULS

Although Moody preached to large crowds, he gave priority to personal work. He demonstrated a practical theology that was, like the ministry of Jesus, focused primarily on individuals. Like the Master, Moody preferred personal encounter of the one-to-one variety. He taught that soul doctors must take each person seriously, listen to each one and to the Holy Spirit, and then introduce Christ to the individual. Moody realized that Christ, after all, is the Healer and Life-Giver. People must meet Him in a personal encounter, usually through a thoughtful and prayerful personal introduction by one who knows Him.

Personal work is apparent in biblical times from Jesus' work in the Gospels through that of the church in Acts. From time to time the emphasis has been lost by the church, especially when its leaders have become overly dependent upon theological discourse, which may have been true of the church in Moody's day. But God has always sent along a Richard Baxter, George Herbert, Michael De Molinos, or John Wesley to call us back to the one-to-one work that became the central theme in the reformation spearheaded by Moody.

It was precisely this deep reforming of true ministry that Henry Drummond referred to twenty years later when he wrote that "time has only deepened the impression not only of the magnitude of the results immediately secured, but equally of the permanence of the after effects upon every field of social, philanthropic, and religious activity." The Moody-Sankey ministry got to the very core—that is, to spirits and souls of individuals. Therefore, Drummond insisted, "it is not too much to say that Scotland . . . would not have been the same to-day but for the visit of Mr. Moody and Mr. Sankey; and that so far-reaching was, and is, the influence of their work that any one who knows the inner religious history of the country must regard this time as nothing short of a national epoch."[34]

MINISTERING TO THE RICH AND THE POOR

One of the major criticisms directed at D. L. Moody during his lifetime and even today is that he aligned himself with the rich or comfortably situated classes, all the while ignoring the plight of the poor. George Adam Smith, an Englishman destined to become a leading Bible scholar, became a friend of Moody during the campaigns. Smith was no toady, however. He disagreed with Moody's understanding of Scripture (Smith was not an inerrantist), and he took issue with Moody on a number of doctrinal issues. Nevertheless, Smith rallied to Moody's defense when the evangelist was criticized for siding with the rich and ignoring the poor. In one of his books he noted that the Moody-Sankey meetings cannot be dismissed with "the classes versus masses" simplicity:

> Like all religious revivals this one had its origin among the merely well-to-do classes, and at first offered some ground for the sneers at bourgeois religion which were cast upon it. But Mr. Moody, who had a knowledge of the city, and the power to bring up before others the vision of its needs, inspired the Christians of Glasgow to attempt missions to the criminal classes and the relief of the friendless. The lodging-houses were visited, with every haunt of vagrants about the brick-kilns upon the south side and elsewhere.

Smith pointed out that countless drunks were rescued, "befriended and reformed." Also, "a huge tent was raised on the Green, and afterward replaced by a hall, which became the scene" for regular Saturday morning breakfasts for the poor, as well as a center for rehabilitation and philanthropic work. Much work was done to help indigent children, and Moody urged the opening of industrial schools and lodging homes—both of which were undertaken.[35]

The Reverend James Scott organized and oversaw Glasgow's "Tent on the Green," as well as the construction of James Morrison Street Hall. He too credited Moody with inspiring this work that for many years fed two thousand hungry men, women, and children every week.[36]

Helping the Material and Spiritual Needs of the Poor

Glasgow was not the only city where Moody helped the church get into social welfare ministry. In almost every city where he ministered, facilities were built, funds raised, and people put to work to serve the material, as well as the spiritual, needs of the poor. George E. Morgan, the son of *The Christian*'s editor, R. C. Morgan, believed that the extensive home mission movement in Britain was a direct effect of the 1873-1875 revival. He wrote that "the vast Home Mission Movement that sprang from the Revival was not only inaugurated and manned, but it was also *financed* to a very large extent by Revival converts and sympathizers." Morgan knew what he was writing about. *The Christian* called for donations to the home mission ministries, and the editors kept detailed records, even publishing donation lists with amounts. Between 1875 and 1908 about 500,000 pounds (British sterling) were donated, with not one penny of this going for administration or advertising. Every cent was put directly into the ministries.[37]

Lilias Trotter's Ministry

London, England, the world's largest and most vice- and crime-laden city, became a target for much of the home missions movement activity. Lilias Trotter, a wealthy, privileged young woman born in 1852, had the direction of her life changed by Moody's preaching and his challenges to reach out to those discarded by polite society. Trotter eventually became a lifelong missionary to North Africa; she also wrote inspirational books that are still read with profit. Her calling to missions grew from a longing to help the hurting that came upon her and many other young women during the revival. In the aftermath of Moody's meetings, hundreds of women started Christian hotels so that working girls and women could live in safety. Other Christian women opened restaurants for the poor—places where wholesome food could be purchased at low prices. Lilias Trotter and several of her companions purchased a vacant night club and turned it into a safe haven for London's prostitutes. As Trotter's biographer phrased it, "In an age when young unmarried daughters of well-to-do families never walked without a chaperon, Lilias decided to be different. She was soon a well-known figure in the night streets of London, recognized, loved and respected. The girls flocked to her shelter and she helped many of these victims of their circumstances to start a new life."[38]

Lilias Trotter eventually went on to North Africa to take the gospel to Muslims. Along with her on the foreign field, according to a knowledgeable British evangelical, was "a host of evangelists and others—who have since become prominent in the Lord's work." Some of these missionaries who ended up in Africa, China, India, or Britain's city missions were converted during the Moody campaigns. Others were already Christians, but they heard the call to full-time ministry during this revival.[39]

Historian George Bebbington convincingly argues that the Moody-Sankey campaign had a prodigious impact on Britain's abstinence movement, as Moody frequently assailed the evils of alcohol during his lectures and sermons. The Holiness Movement, like the abstinence movement, was well underway when Moody began preaching, but the effect of his ministry also gave this movement a big boost.[40]

HYMNODY, MONEY, AND THE MOODY MEETINGS

Indirectly, Dwight L. Moody had a significant impact on hymnody in Great Britain, Ireland, North America, and eventually the entire Christian world. Because Moody brought Sankey, who promulgated his own songs as well as those of other prominent Americans, such as P. P. Bliss and Fanny Crosby, American gospel hymns became popular in the churches and Sunday schools frequented by the masses. Bliss's hymns like "Almost Persuaded," "Hold the Fort," and "Man of Sorrows," or Sankey's music to Elizabeth Cecilia Clephane's lyrics, "There Were Ninety and Nine," plus hundreds of rhymed texts written by the blind but prolific Crosby, were sung, memorized, and maintained as favorites for decades. None of these bore the classical elegance of Charles Wesley's hymns, but they struck a favorable chord with women and men in the late nineteenth and early twentieth centuries.

By the end of World War II more than 90 million of Sankey's hymnals were sold by British publishers alone. J. Edwin Orr wrote that the hymns popularized in the revival of 1873 to 1875 "remained the prime favorites for evangelistic meetings" eighty years later. A Christian newspaper editor concurred, noting that "the remarkable group of American hymn-writers and composers" whose work was brought with Sankey "practically revolutionized the singing both of the sanctuary and of evangelism."[41]

The Hymnal Royalties

The British and Irish campaigns wrought changes that reached back the other way across the Atlantic. Mr. Moody and his American homeland were as profoundly altered as were Britain and Ireland. Moody himself was so broke when he and Emma left New York in 1873 that if it had not been for the last-minute compulsion John V. Farwell felt to give Moody $500, the trip might not have extended beyond New York's harbor. Much has been made of Mr. Moody and money during his 1873–1875 mission to Ireland and Great Britain. Critics charged that he, Sankey, or both were making a fortune selling hymnbooks and little reed or bellow organs. Neither Moody, Sankey, nor even Bliss took any personal royalties from the hymnals, and none of them received a penny from the sale of organs. All three men agreed that their share of the royalties should be overseen by a committee of Christian businessmen who would give the funds to worthy Christian organizations.

In summer 1875 the Sankey hymnbooks had earned a royalty amounting to approximately seven thousand pounds, or $35,000. The Morgan and Scott Publishing Company, which owned the copyright, tried to give this enormous stipend to Moody and Sankey. They refused to touch the money. One of London's business leaders, Hugh M. Matheson, who chaired the committee overseeing the royalties, insisted Britain should not keep the money. There was no way, he argued, that British nationals should charge Moody and Sankey seven thousand pounds for ministering among them for more than two years.

An American businessman who had joined Moody and Sankey in London in the summer of 1875 suggested to Matheson that the money could be sent to Mr. Moody's church in Chicago. If neither he nor Sankey would take the royalties, nothing could be more appropriate than to finish the church building (still unfinished since the 1871 fire) in which both men ministered. The committee readily agreed, and the Chicago Avenue Church eventually acquired a new structure thanks to the 1873–1875 revival.[42]

Money for the Workers

Moody and Sankey not only refused royalties from the hymnals, but they also refused to allow offerings to be taken for either their expenses or honoraria. Besides this, they discouraged collections being taken to cover the other expenses—often quite large—that grew out of the campaigns. In order to avoid all appearances of profit-taking, Moody insisted that invitational committees should assume responsibility for securing their community's expenses—and they must find these funds privately, if possible, so that a minimum of begging would go on.

The only way that Moody and Sankey received money was when someone decided to dig into personal funds and present a gift. This, of course, happened with some regularity. Moody made it a policy never to ask for anything for himself, although he would unblushingly ask for funds to help other ministers or to construct a building for ministry purposes. On the other hand, if someone handed him a gift, he seldom refused it, offering thanks to God for providing for his and his family's needs.

During the two-year British tour, wealthy people such as Lord Kinnaird (the steamline magnate), Lord Shaftesbury (an active evangelical who first met Moody in 1867), and the MacKinnons gave Moody stipends to keep him and his family going. These gifts were accepted with gratitude, as were the envelopes with just a pound or two from the poorer people he encountered along the way. Generally the Moodys' and Sankeys' needs were met when the host committees saw to it that an honorarium was given quietly and privately at the close of the meetings in their community.[43]

Clean Hands

Because Moody never solicited money for himself, and because of his generosity with what came into his hands, he escaped the horrid publicity and scandals that rocked later evangelists.[44] Nevertheless, after 1875 the Moodys were quite comfortable. They never had much saved, but they never went hungry. Money continued to come in from hymnals, but it was used only for ministry; honoraria were steady after 1875, and it was always ample to keep the family comfortably clothed, housed, and fed. Moody's letters show that he frequently used his personal funds to assist ministers in Chicago and he gave away money to help his poor Massachusetts relatives with necessities.[45] His uncle Samuel fell on hard times in early 1878 and asked for a loan of $1,000, offering some property as collateral. Moody promptly sent him $500 with an apology that the family was "a little short," so this was all he could send just then. But Moody sent the money as a gift, not a loan. He said it was a tiny repayment for the generosity bestowed upon a poor nephew many "years ago when he was out of work and money [and] you took pity on me."[46]

God's Provision

What the British campaign had done for both Dwight and Emma Moody proved to them beyond all doubt that God opens doors for ministry and He provides for His workers. There is no evidence anywhere that either one of them ever worried about money or fell short again. Perhaps the litmus test of Moody's indifference to mammon was his attitude toward John Wanamaker, the wealthy department store and dry goods magnate. Wanamaker was a year younger than Moody. A handsome, active Christian who helped bankroll the Philadelphia YMCA and at least one influential church in that city, Wanamaker was in a position to help Moody financially, which he often did. A lesser man than Moody might well have encouraged Wanamaker to earn as much money as possible so that he could underwrite more Christian work. But not Moody. Truly free from worry about finances, he wrote several letters imploring Wanamaker to sell out, give up business, and enter full-time ministry. In one letter Moody said, "I cannot get you out of my mind for the last few days & I thought I must set down to write you & make one more effort to get you out of your business. Why not close out before the [New] Year. . . . You do not know what a blessing you might be to the Work. Oh for consecrated men."[47]

MOODY'S FAME

If the British experience simplified Moody's financial problems, it also became an expensive prescription to heal economic woes. With the widespread sale of "Moody and Sankey Hymn Books" came a rapid erosion of personal privacy. Prior to 1873 Moody's name was rather well known in Illinois, and he was building a national reputation in the limited world of Sunday school planning and YMCA work. Even in this small evangelical bubble, where his name was known, few people would have recognized him if they saw him face-to-face on a street anywhere except perhaps Chicago.

Despite all of Moody's attempts to downplay notoriety, his name and his likeness were now recognizable all over the English-speaking world, including much of western Europe. Considering the nature of his work, Moody did his utmost to keep out of the limelight. He absolutely refused to pose for photographs, even when some photographers offered him thousands of dollars for one sitting. He made public outcries against hucksters who were selling "Moody and Sankey" paraphernalia, especially rings, porcelain statues, and photos pirated from America. He was distressed that profiteers brought out scores of hastily written and usually inaccurate biographies, and he was troubled by unauthorized publications of books of his sermons. In the twentieth century many people, even in ministry, trade on fame to raise money. But this was not Moody's style. He refused to serve mammon, even to raise money for ministry.

Nevertheless, photographs of his balding, bearded face appeared all over the United Kingdom. By the time he and Emma reached home, his portraits were legion in America too. Furthermore, by summer 1875 he was frequently on the front pages of major urban newspapers, among them *The New York Times* and *The Times of London.* Moody was not only regular copy in the secular press, but he was spectacularly newsworthy in the Christian press. Even if all the publicity could have been friendly—and of course it was not—this was hard to bear.[48]

Instant fame did more than erode family privacy—it brought an avalanche of correspondence that never abated until after Mr. Moody's death in December 1899. Even after D. L.'s passing, Mrs. Moody was inundated with mail, and the elder son, William, found answering mail relating to his father to be a time-consuming burden long after his mother died in 1903.[49]

With fame-generated correspondence came all varieties of cries for Moody's time. Gratuitous advice about where he should live and preach, and what he should speak about, came with those streams of uninvited people who always feel a compulsion to be near famous people.

BACK IN NORTHFIELD

On August 16, 1875, Dwight and Emma, with little Emma (age eleven) and Willie (age seven), arrived at Betsy Moody's house with no specific plans. Their goal was to hide out for a few weeks, get reacquainted with family and friends, go through the piles of mail, and reflect on what had happened during the last two years. Moody intended to walk the hills and reminisce about his boyhood, and he longed to pray and seek the Lord's will before he made his next move.

The Farm

It seemed that wherever Dwight Moody appeared—if even for a brief rest—the dust did not stay settled. No sooner had the Moodys unpacked and found sleeping arrangements for themselves in a small house already crowded with Mrs. Moody and three sons, than D. L. Moody had things in an uproar. It seems that some of Mrs. Moody's hens had escaped from her yard and made a way into Elisha Alexander's cornfield. Alexander was an eccentric neighbor who owned a strip of tillable land bordering the Moody property to the west and north. As soon as Alexander saw these birds strolling among his un-harvested corn stalks, he let out an unneighborly roar. Dwight Moody, with all the impetuousness of his younger years, went over to his hot-tempered neighbor and asked him to sell the small plot of cultivated land so there would be no more need to fight over these chickens. Alexander said he would sell, but only if Moody would take all of his land—twelve acres plus the house and barn. Moody inquired of the price and Alexander asked $3,500. Without a pause or counteroffer, Moody accepted his neighbor's terms on the spot.

Thanks to a sizable stipend that Edward Studd had almost forced upon Moody (the evangelist turned it down twice before he realized he was insulting his benefactor), he had enough money on hand to cover the transaction. So several chickens, it turned out, became the catalysts for Moody to purchase a piece of his beloved east Northfield hill country, complete with a house, where he could give his family some room to move about while he worked on sermons and listened for marching orders.[50]

The Options for a Home Base

Even after buying Elisha Alexander's farm, the Moodys were not certain where they would live permanently. They assumed that a traveling evangelistic ministry was in the future, but they were undecided as to a location for their home base. The Alexander farm would be a valuable addition to the Moody homestead in any case, and the house would be a good summer place for Dwight, Emma, and the children. This purchase also enhanced Northfield as an option for their permanent abode.

Chicago was still an attractive possibility. Although their home was never rebuilt and Farwell had disposed of the lot soon after the fire, he offered to provide a house for the Moodys if they would come back to Chicago. Even before they left England he made the offer, hoping to put in a bid for the famous couple before someone in New York enticed them there. Emma Moody had written a thank-you letter to Farwell, telling him they were not going to put down roots anywhere for several months at least. On September 6, Farwell wrote to Moody, "I got your wife's letter about the house, and while it may be the only wise thing to do to be a pilgrim and sojourner for the present, I hope you will find it to be in the Lord's plan when you do settle down to lodge with your most unworthy fellow traveler, though I cannot find it in my heart to deter you from finding a more inviting home than I can give you, if such should seem to be the best

Moody's birthplace, complete with an addition on the west side for Moody's mother

place for the highest usefulness of your time and talents."[51]

To be sure Farwell's offer was tempting. Emma's mother was in Chicago, and so were her married sister and family. Likewise, the Chicago Avenue Church would soon have its roof and final construction completed. Being there for ministry near the YMCA's Farwell Hall all conspired to make the offer extremely attractive. But Moody could also look at things another way. Major J. H. Cole, with the able assistance of Whittle and Bliss, was becoming a superb pastor in Moody's church. Farwell informed Moody that he had made an excellent choice when "you were led in placing him under your Mantle when you left for Europe. He is a star of the first magnitude in faith and purpose" and a superb "teacher of the Word." Added to this, "Moorehouse is here and preaches in the Hall Sunday nights."[52] In short, Farwell wanted Moody in Chicago, but Chicago did not need the traveling preacher. Able men were carrying on the work quite well.

Not being needed in Chicago took pressure off of Moody. He could at least consider staying near his aging mother; and besides, Emma and the children were falling in love with the farm. Both Dwight and Emma found rural Massachusetts to be a tonic for their souls. The greatest ministry opportunities were in the cities, but it was in the country where they settled into the rhythm of God's creation and experienced deepest renewal.

The air of the Massachusetts hills was like a healing balm for the Moodys. Emma and Willie both had been ill before they left for Britain. Neither one had good health during their stay abroad. Even when they spent several weeks on the channel coast, neither Willie nor Emma regained full strength. After four months in Northfield, though, Emma could praise God because they had "so much to be thankful for. . . . We are all so well, and Willie has improved so very much, he is looking quite strong."[53]

While the children played and enjoyed their cousins, and Emma tried to build some sort of a home out of the newly acquired house, Moody quickly grew bored with the restful Northfield life. Within a few days he began a series of protracted meetings that took place every night at the local Congregational church. Once the word went forth that Moody was preaching nightly, people began to take trains up to Northfield and pack out the already crowded church. A young woman who attended one of these meetings recalled that she went to a crowded meeting with her mother, fully expecting to be bored. To her utter amazement, Mr. Moody was a fascinating man. He seemed to be talking rather than preaching, and his message was full of stories that held her rapt attention.[54]

Besides the demands of nightly preaching, Moody was invaded by delegations from several cities. Some men were no longer willing to wait for answers to their letters. So without benefit of invitation to Northfield, they took trains, hired carriages, and found their way to the crowded white-frame house with green shutters. These visitors sought Moody at home in the daytime or in the church at night. Like the aggressive age in which they lived and worked, they pursued Mr. Moody and pressed their claims for extended meetings in such places as Philadelphia, Boston, Washington, and New York.[55]

BLISS AND WHITTLE'S VISIT

More than uninvited people surrounded the Moodys during the first weeks they were at Northfield. Exactly three weeks after Dwight and Emma got home, P. P. Bliss and D. H. Whittle left Chicago for a two-week stay with the Moodys. These friends were not seen as a bother; rather, they were persuaded to come so that the men could pray, talk, and make plans for the future. Major Whittle, who always praised the Holy Spirit "for His goodness in sending the call [to full-time ministry] through Moody to me," kept detailed diary notes on their stay from September 8 to 22. "Bliss and myself received a letter from dear Moody to come at once to Northfield, Mass., and confer with him about the work for the coming winter."[56] Whittle was delighted to go, but one wonders if he didn't feel he was back in the Civil War, with Moody serving as his commanding officer, barking out orders to be obeyed rather than making requests for consideration. Nevertheless, when Moody came on like a regimental commander, he would in the next instance appear as a humble private assigned as an officer's servant. Moody may have virtually ordered Bliss and Whittle to Northfield, but he personally was at the South Vernon station to meet them, grab their bags, and drive them up to the homestead. He "received us with much joy," Whittle wrote, as it had been "over two years ago we parted with him in Chicago."

Whittle said that they passed two weeks "in this beautiful mountain home of our brother." They met his mother, three brothers, Emma, and the children. "We were made part of the family and taken over all the haunts of Moody's boyhood; up the mountain where he used to pasture cows and pick berries and gather chestnuts, and where he passed the last Sunday alone with God before he sailed for England . . . upon his . . . memorable visit." The highly decorated, battle-scared Union warrior confided to his diary that "I love him and reverence him as I do no other man on earth." He wrote that this friend who urged him to devote his life to preaching about Jesus Christ "has seemed for years a man full of the Holy Ghost. The only change I see in him now is a growth of the conscious power and an ability for speaking with added weight and deeper conviction. He is wholly and thoroughly conscious that it is all of God." Two attractive sides of Moody were apparent. "Praying alone with him, I found him humble as a child before God. Out in the work with him I found him bold as a lion before men. No hesitation, no shrinking, no timidity; speaking with authority, speaking as an ambassador of the most high God."[57]

Within a few days Sankey joined the trio and the foursome climbed hills in Vermont and New Hampshire, ate picnics, and looked down on the Connecticut River Valley in awe of northern New England's beauty. On a mountainside the men prayed together, exchanged some of their deepest thoughts, and took turns answering Moody's questions, such as which mountain in the Bible was dearest to each of them and why. Moody's devotion to his frail and sickly brother Sam was also quite apparent as he brought this younger man along so that he could learn about God from these men with robust faith and fascinating ministry experience.[58]

Whittle gleaned from Moody some insights about the revival in Great Britain, especially on subjects related to how God led and provided. "I asked him if he was never overcome by nervousness and timidity" because of the instant fame and success:

> He said no; that God carried him right along as the work grew. He had no doubt that, had he known when he reached England what was before him, he would have been frightened. But as he looked back all he could think of was Jeremiah's experience—that God gave him a forehead of brass to go before the people. He had such a consciousness of the presence of God in his meetings in London, that the people—lords, bishops, ministers, or whoever they were–were as grasshoppers.
>
> It troubled him some in going to London that his sermons and Bible talks would all be reported [often entire messages were printed in the daily press], and his entire stock, the same that he had used in other places, would thus be exhausted, but as he expressed it, "There was no help for it, so I just shut my eyes and went ahead, leaving it with God." He told me he spent but comparatively little time in secret prayer and had no experience of being weighed down and burdened before God. He did not try to get into this state. His work kept him in the spirit of prayer and dependence upon God, and he just gave himself wholly to the work.

Whittle remembered that a year or so before Moody went to England he was always burdened and crying out to God for more power. Sometimes he would call several men together and spend a half day in prayer, and he "would groan and weep before God for the baptism of the Spirit." But Whittle observed that Moody seemed to feel no need for such agonizing prayer now. Indeed, Whittle admitted,

> I wanted such a season while with him, feeling my own need, but he was as one who had passed through that experience, and had just put himself wholly in God's hands, received the baptism of the Holy Ghost, and was being led in all things by Him. His prayers while I was with him were as simple as a child's full of trust, humility, and expectation that God would not disappoint him. There seemed to be an understanding established between the servant and the Master which made long prayers or the importunity of repetition unnecessary.[59]

THE STRATEGY DEVELOPED AND IMPLEMENTED

Hikes, picnics, prayer, and nostalgia were woven together with a strong thread of hard work. There was ministry every night "with very blessed results. The whole population attended, and hundreds came from surrounding towns." Moody's mother and brothers, though still stubbornly "connected with the Unitarian Church, were much blessed," and "many brethren from different parts of the county "found their way to the meetings." Also while Moody, Bliss, Whittle, and Sankey were together they arranged a "compilation of hymns for our common use." And finally they laid out a strategy for the next few months.

Like generals in a war, they looked over their maps. They identified cities as the locations where the enemy was most entrenched —where he was inflicting the most devastating damage to entire communities and individual souls. Therefore, they planned an assault on enemy urban strongholds along several fronts. Rather than all battling together in the same locale, Whittle noted, "we all agreed that it would be best to distribute our forces in different parts of the country." Moody used a striking metaphor to explain their battle plan: "Water runs downhill, and the highest hills in America are the great cities. If we can stir them we shall stir the whole country."[60] It was decided that Whittle and Bliss would take on the midwestern and southern "hills," and Moody and Sankey would invade the massive cities on the Atlantic coast.

Just as New England's leaves were turning to their rich hues of red and gold, Whittle and Bliss moved out for predetermined cities in Michigan, Illinois, Kentucky, and Georgia; while Moody and Sankey made assaults upon Brooklyn, Philadelphia, and New York. On October 2, 1875, Moody and Sankey's coastal campaign began. It lasted until May 1876. They had a brief strategy session in New York City in early October, and then four full weeks of ministry took place in Brooklyn through mid-November. The next place the team moved was Philadelphia, where it did a nine-week campaign that carried on through Christmas and into the new year and culminated on January 20, 1876.

There was a brief respite in Northfield for two weeks, and then they moved into New York City (Manhattan) for an extended campaign that spanned nearly three months. This last leg of the campaign was scheduled to end on April 30.[61]

During the months and weeks preceding this seven-month, three-city campaign, there was a sense of expectancy within the evangelical Christian community. The editor of one Christian newspaper said that many people were praying for and expecting a blessing to spread to America after what happened in Britain. "Great meetings have been held" to pray for an outpouring of God's grace on America, especially on her cities, and "all look toward Moody as the messenger of God to strike the rock and set free the waters of salvation. . . ."[62]

Because of British momentum and weeks of prayer meetings, the campaign got off to a better start than the one in England. Local committees of pastors and lay leaders were already organized. These committees were genuinely nonsectarian, with representatives from almost every denomination. As always, opposition raised its head— a few outspoken pastors pointed out that Moody was neither ordained nor a student of theology. Skeptics, too, hammered away at any attempt to talk of a resurrected Savior who could make a difference in a community or a person's life. But by and large, according to *The New York Daily Tribune,* "interest was intense" and thousands were turned away every night in Brooklyn, Philadelphia, and New York City. "Interest and enthusiasm . . . greeted [Moody]," and no one could measure the massive "awakening of the people, the quickening of the Churches and the conversion of the multitudes."[63]

The meetings were organized in much the same way they had been developed in Britain. There were special meetings for men, women, and children, as well as daily prayer meetings, question-and-answer sessions, and Bible talks. Evening sessions featured hymn singing, well-prepared choirs comprised of men and women from scores of churches, at least two Sankey solos, and a twenty-five or thirty-minute sermon by Moody. Mr. Moody always shared the platform with a representative group of pastors, YMCA leaders, and laity who had helped bring the program together. No offerings were taken for Moody and Sankey, and no stipends were given to them. After the message came a closing hymn with an invitation to people who would like to be counseled and prayed for in an inquiry meeting.

Favorable Press

Secular newspapers and the Christian press were generally quite favorable to Moody and Sankey. They were impressed that the Irish and British watchdogs had found no irregularities and no attempts to line the pockets of the evangelists, musicians, and churches. Here in the United States, as well, there was no emphasis on money except to defray facility-related expenses. This fact utterly disarmed many cynics and critics. Moody, in fact, was so intent on keeping the money issue at bay that he opened his New York City services on the first night with a pointed attack on anyone seeking to make money from meetings designed to rescue and heal souls. "And right here, before I forget it," he said in his familiar and homespun way, "I want to urge the people of New York—the Christian people—not to buy anything of these people on the street. I am told that 65 men have come from Philadelphia to sell photographs and medals, and I don't know what not, and they are hawking them in the streets."

He expressed surprise that people would come to meetings when men were selling products bearing the names and likenesses of Christian leaders. He implored the people to boycott these sellers who were "doing the cause of Christ a great injury. I don't know that anything is hindering the work more than these men, that are making money out of us." He went on to say that if people wanted to buy a hymn book, they should go to a bookstore and buy it. And "don't buy these photographs. They are no more photographs of us than they are of you." The crowd of twelve thousand roared in laughter as Moody assured them he had not had a photograph "taken for eight years," so what they got would be counterfeit.[64]

Souls, Not Labels

In these East Coast meetings, Moody won an amazing amount of support from the Roman Catholics, who comprised a sizable portion of the population of Brooklyn, Philadelphia, and New York City. Similar to his stand in Ireland and Britain, he refused to attack Catholics for two reasons. First, they represented a large percentage of the urban population; and second, he never assumed a priori that anyone was lost because of his tradition.

Moody had talked to enough men and women over the years to know that most people have little true understanding of their church's theology. And in any case, to Moody it was only the issue of one's soul that mattered. Either Christ's Spirit had been birthed in a person or He had not. Labels were irrelevant. *The Tablet,* an eastern-based Catholic paper, published a lengthy editorial generally supportive of Moody, and a number of leading Catholics gave forth words of encouragement and support. Moody, of course, wanted *everyone* to attend the meetings so they could hear the gospel preached and sung. He was not about to attack a group and drive it away.

No doubt every priest in New York learned that one night Moody used a story about a French Catholic Archbishop as an illustration. The man had been thrown in a prison during a recent war, and there was a window in the door of his cell in the shape of a cross. With a pencil "at the top and the bottom [he] marked the height and length and depth, and at each end of the arm the length and breadth. Ah, that Catholic bishop had been to Calvary," said Moody. "He could realize the breadth and length and depth and heighth of God's love, and that Christ gave himself up freely for us all." Moody undoubtedly alienated some separatistic fundamentalists with this illustration, but it surely endeared him to many American Catholics as his inclusiveness had endeared him to people in Ireland.[65]

For Moody, his attitude toward Catholics was not merely a ploy to attract hearers. He was no hypocrite. Over the years he demonstrated a consistent love and fellowship with all Roman Catholics who would accept his extended hand. In Northfield he employed as a handyman an aged Catholic who was in a life-and-death struggle with alcohol. Moody hired him, spoke to him about how Jesus Christ could help him stop drinking, and also encouraged him to worship at the Catholic church. And when the Catholics built a new building, Moody gave the priest $500 for a new organ. At a later time the priest, in turn, loaned Moody and his friends some wagons and gave them materials for one of their building projects.[66]

No wonder when Moody died many Catholic spokespersons mourned his passing. *The Catholic World* noted that "his prevailing qualities were tireless energy, amazing common sense, unquestioning faith, and a human sympathy rarely equaled. [He was] a powerful leader of men. Protestantism has lost its best apostle. . . ." Elsewhere Moody was labeled "a genuine soul."[67]

Moody was extremely encouraged by the following letter he received from a Catholic monk in Wales. He took it as a sign that the Holy Spirit would one day unify the faithful. He also believed that the brothers' prayers were one of the reasons the campaign was going so well:

Abegavenny, March 17, 1875

My very dear Brother in Jesus Christ our God,
    I must send you one word of affectionate greetings in our Precious Redeemer's name, to say how rejoiced I am to hear and read of your powerful gifts from "The Father of Lights," "good and perfect gifts" indeed; and the blessed and faithful use you are making of them. In these days of tribulation surrounded by rationalism and infidelity without, and sectarianism within, yours is a work to confound the one and break down the other; and the saints of Jesus must rejoice exceedingly at "the showers of blessing" which accompany your progress through our land. You are but mortal man, and one of Jesus' plainest marks upon you is your simple humility in spite of the popularity which God wills should attend you. . . . [We are Catholic and ritualistic, and we] have in our Houses the perpetual adoration of the Holy Sacrament; but we preach Jesus only as perfect, finished, and present

salvation to all who are willing to receive Him. And the only work of the evangelist is to give knowledge of salvation to His people.

I have prayed and shall pray for a blessing upon you and will ask your prayers for me. . . .[68]

It was the prayers of this monk, as well as the prayers of thousands of other lovers of the Lord Jesus Christ, that Moody cited as a major cause of the large crowds and their receptivity to the gospel message. In his opening message in one eastern city, he made clear that only prayer and the visitation of the Holy Spirit can bring eternal results. Great choirs, important or famous ministers, large congregations—none of these makes the difference. "We must give all the glory to God. . . . It is not by might and power, but by God's spirit, and we have got to get our eyes off of all those things, and there will be no work and no blessing until this is done." He made clear that "we have not come with any new Gospel; it is the old Gospel, the old story, and we want the old power, the power of the Holy Ghost, and, if it is anything less than that, it will all come to naught and be like a morning cloud—soon pass away."[69]

Moody went on to underscore the ultimate importance of the renewing work of the Holy Spirit. He said that if the ministers in attendance did not get "quickened" once again by the Holy Spirit, they would say in the days ahead that the work had failed. Those people who "get acquainted" would know that the work had been a success. "There is no true revival until God's own people are lifted, until they are quickened. It will be superficial until then. It will be counterfeit. If you attempt to begin work among the ungodly and unconverted before you get quickened yourself, God won't bless you. . . . Here and there we will hear of one converted, but it won't be deep and thorough unless the Church of God is quickened." Moody called for an outpouring of the Holy Spirit on humble Christians "here to-night in our hearts; that we may be quickened first, and then how quickly the Lord will bless us." If you want to introduce two people to each other, you need to stand near them to make the introduction. In the same way, he argued, you cannot introduce others to the Lord if you are not standing near Him.[70]

A Focus on God, Not Man

Throughout his Atlantic seaboard city meetings Moody cautioned against "so much man-worship." Praising Moody, Sankey, or other Christian leaders would not be tolerated by God, who must

Betsy Moody (D. L. Moody's mother) circa 1880

have all of the glory. "We have got to sink self. . . . We have got to get rid of this man worship before [we see] deep work." Finally, God will only use weak things. "We want the great, the mighty, but God takes the foolish things, the despised things, the things which are not. What for? That no flesh may glory in His sight." If we lift up ourselves "and say we have got such great meetings and such crowds are coming, and get to thinking about crowds and about the people, and get our minds off from God, and are not constantly in communion with Him, lifting our hearts in prayer, this work will be a stupendous failure."[71]

Certainly Moody's determination to focus on God and not on himself, plus the tremendous prayer support before and during the meetings, were significant factors in the ensuing blessing. Lives were transformed. Even the *New York Times* had to admit that "the work accomplished this winter day by Mr. Moody . . . will live. The drunken have become sober, the vicious virtuous, the worldly and self-seeking unselfish, the ignoble noble, the impure pure, the youth have started with more generous aims, the old have been stirred from grossness." "New hope" and "consolation for the sorrowful" were other results.[72] Several years later there were amazing testimonies of the long-lasting effects.[73]

Moody's reaction to all assessments of cause and effect were to one point. If the Holy Spirit was working through the workers, and if the listeners were open to His promptings, glorious results would follow. Moody himself was at least as open to the Spirit as he knew how to be by the middle 1870s. The true seekers who heard him speak overlooked the poor grammar and lack of sophistication because he did what few ministers were able to do—make the Bible come alive so that the stories, and the truths these stories illustrated, pierced the very soul of the sincere person.

MOODY'S SECRET OF POWER

A religion editor for a Chicago paper noted the irony that Moody—untrained and unschooled—"knows how to handle a Bible. It is a singular fact that with all our theological seminaries and learned treatises on homiletics, it should fall to the lot of laymen to teach the ministers of this generation how to 'preach the word.'" It had taken D. L. Moody, Major Whittle, and Harry Moorhouse—all laymen filled with the Spirit—"to open the biblical era of preaching in America." In an unusual bit of insight for a busy newspaper editor, the writer caught the essence of Moody's biblical preaching skill and technique—he was "expounding the word of God from the inside thereof; trying to find out what was in the heart of Christ, and of his prophet or apostles when they spoke and wrote it, and to bring forth that power and infuse it into the hearts of their hearers."[74] Here it was; heart to heart—Spirit to soul—done with the aid of stories. It was not the erudition and talent of the preacher that was to be paraded. No. It was the Spirit's message that must be delivered to dying or sick souls. The preacher must be incidental and unobtrusive in the same way that the inquiry-room workers must be a mere dwelling place and channel for the One doing the work.

Not everyone understood the secret of Moody's power, at least in the way he understood it. To him it was a simple matter of the sacred anointing that falls on the available man or woman who is willing to become less so that Jesus can become more. He frequently pointed to John 3:30 and 2 Chronicles 16:9 to prove his point. But to many observers this was too simplistic. To them, there must be special techniques that can be observed, explained, and then taught to others. Seminary professors studied Moody's sermons and then passed on to students their observations of his methods and techniques. Still others compiled files of his stories and used them as their own illustrations. By far the least attractive of many imitative efforts were the men who read Moody's sermons verbatim to their own congregations; and decorated both ends of the sermon with someone who aped the style and tone of Ira Sankey.[75]

Overall the ministry of Moody went well—so well in fact that thousands of practicing and aspiring pastors and evangelists wanted to imitate the man from Massachusetts. Moody and Sankey filled the Brooklyn Rink (5,000 seats) to capacity for a month, and thousands of people from this city of more than 400,000 were turned away each night. In Philadelphia, a city of nearly 800,000 people, locals packed the recently vacated 10,000-seat freight depot of the Pennsylvania Railroad that was hastily transformed into a tabernacle by John Wanamaker and other business leaders. Then in New York City the massive Hippodrome that seated 14,000 (7,000 in each of two facing halls) was filled to capacity for ten weeks in this metropolis that had soared to more than 1 million people.[76]

To the eyes of many onlookers, Moody was a conqueror who had claimed the cities in Ireland and Great Britain for the Lord, including such prestigious and historic giants as Dublin, Edinburgh, Glasgow, and London. Now he had vanquished massive and booming Brooklyn, Philadelphia, and New York City for Christ. Only Boston, Washington, San Francisco, and Chicago remained to be captured.

Whittle, Sankey, and a few other insiders saw these successes as the Holy Spirit's loving partnership with the communities of believers on both sides of the Atlantic. Christians had asked Him to come, and He honored their prayers. The sovereign work of God, yes, but it was in response to a free body of Christians who had chosen to confess their sins, repent, and exercise their responsibility to invite the Christ who is knocking at the door to come in. The theological presuppositions were more like those of John Wesley and Charles Finney than they were like Jonathan Edwards or George Whitefield, but Moody and the men he mentored paid little attention to historical or systematic theology. What they were supremely confident about, however, was that God raises up men and women in every era—those who are open to Him and willing to be used to glorify Him and further His kingdom.

MOODY'S RELATIONSHIP WITH GOD

Somehow, Whittle, Moorhouse, Varley, Cole, Farwell, and a few other insiders who knew Moody well were convinced Moody had a special relationship with God, through the Holy Spirit, that originated with his conversion in the 1850s, but was accelerated during those hours of special blessing in New York in 1871. Torrey maintained Moody was "definitely endued with power from on high" after "the baptism with the Holy Ghost" in 1871. And Whittle admitted when he was in Northfield in September 1875 that he hoped Moody would pray with him as they had prayed in Chicago in 1870. Whittle confessed that he wanted what Moody had, and he believed it would come through a "season" of wrestling with God. Moody, he said, "put himself wholly in God's hands, received the baptism of the Holy Ghost, and was being led in all things by Him."[77]

FLARE-UP IN NEW YORK

There is no doubt that Moody had received a special blessing in 1871. It is apparent as well that God had used him in ways that defy simplistic rational explanations. But it is equally true that Moody did not always have perfect peace, even after his 1871 experience and the ensuing ministry victories. Precious experiences with the Spirit and glorious meetings notwithstanding, his old nemesis, abrasiveness and short temper, appeared from time to time. In New York City a horrid outburst erupted. Several of the pastors decided to take their long-scheduled spring vacations after the busy schedules leading up to and through Holy Week. Moody was markedly and openly distressed that they would leave the city before the campaign was over. "I thought this rather hard," he complained. "They should have been as much interested in the conversion of the town as I was. But apparently they were not. So I lost my nerve—and I lost my good sense."[78]

It never occurred to D. L. Moody that some of the men needed rest. It never passed through his mind that perhaps they had promised to get away with their wives on those dates long before Moody got around to committing to going to New York City. In the same self-centered and insensitive manner he hurt, if not insulted, Dr. John Hall, a Manhattan pastor, who was the chairman of an afternoon Bible reading session and was on the platform. While doing his exposition of a text, Moody interjected a snide comment about a newspaper, *The New York Ledger,* which catered to many upper-class church people. No doubt still rankled by pastors who were heading off to the shore and other exotic vacation spots, he launched an attack on pastors who would write for the *Ledger*. Dr. Hall was one of those fashionable clergymen who occasionally wrote for the paper. As soon as Moody finished his message, Hall left the platform with noticeable displeasure toward the speaker. Hall himself was off to Europe, and Moody was unable to extend an apology. "I didn't mean to say anything against the paper but somehow it popped up."[79]

The desertion of several pastors, as well as his break with Hall, which he was not able to patch up for months, if ever, caused Moody to act in a fit of temper. He had agreed to stay in Manhattan, at the Hippodrome, through April 30. But angry, hurt, and without benefit of prayer and counsel, he acted in commanding-general-like fashion and unilaterally closed the campaign two weeks early. There is no way to calculate the embarrassment, cost, or inconvenience this caused the people who had contracted for all the facilities and arrangements. Likewise, there must have been thousands of disappointed ticket holders who had planned to come to those meetings. Many people evidently had traveled long distances only to be turned away. Moody, in retrospect, sensed he had been terribly wrong. "I closed the meeting in the Hippodrome. In doing so I grieved the Holy Spirit." And even though New York City had been "the best [campaign] he ever had" (approximately a million people attended in more than ten weeks), he was convinced God would never bless his work in that city again.[80]

SOUTHERN INVASION

It was more than this New York fiasco that showed Moody to be an ordinary man despite his special anointing. He exuded a restlessness that must have been exasperating to Emma and to those who worked with him. When he closed down the Manhattan meetings, he immediately packed up the family. Rather than go back to Northfield for solitude and rest, he announced that the weather in Georgia would be best for his wife and children's health. Whittle and Bliss were already in the midst of their Georgia meetings when Moody showed up, barged in on their work, and caused a brief time of tension as he immediately stole the show from his loyal friends.[81]

Segregation

In some ways Moody paid a heavy price for his invasion of the unreconstructed South. Whites in Georgia were still reeling from

General William T. Sherman's march through their land. There were wounds aplenty that had not yet healed. The congregations were filled with ex-slaves, former Confederate soldiers who still carried scars of war, and many a war widow who came to meetings to see if God was still the protector of widows and orphans. The Georgians accepted Union veteran Whittle with no problems, but Moody caused a fight that left him more shaken than in New York City. In the North his meetings were integrated, and no one thought much about it. At the Hippodrome in Manhattan, a reporter said, "the hall is nearly full—a mixed assemblage of all classes; some very poor. . . . Many black faces dot the congregation."[82]

But in Augusta, Georgia, Moody was shocked to find blacks and whites segregated by the white power elite that arranged the open-air meetings. Memories of abolitionists in Boston came to his mind, as did the torn bodies he had witnessed in many Civil War battle hospitals. Therefore, he decided to take on the leaders. He publicly decried the affront to blacks, asserting that one day some of these white folks might be surprised to see these same blacks in "heaven while they themselves are shut out." In response the white leaders let Moody know in unguarded language that if he had come to Georgia to bring social revolution rather than the gospel, he should go home. Moody knew in his heart the distinction was not so simple. He, after all, was a preacher of God's love for all people. But the pressures were too great for him to withstand. Reconstruction had not ended. Union soldiers still occupied the South. Much bitter enmity lingered between North and South, and this social issue symbolized the animosity. He considered holding his position and refusing to back down. But after much counsel he surrendered. The audiences remained segregated.[83]

Civil War Battlefields

When the Whittles and Moodys left Georgia, D. L. Moody was limping emotionally from many wounds. He told Whittle he was "entirely bankrupt as to sermons and material." He needed time to study and rest. On the way back North, Major Whittle triumphantly took both families through the path of General Sherman's march. Whittle had been with the General, and he could give stirring firsthand accounts of scenes enacted just eleven years earlier in Georgia and at Lookout Mountain near Chattanooga, Tennessee.[84]

The personal tour of Civil War battlefields and fortifications helped take Moody's mind off himself and the humiliations in New

York City and Augusta. People reminded him along the way that he was the most influential religious leader in the English-speaking world. He soberly responded, "I am the most overestimated man in America . . . only the mouthpiece and expression of a deep and mysterious wave of religious feeling now passing over the nation."[85]

There indeed was a "deep and mysterious wave of religious feeling . . . passing over the nation" and it was to continue for many more years with D. L. Moody as the leading spokesman. Although "entirely bankrupt" by summer 1876, he did not give up. He took Emma and the children and they retreated to Northfield. There was always a time of refreshment when he climbed his favorite northern New England hills.

CHICAGO: A HOMETOWN WELCOME
—AND UNWELCOME NEWS

After spending the summer and early autumn in Northfield, the Moodys made their first trip to Chicago in three years. If Mr. Moody was still bruised from his struggles in New York City and Georgia, he did not show it. He had promised a three-month campaign in the Windy City, and this time he planned to stay the duration. No matter how he was received—and prophets are not always honored in their own country—he intended to stay and accomplish whatever God would allow.

To the surprise of some observers—perhaps even Moody himself—Chicago provided the greatest reception he had received anywhere. Exceptional unity among clergy and laity existed from beginning to end. The press stood enthusiastically with the famous evangelist and Sankey. At every level of the campaign, hearty cooperation and quantifiable results were exceptional and apparent. A ten-thousand-seat tabernacle was constructed by John V. Farwell specially for Moody and Sankey meetings. The opening session was a time of celebration. Moody was welcomed to Chicago like a conquering hero, and two hundred pastors sat on the platform in a powerful display of Christian unity. A several-hundred-voice choir was assembled by George C. Stebbins, a singer and song leader that Moody and Sankey had located, auditioned, and then hired to help with the Chicago campaign.[86]

The sometimes unruly crowd that tried to hear the hometown men who had become international celebrities could not be crowded into the new tabernacle. Eventually some six thousand disappointed people were left outside, and they blocked the entryway so completely that scores of choir members had to enter through windows at the back.[87]

Moody played general on opening night. From the platform he directed the throng, finding seats where there did not seem to be any. He had his eye on everything because the first night, he insisted, must be done well. If not, half the battle would be lost. He spotted one usher, among hundreds there, who was moving crowds with a wand in his hand. Something about the man bothered Moody. He asked the committee chairman for the man's name. Moody was informed it was Charles J. Guiteau. The name meant nothing to Moody. All he knew was that the man bothered him. Five years later a few people were amazed at Moody's sensitivity to human spirits. On July 2, 1881, Guiteau, a mentally deranged disappointed office seeker, assassinated President James A. Garfield.[88]

Moody turned attention from Guiteau to the choir. He urged them, as a local reporter heard him, "to sing as [if they] meant it. He did not want any lagging. The organist must make the organ thunder. He told two hundred preachers who sat on the stage that they were there for work—not dignity. He was, to use one more of his military metaphors, "going to turn the battery [of artillery] towards Sinai."[89]

Mr. Moody loved Chicago, and the people loved him. The tabernacle was filled for nearly every session for three months. Many came to see the famous duo; others came merely to shake Moody's hand and see his face again. Thousands of others came to find inner peace. No one knows how many people made professions of faith during the twelve-week campaign, but at the closing night farewell service, reserved only for people who had come to Christ during the mission, six thousand people turned out. That many of these people were quite serious about discipleship was apparent when local churches reported more than two thousand new members added to their rolls during the crusade.[90]

Samuel's Death

The Chicago campaign exceeded the most optimistic expectations. The organizing committee was grateful, Farwell was elated, and Christian Chicagoans in general seemed warmed and inspired. Moody was deeply touched by the love he received and the impact of the meetings on the local churches, but he could not, it seemed, get through an extended time of ministry without spiritual or emotional trauma. Less than two weeks into the crusade his infirm brother, Samuel, died. Four years younger than Moody, Sam was always more frail and more dependent than anyone else among the rather robust Moodys. For a variety of reasons—not the least of them Sam's ardent love for Dwight and his family—Moody was closer to Sam than any of his other siblings. When word came to Chicago, the distraught preacher passed the preaching responsibilities to Whittle for a few days and went home to bury Sam and comfort his mother.[91]

P. P. Bliss's Death

The Chicago meetings ended on a note of tragedy that was perhaps even more painful for Moody. Back in Northfield in September 1875, when Moody, Sankey, Whittle, and Bliss planned their campaigns, it was agreed that Moody and Sankey would do Chicago, but Whittle and Bliss would join them for a finale in late December. Then when Sankey and Moody headed for Boston—the location of their next extended crusade—Bliss and Whittle would carry on in Chicago and do the follow-up meetings.

Everything was going as planned. Paul P. Bliss, his wife, and their two children went to his widowed mother's home in northern Pennsylvania for the Christmas holidays. A raging blizzard caused Bliss and his wife to leave their two children with a relative in Avon, New York. Because of their commitment to be in Chicago no later than New Year's Eve, the couple sent Whittle a telegram on December 28, "We're going home tomorrow." On the 29th they took the train heading for Chicago. Late on Friday night, just outside Ashtabula, Ohio, an iron bridge gave way because of the weight of the snow and the train. The Pacific Express passenger train plunged seventy feet into an icy creek, where it was mangled and then burned. Nothing of their remains was ever identified.[92]

On Sunday, December 31, a memorial service was held in the black-draped tabernacle. A choir sang several of Bliss's favorite hymns to a hushed congregation. After the singing Moody took his place at the podium. With an effort to hold back the tears, he read the words of David, "Know ye not that there is a prince and great man fallen in Israel?" Then, in a voice that was nearly inaudible for weeping, he said, "Let us lift up our hearts to God in silent prayer." Moody then gained his composure and spoke some words about how this godly man in the prime of life, only thirty-eight years old, had written words and music to some of the most widely sung gospel songs. Moody later asked for subscriptions for a memorial for Mr. and Mrs. Bliss. Ten thousand dollars was immediately forthcoming, with five thousand dollars given by London's R. C. Morgan, whose firm held the copyright of Bliss's songs.[93]

Moody was deeply wounded by Bliss's death. He loved this man whose disposition always seemed sensitive, encouraging, and hopeful. Moody had backed both Bliss and Whittle, sensing a powerful anointing on the twosome. Moody was edified by Bliss's ministry and his songs. Especially inspirational had been the Blisses' unwillingness to take even a small portion of the hymnbook royalties (their share was already $60,000) to build or buy a house. They were still renters when they died.[94]

ON TO BOSTON

Staggering from these unexpected blows, Dwight, Emma, and the children retreated once again to Northfield. In the snow-blanketed hills,they rested and prayed for the strength just to do the next thing—to get down to Boston by January 28 to do a two-and-a-half-month visitation of proclamation and song. Moody and Sankey met in Philadelphia and were joined by George C. Stebbins. They had liked what they saw of him in Chicago and they urged him to become a permanent member of their team. Although he traveled from time to time with other evangelists that Moody was encouraging, the thirty-six-year-old New York native preached and ministered alongside Moody regularly until the great preacher's death more than two decades later.[95]

The Boston campaign went well. The extended series was organized in a fashion similar to the others, with emphases on union of churches, preaching and singing services, inquiry rooms, Bible-reading sessions, and special meetings for men, women, children, and people who sensed a calling to full-time ministry.

Three Important Friendships in Boston
Adoniram Judson Gordon

Three important relationships developed for Moody in Boston. First of all, he worked closely and became lifelong friends with the Reverend Adoniram Judson Gordon. Moody's senior by ten months (A. J. Gordon was born in New Hampshire in 1836), Gordon hit it off well with Moody from the outset. Gordon was the son of a woolen miller who brought his children up in the Baptist faith. A. J. was converted as a teenager, and then went on to receive two degrees—one from Boston University and the second from Newton Theological Seminary. After seminary he took a Baptist church in Roxbury, Massachusetts, and when Moody opened his Boston meet-

Will Moody

ing in 1877, Gordon was pastor at Clarendon Street Baptist Church in the city.

One of Moody's staunchest supporters, Gordon had been convinced of the truth of premillennialism and urged Moody to keep pressing that line. Gordon had been under heavy Brethren influence when he and Moody met, so he did not, to Moody's mind, embrace a biblical view of the Holy Spirit's work in this age. Moody nudged his new friend toward a love for the Holy Spirit. In turn, Gordon set Moody afire with a desire to encourage worldwide foreign missions. Moody, to be sure, was always interested in missions, but it was Gordon, active on the American Baptist Missionary Board since 1871, who got Moody's attention on this issue. He would partner with Gordon much in the future, especially as conferences for students, missions, and the deeper life were held in Northfield. Gordon, for his part, would slowly push Moody to an interest in divine healing, the very line Emma Dryer was pushing from her vantage point in Chicago.[96]

Henry F. Durant

During the Boston campaign, Moody also developed a close personal friendship with Henry F. Durant. Moody and Durant first met in 1867. Durant admired Moody's ministry, kept an eye on his progress, and enthusiastically served with the leaders who brought the evangelist to Boston. Durant, an extremely successful lawyer, lost a son to an early death and was ministered to by Moody. Eventually Durant gave up his law practice and devoted his life to lay evangelistic causes and educating young women within a decidedly Christian context. Besides offering hospitality to the four Moodys during the 1877 campaign (the Moodys lived in the Durants' spacious and elegant home from January 28 until April 8), Durant connected Moody with several important Boston businessmen and philanthropists, among them H. N. F. Marshall. Also, as the founder of Wellesley College, Durant encouraged Moody to think more about educating women. Soon the men would assist each other in significant educational ventures. Toward this end they spent many weeks together—sometimes as much as a month at a time—praying and planning ways to educate young women.[97]

Frances Willard

A third person Moody worked with in Boston was Frances E. Willard, the head of the Women's Christian Temperance Union (WCTU). Moody first met Willard during the Chicago campaign, in late 1876. By that time she was well known in Christian and temperance circles. In her late thirties by the time she and Moody met, she was well educated, bright, urbane, and quite sophisticated. She had been on the faculty at Northwestern University in Evanston, Illinois, just north of Chicago. Having served as the head of the Northwestern College for Women, she became dean of women when the school merged with the university. Just before Moody arrived for the Chicago campaign, Willard had severed her ties with Northwestern. It appears that she and the president, Charles Fowler, had butted heads over policy.[98]

Moody had relied upon leaders in the Chicago Christian community to locate able men and women to minister in the inquiry rooms and to lead Bible readings and special sessions. Well known among evangelicals, Willard was tapped to lead women's meetings. Moody slipped into one of her sessions. He was deeply moved by her prayers, her articulate speech, and her ability to engage the congregation. Consequently, near the end of his campaign, he urged the vivacious Willard to join his staff for the upcoming Boston series. Willard prayed with Moody and then promised to go home, discuss it with her mother, and give the offer more thought and prayer. By December she promised to join Moody in Boston by late January.

During the Boston campaigns, Willard made a splendid contribution. She did inquiry-room work, spoke to many well-attended women's meetings, and overall made a good impression. But before the ten-week campaign ended, problems developed, and she and Moody had an amicable but permanent parting. Although they respected and never attacked each other, they were never to minister together again.

The wedge was a two-edged sword that Willard carried with her into evangelistic work—temperance and feminism. She insisted on pushing temperance (actually total abstinence from alcohol) in almost every gathering where she presided. Moody agreed that "demon rum," as he labeled all alcoholic beverages, was at best harmful to the body and at worst a destructive demon that ruined individuals, families, and communities. His bias notwithstanding, he did not think it wise to push the issue to the extent she did, because it might be divisive and get in the way of reaching souls. Further, many mainline clergy and laity did social drinking, and Moody was more interested in unity than the cause of prohibition. Nevertheless, Moody tried to be patient with Willard's agenda. After all, he respected her and valued her contribution to the work.

Their attempts at working together were valiant but doomed from the start. It became obvious after a few weeks that the temperance movement was primary to Willard, and evangelism was a tag-on. During the Boston campaign, when she held a WCTU meeting and openly shared the platform with Unitarian women, Moody was outraged. He would not compromise with people who would not uphold the divinity of Christ. Unitarianism had held his own family in a firm grip for years, and one of his brothers still attended a Unitarian church. Large parts of New England, to Moody's view, were still in bondage to Unitarianism, so he felt he must ask Willard to sever relations with non-Trinitarians. Willard was incensed. She would associate and share a platform with whomever she chose. If Unitarian women wanted to abolish the sale of alcoholic beverages, she would welcome their partnership.

Rather soon she sent off a long letter to Emma Moody. She realized Emma handled the correspondence, and she probably misjudged

Moody's wife and expected her sympathy. At great length she set forth the importance of her cause, then rounded it off with a strong attack on Moody's entire philosophy of special meetings for women and men. Beyond this practice that she considered insulting to women, she criticized what she considered Mr. Moody's antiquated style of having only men preside at the mixed plenary sessions.[99]

Moody never responded. He believed he was open to women, using devout Christian women for everything except preaching and presiding at the joint sessions of men and women. It astounded him that anyone could think he failed to be an advocate for women when he had battled on both sides of the Atlantic to have women's meetings where women were free to discuss issues applicable to them. Also, had not he been the spearhead in Britain and America to open the YMCAs up to women? To Moody, he had gone as far as he could. Too many pastors believed women should not teach men. Over this issue, which he saw as a secondary one, he would not blunt his evangelistic arrow point.

What Moody learned from his association with Willard was that he would be even more careful in the future. He would keep the rescue and healing of souls as his primary objective, and he would not allow any other issue, regardless of how worthy it might be, to become a fellow traveler. For better or worse, he would not allow anyone to tie another cause to his understanding of the Great Commission.

Willard learned her lesson too. Despite her interest in evangelism and Christian work, she would let nothing become a cowbird to push the eggs of temperance (and eventually full equality for women) out of the nest. She and Moody had learned much from one another. They parted as friends.

Other Relationships in Boston

The time in Boston was full of relationship-building. Moody got well acquainted with H. N. F. Marshall; he also became quite friendly and found support from a famous Episcopal priest, Phillips Brooks, who wrote, among other things, "O Little Town of Bethlehem." Brooks became an admirer of Moody, if not a close friend. He even preached for the evangelist one night in Boston when Moody could not fill the pulpit.[100]

By almost every angle of vision, Boston was another great success. Hundreds of thousands attended the meetings, thousands made commitments of faith in Christ, and many churches gained new members. One of the remarkable success stories came to A. J. Gordon's church. Moody had pushed the pastors and lay leaders to look to the hurting masses. He especially urged them to reach out to alcoholics, prostitutes, the poor, and dispossessed children. Thirty alcoholics who were rescued by Moody's zealous program were baptized and became members of Gordon's city church. Nearly twenty years later, twenty-eight of these ex-drunkards were still on the wagon, and they were loyal disciples and faithful churchmen. This phenomenal success story caused Gordon to spend the remainder of his life preaching and teaching that "God can instantly change a man."[101]

To be sure, there were scoffers aplenty in historic and snobbish Boston. Not the least of them were some secular newspaper editors who had a field day painting Moody and Sankey as boors, bumpkins, and buffoons. Perhaps the most biting and sarcastic was poet Walt Whitman. But the opponents, in the final analysis, made little difference. When alcoholics got sober, and when respected intellectuals like Wellesley's founder Durant, or the well-published and widely read Phillips Brooks, came publicly to Moody's support, most Bostonians were objective. They were willing to give Moody and Sankey a hearing—and for the most part they liked what they heard.[102]

Much happened in Boston to make the Moodys joyful, but once again they experienced a rough shaking. While the Moodys were living with the Durants, eight-year-old Willie came down with a savage case of scarlet fever. To protect twelve-year-old Emma, she was whisked off to relatives at Winchester, Massachusetts. Once again death hovered over the beleaguered Moody family as a dreadful sickness struck with vengeance. Because the Durants were used to hardship, they rushed alongside with support, paying no attention to their own exposure. They helped nurse little Willie back to health, and they also gave Emma some much needed rest.[103]

D. L., as many people in Massachusetts called him, carried on with the campaign despite his heavy heart and the cloud of darkness that had pursued them so long. Finally Willie rallied and was restored to good health. Young Emma returned to her parents, and they all went back to Northfield for a much needed rest from the pressures of public ministry and the hurry of urban life.

Where success had sometimes made Moody domineering, this succession of crises made him, according to Whittle, "very kind and tender."[104] Moody gradually learned to cope with the strains of life by telling stories and jokes, allowing laughter rather than the old outbursts of temper to be his safety valve for tension and strain. Whittle said Mr. Moody "found relief from the strain that is constantly upon him" through "hearty" laughter. He would "shake all over and hold his sides over jokes." In all this levity "he is as natural as a child," and he "knows how far to go with a joke—never [laughing] about sacred things," and astutely able to "turn to the subject of Christ" in a moment.[105]

CHAPTER TEN

CONSOLIDATING THE GAINS
D. L. Moody the Educator

1878–1889

*"I Think If God Should Spare Me . . . I Would
Get into the Field 2 to 3000 Splendid Workers."*

The Moodys returned to Northfield after the Boston series, eager
to spend time together as a family in the comfort of their new
home. Less than a year before, they had built their own place by ren-
ovating and adding on to the four-room farmhouse situated in the
midst of the land D. L. purchased from Alexander. The end product
was spacious but not luxurious. With gifts from generous friends, the
Moodys settled into a solid middle-class house.

The most extravagant aspect of the place was the view. The
house was located in a lovely spot about a hundred yards below the
Moody family homestead. Betsy Moody had a more commanding
view of the Connecticut River from her loftier vantage point, but on
a clear day Dwight and Emma could get a glimpse of the water, and
they always had a panoramic view of the majestic mountains of
Southern Vermont and New Hampshire. Emma told their Scottish
friend Jane MacKinnon, "We are in our own home" finally, and "in
a most delightful spot with such beautiful scenery." Their house was
located in "the pretty spot that Mr. Moody played when a boy, and
that he loves to call *home* now. It is a very happy place though more
humble than many other homes where we have been so kindly entertained."

In all of their letters the Moodys celebrated "the farm," as they
frequently dubbed it. Emma's only complaint centered on the difficulty of finding domestic help. This in itself might not have been such
a problem except that she had her children to tend as well as a con-

stant stream of overnight visitors. In an era and location where water was pumped and laundry done by hand, keeping up with the towels and bed linens was nearly a full-time job, even if one did not count the hours spent gathering eggs, cultivating a garden, and preparing from scratch enough food to feed at least six to a dozen people per meal.[1]

D. L.'S YOUNGEST: SON PAUL

During the next months Emma's life grew even more complicated when she became pregnant with their third child. Paul was born April 11, 1879, during the extended Baltimore campaign. Emma Moody and the two children were with Dwight at the time of Paul's birth because the parents had committed themselves to keeping the family together as much as possible. On extended campaigns like Baltimore, which lasted nearly eight months, this was relatively easy to do. The children could be placed in area schools, or sometimes a tutor could be brought to the home. In Baltimore it was Emma's good fortune to be in a quiet and protected living arrangement, complete with domestic help. But once the enlarged family returned to Northfield, Mrs. Moody needed assistance at home more than ever.

"THE FARM"

The two older children did their part to relieve their mother's burdens (young Emma was now a teenager, and Willie was ten). Mr. Moody also helped, but he was probably more of a work maker than an asset. He loved gardens and farm animals and was convinced that he saved the frugal family a small fortune. A garden plot of 100 feet by 100 feet would have served his family and guests nicely, but he always put four acres under cultivation. It became a family joke that he grew enough asparagus and strawberries to feed most families within a three-mile radius, and he was so devoted to chickens and fresh eggs that he kept hundreds of hens. These numerous birds had voracious appetites; it required two full-time workers to maintain them and all the geese, Jersey cows, and bees that Moody insisted they needed to have a proper farm.[2]

Moody took much ribbing about his part-time farming skills, but the truth is he loved to see things grow and he reveled in the company of animals. Emma always said that his "farming" cost them a fortune because of their need to hire workers and buy feed to sustain Mr. Moody's menagerie. Dwight, on the other hand, boasted of his earnings whenever one of the children sold a few eggs or a jar of honey.

D. L.'s Beloved Dogs and Horses

Moody loved dogs as well as animals that provided food. The farm was never without a dog or two, and he was especially proud of a pair of English mastiffs given to him by John Wanamaker. Paul remembered his mother's good-natured complaints that the female of the pair always delivered a large litter of pups whenever the family was busiest with guests and conferences. But Mr. Moody took a quiet delight in giving away dogs and seeing tracings of mastiff in many of the canines that roamed the Northfield and Vernon region of the Connecticut River valley.[3]

Horses were equally high on Moody's list of simple pleasures. He always had a spirited saddle horse for his personal riding enjoyment, and he gave each child his or her own pony—graduating them to horses when they were old enough to ride. "It was part of my father's plan to accustom us to horses," recalled Paul. Moody's own favorite horse was a gray mare, "Nellie Gray," given to him by a good friend, Julius J. Estey, a businessman from a dozen miles away in Brattleboro, Vermont. Nellie Gray became part of the family in 1877, lived to old age, and bore three colts.

There were usually anywhere from eight to a dozen driving horses on Moody property at any time. They had no plow horses be-

Moody's canine companions (circa 1880)

cause "the farm" was not really a working farm. Their horses were for driving carriages or saddle jaunts, and most of the animals were quite spirited and fast. Mr. Moody had a well-earned reputation throughout the valley as a man who drove his horses fast. He never shared the reins with anyone because he considered himself the world's best driver, and in any case other people drove too slowly to suit him or they refused to take cuts across uncultivated terrain. People cherished amusing memories of farmer Moody riding the countryside at a fast gallop, sporting a dark brown velvet jacket, bedraggled tan trousers, and an old slouch hat—a getup his family derisively dubbed his "Bumblebee" suit.[4]

D. L. and the Nature/City Conflict

Throughout his life Dwight Moody maintained the attitude that humans were meant to be close to nature. As men and women were flocking to cities in the United States and Europe, Moody, like the majority of his contemporaries, believed they might find economic opportunity but, in the bargain, they would give up a lifeline to nature that provided physical and emotional nourishment. Too orthodox a Christian to believe that being close to the soil brought salvation, Moody understood the inherent sinful nature of his fellow rural New Englanders. He knew their needs for spirituality, and it grieved him to see so many turn to spiritualism or Unitarianism because nature did not meet their inner cravings. Nevertheless, Moody firmly believed that God poured out common grace for all mankind through nature. Moody personally experienced renewal—both spiritual and physical—when he traversed the hills and fields of rural New England.[5] This is one of the reasons he maneuvered his wife into making a permanent home in Northfield rather than returning to Chicago where her family lived.

It is impossible to understand D. L. Moody without grasping his love-hate relationship with the great cities of the Western world. Most of his preaching and teaching hours were spent in cities. He actually lived approximately nine months of every year in cities. He knew that urban places were the wave of the future, because it was to these metropolises that men and women were flocking in search of jobs, prosperity, and quality of life. From these cities emanated a vast railway network that interconnected entire continents and enabled people to travel with unprecedented speed and comfort. He recognized these trends, experienced them, and enjoyed the benefits.

Advice and Commands About the Farm

On the other hand, his soul craved the country. Virtually hundreds of his letters, written to family in Northfield while he was off preaching in cities, ask for information about "the farm." "Send me a good farm letter," was one of his constant refrains. It is significant that he could be in the midst of a demanding campaign in an English or American city, and yet find time to send orders (seldom suggestions) to Samuel while he was alive, and later to his brother George, regarding what to do about the gardens on his and his mother's property. He took time out of grueling schedules to buy seeds or asparagus starts and send them home for planting. He had advice for what to plant and when to plant it. He dispatched orders by mail on buying and selling livestock, and he let his brother and nephew know when to hire studs and kill chickens.[6]

It is not that he took advantage of his brothers and his nephew. On the contrary, he sent them money and kept them gainfully employed. To young Ambert, his brother George's son, he sent money to repay his labor. He also encouraged the lad to go to school. D. L. even found a well-established Boston family to take Ambert into their home and place him in a city school. D. L. wrote that "Mr. Marshall says he would like much to have Ambert stay in Boston this winter and go to school. I would have him do it by all means if he can have Mrs. Marshall look after him. It will be just the place for him and he could not get a better chance in my opinion."[7]

Dwight Moody recognized the tremendous advantages the city and its educational opportunities would offer his nephew—advantages that he and his siblings never had. Yet he wanted the refreshment of the country, for he hastened to rural New England and remained there most of each summer, with intermittent visits during the other nine months, as his ministry and travel schedule allowed.

Early Mornings at Northfield

A common pattern for Dwight Moody at home was to get up two or three hours earlier than most of the family. He never seemed to require much sleep. Some mornings he studied in his little library until breakfast was ready, but when the weather was decent, he rode horseback or walked for an hour or two. During these solitary outings he refreshed himself by listening to birds, smelling the pines or freshly mown hay, and watching the fog slowly rise from the river and mountains. It was during these more leisurely days at Northfield that Moody listened to God and did his most careful thinking.

MOODY'S BELIEFS, POLITICS

Moody was not an abstract thinker. He seldom reflected on contemporary issues from a philosophical perspective, and he had not done enough reading to place local or world problems into a historical context. He never read poetry or fiction; in fact, he assumed novels and the theater to be instruments of the devil. Although he greatly admired President Lincoln and was supportive of General U. S. Grant when he served in the White House for eight years, he showed only a hint of interest in politics. He was loyal to the party of Lincoln and, therefore, could not support Democrat William Jennings Bryan in 1896 when he ran for president, even though the great orator from Nebraska shared his dim view of cities and his great love for God and the Bible. Paul Moody declared that his father "was a Republican all his days, to the deep disgust of some of his prohibitionist friends who felt he might have been a tower of strength to their party."

As his son discerned, "he believed that [prohibition] as well as most issues should be decided and controlled at the local level."[8] A product of Revolutionary New England, the cradle of local autonomy and the birthplace of town meetings, he took a markedly dim view of strong central government. He never believed that the federal government should regulate wages, hours, working conditions—or much else, for that matter. This is why his sermons and letters say almost nothing about national politics, and it no doubt explains, in part, why he could ignore the plight of workers, refrain from public mention of Chicago's Haymarket Riot, and pay no attention to increasing demands for railroad and corporate and industrial regulation.

People's Greatest Need

Middle or late twentieth-century historians are sometimes hard on Moody for not becoming a Christian Socialist or at least taking a strong stand on the side of labor against the industrialists, some of whom were Moody's close friends. But Moody would have answered that he had great concern for the weak and downtrodden. Their bigger need was to be freed from the bondage and guilt of sin. They needed the Holy Spirit to breathe life into them and give them hope. He would have said that he concentrated much effort on liberating children and adults from the chains of alcohol and abuse, and he could show many a changed life to prove the efficacy of his panacea. He preferred to help people one-to-one. Tinkering with economic and political structures seemed impractical and less effective in the final analysis. Anyway, Moody would have said that he had no confidence in political solutions to social problems because until people's hearts were transformed they would still be in darkness and spiritual slavery. And as for those so-called "Robber Barons" who made fortunes off the backs of workers in urban-industrial America, he would say that the ones he personally knew—Farwell and Wanamaker (the dry goods magnates), McCormick (the farm equipment manufacturer), T. W. Harvey (lumber and real estate)—gave hundreds of thousands of dollars to build schools for the poor, help them get free from alcohol and drugs, and most important (to Moody's view), help them meet and learn about the only ultimate hope—the Lord Jesus Christ.

Moody believed, because of his experience, that if people stayed sober, worked hard, and became loyal followers of Christ, they could make a living and survive quite well. He had no use for anyone who had greedy appetites and desires to merely get ahead and live luxuriously. On the contrary, he talked several men out of lucrative careers and into full-time ministry, and with several others he attempted to do the same.[9] He believed too that the Christian community should take care of people who were sick or had abusive spouses or parents, or those who were destitute, like widows and orphans, until they could get on their feet. Give the downtrodden a leg up, to be sure, but then they must climb the ladder on their own. Moody could never have imagined twentieth-century welfare programs; he was not among the nineteenth-century minority that advocated federal responsibility for social and economic change. Moody had what he interpreted as biblical solutions to social problems. Not everyone agreed with his views, but he was not insensitive to the social problems he encountered.

Pondering

As he rode Nellie Gray on those early mornings in the late 1870s, and as he sat on granite juttings and watched the morning sunshine melt the mountain mist, he talked with God and sought direction for the months and years ahead. As Whittle had pointed out, the deaths of Sam Moody and the Blisses, as well as the personal hammerings he took quite frequently, were softening him.

Moody also had a sense that something like the Sword of Damocles was hanging over his head, threatening to drop at any moment. Little Willie, who was ten in 1879, went from one illness to another.

The boy was especially susceptible to throat and bronchial infections of the variety that were often fatal to children in the nineteenth century. Mrs. Moody, too, was often weak and run-down, despite her heroic efforts to keep up with an inexhaustible husband. Whittle said that she learned from a Chicago physician in 1876 that she was suffering from a weak heart, but she never told her husband for fear of adding to his burdens. Mr. Moody may not have been privy to details, but he was no fool. Anyone could see that Emma was not strong. He urged her to take only the trips with him that she felt would be invigorating and healthful. He hired a niece, Fanny Holton, to be a live-in nanny for the children. And Mr. Moody engaged the services of several men to help with correspondence, especially after Paul's birth in 1879.[10]

Developing a New Strategy

During his sojourns to Northfield in 1877 and 1878, Moody began to formulate the second stage of his overall plan. He would fulfill his commitments made far in advance to do extended city campaigns of more than a month. New Haven, Connecticut; Baltimore, Maryland; and St. Louis, Missouri, were already scheduled, taking up three blocks of time into 1881, and he had promised to go back to Britain in October 1881. He would continue to do evangelistic meetings of shorter duration—anywhere from a day to four weeks maximum. But the extended campaigns, he believed, must be phased out as soon as possible. His experiences in large cities were anything but discouraging, but he sensed some flaws in his overall strategy.

Always alert, and continually trying to improve his ministry, Moody could see several things. First, to reach the most people required an urban strategy. Rural Americans, as well as immigrants from Europe, were moving into the major metropolises in ever-increasing numbers. Several million farmers moved to the cities between 1860 and Moody's death in 1899, and the trend was growing. During those same years, almost 14 million immigrants came to America's shores, the numbers increasing dramatically in the 1870s and 1880s, with approximately 3,500,000 coming in the 1890s alone.[11] Moody recognized that when these newcomers arrived they were poor, maladjusted, and frequently lonely. He grew especially concerned about Germans and Swedes (two of the largest immigrant groups in the 1870s and 1880s), arguing that the church had a responsibility to reach these people.[12]

Moody's second observation from a decade of preaching was

D. L. Moody at age 45

that the truly effective work had to be done in the inquiry room—it must be personal work. The problem was that most cities did not have churches with enough spiritually mature and biblically informed people to get the job done well. Moody was willing and able to run brief training sessions for workers, but he increasingly found this to be insufficient. He recognized a great need for "gap men," as he phrased it—men and women who did not need the extensive training of ordained ministers and clergy, yet were knowledgeable enough about souls, basic doctrine, and the Bible that they could teach the ordinary lay person and also evangelize the unchurched that the laity would not reach and the pastors had no time to gather in. The cities needed a huge army of "home missionaries"—people who were willing to live simply, walk by faith, and devote their lives to evangelizing the poorest and most neglected class of urban dwellers.

These observations led to Moody's third point in a developing strategy: to equip people who were not far removed from the lowest economic level themselves for city mission work. People recently arrived from the farms were best able to reach the farm-to-city migrants. They spoke the same language and understood the background and problems. In the same fashion, recently converted alcoholics, addicts, and prostitutes were the very ones who could win the confidence of people locked in the same bondage, as were recent escapees from the tenement houses and slums most likely to bring Christ to the folks living in similar environments.

This class of workers needed training. They did not have to go to college, and certainly they did not need seminary. They would not even have to be high school graduates. What they needed was training in evangelism, personal work, the English Bible, and basic doctrine. This could not be provided in a one-time training session, and it was not being done by local churches. Some program of education needed to be developed to train and place such city missionaries.

A fourth piece of the new strategy was to train and set out an army of missionaries to go to the uttermost parts of the earth. The home missionaries could take care of Jerusalem and Judea, but workers were desperately needed for Samaria and the far-flung corners of the world.

A fifth pillar of Moody's emerging strategy was partly sentimental, but certainly related to his other four pillars—that is, he wanted to help poor children, in particular little girls trapped in the rural poverty of northern New England. This vision first came in summer 1875 when Dwight and Samuel took a drive through the nearby country. The brothers came upon two girls whose situation became the impetus for a plan. William Moody remembered the story from his father this way:

> One day [D. L.] was driving with brother, Samuel . . . over one of the mountainous roads near Northfield, when they passed a lonely cottage, far distant from any town or neighbor. Sitting in the doorway were the mother and two daughters, occupied in braiding straw hats. The father was paralytic, and could do nothing for the support of the family; thus the burden rested on the women. But though the father was physically helpless, he was an educated man, and his daughters had an ambition that reached beyond their present narrow horizon.
>
> The limitations of their condition and the apparent helplessness of their future deeply impressed Mr. Moody. The sight of those women braiding hats in that lonely, out-of-the-way place resulted in his determination to meet the peculiar needs of just such girls in neighboring hills and communities.

Samuel Moody was as touched by the mountain scene as his brother. He, like D. L., bemoaned the lack of inexpensive, high quality educational opportunities in rural northern New England. They both regretted that their sister Elizabeth (Samuel's twin) could not afford better schools than the poor, local ones; and they talked during the months ahead of their determination to do all that they could "to put such educational advantages within the reach of girls living among the New England hills as would fit them for a broader sphere in life than they could otherwise hope for."[13]

One more element was required in D. L. Moody's new strategy. Money must be raised to build educational facilities, pay teachers and administrators, and underwrite a sizable portion of the tuition, room, and board.

The Continuing Popularity

Years after Moody's death, some historians argued that by 1880 Moody's popularity had peaked and his evangelistic ministry was beginning to run out of steam; therefore, he switched over to education, seeking a worthy outlet for his soul-saving energy.[14] Nothing could be further from the truth. By the late 1870s and early 1880s his popularity was higher than it had ever been. Invitations inundated Northfield, right up to the time of his death, urging him to preach in cities all over the world. He was on the brink, by 1880, of launching a worldwide evangelistic ministry that no one had ever attempted or would undertake until Billy Graham emerged as the leading evangelist in the second half of the next century. Moody received invitations to preach in India and the Middle East, but he and Emma prayed and turned down the offers. He was implored, too, to do an extended campaign throughout Australia and New Zealand, and that invitation he also passed up.

The only overseas invitation he accepted was to Britain, where the leaders had begged him to return every year since he left in 1875. He and Emma returned to Britain in 1881 for nineteen months. The results there were not as astounding. Nevertheless, crowds were massive, personal work went well, and contemporary reports suggested a tremendous success. Moody also received money for his schools, and he procured good British speakers for his work in the States. He also spoke for a month in San Francisco in 1881 and 1889. Each time the church leaders were upset that he stayed only four weeks—hardly evidence of an evangelistic ministry running on its last legs.[15]

The evidence suggests that Moody took a serious look at his

work in the wake of the well-received Chicago and Boston campaigns. He had already accepted many obligations for the next two years, and he had piles of invitations that implored him to preach for two months or two days—but to please come. He had years of successful work behind him, but the follow-up and consolidation of gains had not been nearly as effective as he believed it should be. Furthermore, he watched good young people around him die, and he saw his own wife's failing health. Both he and Emma were gaining weight by 1879, and both showed signs of prematurely gray hair. He was only forty-two and Emma just thirty-six, yet friends and family feared for their health and cautioned them against dying young from sheer overwork and the strain of mental and physical exhaustion. To Moody the priorities were becoming more focused. "I think if God should spare me ten years longer I would get into the field 2 to 3000 splendid workers."[16]

D. L. Moody's vision had not changed since he left business for full-time ministry in 1862. The only difference now was that he had a clearer strategy born out of experience, prayer, and the necessity of limiting his activities. Countless opportunities were before him now that he was internationally renowned and in constant demand. But every need was not a call, and he could rest with the assurance that he was choosing the best options.

TRAINING A NEW GENERATION

By 1878 the die was cast. Moody would, with God's help, put plans in motion to train up a generation of youthful workers. This desire to educate and equip young people for ministry was, of course, not new to Moody. In a way, Christian education had been a significant part of his work since he started his own mission Sunday school in Chicago's Sands back in the late 1850s. This early educational ministry expanded when he used Sunday school conventions and publications to encourage and train teachers of children. Moody as an incipient educator can be seen in his training sessions for inquiry room workers during his campaigns, and his vision for training "gap" men and women was evident when he hired Emma Dryer to start a deaconess ministry in Chicago in the early 1870s. The difference by 1878, however, was Moody's determination to make this educational program his primary work and to establish it on a strong and permanent footing.

Once D. L. Moody set his course, he went forth with determination, diligence, and almost incredible enterprise. In a fashion typical of his era, nothing would be modest in vision, size, or scope. During this so-called Gilded Age—an era of large corporations, spacious and gaudy houses, huge buildings with names like Hippodrome, massive cities, and the advent of larger and thicker books—Moody adopted a similar stand. He was confident his plan was inspired by the Holy Spirit, and the evidence suggests that God greatly used his vision that had some of the markings of the boldness and strength of America's late nineteenth century.

THE FIRST TWO SCHOOLS

To Moody that meant launching the schools on several fronts almost simultaneously. No doubt his loyalty to Samuel's memory and the plan they conceived together caused him to take the first step at Northfield, where a preparatory school for girls and young women was opened in 1879. No sooner was this Northfield Seminary opened than a plan was unveiled for a boys' and young men's school, the Mount Hermon School, across the Connecticut River near the town of Gill. Once these two institutions were opened, albeit still in their developing stages, he began work in earnest in Chicago on what was to become Chicago Bible Institute. Then finally he returned to Northfield and built a separate Bible training institute there, along the line of his school in Chicago.

Moody still carried the marks of the Civil War, so it is not surprising that he frequently explained his new missions and evangelism strategy with military metaphors. He was launching an offensive against the cities, and he was pushing the assault on two fronts. Men and women would be recruited, trained, and equipped in two separate regions, and, once combat-ready, they would be deployed to either urban American or foreign fronts.

This new phase of his life's work brought out the best and the worst in Moody. His schools were going to require enormous outlays of human and material resources, all gathered, organized, and put to efficient and effective use. From the perspective of 1894, Henry Drummond maintained that "if Mr. Moody had remained in business, there is almost no question that he would have been to-day one of the wealthiest men in the United States. His enterprise, his organizing power, his knowledge and management of men are admitted by friend and foe to be of the highest order; while in his generalship—as proved, for example, in the great religious campaigns in Great Britain . . . [he shows] that, had he chosen a military career, he would have risen to the first rank among leaders."[17] General O. O.

Howard, who had been close to Moody since they were together at the front in Tennessee in 1864, agreed that after the Civil War Moody "acted as a general." Howard acknowledged "I became his subordinate in the great war for the liberation of captive souls."[18] Lord Kinnaird, one of Britain's and the world's leading merchants, closely observed Moody during the 1870s and 1880s. He said he had "never met a man with more business capacity and sheer executive ability than D. L. Moody."[19]

MOODY'S NEED TO CONTROL

The story of the founding of these institutions reveals Moody's genius, and it also uncovers a need to control—perhaps a bent toward authoritarianism. Tendencies in this direction could be seen early in the 1870s when Moody took it upon himself to tell men like Whittle, Revell, and Sankey, and women like Dryer and the future Mrs. Fleming Revell, to change direction and devote their lives to careers in ministry. Moody always urged such people to pray about their decisions, but there was an attitude about him that suggested he already knew the will of God in the matter. Usually Moody's promptings rang true—prophetically true—and the people he confronted were quite thankful and fulfilled in lives of ministry. But there is a fine line between the biblical exhortation to stir up people's gifts and playing God in their lives, and Moody seemed to have crossed that line at times.

That Moody showed tendencies in the latter direction can be seen in letters to Northfield from the 1860s onward. Many of these epistles reveal his need to father his siblings in Massachusetts. To be sure, there was no father figure at home, and Isaiah, the eldest, showed little inclination or ability to help his mother or the youngsters as they grew up. So over the years, as Moody's confidence grew, he played the patriarch. He sent money and suggested the best places for each one to live.

He badgered poor Samuel to move to Chicago until the timid younger brother came out and revealed his epilepsy and other ailments, thereby showing his well-meaning but sometimes domineering brother why he had never wanted to leave the refuge of his mother's home in the first place. Once Dwight discovered the nature and complexity of his younger brother's infirmities, he backed away and supported Sam's desire to go home. From that time on, D. L. encouraged Samuel to care for the livestock and gardens, and he helped him with money and instruction so that he could begin a Northfield

YMCA and a mission Sunday school.[20]

As soon as Samuel died and brother George (four years D. L.'s senior) agreed to oversee "the farm" and their mother, D. L. sent him letters at least every two weeks telling him how to manage the animals and gardens. Dwight did bankroll the homestead and the various parts that were added on. Perhaps George welcomed the guidance (they were extremely close while growing up, and George gave D. L. five dollars when he headed out to Boston in 1854). It is also possible he asked D. L. to find his son Ambert a school in Boston. But the letters as a whole exude an attitude of wisdom and control that must have been difficult to accept, even in a family that was as close-knit as the Moody clan.

It is possible that George understood Dwight so well and loved him so unconditionally that the absentee landlord posture of D. L. never caused a problem. But out in Chicago, the story was different.

The Chicago Avenue Church

Dwight L. Moody, with the invaluable assistance of Emma Moody and John Farwell, was the founder of what became the Chicago Avenue Church. When he and Emma left in 1873 and did not return for three years, the church went forward with a succession of unusually able pastors. J. H. Harwood was the pastor from 1866 to 1869, despite Moody's frequent occupancy of the pulpit. Several of Moody's disciples, among them Whittle, Morton, and Cole, oversaw the flock when the Moodys were away for the next half decade. William J. Erdman served as pastor from 1876 to 1878, and Charles Morton led the church from 1878 to 1879. George Needham took the helm between 1879 and 1881, Charles F. Goss (a first-rate Moody biographer) from 1885 to 1890. Several interim pastors stood in the gap in the early 1880s and early 1890s, and Dr. R. A. Torrey became senior pastor in 1894 and continued until after Moody's death.[21]

The turnover in pastors at the Chicago Avenue Church from the 1860s until the turn of the century suggests serious problems. Although this can be explained in part by the citywide fire and the general growing pains of a new church in a new city, it is significant that the church could not keep a senior pastor very long until Moody died. After he died, the Chicago Avenue Church (later Moody Memorial Church) became one of the most prestigious and most sought-after pulpits in the United States. Prior to 1899 the Chicago Avenue Church pastorate looked attractive from a distance, but up close one could detect the tensions.

During the early years, Moody was in and out of town so much that no one seemed to know who was in charge. When he was gone the staff carried all the responsibilities, but when he returned he took controls back into his hands. Likewise, even though he and Emma made their move from Chicago permanent by 1876, Moody's correspondence makes perfectly clear that he intended to run the church from Northfield or any city where he happened to be preaching. His letters are replete with gratuitous advice about how to manage finances or whom to hire for different positions and with announcements of men he was sending out to preach at the church for a week or two. He also sent directions on how to conduct the Sunday schools, as well as how to "go after the Sweeds or any foreign parents." Finally, Moody was never reticent about pronouncements such as that he could not be at the annual meeting "but as I can not I will write you what I would say," followed by a lengthy list of instructions. Charles Blanchard, who often preached at the church in the early 1880s, noted with sadness that in those days "the church was a good deal shattered."22

As much as the Chicago Avenue Church leaders admired Moody, and as grateful as they must have been to him for channeling hymnbook royalties and his own money for construction and staff salaries, it was tiresome to be controlled by a man who was not living in the community. No pastor could develop his own God-given potential with an outsider, however well-meaning, constantly meddling in the programs and disrupting preaching schedules. For better or worse, D. L. Moody was incapable of letting go and delegating responsibilities for the Chicago Avenue Church that he no longer felt led to pastor.

Dryer Waiting on Moody

His overeagerness was exacerbated by the entanglement of several ministries that he inaugurated and supported in Chicago. After the church was organized in the 1860s, Moody encouraged Emma Dryer in 1873 to begin a home missions training and ministry program among women. She promptly surrendered her secular teaching career and devoted herself full-time for many years to the work. All the while Dryer believed that Mr. Moody would return to Chicago and oversee the construction of a building for a wide-ranging home missions training school.23

Moody did not return until 1875. He approved Dryer's selection of a building site, and he drummed up some initial support for her work. His letters reveal that he sent one thousand dollars to the church every year to keep Dryer financially secure enough to continue her ministry. (This stipend was a typical salary for a full-time senior pastor, about $400 above the average wage earner's annual income.) For her part she contributed first-rate effort, training women workers in and for Chicago and preparing a series of home Bible studies. Nevertheless, the building was not constructed, and the work remained underdeveloped. Although Dryer never publicly criticized Moody, and although she remained a close friend with the Moody family (especially Emma), she clearly felt betrayed by Mr. Moody. He talked her into heading up a work that he neglected to promote vigorously—not because he did not care, but because he was simply too busy to keep it all going. Moody paid lip service to the concept of a program that he relegated to a low place on his priority list. Dryer did all she could to get a Bible-training institute going, but the potential financial supporters made clear they would not fall in behind the plan without Moody's serious commitment.

By autumn 1879, Emma Dryer's health broke under the strain of her demanding and undersupported work. Moody felt compassion and responsibility toward this forty-five-year-old warrior, so he sent her on an expense-paid retreat for six months in Great Britain. She lived part of the time in the Mildmay Deaconess Home, traveled in England and Scotland, and was able to return to America with restored health and vigor. Finally, in 1886, D. L. Moody went to Chicago and made an all-out effort to raise funds and put quality time into the founding of the Chicago Evangelization Society, the forerunner of the Chicago Bible Institute.[24]

THE CHICAGO EVANGELIZATION SOCIETY

The Chicago Evangelization Society was the product of D. L. Moody's early vision, Emma Dryer's energy and hard work, and the generous gifts of several Chicago philanthropists, especially the McCormick family, T. W. Harvey, and John V. Farwell. In 1886 Moody publicly called for $250,000 to launch the CES. The amount would provide for building on a lot just north of the church, as well as staff and other overhead, including tuition for students. Mrs. C. H. McCormick, whose husband had died two years before, pledged $100,000, and her son took the position of secretary of the board. Moody himself became chairman of the board. Other board members included lumber magnate T. W. Harvey (vice president), banker E. G. Keith, John V. Farwell, steel manufacturer N. S. Bouton, and Robert Scott, who went into dry goods with a firm named Carson, Pirie and Scott.[25]

In summer 1887 Moody and the majority of the board had a disagreement over some fund-raising and construction strategies, as well as the size of the board of directors. He impetuously dashed off a letter from Northfield to Mrs. McCormick—a loyal friend who had contributed much to all of his work. "I am opposed to increasing the board until we get the building up and the work well in hand. I think seven is far better than sixteen to get things in motion. I have had some experiences with large committees and I feel convinced that they are not so effective as small ones when there is any building going on." He went on to add that he was now at loggerheads with the board, so there were only two choices left to him, "either to go against my judgment and join with my board or stand aside and let the work go on without me. After due consideration I have decided to resign, and let me say in doing so, that I do it with the best wishes for the society."[26]

Moody's refusal to cooperate unless he could dictate the terms confused and pained his friends. Mrs. McCormick felt betrayed and insulted, and the blow stunned the board. Emma Dryer, who had been waiting thirteen years for the program to go forward, knew it could never materialize without Moody's enthusiastic endorsement and titular leadership. Sensing that her dream was about to be shattered, she mailed a caustic letter to Moody and chastised him for hurting the McCormicks and for acting without respect for others. She likewise sent an appeal to Emma Moody, asking her to talk sense into her husband.[27]

Moody had the humility to confess his errors and make amends. Once the reaction reached him and Emma from Chicago, he telegrammed Dryer and McCormick that he was "very sorry for the letter. Will withdraw it. Tell the trustees to do as they please . . . and I will come [out to Chicago] soon."[28]

Moody then took off for a short preaching mission in Montreal. Eventually Emma and Major Whittle had to enter the fray to smooth feathers and salvage the program. Moody, by now humbled and repentant, wrote to Mrs. McCormick and begged, "if I have done wrong will you not forgive me? . . . I am willing to work at the front or behind, or outside, or inside, and will go where you say[;] only for the sake of the Master let us have the work finished."[29]

By summer 1887, the Chicago Evangelization Society was formally constituted with D. L. Moody as president. The board of directors and he were once again harmonious, and a separate nine-member board of managers was put in place to help oversee day-to-day operations. Only two men were among the managers. The seven women managers included Emma Dryer, Nettie (Mrs. C. H.) McCormick, and Mrs. T. W. Harvey.[30] What had begun as a deaconess program to evangelize the poorest women and children of Chicago eventually evolved into an evangelistic ministry with a concomitant program to train lay women to minister to women and children in Illinois.

Always emphasizing a thorough knowledge of the English Bible with an interpretative or hermeneutical approach that assumed the imminent, premillennial return of the Lord Jesus Christ, this school that was at once academic and practical became an even more ambitious program by 1887. By then the Chicago Evangelization Society's goal was to "educate, direct, and maintain Christian workers as Bible readers, teachers and evangelists; who shall teach the gospel in Chicago and its suburbs, especially in neglected fields [among the immigrants and poor]." With the founding of CES's army of "personal workers" was also the establishment of the Bible Work Institute (later Chicago Bible Institute and eventually Moody Bible Institute), which by 1889 was designed to train women and men "familiar with the aggressive methods of work, to act as pastor's assistants, city missionaries, general missionaries, Sunday school missionaries, evangelists, and in various other fields of Christian labor, at home and abroad."[31]

Dwight L. Moody's willingness to admit he was wrong—and mean it—paid rich dividends. When the people he had walked roughshod over experienced his genuine repentance, they forgave him and got on with making the vision a reality. These board members, after all, believed deeply in it. Their contributions were much more than favors to Moody. They saw the society and its school as essential instruments for building Christ's kingdom. Because they lived and labored in Chicago, they probably felt more urgency than Moody—certainly Emma Dryer did. Finally, the philanthropists and board members were eager to restore harmony because it was a command from God, and, quite frankly, Moody's involvement brought credibility to the effort.

THE PRESSURES ON MOODY

One of the reasons D. L. Moody lagged behind Chicago evangelical leaders on bringing the society and school to fruition was his heavy traveling and preaching schedule. He was on the move and living out of suitcases and hotel rooms nine to ten months out of the

Mr. Moody reading correspondence in his Northfield study in the 1890s

year. Despite the fact that he had cut down on the extended campaigns, he was probably even busier than before. Shorter stays meant more travel. Wherever he traveled he met more people and made new friends. As his circle of influence widened, so did the correspondence. By the late 1870s, he regularly employed someone to help him and Emma answer the hundreds of letters they received daily, but he still wrote scores of letters each week. Besides these, he put his signature on hundreds more that were written weekly by Emma or a secretary.[32]

As the correspondence increased, so did the numbers of people who wanted personal time with Mr. Moody. The stream of pilgrims who showed up at his door—whether he was at home or away—increased with every passing year. Some of the visitors were invited, but many stopped by on the chance that the man whom God had used to transform their lives might have a "free" minute to hear their stories and bless them with prayer. Neither Dwight nor Emma complained publicly about the crush of people and piles of mail, but sometimes they must have felt overwhelmed. "I have been a very busy woman," Emma informed one close friend to whom she had not written for months. "My husband's urgent letters [take] most all my spare time" and "we have had company every day." This was not a complaint or a fit of self-pity, but an appeal for understanding from someone who might feel forgotten or neglected.[33]

The demands on Moody's time contributed to occasional outbursts of temper and probably prompted impetuousness such as the resignation letter to Chicago. Moody, after all, had limits like everyone else. What was remarkable, however, was his overall good humor and sound judgment in the midst of so many pressures. And it is impressive too that he wrote regularly to his mother, and that seldom a week passed when he did not pen a note to each of his three children.

THE NORTHFIELD SEMINARY

Travel, visitors, and correspondence contributed to Moody's tardiness in promoting a Chicago enterprise that he truly wanted developed, but the planting of schools in Northfield was the primary reason the Illinois school did not materialize earlier. Moody fully expected to build a school in Chicago, but it was, so to speak, out of sight and out of mind. Northfield, on the other hand, was where he spent two to three months of the year, so his initial and most profound energies went there. Furthermore, these schools, like the hills they were planted upon, became near and dear to his heart. His correspondence in the last two decades of his life show that he increasingly gave time and energy to the Northfield and Mount Hermon schools. He told his son Will, "They are the best pieces of work I have ever done." It was not that he was forsaking his gift of evangelism, but that in the schools thousands would be prepared to do more than he could ever accomplish on his own. "I have been able," he told Will, "to set in motion streams which will continue long after I am gone."[34]

Henry Durant and Wellesley College

In Northfield, by the late 1870s, D. L. Moody's talents began to shine even brighter. Armed with the vision to help impoverished New England girls, he set out to find a group of supporters such as he had found for everything he had done in Chicago. Moody needed money to buy land and build on it. He also needed teachers and administrators, because he admittedly knew nothing about the practical operations of a school.

The first person to become part of the team that built Northfield Seminary for Young Women was Henry F. Durant. A wealthy Boston lawyer who had known Moody since the late 1860s, he had taken a keen interest in the Mount Holyoke Seminary. Durant wanted to build a college for economically deprived young women. To his mind the college should be steeped in the liberal arts, but it also must be well-grounded in English Bible and Christian doctrine. Added to these basics he wanted to see the women taught how to do domestic chores by requiring all students to help with the cooking, laundry, and general housekeeping of the school. He inaugurated his experiment in 1875, calling it Wellesley College. He took Moody to see the school several times after it opened and stressed to the Northfield visionary that he wanted "calico girls" at Wellesley, not "velvet girls."[35]

Moody was elated by what he saw at Wellesley; he especially applauded the Christian underpinnings and the recruitment of the poor. Durant, who had housed the Moodys during the Boston campaign, drafted Moody to join Wellesley's board of trustees. Moody's name gave the school credibility within conservative Christian circles, and Moody could help find good teachers for the Bible portion of the curriculum. During June 1878 the Durants invited themselves to Northfield for a three-week visit. Moody assured them that he and Emma would love to have them in their home for an entire month. They enjoyed the Durants' company and the Moodys had previously been treated to gracious hospitality in the Durants' Boston home.

The Board of Trustees for the Northfield School

When the Durants came, Henry and Dwight walked about the hills and discussed Christian education. They talked about Wellesley's future, and Moody revealed his ambition to start a preparatory school for young women who should go to a college like Wellesley but could never afford access to the necessary academic preparation. During the middle and late nineteenth century, as both men realized only too well, there were hardly any college preparatory schools for young women. The few that did exist were extremely expensive, and they were not located in the northern regions of New England. Durant urged Moody to start the preparatory school; he promised to help financially and serve on Moody's board. Both men, it should be noted, vigorously rejected a prevailing educational view during the middle 1800s that women had delicate brains and would suffer mental damage if they studied the same subjects as men.[36]

With a respected lawyer and educational institution founder on the board, Moody set out to secure the second member of the team. Within a few weeks he found H. N. F. Marshall, a retired Boston merchant whom one of his contemporaries described as a man "who, having been led to consecrate himself and all his property to the work of the Lord, and feeling a strong personal attachment toward the evangelist, to whom he was a spiritual debtor, found that no occupation could be more congenial than to assist the educational schemes of his friend."[37]

Marshall was a perfect choice to be financial manager and general overseer of this new venture. He had wide-ranging business experience, plus an extensive background in construction of buildings and property management. He and his wife enthusiastically joined the Moody team, sold their home in Boston, and promptly moved to Northfield.[38]

Buying Property for the Northfield School

While the Northfield Seminary was still in its planning stages, Marshall and Moody were walking Moody's land and looking for the best site for building a classroom facility. In what Moody quickly concluded was an obvious act of God and, therefore, a clear sign that the seminary vision should go forward in all haste, he and Marshall cast their eyes on some sandy, hilly land adjacent to Moody's property. It was barren soil, seemingly unfit for cultivation and even worthless for pasture. Just as they were surveying this bleak hill with apparently little going for it except a spectacular view of the Connecticut River, the owner rode up. Moody inquired how much land he owned there; the neighbor guessed about sixteen acres. Marshall and Moody immediately asked him if he would sell. Having no use for the property himself, he signed it away that day for a reasonable price.[39]

That was autumn 1878. Within a few weeks several adjoining lots of similarly marginal land were purchased before people in the neighborhood suspected the land to be in demand by anyone. Before another year passed a campus site of nearly one hundred acres near Moody's own property had been purchased. Now all they needed were facilities and students.[40]

Friends and Supporters of the New School

With attorney Durant's help, the Northfield Seminary was quickly incorporated, complete with a first-rate board of trustees. Among the indispensable members of Moody's team was William E. Dodge, Jr., a New York businessman and philanthropist who made a fortune in the copper industry and held investments in a host of other enterprises. Dodge admired Moody, and he had chaired the New York committee that persuaded Moody to do the Hippodrome campaign. He, along with several others, oversaw the trust where the Bliss, Moody, and Sankey hymnal royalties were placed. Influential in Christian and financial circles throughout America, he brought tremendous respectability to the Northfield project.[41]

Along with this powerful New Yorker and Bostonians Durant and Marshall, Moody astutely brought to the board some prestigious northern New Englanders. One was Franklin Fairbanks, a manufacturer of scales from St. Johnsbury, Vermont. Julius J. Estey, from nearby Brattleboro, Vermont, also agreed to serve. He became one of the school's ablest and staunchest allies.

Estey, only thirty-four years old, was the only male heir to the Jacob E. Estey family fortune. Jacob Estey, Julius's father, moved to Brattleboro from his New Hampshire birthplace in the 1830s. From that southern Vermont town located on the Connecticut River, he began manufacturing melodeons of the variety played by Ira Sankey.

The Estey Organ Company became famous for its beautiful black walnut reed organs, all handmade with care by craftsmen and musicians from Scandinavia. By 1879 Julius was a partner with his father and brother-in-law in a company that sold large quantities of organs all over the United States and Canada. Both Julius Estey and his father were well-known in northern New England. They were partners in the Vermont People's Bank (later Vermont National Bank), and they built a handsome Baptist church in Brattleboro.[42]

Julius Estey quickly became to Northfield Seminary what Mrs. McCormick became to Moody's Chicago ministries; he could always be counted on to make an initial, large donation to a building fund and allow his name to be used to add credibility and thereby help bring more funds to the project. He also became one of Moody's closest friends, praying with the evangelist and listening to him when he needed a sympathetic ear. Estey, who wanted to see young people led to Christ and equipped to work with souls, was a quiet but continual supporter of the tuition funds for indigent students who attended Moody's Northfield schools.[43]

The board had several other committed men and women, among them Ira D. Sankey, Mrs. Betsy Moody, and eventually Moody's wife, Emma. The Moody women were particularly helpful on a board that was weighted with preachers and businessmen—none of whom knew much about young women's needs in a residential, academic environment.

With a strong team assembled and money in place from hymn-book royalties and board-member donations, construction started on Northfield Seminary's first building in spring 1879. Typical of Moody, he did not expect others to give sacrificially if he did not make a significant contribution of his own. To be sure, he and Sankey were giving up royalties that were legally theirs, but for Moody that was not enough. He and Emma donated the privacy of their home. The first building was to be a "recitation hall," with space for up to one hundred students. President Moody also ordered alterations to his own house so that the expected eight students would have a place to live.[44]

Classes Begin

The Northfield Seminary for Young Women officially started classes on Monday, November 3, 1879. To everyone's surprise, when the girls arrived the weekend before classes were to start, they were welcomed by nearly a foot and a half of snow. Also, instead of the projected eight young women whose rooms and beds were readied, twenty-five showed up, including the two impoverished sisters D. L. and Samuel had met in the mountains four and a half years before. To complicate crowded conditions even more, the recitation hall was not finished. For another month classes were held in the Moody dining room, and for the entire academic year more than twenty women were squeezed together in a wing of the Moody house designed for no more than ten or twelve people.[45]

Somewhat typical of D. L. Moody, he and Emma were in St. Louis when the school opened. He was preaching one of his few remaining multiweek campaigns that had been promised more than two years before. The chore of getting sleighs to the train station, turning the house into a dormitory, and arranging logistics for classes in the dining room that would also serve as a mess hall for the school was left to Mr. Marshall and the new principal, Harriet Tuttle. They never complained; rather, they joined hands, recruited local help, and carried on quite well until the Moodys came home the next summer.[46]

As soon as the ground thawed in spring 1880, H. N. F. Marshall directed construction for Northfield's first dormitory. East Hall was completed in August, furnished and ready for the next year's class.[47] With this second building opened, several things became apparent by September 1880. First, although Moody was gifted with vision, the ability to find human and fiscal resources, and the skill to get things moving, he could not be counted on to help with the administrative efforts required to keep his dreams alive. Second, Moody's staff was dependable and talented. The Northfield Seminary went forward quite well with or without the Moodys in Northfield. Third, the students loved the seminary and their numbers increased annually. The Northfield Seminary for Young Women was obviously meeting a need.

Doctrinal Disputes at Northfield

One other factor about D. L. Moody and his enterprises became only too apparent by the early 1880s. The Northfield-born seminary president celebrated the union of Christians of diverse doctrinal positions, but he did not have the executive skill or will to take stands and end disputes among people who disagreed. This problem that would plague Moody, and harm his schools in the years ahead, became apparent from Northfield Seminary's inception.

H. N. F. Marshall served as board member, treasurer, and chief operating officer of the school. He and Moody were close friends. Like Moody, Marshall was a premillennialist in his understanding of biblical interpretation. Harriet Tuttle, on the other hand, a first-rate principal, excellent teacher, and friend of Henry Durant, was amillennial or postmillennial in her hermeneutical approach to Scripture. They could agree to disagree and respect each other's differences only up to a point. When Tuttle began teaching her own perspective, Marshall objected strongly. The sometimes authoritarian Mr. Moody refused to take sides. The issue became so large by spring 1882 that Miss Tuttle threatened to resign. When she wrote to Moody for help (he was in Britain on a mission) he refused to intervene. Instead, he took money from his own pocket and sent Tuttle and a teacher, Alice Hammond, off to Europe. He maintained that if Tuttle got away for the summer she would be able to cope with Marshall when the new term began.

Tuttle and Hammond returned refreshed. But the problem was still there. As soon as the semester began, she and Marshall were at loggerheads again. Moody dodged the issue once more, so in midautumn Tuttle resigned.[48]

Moody's deaf ear to a serious problem did not paralyze the school. A new principal, Evelyn S. Hall, stepped into the gap. A Wellesley graduate, she turned out to be a brilliant educator. Although young and relatively inexperienced, Hall was a natural leader. By 1886, only four years into her tenure, she had 217 students under her care, a faculty of twelve women, plus four matrons to handle nonacademic responsibilities.[49]

A SCHOOL FOR YOUNG MEN

Dwight Moody's vision for Christian education that began

years earlier in Chicago and came to flower in Northfield Seminary quickly reproduced into new fruit in the early 1880s. No sooner had the women's school opened than people in the surrounding region began to agitate for a school for boys and young men. Moody mentioned it to his Northfield board. Almost everyone agreed that it was a worthy endeavor, but it should not be a part of the women's institution. For better or worse most preparatory schools were segregated by gender. Moody and his board were not even tempted to challenge this conventional wisdom; instead, they determined that the boy's school should be convenient to Northfield, but far enough from the female seminary to discourage temptations and avoid appearances of impropriety.

Hiram Camp's Assistance

Hiram Camp, president of New Haven Watch Company in Connecticut, had been on the seminary board since its inception. A devout lay leader among New Haven's Christian community, he had been instrumental in forming a union movement to invite Moody to speak to Yale students and the wider industrial city. When Moody went to New Haven and conducted nearly two months of well-received meetings in early 1878, Camp and Moody's acquaintance blossomed into what became a lifelong friendship. In the wake of the New Haven campaign, Mr. Camp agreed to join the Northfield Seminary board. He further promised to provide long-term financial aid.

This amiable, eccentric industrialist, nearly seventy at the time, seemed to be loved by everyone. He had warm eyes and an engaging smile. Almost always dressed in a black suit with a black tie, he invariably sported a matching black vest to accommodate his New Haven pocket watch and dangling gold fob. His snow-white beard was similar to Moody's in length, and his balding head was ringed on the sides and back by a flowing gray mane of nearly shoulder-length hair.[50]

When the boys' school discussion became serious, Hiram Camp had a private talk with Moody. Camp told Moody he had provided well for his family and now he wanted to do something significant for Christ with the money he had earned. At this precise time Moody had learned that the Ezra Purple farm was going up for auction. It was exceptionally good land for northern New England, located in Gill township, just across the river from Northfield. Purple had tried to take the Widow Moody's house over a $400 debt when her husband died. The land had long since passed from greedy old man

D. L. Moody with Mount Hermon students (circa 1892)

Purple to his two sons. In August 1880 a surviving widow of one of the sons got word to Moody that the land would be auctioned, but she would prefer he get it for school or ministry purposes rather than have it go to anyone else.

The irony of this providential turn of events was not lost on Dwight L. Moody. He laid the opportunity before Hiram Camp. Before the sun set on September 11, the two friends rode over to the Purple farm, walked the land, prayed, and envisioned young men tilling the soil to help pay for their schooling and keep. That night Camp wrote a check to Moody for $25,000. Although Mrs. John Purple had hinted it would require $20,000 to secure her property before it went before the public at auction, Moody owned the more than four hundred acres of highly sought after farmland eight days later for $12,500.[51]

In mid-September, 1880, the Northfield Seminary board and a small crowd of well-wishers gathered around East Hall, the new female seminary dormitory. Mr. Moody gave a dedicatory address. At the conclusion of his talk Moody stood smiling and silent. There was an unusual twinkle in his eyes when he said:

> You know that the Lord laid it upon my heart some time ago to organize a school for young women in the humbler walks of life, who never would get a Christian education but for a school like this. I talked about this plan of mine to friends, until a number of them gave money to start the school. Some thought I ought to make it for boys and girls, but I thought that if I wished to send my daughter away to school I should prefer to send her to an institution for girls only. I have hoped that money might be given for a boys' school, and now a gentleman who has been here for the last ten days had become interested in my plans, and has given twenty-five thousand dollars toward a school for boys.[52]

Hiram Camp agreed to serve as president of the new school's board of trustees; to thank him Moody asked Camp to name the institution. His choice was Mount Hermon Boys' School. He took the name from Psalm 133:3, "As the dew of Hermon, and as the dew that descended upon the mountains of Zion: for there the Lord commanded the blessing, even life for evermore" (KJV).

Julius Estey agreed to join Hiram Camp on the Mount Hermon board, as did several other ministers, businessmen, and philanthropists. By May 1881, they had hired a principal and admitted the first group of boys.

Beginning Problems

But Mount Hermon got off to a poor start. Because there were so many orphaned and indigent boys in the area, the board decided to take in younger ones from ages eight to twelve, as well as older boys and young men. All students were housed family-style in farm houses already on the property, and a frame classroom building was hastily constructed. The littler boys were undisciplined and inexperienced in schooling and farmwork, and the bigger lads sometimes bullied them.

To complicate matters more, five months after the students arrived the Moodys sailed for England to raise money for schools, find
fresh speakers to bring to America, and fulfill a promise to preach
again in the United Kingdom. Julius Estey promised to make daily
runs from Brattleboro to Northfield to keep an eye on everything.
But the headmaster became seriously ill soon after Moody left, and
within a year he resigned. Estey made herculean efforts to hold the
fledgling school together, but he had a business to run, and New England winters sometimes made daily visitations impossible. The board
rallied. By 1884 it hired a new principal, Henry E. Sawyer. Sawyer,
a Dartmouth graduate, held an Ivy League master's degree, possessed a keen grasp of educational theory, and had experience.
Within a year he turned the school around. The first thing he did was
to refuse admittance to anyone under age sixteen. Then he revamped
the curriculum to make it a genuine college preparatory school. He
maintained teaching of the English Bible and Christian theology, but
he instituted a program in the liberal arts.[53]

Once again Moody's role was limited yet crucial and clear. He
had the vision, he found supporters, and he got the program underway. For Northfield and Mount Hermon both, he continued to court
supporters who provided funds to add buildings and keep poor students in school. Room, board, and tuition alone cost between $160
and $200 per student per year. Moody never expected them to pay
more than half. He always found someone to pay a poor youth's fees,
even if he had to dig into his own pockets.

Emma Moody became an ingenious fund-raiser for student
needs. She organized a Ladies' Aid Society, thanks to the suggestion
of a campus visitor. A woman could join the society for two dollars a
year; thirty dollars would purchase a lifetime membership. The purpose of the fund, which Emma oversaw, was to "lend money to needy
and deserving students, to enable them to meet the expenses of the
course without impairing their independence." In typical nineteenth-
century New England style, the Ladies' Aid Society eschewed
harming a student's pride or spirit of self-reliance with a direct dole.
Loans were provided and students were expected to repay their debts
once they had left school and could gainfully earn their own way.[54]

Moody kept out of the daily running and educational policy-
making of the two Northfield schools. He had neither the time nor
the expertise to say much about these matters. But he had delegated
the work to extremely able people, and, therefore, the schools prospered. There were approximately five hundred men and women on

both campuses combined by 1886, and hundreds were turned away for lack of space. By 1892 the men came from twenty-three states and ten foreign countries; the women from twenty-two states and four foreign countries. Mount Hermon eventually sat on approximately 750 acres, and Northfield Seminary embraced another 250 acres, as the boards acquired adjacent land when it became available. The real estate properties alone were valued in 1892 at $275,000, and an endowment of $236,000 was in place and carefully invested by the two boards of trustees.[55]

MOODY'S SCHOOLS FOR THE POOR

Moody himself was largely responsible for raising the funds, but he was also the primary impetus behind the remarkable diversity, Christ-centeredness, and mission-minded atmosphere on both campuses. He frequently stated that his purpose for both schools was "to help young men and women of very limited means to get an education such as would have done me good when I was their age. I want to help them into lives that will count the most for the cause of Christ."[56]

Because Moody reached out to the poor and least advantaged, students who could afford expensive preparatory schools were asked not to apply. Also in line with his determination to assist those from the lowest rungs of society, both Northfield and Mount Hermon were unusually well-integrated racially. Modern historians or Moody's contemporaries who have charged him with racism because of his surrender to southern white demands for segregated meetings have no idea of the efforts he made to integrate his schools in an era when all of the South and most of the North reserved preparatory education for wealthy whites. That Moody was decades ahead of most educators can be seen, first, by the fact that his initial efforts to educate students in Chicago and Northfield were directed toward women. Second, in all of his schools there was racial diversity. Almost from the beginning Northfield had Native American Indians. Young women were recruited from Indian Territory and then sent back to be teachers and missionaries to their own people.[57] This was, of course, consistent with Mr. Moody's belief that the most effective personal workers are those who can personally identify with the people they hope to reach.

Diversity Within the Schools

Mount Hermon, like Northfield, had Native Americans, and

both institutions encouraged the enrollment of blacks and Asians. A study of class photographs shows a sprinkling of blacks and Asians in both schools. Many of the blacks were evidently Americans, given their names; but a few were probably native Africans, because during some academic years the records reveal that promising students were brought to Northfield and Mount Hermon from Africa and Asia. There seems to have been no discrimination against minorities in any way. Photographs reveal more black men in literary societies than on football teams. All students lived, ate, attended chapel, played on sports teams, and served in clubs or societies together. Chapel speakers at both schools were men and women, and non-Caucasian men and women spoke. Booker T. Washington was brought to campus by Moody, and on one occasion a husband and wife team—natives of Zululand—spoke to the students, urging them to consider a career in missions to Africa.[58]

Diversity at Northfield and Mount Hermon is astounding considering the lack of opportunities offered to women and ethnic minorities in the late nineteenth century, but it is not surprising given D. L. Moody's predisposition. In the late 1850s and early 1860s, after all, he had an integrated mission Sunday school in Chicago. Likewise, two of his closest friends, Major D. W. Whittle and General O. O. Howard, worked tirelessly for the betterment of blacks both during and after the Civil War. Both of these men spoke frequently at Moody's Massachusetts schools, and their attitudes and influence would not have been lost on the student body. These men no doubt had a hand in recruiting some of the black students. Certainly their impact caused several Northfield women to go forth to found orphanages for black children in the war-torn South.[59]

Attitudes Toward Jews

Moody's hand in promoting diversity and tolerance at Mount Hermon and Northfield can be seen in the schools' attitudes toward religions other than Protestant Christianity. Jews and their traditions were celebrated at the schools in a way that was unusual, considering the widespread anti-Semitism of the late 1800s.[60] Deliberately moving against the tide of bigotry toward Jews, students reflected what they were learning at Northfield and Mount Hermon.

Moody offered twenty-dollar prizes for outstanding essays at both schools, and it is fascinating to see how many published student essays and articles criticized predominant pejorative thinking about Jews. One article entitled "Shylock: A Character Sketch" maintained that Jewish manhood as stereotyped by Shakespeare is distorted and hurtful, and the author concluded that Jews and Gentiles are equally loved and created by God. In a still more pointed essay entitled "A Plea for the Jews," a Northfield Seminary woman argued that Jews are misunderstood and misjudged all over the world. She wrote that it is deplorable to take the noble label *Jew* and turn it into a verb, noting that dictionaries say "to jew" is to cheat. She argued that many Christians have been taught to loathe Jewish people because of their rejection of Jesus, when most of the world has rejected the Messiah as well. The thoughtful student concluded that Jews gave the world not only Jesus but much of what we enjoy in modern civilization.[61]

A few of Moody's sermons show ambivalence toward Jews, revealing his inability to completely escape the anti-Semitic sickness that infected American culture. Nevertheless, he was far ahead of his times in attitudes toward Semitic peoples, as were many premillennialist Christians who understood the Bible to predict an end-time mass conversion of Jews to Christianity.[62]

Roman Catholics and Various Denominations

Roman Catholics were held in high esteem as well at the Northfield and Mount Hermon schools. Again this made Moody and his educational community unique among private preparatory school educational institutions, where Catholics were usually seen as un-American. Moody's schools were likewise singular within conservative Christian circles, where Roman Catholics tended to be viewed as hell-bound religionists. F. B. Meyer, the English Baptist preacher and author whom Moody brought to Northfield many times, was markedly impressed by D. L.'s relationship with Roman Catholics. In a memorial address delivered in 1899, Meyer recalled how Moody gave support to a local priest, and "when [Moody's] old mother died . . . and was carried through the snow to her resting place, the Roman Catholics asked that they might furnish a pallbearer."[63]

Moody clearly set the tone at his schools about Roman Catholics, so it is not surprising to find so much goodwill expressed among the students. Student publications contained many favorable articles on Catholics. One positive article on Roman Catholic monks appeared by a student in *The Hermonite*, and other essays were published celebrating the Jesuits, as well as such men as Bernard of Clairvaux and Ignatius of Loyola. Obviously Moody's students in Massachusetts were not taught that nothing much worthwhile in Christianity existed between the time of Saint Augustine and the Protestant Reformation.[64]

As F. B. Meyer phrased it, "What were Roman Catholics, or Congregationalists, or Baptists, to him? The one thing he cared for was the glory of God. These were the things that attracted people."[65] And attract people he did—a diverse lot of them. In 1897 Mount Hermon surveyed the denominational affiliation of its men. More than eighty had no church membership. Those who claimed membership reported the following:[66]

> Congregational 82
> Baptist 38
> Methodist 35
> Presbyterian 34
> Episcopal 11
> Independent 5
> Roman Catholic 4
> Reformed 3
> Christian 2
> Swedish Lutheran 1
> Union Church of Christ 1
> Disciples 1
> United Presbyterian 1
> Friends 1

A similarly diverse breakdown among men and women students was tabulated in 1898, making it understandable why so many Northfield and Mount Hermon students went to the mission field with independent rather than denominational missions. Moody and his schools gradually undermined denominationalism—even loyalty to a sectarian tradition. Graduates from these two schools typically became nonsectarian, union people. They played a large role in the promotion of independent churches and of nondenominational parachurch organizations. And no wonder. Their experiences during these formative years included living and studying with a diverse student body. Speakers represented a wide range of traditions and emphasized the importance of being "biblical" rather than creedal. The speakers Moody brought to Northfield and Hermon focused on evangelism, missions, and disciplemaking rather than denominational distinctives. There were campus clubs for Wesleyans and those of the Reformed persuasion, but Moody and his faculty cared nothing for these distinctions, and they made their view known. Finally, a major cause of this eclectic mind-set was the fact that students attended interdenominational chapels and church services nine months out of the year. This was partly from design, but also the result of necessity. There were only three churches in town—one Congregational, one Roman Catholic, and the other Unitarian.[67]

Speakers at the Schools

Thanks to the efforts Moody made to recruit inspirational and challenging speakers, students at Northfield and Mount Hermon were treated to sermons by some of the best preachers in the English-speaking world. From both sides of the Atlantic they came, regaling young people with true stories from evangelism campaigns and mission outposts. Among the many preachers from Great Britain were Henry Drummond, F. B. Meyer, G. Campbell Morgan, C. T. Studd, George Adam Smith, John T. McNeill, and Henry Moorhouse. An equally talented and diverse group came one and two at a time from all over the United States, including D. W. Whittle, O. O. Howard, R. A. Torrey, A. J. Gordon, A. T. Pierson, John R. Mott, Henry Van Dyke, Robert E. Speer, C. I. Scofield, Graham Taylor, A. S. Steele, and Phillips Brooks. Many women spoke too, but their names, with the exception of the writer Margaret Sangster, were not as well known. Most of the women speakers were home or foreign missionaries or some of the stimulating Bible teachers from the schools' own faculty and administration.[68]

One speaker Moody worked hard to recruit to speak at Northfield was Charles H. Spurgeon. The famous English Baptist never came to the United States, but when he died in the early 1890s, his wife sent Moody his pulpit Bible with the following inscription:

> Mr. D. L. Moody from Mrs. C. H. Spurgeon, In tender memory of the beloved one gone home to God. This Bible has been used by my precious husband and is now given with my unfeigned pleasure to one in whose hands its blessed service will be continued and extended.

> S. Spurgeon, Westwood,
> November 20, 1892 [69]

Northfield students never heard the brilliant Englishman preach, but they did see his Bible and they heard Moody, their favorite and most famous speaker, tell stories about this departed brother and his wide-ranging ministry.

No one wielded a more profound personal influence on both Northfield schools than Moody himself. Because of him the institutions were permeated by an atmosphere unlike any other preparatory schools in the region. Both Northfield and Mount Hermon embraced the English Bible as the most important subject of study. To Moody the Bible was necessary for the illumination of all other books and subjects. Beyond this, the institutions were Christ-centered with a view of the Holy Spirit as a constant Companion, Counselor, Guide, and Teacher.[70] And finally, both academies were distinctive in the way that they celebrated the importance of missions and evangelism as lifestyles and callings.

Moody brought these distinctives to the schools and helped make them part of the very fabric and ethos of the community. He did this through his hand in selecting teachers and by bringing a continuous stream of speakers. Also, the sheer power of his personality caused his point of view to be impressed on the schools.

D. L. Moody–From the Students' Perspective

It would be difficult to overestimate Moody's personal impact on the community. He was internationally famous by the late 1870s. Odds are high that all students, regardless of their cultural and social disadvantages, were aware of his fame. That he was not always on campus—but often away, as he phrased it, on his "campaigns"—added to his mystique and the students' sense of his importance. Indeed, when some students were asked in 1891, "What do you see of Mr. Moody?" their response was, "By no means all that we wish, but more than we could well expect. Some one has said, 'The *world* is Mr. Moody's parish,' and we would add that Northfield and vicinity is his parsonage; and in a sense the schools here founded are his seminary, and no man living receives from six hundred young men and women a love more nearly *filial* than he receives from them."[71] This man who was much in demand everywhere graced the students with his presence at least a day or two each semester, except when he was in Britain from October 1881 to April 1883. To the students he was absolutely unforgettable. He made a lifelong impact on them.

Moody's relationship with students was inspired by his past. Through his life, he carried lasting impressions of one woman teacher in Northfield, an old man in Greenfield, and a Sunday school teacher in Boston. Each of them took time to look him in the eye, affectionately lay a hand on his shoulder or arm, and then offer words of encouragement and hope. With these indelible memories, Moody set out to do the same for Northfield and Mount Hermon students. He knew that most of them were poor, lonely, and neglected. Like him, they craved parental touch and attention. These blessings he imparted whenever he was there, and they never forgot him.

Praise for the Schools' Founder

Thirty-eight years after D. L. Moody died, and in commemoration of the 100th anniversary of his birth, John McDowell compiled an anthology of "Appreciations and Appraisals" entitled *What D. L. Moody Means to Me*. A striking theme in many of these remembrances is Moody's personal impact on individual lives. One young man who met Moody during his Dublin campaign in the early 1880s recalled how he asked Moody if he could come and study in his school. "After a brief conversation and then a pause that seemed to me ages long (though not more than a minute or two), he said in his own earnest way, 'Do you really want to come?' to which I answered with an eager, 'I do, Sir.' He said, 'Very well, then, I will take you.'" T. B. Hyde went to Mount Hermon and graduated in 1887.[72]

During that same British campaign Moody met a young English carpenter named Joshua Gravett, who inquired if there was any way a poor tradesman could work his way through Mount Hermon. Moody chatted with him for a few minutes and then said, "Come on, the School was founded for just such men as you." Gravett went, Moody found him transportation funds and tuition, and then, as Gravett phrased it, "his commendation led to my being called to the church [in Denver, Colorado] I have served as pastor since 1891." When Gravett graduated in 1889, Moody opened a door for him to serve as an assistant pastor in Springfield, Illinois, and, as Gravett put it, "in two hours of great need, by most liberal gifts, he proved [a] noble benefactor."[73]

American as well as British young people were touched by Moody's sincere interest in their lives. J. Collins Caton, from the class of 1891, said Moody "is a life-long heroic influence. His personality is a call from the heights to 'come up higher.' . . . To me he was the embodiment of the healthiest interest in all humans and not the least in youth. He was a partner in any play, our work and our future. His interest in each was that one should be a good citizen and a good Christian."[74]

Frederick E. Newton, class of 1888, entered Mount Hermon at age thirteen. He, like many others, was an orphan. "It was Mr. Moody's loving ambition to take the place of parents [to us]. This he did with keen, unfailing interest, which continued not only during the years at the School, but through college years and into later life."[75]

Mr. Moody on the Northfield campus

The Reverend Thomas Cole, who graduated in 1888, said, "D. L. Moody was the friend of my boyhood." He met Moody when Moody spoke in Rhode Island. "I was an unpromising specimen but he must have liked that kind and the proof is, he took me into his heart, for not only did a single $50 pay my tuition from 1881-1888, but after graduation from Hermon he sent me $300 a year to put me through Amherst."[76]

E. A. Yarrow, like many young men who went through Hermon, remembered that Moody encouraged them to lead lives of simplicity—"learn to eat soup with a one-tined fork." This philosophy "has helped me in many extremely difficult and dangerous situations. The implication that the effort and material saved in this process should be put to the service of others, has . . . been a guiding star in my life's activities."[77]

Edward H. Newcomb planned to be a lawyer. But before he graduated from Hermon in 1891, Moody challenged him to consider ministry. In 1897 the former aspiring lawyer was ordained to the gospel ministry. He spent his life in ministry after Moody "paid my carfare and arranged for my admission" to the Bible institute in Chicago.[78]

Patty White Smith was in Northfield Seminary's class of 1889. "We all have a dual personality I believe—and the quiet influence of those five characters [D. L. Moody and others] drew out the best in us all."[79]

Another student, Mrs. Robert Sheffield, said she could never forget the impact of Mr. Moody's chapel demonstration of how they should be filled with the Holy Spirit. "I can still see Mr. Moody with his pitcher of water on that platform." He poured it into a clear tumbler, "clogged with chaff and dust, until the overflowing water cleared away all the impurities. Don't 'bother about the devil,' but be continually filled with the Spirit's overflowing love."[80]

Moody's Interaction with Students

Evelyn S. Hall, for many years the principal of Northfield Seminary, said that phrases such as "He was a father to me!" or "It was worth coming all the way from China to hear him say, 'God bless you, Nellie'" were typical of the feelings of Northfield women. When he was in Northfield he could be seen cheerily driving about the seminary grounds with "a word of greeting for everyone, sometimes a playful salute of the whip and an invitation to 'get in,' until the back of the express wagon was filled with girls." He loved to take the new girls up to the spot where they could get the most commanding view of the countryside or invite them to his home for apples or ice cream. Sometime he appeared unexpectedly in the seminary kitchen to test the coffee and sample the breakfast being prepared for the morning. One treat they always counted on when he came to Northfield was his declaration of an unscheduled "Mountain Day"—a day when all the students laid aside books and study, classes were canceled, and everyone climbed the nearby New Hampshire mountain. On it, Moody would tell stories, do a Bible reading, and then take 350 girls down to his house for a surprise clambake dinner.

Moody loved to play games and sing songs with the young women, and he was especially attentive to those who were ill or homesick. He made them feel like a part of his evangelistic work too, because before departure on a campaign he spoke in chapel, explaining his itinerary and soliciting their daily prayers for the work. He urged them to send him letters while was away, and he usually sent Miss Hall a letter to be read to the girls in chapel. Typical of his epistles to the seminary were these:

> Next Tuesday will you have a special prayer for New York? I think the work has grown deeper and deeper from day to day, but I want to see it spread all over the land. On Tuesday I am to take up the subject of the Atonement, and will you all pray that the Holy Spirit may make it real?

Another letter said:

Will you thank the students for their prayers, and will you say to them
I think God is answering prayer, for I have never seen the work take
so good a hold in so short a time. I do believe it is an answer to prayer.
Next week I am to be on the Spirit all the week, and I do need your
prayers far more than I can tell you.[81]

Moody behaved on the Mount Hermon campus in much the
same way he coursed through Northfield Seminary. He took the boys
on hikes, played games with them, and declared a holiday for outdoor activities once each term. He gave the young men special
lectures on staying fit physically, and he encouraged them to personal purity and habits that bring glory to God. He urged them to live
frugally and simply, and no young man went through Mount Hermon without a challenge to consider full-time service as a missionary
or pastor.

Moody also gave personal attention to boys who were ill, and it
was not unusual for him to take seriously infirm youngsters into his
own home. One young man's illness turned out to be tuberculosis, so
Moody raised money to send him to the Adirondacks for a time of
rest and healing. As one Hermonite put it, "This was only one case
out of many" where Mr. Moody stepped in and provided special care.
Moody, according to this witness, had one "chief concern . . . the
spiritual life of the school." This concern he nurtured by giving of
himself and bringing in the best of Bible teachers from home and
abroad to encourage the students to study Scripture, love Christ, and
serve Him all their days.

The boys could never forget the preaching of men with British
accents, or the stirring words of General O. O. Howard who, with
one arm missing from a battle wound, told them how God brought
revival during the Civil War. Most of all, however, "Mr. Moody himself . . . knew his boys through and through. They knew him, believed
in him, loved him. He had a burning desire that every new boy
should take an out and out stand for Christ. When at home he always
spoke on the first Sunday night of the new term, and followed his address with an after-meeting and personal work." Hundreds of boys
were thereby converted. Countless more were encouraged to grow in
their faith, and others were inspired to devote their lives to the front
lines of the raging battle for souls.[82]

Some Teachings of the Schools

Because the Mount Hermon school and Northfield Seminary were not restricted to Christian students, Moody was continually on the alert for nonbelievers who could be loved into Christ's kingdom. Evangelism, however, was only a small part of the effort to work with souls of students. The curriculum, as well as extracurricular activities, was designed to help Christian students mature in their faith.

Moody actually took a dim view of conversion without purposeful follow-up and disciplemaking. He encouraged faith development in several ways. First, there were daily chapel messages designed to help young people apply Scripture to their lives. Second, there was an emphasis on regular worship, including singing of hymns. Moody made clear wherever he ministered that worship services, especially on Sunday nights, "should be preceded by a half-hour's service of praise." He also suggested evenings be set aside periodically for the community of believers to "practice in unison and harmony the singing of hymns and tunes they know, and learn new ones." Moody maintained that intercessory and confessional prayer were always important to keep the believer God-centered and growing, but "strange as it may seem to those who have not thought of it, yet it is true that more is said in the Bible about praise than about prayer."[83]

A third practice that the educator-evangelist stressed for the spiritual health and maturation of his students was regular celebration of Holy Communion. Moody argued the importance of the Lord's Supper along biblical lines. "It was the dying request of Christ that we should eat of the bread and drink of the wine in remembrance of Him; yet many young converts say to me, 'I need not go to the Communion table, need I?'" He went right to the heart of the matter in his typically blunt and illustrative manner. "I tell them they need not go unless they want to, but if that was the dying request of any friend they had they would be willing to do it all their lives; why, then, should they not desire to do it in remembrance of their Saviour?" Moody stressed that during Communion "we must pray to God to fill us with [Him] and help us get rid of self."[84]

After the Students Moved On

Moody's ambition to "get into the field 2 to 3000 splendid workers" was well on the way to fruition by the 1890s. Some students came to faith at the two schools, most students became stronger and more devout Christians, and scores of young people committed their lives to full-time Christian service. Many Northfield women went on to college, the majority going to Wellesley. Of the Hermonite men, many of them went to college as well, with the majority going to Amherst. Some Mount Hermon men went to Yale after graduating.

Although D. L. Moody trusted Wellesley College, he was fearful that Amherst or Yale might ruin the faith and dispositions instilled in the young people. But he need not have worried. Amherst in the late nineteenth century was a college that recruited strong Christian faculty. Calvin Coolidge, for instance, a Vermonter who graduated from Amherst in 1895, spoke often of his philosophy professor, Charles Garmen, whom he said "walked closer to God" than any other man he ever met. Coolidge entered politics after graduation, becoming mayor of Northampton, Massachusetts, and eventually serving as governor of Moody's state. After becoming president of the United States, Coolidge, a sincere Christian, looked back on Amherst with fondness. He said all of the students there were told that by getting a college education they were receiving an advantage well beyond the reach of most Americans. This blessing was a sacred trust to be dedicated for the good of mankind, never something to be used for self-promotion or material gain. The men at Amherst, according to Coolidge, were instructed to devote their lives to the service of others. They were encouraged to be ministers or missionaries, but if they sensed no such calling, they should consider devoting their lives to public service.[85]

Yale was more secularized than either Amherst or Wellesley, but Moody's worries were unfounded, at least during his lifetime. Both of the Moody boys, William and Paul, graduated from Yale (classes 1891 and 1901 respectively), and both men were sincere Christians who spent their lives in ministry and education.[86]

Numerous Northfield and Mount Hermon students, whether they went on to college or not, made their way to foreign and home missions. Moody's hopes were being realized; his prayers were being answered. Truly he had "set in motion streams which will continue long after I am gone."[87]

THE NORTHFIELD BIBLE TRAINING SCHOOL

These two college preparatory experiments were so successful that Moody found the will to launch one more school. During his extensive preaching tours of New England and eastern Canada in the late 1870s and 1880s, Moody encountered a class of women he wanted to help. Typically they were born and raised in rural New

England or eastern Canada with little or no formal schooling. They converted in one of his meetings, and immediately, or within a year or two, felt a persistent call to foreign or home missions. There was a growing demand for women to serve in foreign missions, and there was a particularly pressing need for women to serve in North American cities. Urban churches were short on workers to do evangelism and house-to-house personal work among the urban poor. Moody wanted to connect those who were called with the locations needing workers.

The Northfield Seminary was not an option for these women because many were barely literate. In any case many women in their late twenties and thirties would not have felt comfortable among the teenagers at the seminary. Furthermore, because of their ages and the urgency of their call, the investment of four years in a college preparatory program was impractical. What these women needed was intensive study of the English Bible, the central truths of Scripture, and the life and teachings of Jesus, as well as practical training in how to lead people to Christ, conduct prayer meetings, do Bible readings and teachings, and work with children. These women also needed to learn how to support themselves and do social work among the poor. Sewing, cooking, and housekeeping were ways to accomplish two goals: earn money and aid the sick, the aged, and shut-ins. Therefore, training in home economics was viewed as a necessary concomitant with a Bible school program.

For years Moody had seen the needs for women missionaries in America's cities, and he frequently sent forth challenges when he preached across the continent. By the 1880s he was meeting women during his campaigns who told him they were called but needed some help to get into missions work. Added to these personal encounters came an increasing flood of mail from women who worked as domestic servants and had very little money, no Bible training, and a desire to accept Moody's challenge. Typical of the letters Moody received was one from a young woman who grew up in rural Massachusetts. She was converted at a Boston meeting, and two years later she felt a call to missions. She was being discipled at A. J. Gordon's church, but required training before she was ready to serve. Could Mr. Moody help?[88]

Once the Chicago Bible Institute was opened with full facilities for men and women in 1889, Moody could recommend people to go there—and he did. But by 1890 there was only room for fifty women and two hundred men at CBI. These places were filled quickly, still leaving scores of prospective students with no place to go for training. Furthermore, not all eastern women felt comfortable going west to Chicago for school.[89]

The Facility for the Fourth School

Moody, for all of his optimism and zeal, did not have the heart to start a fund-raising campaign to build another school, especially since the two schools at Northfield and the one in Chicago continually required funds for more facilities and student support. Consequently, he came upon an ingenious idea to use the Hotel Northfield during the off season. In the 1880s some wealthy Christians from New York, Philadelphia, and southern New England pooled resources to construct a first-class hotel at Northfield. They did so because, beginning in 1880, Moody held deeper life conferences at Northfield similar to the Mildmay conferences he had attended in England. In the early years, a few people found lodging at Moody's home, but others were forced to rent rooms from local people, live in school dormitories, or put up tents. Although such accommodations suited most summer conferees, an elite element wanted the comfort and luxury of northern New England's finest mountain resort inns.

When "The Northfield" was available by the middle 1880s, this three-story, red brick structure was graced on three sides with lounging verandas that overlooked lush, spacious lawns. Most of the rooms were large and well appointed, complete with massive windows, dark natural woodwork, oriental carpets, elegant draperies, writing desks, and comfortable furniture.[90]

Like most New England inns, this elegant, expensive resort was open from April through September, leaving it vacant six months of the year. It occurred to Moody that he could put two women in each of the larger rooms and offer two three-month school terms, divided by a brief Christmas and New Year holiday. Inasmuch as Ambert G. Moody, George's son and Dwight's nephew, was the manager of the hotel and the shareholders were all friends of D. L. and his work, it was a simple task to hire Ambert as treasurer and secure access to the building for a nominal fee plus maintenance costs. The only other task was to find a principal and faculty, which Moody's extensive contacts enabled him to do with relative ease.

The Northfield Bible Training School turned out to be one of Moody's most successful educational ventures. With no endowment and no buildings of its own, the NBTS opened its doors in October 1890. Fifty-six women arrived, coming from eleven states and seven

Christian denominations. The following year seventy-three students attended, representing nine states and three foreign countries. By the turn of the century more than seven hundred women had completed one to four terms at NBTS.[91]

Unlike the two college preparatory schools where students studied four years of Greek and Latin, plus a wide range of humanities courses including history, philosophy, and literature, NBTS was strictly a vocational school. Lila A. Halsey, the principal at the time of Moody's death, wrote that the school was designed to train Christian workers: "While this is neither an industrial school nor a training schools for nurses, it recognizes the truth that ministry to physical needs is often the wedge which opens the door for ministry to spiritual needs. Sewing, cooking, music and hygiene, therefore, have a prominent place in the course of study." But the greatest stress is laid upon "deepening of spiritual life, and study of the English Bible." The Bible courses covered structure and interpretation of Scripture, with emphasis on "application of the truth to individual souls." Students took classes that specifically related to the rescue, healing, and care of souls, plus related classes in personal work, character study, and analyzing Bible characters. Students also learned how to teach and work with children, pray, make clothes for the needy, and prepare food for the sick.[92]

Practical Ministry for Students

NBTS women did more than take classes in the hotel; they also went into the adjoining towns and rural areas, making house visits under the supervision of pastors, evangelists, and teachers. Many pastors and evangelists donated their time to this program, and by the end of the first year there were a dozen full-time teachers. The bulk of the faculty was comprised of women who were experienced in home or foreign missions and willing to live at the school for six months in exchange for room, board, and a small salary.[93]

D. L. Moody always called on this school when he was in Northfield, but it was Emma Moody who worked regularly with the women and who is seen in most of their class photographs. Once again it is apparent that Dwight Moody had the vision, found able administrators and teachers, and raised the money to cover the costs, while others kept the work alive through day-to-day hard work and dedication.

Students were theoretically required to pay $100 per term, but school records reveal that most of the students were too poor to raise even half their fees. Student files suggest that Moody either went into his pocket or the royalty fund or tapped wealthy friends to under-write the women's fees. A letter to a prospective student reveals what typically happened. She inquired about admission but confessed to having scarcely enough money to get to Northfield. A staff member wrote and told her to come anyway, and "meet Miss Sherman," who would have charge of the school. "Do not worry about [the] finan-cial part: I saw Mr. Moody about the matter this evening and he says you can come and have the tuition and board free. We will thank the Lord for opening the way."[94]

Students As Answers to Modern Problems

NBTS was absorbed into the seminary in 1908, but for the eigh-teen years of its independent existence, the fulfillment of Moody's vision is impressive. In autumn 1895, Moody reflected on the criti-cal role of NBTS. The late nineteenth-century church, he noted, was not living up to its potential. Many people were standing idle while labor for souls needed to be done. Formerly in our nation almost everyone went to church, enabling pastors to present the gospel to most people. But, alas, observed Moody, in this growing nation of large cities it was harder to get people to go to church, "so we must get into their homes. . . . Women can best get into homes by serving mothers and children. . . . There ought to be thousands of women giv-ing their lives to this work in the cities and large towns of our land, and more and more churches are calling for such workers."

He went on to describe another deplorable change—the decline of churches in rural areas. In many places the lure of cities was drain-ing away the population. "The churches are becoming empty," he observed, and pastors were moving elsewhere because these dwin-dling congregations could not pay them a living wage. One solution, according to Moody, was to get teams of people to clean up decrepit church buildings and make them attractive again.

If the little congregations could not afford to support a pastor who had a wife and children, single women who were trained could go in there and "stand in the gap." These trained women could bring spiritual leadership back into rural communities by living among the people, conducting Bible readings and prayer meetings, and visiting the sick and shut-ins. These women could do "Bible readings at their homes, and preaching in the church." He concluded his talk by say-ing that women were especially needed for ministry in the West and South, and "we can train them" at NBTS. He then promised to cor-

Mrs. D. L. Moody, circa 1883

respond with any woman who had an interest in such work.[95]

Moody's call for women was bold and wide-ranging. Precisely what he believed about the ordination of women is unclear. His sermons and lectures are not revealing. We do know that he never wanted ordination for himself, so he believed it unnecessary for ministry. (Not being ordained, however, never made him shy about administering holy communion or baptism. Indeed, there is a striking photograph of Moody baptizing the infant twins of the principal of Mount Hermon School.)[96]

Moody's silence on ordination of women was consistent with his posture on most issues that were, to his thinking, secondary, especially when the major traditions were not in agreement. He worked closely with the Brethren who allowed no women elders; on the other hand, he ministered equally close to Methodists of various stripes (especially Free Methodists or Wesleyan Methodists) who frequently ordained women into pastoral ministry. The Chicago Avenue Church had no women pastors, and presumably if Moody had wanted one he would have opened the way for such an appointment. Nevertheless, he was openly supportive of women in all types of ministry, including teaching Bible to men and women and having women in pastorates. His public remarks in September 1898 show beyond question that he wanted women to take vacant churches in rural America—he even offered to train them for the work.[97] Likewise, although the bulk of the women trained at NBTS were home and foreign missionaries, some of them became pastors of churches—a fact that was celebrated in NBTS literature.

In *Northfield Echoes*, NBTS principal Lila Halsey, a woman Moody personally knew and appointed, boasted about the wide-ranging ministries NBTS women held while they were in training. Two students did house-to-house visitation, and in the process one hundred and thirty persons "signed cards stating that they wished to become Christians." Seven young women worked for the Vermont Domestic Missionary Society "to visit and hold special services in remote communities of that state," and one of them "has remained to supply a small church."[98]

Among NBTS graduates by the turn of the century were thirty full-time foreign missionaries, serving as far away as China, Japan, Africa, and India. Even more graduates were serving as full-time home missionaries, including workers in rural New England, South Carolina, and Florida. Some were involved in YMCA work, two went to "a colored orphanage" in Chattanooga, one assumed "the care of an orphanage in Atlanta, Georgia," and one assumed "charges of two churches in Colorado, her parish covering a circuit of ten or more miles."[99]

There was an attractive consistency about Dwight Moody. He was called to search for lost and wounded souls and conduct the one-to-one work essential to the task. He was also called to encourage and train workers to do this kind of personal work. Gender, age, race, or economic class meant nothing to him. More laborers were needed, and he would do all he could personally and through his schools to get them into the work. Until his death this angle of vision dominated every one of his schools; he would have it no other way. The result was a flood of Christian workers who poured forth into home and foreign work. Before he died he had been instrumental in realizing his dream of getting "into the field 2 to 3000 splendid workers." And most of all, he had fulfilled his ambition "to set in motion streams which will continue long after I am gone."[100]

CHAPTER ELEVEN

LANDMARKS IN NONFORMAL CHRISTIAN EDUCATION

D. L. Moody's Contributions to Worker Training, Publishing, and the Conference Movement

1889–1895

"I Have Never Been So Hopeful About Anything I Have Ever Undertaken."

Dwight L. Moody never thought systematically or philosophically about education. He would have been amused at categories such as formal and nonformal education. For him, there were two educational tasks. First, socially and economically disadvantaged young people needed education within a decidedly Christian context in order to go into adulthood better equipped to serve church, family, and society. Second, trained workers were needed to fulfill Christ's commandment to make disciples at home and abroad. Moody recognized that some prospective workers needed encouragement and vision; everyone needed books and other study materials; and most people required various levels of special training. Specific educational needs varied so much from person to person and place to place that all Moody fully grasped was the urgency and scale of the task.

The three schools at Northfield—thanks to able staffs—were rapidly well-defined and organized as formal educational institutions. The first two were designed to educate young men and women to live Christianly and to prepare some of them to go on to college or seminary and perhaps full-time Christian service. The third functioned to equip more mature Christians for full-time service in home or foreign missions. His fourth school was the one Emma Dryer worked so hard to begin in Chicago.

Ironically, the only one of the four educational institutions planned by Moody that has remained focused close to its founder's vision started off in an extremely eclectic if not an unplanned fashion. The Chicago Bible Institute had an inauspicious beginning to say the least—in part because Mr. Moody was so far away, but primarily because too many things were undertaken at one time. Once Moody had Northfield Seminary and Mount Hermon up and running, he turned serious attention to training Christian workers in the Midwest.

Originally, and with Emma Dryer in charge, the extent of Moody's purpose was to get women evangelists and personal workers into the homes of unchurched residents of Chicago. By the middle 1880s, Moody enlarged the vision to include spring or summer seminars for pastors. The goal was to bring pastors from all over the United States to Chicago for several weeks. They would be on their own for housing and food, but Moody, some of his friends, and the Chicago Evangelization Society would offer classes and practicums on how to reach the unchurched in the poorest neighborhoods.

FOCUSING THE VISION IN CHICAGO

Moody gradually sharpened the focus. In winter 1888 he said: "I will start in Chicago the first of April [1889] a training work, and all who would like can come free." There would be lectures on personal ministry each morning, personal house-to-house visitation in the afternoons, and then preaching meetings at night. "Young ministers and theo[logy] students, . . . also ladies who would like to devote their life to Christian work can have the training free, but all must board themselves." At the end of sixty days, the teachers "can tell who had the gifts for Christian work." Those who are gifted "can take a more thorough course, and others can drift back to their old place and work evenings" in ministry. The administration would help "any man or woman who has got gifts" find a position helping established churches and ministers do city "mission work." At the same time "a good many [established] ministers [can] come and learn how to get hold of the masses. I find so many are sick and do not know what to do" to reach these newcomers to the cities.[1]

Moody exuded tremendous enthusiasm for his plan. "I feel the fire in my bones," he wrote. "I think a good work has been done [in earlier seminars] only not enough of it."[2] This nonaccredited, nonformal seminar, he argued, if the people could come "for 60 days, [would] be worth more than a year's study" in any formal program.[3]

The exuberant visionary from Northfield urged the Chicago

Evangelization Society and the society's secretary, F. G. Ensign, to get behind this venture, talk it up, and advertise it in *The Christian Record* and other Christian newspapers and periodicals. "Get out the call [letter] and send it to me and I will sign it and you can put it in all the religious papers and dailies." Moody offered to speak every weekday morning for one month, and he promised to find first-rate speakers for the other morning and evening sessions.[4]

Early Success of the School in Chicago

The response in 1889 transcended everyone's highest hopes. Moody told Whittle they had had "a great success this spring. We had over 500 ministers. They came from Miss., Ala., Ark., Tenn., Ky., and all over the northwest and some from Wash[ington] Territory." He said he expected more than a thousand to come to the next "school" in the autumn. "I am expecting great things. The hour is now come for us to raise up a class of men and women that will go for the 3/4 that do not go anywhere to church, and I am inclined to think I am going to succeed and get a lever under all the churches. I have never been so hopeful about anything I have ever undertaken."[5]

Moody's years of experience showed him that every innovation—especially when it is successful—threatens the guardians of formalism and engenders opposition. He confided to Whittle, "I will have some trouble with the seminaries but if a few of my friends will stand by me it will come out all right."[6] As long as the conventions and training seminars were billed as nothing more than continuing education for ministers, or as preparation for deaconesses and assistants to ministers and churches, the opposition was minimal. But as soon as the Chicago Evangelization Society began to formalize courses and offer sophisticated programs on a regular, ongoing basis, a few heads of seminaries and some clergy began to turn on him. Vocal critics were heard as soon as The Bible Institute for Home and Foreign Missions was launched in 1889. To deflect criticism and give the institute intellectual respectability, Moody tried to recruit W. G. Moorehead, a Xenia Theological Seminary professor and highly regarded teacher, to oversee the school. Moorehead, already on his way to the presidency of the Presbyterian Seminary in Ohio, declined the offer.[7]

Failing to attract Moorehead, except as an occasional teacher, Moody turned his attention on R. A. Torrey. A powerful preacher, stimulating teacher, and proven administrator, Reuben Archer Torrey was Moody's second choice, although he probably never knew it.

Second fiddle or not, Torrey proved to be the ideal man for the task. Nineteen years younger than Moody, he was born in New Jersey in 1856. Extremely well educated for his time, he had earned a B.A. at Yale University in 1875 and a B.D. from Yale's Divinity School three years later. Torrey knew his Greek and Hebrew as well as any seminary professor, and he had a keen grasp of historical, biblical, and systematic theology. Added to these strengths, he possessed fluency in German, complete with post-graduate level studies in biblical criticism at two German universities (Leipzig and Erlangen) in the early 1880s.[8]

Superintendent R. A. Torrey

Torrey first fell under Moody's influence at Yale, where Moody encouraged the young seminarian during the extended New Haven meetings in 1878. After divinity school Torrey went on for ordination in the Congregational Church, taking a pastorate in Ohio. Married in 1879, he pastored for a few years, flirted with liberalism for a season, and studied in Germany. By the middle 1880s, however, Moody had helped lure him back to a conservative view of Scripture, even managing to convince the brilliant young intellectual (he was not yet thirty years old) that there was a greater need for evangelists in cities than for parish pastors of the stripe Yale prepared him to be.

Torrey's servant heart and humility were manifested in his bypassing attractive pulpit opportunities to take the helm of a city mission in Minneapolis, Minnesota. Many people assumed Torrey to be suffering from a mild form of lunacy. A well-educated intellectual, they said, should not expend his energies and gifts on the down-and-outers in an urban mission. But Torrey had more than intellect and education; this powerfully built man, who had a body and beard almost identical to Moody's, possessed a keen ear. He heard God's call to work among the lower walks.[9]

More than half a decade of evangelistic and administrative experience in Minnesota's major metropolis splendidly equipped him to be the superintendent of the new Bible institute with a strong emphasis on urban ministry. He took over in September 1889 and stayed at his post until 1908. Along with Torrey, who served as general superintendent and the school's Bible teacher, as well as supervisor of the men's department, was Sarah B. Capron, a veteran missionary who superintended the women's department. Her assistant was Gertrude Hurlburt. Emma Dryer quietly and without bitterness resigned at this time, in part, at least, because of her dif-

Reuben A. Torrey

ferences with Capron and the board over leadership style and programs.[10]

In a fashion similar to what he had done in Massachusetts,
Moody pulled together an unusually able faculty and staff. Besides
Torrey, whom he labeled "the man for the place," he had F. G. Ensign
as a superb utility man who served as secretary for the CES and oversaw fund-raising, advertising, and liaison work between CES and the
institute. He also had T. W. Harvey, the wealthy entrepreneur and
philanthropist, to tend to all sorts of problems and plans, especially
raising money from men like Armour, Swift, Pirie, Palmer, Scott, and
McCormick.[11]

The men and women Moody turned the CES and Bible institute
over to by 1889 were as strong a team as could have been found anywhere. Once again Moody's genius in finding loyal and gifted people
to carry out his dreams was markedly evident. He not only found
good people, but he also knew how to keep them happy. He insisted
that Torrey be paid $200 a month at a time when the average wage
earner brought in no more than $600 a year. (CES paid its full-time
Bible workers $600 per annum.) He also took time to write and tell
board members to encourage and praise Torrey for his excellent

work. Moody personally guaranteed and paid from his own pocket 10 percent of every dollar Ensign could raise for the institute as a bonus, and he personally guaranteed for Emma Dryer, and eventually for the other women on staff, annual stipends between $1,000 and $1,500 a year.[12]

MOVING AHEAD WITH INCREASED CONFIDENCE

A combination of Moody's ever-expanding vision, plus the goals and considerable talents of the faculty, caused the institute to expand its educational ambitions by the early 1890s. No longer did its leaders cower in fear that they might threaten or be looked upon with disdain by theologians and seminarians. The world needed Christian workers to go to the cities, rural areas, and foreign fields, but traditional institutions either could not or would not train them.

The Purpose and the Need

The institute continued to recruit students who wanted to be pastors' assistants, urban workers, foreign missionaries, and English Bible teachers, but it expanded its program by formalizing men's and women's departments, and also a music department, complete with ever-growing lists of courses and classes that were theoretical as well as applied. The institute offered a special welcome to older men and women who could not go to college and seminary to prepare for the call they received from God in middle life. Then in 1893 the institute boldly advertised as one of its objectives: to prepare "men who expect to enter the pastorate in fields where a knowledge of the Word of God and a knowledge of men is regarded as more important than a thorough scholastic training."[13]

R. A. Torrey stood fearless. Like his friend Moody, he possessed the courage to do what needed to be done regardless of the opinions of the theological and educational elite. Torrey and Moody were in perfect agreement about the needs of workers in the late nineteenth century. To their mind, the divinity schools, seminaries, and colleges were providing academic training that simply failed to equip ministers and missionaries for the realities of wretched humanity at home and abroad. Increasingly, the formally trained clergy were steeped in academic disciplines such as history, philosophy, and theology, as well as biblical languages. They had enough Greek and Hebrew to exegete almost any text, but no one had encouraged them or taught them how to let the inspired Scriptures exegete their own hearts, let alone how to point the texts to the hearts of congregations. Except for rhetoric and homiletics, little was offered in practical theology.

The divinity school graduates, Torrey knew from experience, were laden with critical tools to carve up the Bible, but they came to ministry with decreasing confidence in the ability of the Scriptures to transform souls and lives. Furthermore, little was taught in the formal training centers on personal work, prayer, evangelism, and missions.

Torrey himself had to learn about evangelism, inquiry rooms, and personal work from Moody in 1878, because Yale's focus during his student days was almost completely devoted to an academic approach to ministry. Finally, from Torrey and Moody's perspective, the Holy Spirit was sadly and perilously overlooked in most of the other institutions. Moody believed in the baptism of the Holy Spirit as a gift of grace that was available to all people regenerated by the Holy Spirit. Moody had introduced Torrey to a more robust view of the Holy Ghost, and he constantly urged him to preach and teach on this subject. Both men were unalterably convinced that men and women in ministry—of all people—needed to be "endued with Power from on High." Moody's son Paul argued that his father's stand was not one of opposition to trained ministry; rather, it was a revolt against "the dryness of the seminaries of his day."[14]

Moody often went to Torrey and said, "Torrey, I want you to preach on the baptism of the Holy Ghost." The Bible institute superintendent recalled that

> Once, when I had been invited to preach in the Fifth Avenue Presbyterian Church, New York (invited at Mr. Moody's suggestion; had it not been for his suggestion the invitation would never have been extended to me), just before I started for New York, Mr. Moody drove up to my house and said: "Torrey, they want you to preach at the Fifth Avenue Presbyterian Church in New York. It is a great, big church, cost a million dollars to build it." Then he continued: "Torrey, I just want to ask one thing of you. I want to tell you what to preach about. You will preach that sermon of yours on 'Ten Reasons Why I Believe the Bible to be the Word of God' and your sermon on 'The Baptism with the Holy Ghost.'" Time and again, when a call came to me to go off to some church, he would come up to me and say: "Now, Torrey be sure and preach on the baptism with the Holy Ghost." I do not know how many times he said that to me.[15]

From Moody's and Torrey's viewpoint, men and women could only mature in Christ through a personal relationship with the third person of the Trinity. And equally important, to their way of thinking, everyone called to work in the rescue, healing, and care of souls needed training to work in ways that were experiential and practical—not merely academic. To this end in 1892 the Bible institute boldly offered classes to "graduates of colleges or theological seminaries who wish to supplement the valuable education received at these schools by a thorough study of the English Bible and methods of aggressive Christian work."[16]

The Developing Gulf

An unfortunate but perhaps inevitable gulf started developing at this time between the Chicago Bible Institute and institutions that would follow it, on the one hand, and more academic institutions like Princeton Seminary, Yale Divinity School, and McCormick Seminary in Chicago, on the other. The former would be perceived by the latter to be separatistic, practical, and unacademic—even anti-intellectual; the latter perceived by the former as heady, overly scholastic, arrogant, and liberal or unbiblical. By the early twentieth century, the seeds of different emphases took root. And while most institutions of both stripes were more diverse than their critics realized or acknowledged, stereotypes sometimes became self-fulfilling prophecies.[17]

Debates and differences aside, the truth is that D. L. Moody put the considerable weight of his international notoriety and personal talents behind the Chicago Bible Institute. The result was the development of an educational enterprise (always both formal and nonformal) that has met a major need for more than a century. CBI from 1889 forward was phenomenally successful in attracting students. Classes were filled from the 1890s onward. Hundreds of students annually went to the ever-growing physical plant and faculty at Institute Place in downtown Chicago. There they were trained for home and foreign missions, as well as pastorates in rural areas, small towns, and cities.

The secret of initial and long-lived success at CBI was manifold, including a superb faculty in an easily accessible large city. Also, Moody's prestige and deep involvement were absolutely essential for success. It is true that he spent much more time in Northfield than he did in Chicago. He never had the level of involvement with students at CBI that he maintained with the schools in Massachusetts. Nevertheless, he was in Chicago without fail at least once and usually several times every year between 1886 and two months before his death in 1899, with the exception of 1896. When he was in the Windy City he made purposeful pilgrimages to the institute. He usually talked to students, met with faculty and administrators, and preached at the Chicago Avenue Church. This is a remarkable record of faithful interest, considering his demanding travel schedule that took him in the first decade of CBI's history all over the United States, across Canada, into Mexico as far south as Mexico City, and to Great Britain, Ireland, Italy, France, Egypt, and Israel.[18]

Moody's correspondence was voluminous, especially in the 1880s and 1890s. His letters reveal that he maintained close ties with R. A. Torrey, T. W. Harvey, F. G. Ensign, A. F. Gaylord, and others at the institute. His correspondence shows that he was well-informed about the school and the church, and he maintained a loving and helpful relationship with the institution until his death.

MOODY'S CONTINUING INVOLVEMENT
WITH THE CHICAGO SCHOOL

The founder's involvement was deeper than annual visits and letter writing. He continued to raise money for CBI, and he channeled his own resources there as well. Students were recruited by Moody whenever he traveled and preached, and it is clear that he found placement for many a CBI man and woman when he was out in the field preaching and teaching. Two letters written from Colorado in 1898 are typical of his continued interest in building the kingdom of God through CBI. He wrote that he had met "a splendid girl in Pueblo who wanted to go to the Institute," but she was told they were "full" now. Moody was not pleased about what she had heard from Chicago. "I want to see 1000 students at the Institute," he protested. He insisted that they stop turning away students who were called to ministry and needed training.[19]

Moody also urged innovations at the institute. In 1894 he suggested to Torrey that an evening school could be started as a way to bring in people who could not otherwise take advantage of the programs. Some experimentation was done along these lines in the later 1890s. Although the institute did not launch a regular evening program until 1903, it is clear that Moody consistently maintained vision and stayed at least a step ahead of his times. Moody's suggestions demonstrate a thoughtful interest in the Chicago school, as well as a consistent determination to find ways to prepare nontraditional students for ministry. Everything considered, the institute was a marvelous success. C. R. Erdman, the son of Moody Church pastor William Erdman, wrote that by 1899 "students were in attendance for all quarters, and representing all races of the world. More than two hundred [graduates] were engaged in home and city missions and rescue missions; 186 were on the foreign field."[20]

MOODY'S FAMILY AND THE NEED FOR REST

Dwight Moody's preaching and traveling schedule alone would have been beyond the endurance of most people. Typically Moody traversed twelve to fourteen states and approximately thirty cities each year, delivering multiple messages and talks six days a week. The pace gradually escalated until in 1895 he visited fifteen states, two Canadian provinces, and more than thirty cities.[21]

Constant traveling by train and buggy, living out of suitcases, sleeping in strange hotel rooms, meeting a seemingly endless line of local leaders at each stop, continually speaking to large groups without benefit of a microphone, and following up with extensive one-to-one soul work in the inquiry rooms utterly exhausted Mr. Moody. He desperately needed rest and quiet time alone. No preacher or teacher—not even one as talented, anointed, and experienced as Mr. Moody—could carry on effectively without rest and regular quality time to study, pray, and think. In 1878, Mrs. Moody wrote to a friend that her husband "has made quite a rigid rule whereby he takes six hours each day for study."[22]

Emma's Protection of Her Husband

Emma Moody did all she could to help her husband with his demanding schedule. She made clear that she would do all in her power to protect him from intruders who would take away the precious time he needed by himself and with God, so that he would have something worthwhile to give to his family and his public. Mrs. Moody was rather quiet and reserved compared to her extroverted, public husband, but she was no weakling. Underneath her genuinely serene exterior was a will of steel. If people tried—and they often did—to squeeze one more talk or another half hour out of his schedule, she stood in the gap as courageously and effectively as those Union soldiers she visited and nursed during the Civil War. In 1889, for instance, she sent off a strong letter to F. G. Ensign in Chicago:

Los Angeles

March 19, 1889

Dear Mr. Ensign:

I am writing for my husband to ask you to make no appointments for him to preach or hold services himself personally in any of the churches. He wants to be in Chicago to help in the work of the Institute and expects to be there, but he cannot undertake to preach in any of the churches in the evening.

I am writing for him to Dr. Barrows to say that he will not be able to preach in his church. Since the month of September Mr. Moody has been preaching constantly, and is very tired, and ought not to undertake any preaching in Chicago. The Institute meetings are more than I think he is able for, but this of course he does not think he can forego.

I hope good work may be done, and preaching by others be greatly blessed.[23]

Moody's strong self-discipline, his ability to get by on only five or six hours of sleep, plus his adherence to clear priorities enabled him to accomplish more than most people. By the late 1880s his schedule still included evangelistic preaching and equipping pastors and lay leaders to do personal work and disciple-making, plus finding ways to educate young people to rescue and care for souls. Besides these priorities, Moody never compromised his determination to be a good husband and father. Unlike far too many people busy in ministry, Moody had time for Emma and all of the three children. The family members all genuinely enjoyed one another, and the relationships were not scarred by deep wounds of resentment from neglect.

The Family Bond

The Moodys avoided the pitfalls that befell so many evangelists and missionaries because he and Emma made deliberate choices to be together. Making Northfield a home base ensured their having a place where the children always had relatives surrounding them. During the summers there were extended periods when the entire family, including Mr. Moody, were together. They gathered for meals and family worship around their ornate Estey organ. They also shared chores, and they found time for exciting boat rides, picnics, and games. Both of the Moody sons, William and Paul, wrote extremely fond memories of their life with father, mother, siblings, and extended family. Granddaughter Emma Moody Powell recalled love, joy, and tenderness within the family circle, as did son-in-law A. P. Fitt.[24]

Paul Moody, the youngest of the three children, filled his memoirs with references to the attractive qualities of his father. "He seems to me in retrospect the most generous man I ever knew," or "I cannot think of a more ideal companion," were representative comments. Paul did reveal a slight tinge of sadness about how his father's work caused periods of separation: "When his own children were young he was too often away from home or too busy to extract from them all the pleasure he did from his grandchildren."[25]

It is true that D. L. Moody was frequently away from his family. Given the calling to itinerant work, however, he and Emma arranged family affairs as well as anyone could have. The secret of their family unity seems at core to reside in a keen sense of God's calling—His call on Mr. Moody to preach and His call on Mrs. Moody to serve God by supporting her husband and serving her children. Each member of the family had his or her own responsibilities before God and one another.

Carrying out difficult responsibilities was sweetened by the assurance that the parents genuinely loved each other and the children. Furthermore, whenever possible the family stayed together. The summer family times in Northfield were never violated unless everyone went away together. Even during the trips to Britain from October 1881 to April 1883, and again in 1891 to 1892, all five of them made the voyage. This was a remarkable commitment of togetherness, considering that Emma was in her late teens and late twenties on the two journeys, and William was in his early teens and early twenties respectively.[26]

When D. L. campaigned in one city for several months, Emma and the children came along and lived with him. Dwight and Emma made this choice for several reasons. First, they believed God wanted them to be together as much as possible because the children needed both of their parents. Second, D. L. needed Emma's help to fulfill his calling. She answered the bulk of his correspondence, and she shielded him from intruders and the constant pressures to take on more than was wise.

Emma Moody no doubt helped keep D. L. alive longer by reminding him of priorities, saying no for him to others, and being his refuge when the pressures were strong and the opposition disconcerting. Emma Moody tended to many of the details, organization, and interpersonal issues that Dwight simply could not perform well. She also made those invaluable contributions that no one but her husband and family saw. Just before they undertook the Mexico City campaign in spring 1895, Emma read through five volumes on Mexican history and culture. Although neither she nor D. L. spoke Spanish, at least she was able to help her husband understand the nation and the people. No doubt the tutoring sessions she provided on trains and in hotel rooms enabled him to avoid horrible blunders and have a better sense of the context in which he was to minister for two weeks. In brief, without her continuous involvement on many levels, it is certain his ultimate contributions would have been considerably diminished.[27]

The Children's Schooling

When the entire family went to such places as Boston, Baltimore, or St. Louis, the children were placed in local schools. In most cities they were ensconced in private academies. Once Emma acknowledged, "I have put Willie into school here in New Hampshire. I found there was no private school in the place, so I put him into public school under a very nice teacher and [in] a school that is very near the hotel. A little granddaughter of the proprietor of the hotel [where we live] goes to the school with Willie and is in the same class with him." She concluded that "he seems quite happy in going there."[28]

Although family togetherness remained a high priority, Emma and Dwight remained flexible. Sometimes decisions about locations and schooling were made in light of what seemed best for one child's health or another's education. During one period, when D. L. was ministering throughout New England, Emma was placed in a good private academy that she especially liked in Amherst, Massachusetts. On another occasion, when Willie was suffering from the pulmonary distress that frequently haunted him, Mrs. Moody packed up the two children and left D. L. on his own to tough out a northeastern winter. She took Willie and Emma to the balmy climate of Georgia, and their father visited them in the deep South whenever he could get away.[29]

The poor health of both Mrs. Moody and Willie became a factor that dictated which members of the family would be together and where. As she typically wrote to friends and relatives, "the children are well and busy with their lessons, though we need to be very careful of Willie, as he is not strong."[30]

To protect Emma's health and keep her free to be with the children when they were all together on a campaign, Mr. Moody urged her to skip his meetings and stay home with the children. "I hear about the meetings from him but do not get there myself," she wrote to a friend, "as Mr. Moody tells me he wants the room I would take; and besides this, the air [in large cities] Mr. Moody thinks is too bad for me." She assured her friend, "I am not ill," but D. L. was protective. And rightly so. She was obviously quite busy. If there was to be any time for the children, she could not be on an endless treadmill of meetings, listening to sermons she had heard her husband preach before. Offering her friend a glimpse of her life, she wrote, "I am always surprised in looking back" at how quickly the time slips by. "We have been in our home [in Baltimore] for the winter just two months and are quite settled, Mr. Moody at study and work in the meetings, the children in school, and I in all sorts of work, writing for my husband, attending to some of his calls, and helping him where I can, besides a variety of other things which don't amount to much yet make me tired by night."[31]

Letters Home

During times when Moody had to travel alone, he remained in close contact with his entire family by mail. Seldom a week went by without letters to his wife, mother, and each of the children.

Scores of letters have survived that Moody wrote to their first-born child and only daughter when he could not be in her presence. These epistles span more than a quarter of a century. One of his first letters to her was a three-page communiqué that contained a drawing of his feet, with this note attached:

> My dear Emma,
>   This is my right foot turned toward Northfield. I expect my boots will get into town about thirty or forty days from now.
>   This is my left foot after my right foot and I expect them to get me to town together and you must come to the station to see me unless I come on the late train.
>   I send you sweet kisses.[32]

Several years later he wrote, "I am real homesick, and shall be glad to get back and see you all again. . . . the books [I'm sending] will interest you." Still later, when Emma was embarking for Europe with her aunt and uncle Revell, he wrote "I am feeling quite lonely with you going off this week and we will be glad to get you back again. . . . And now dear Emma, goodbye. May the 91st Psalm be your comfort and stay all the time you are gone from your loving [Father]." The next day he could not resist writing again: "I must write to you once more before you leave this land. I have no news to tell you but I am real lonely at the thought of your going. It has seemed so nice to me to think of you safe and happy at Northfield. And now it seems as if a part of myself was gone. . . . I need not tell you that I love you very much[,] far more than I can tell you, and you are in my thoughts so much of the time. I never loved you more than I do tonight . . . so I can say go and may the angels of God hover over you by day and by night is my most earnest prayer. . . . Your own loving father."[33]

Emma Moody Fitt

The Child Emma

Emma was a bright and lively child, full of zest for life. Her keen sense of humor and independence of thought were most of the time appropriately channeled, and it is apparent that she never became rebellious enough to cause her parents any worry. When her self-determination manifested itself, it usually came out in ways that were, in retrospect, rather humorous. When Emma was about twelve years old, the Moodys were house guests of the Wanamakers in Philadelphia. Rod Wanamaker (who was Emma's age) and Emma were given money by Mr. Wanamaker to go to an afternoon concert. The adventurous twosome, however, left the house and promptly concluded that a circus would be more enjoyable. But when they returned home, the parents had already discovered the "misappropriation of funds" and sent them off to bed with a spartan supper of milk and bread, topped off with a good scolding.[34]

Over the years the Moody family loved to remind Emma of her father's ability to get the last laugh, despite her usual foresight and resourcefulness. In April 1893 he came into the Northfield family parlor and announced that a young university student whom he had met in Dublin the year before was on his way to America to be Moody's secretary during the great evangelistic ministry planned for the World's Fair in Chicago. When Moody said his name was Arthur Percy Fitt and "I call him Arthur," Emma roared with laughter, saying, "Who ever heard of such a name! I wouldn't have that name Fitt for anything." Her father warned her, "Take care, young lady! You better wait till you see this young Irishman before you say that."[35]

Dwight L. Moody revealed an unusual prescience. Thirteen months later Emma Moody became Mrs. Arthur Percy Fitt.

William, the Firstborn Son

William Moody was an object of his father's affections every bit as much as his sister was. Letters to his elder son issued forth from his father's pen with uninterrupted regularity. There were lines of tender remembrance: "I am thinking of you at home and I wish I could drop in on you," and encouragement to be kind to his baby brother: "Kiss Paul for me. Do all you can to make him happy." There were usually words of spiritual challenge and direction, among them "learn Isa. 57. . .15" or "I hope you will do more for Christ this year than ever before is my earnest prayer that God may make you not only his but a very useful man." Sharing from his own past, the loving father wrote, "I am sure the happiest days of my life have been when I tried to do the will of God as far as I knew it to be His will. May God of the prophets watch over you and keep you is the earnest prayer of your own Father."[36]

It delighted Mr. Moody that William attended Mount Hermon School, and his letters are full of suggestions on how to have the boys raise more of their own food and thereby "stop the meal bill." "I am ashamed to send in a bill for butter when we have so many cows," he continued, and "you had better read up and find out what makes hens lay." He also urged Willie to "write me a letter about the schools. I will be anxious to hear all about them, how they have opened and tell me about the new boys."[37]

Moody wanted William to do more than study and tend livestock: "I hope you will grow up to love the Bible." He also urged him to take time to play—"I am in hopes you have had a good deal of good skating. I also hope you have an ice bridge to go across the riv-

Will Moody

er now," and "I have got a man on the track for a dog. I am in hopes we will soon have one."[38]

Always attentive to important dates in his family's lives, Moody wrote to Willie from Jacksonville, Florida:

> By the time this gets to you you will be seventeen years old, and I want to tell you I am thankful to God for keeping you in so good health all these years. Ten years ago you were in this city a sick boy, and now by the blessing of God you are well and healthy. Let us thank God and show it in our lives.
>
> I wish I could I write you all I feel this morning, but I cannot, so you have to wait until you get to be a father before you will know how much I love you.
>
> I cannot get you any present here, so I am sending [some money].[39]

Moody continually exhorted Willie to stay fit spiritually. "I think you should go to one prayer meeting a week if you want to grow." Consider "taking a class in the Sabbath School, I think it will be such a help to you. You cannot help others without helping your-self, and it will help you to confess Christ."[40]

Spiritual Rebellion

Despite his father's guidance, Willie entered into a period of spiritual rebellion. He experimented with smoking, and he expressed serious doubts about the faith. D. L. wrote and warned, "Dear Willie, the world will deceive you but never satisfy you. You have not been happy for a year and your discontent has increased. . . . I have never prayed for you as I do now."[41]

Busy as Moody was with his travel, meetings, and other corre-spondence, he did more than write to Willie. He also sent letters to one of the Northfield Seminary teachers whom Willie respected. He urged her to get a horse from Ambert and "go over and see Willie [be-cause] he's greatly cast down . . . and I am so far away." On another occasion he begged her again to look after him, because "you have more influence over Will than anyone and if he is not reached this season I do not know what I will do. I do not want him to go to col-lege until he is a Christian."[42]

Dwight Moody was so disturbed about his son's spiritual well-being that he canceled meetings in Chicago and went to Northfield on the pretext of burying a dear friend, but Emma and he knew the major purpose of the visit.[43] Still Will (he dropped "Willie") re-mained unmoved. The young man went on to Yale the next autumn, and his father made a trip to New Haven in November to plead for the young man to surrender his life to Christ. But once more the fa-ther's wishes were not granted, perhaps because he came on so strong that he evidently became upset and distressed Will. Moody wrote to Will and apologized, expressing sorrow that he "could not keep cheerful during the visit, . . . but the thought that you may be cut down unsaved troubles me."[44]

A New Strategy

Moody switched strategy by Thanksgiving of 1887. He merely wrote and congratulated Will that Yale had beaten Harvard in foot-ball, and he told him to keep up with studies as well as sports. "I am glad that you like your new room and the men you room with."[45] A year later he was reporting news of campaigns, wishing Will well, and carefully avoiding any mention of the young man's faith.[46] Will was taken down with such a horrid throat infection in early 1890 that he had to go home to Northfield for Emma to nurse him. But once again his father only inquired of his physical health and ignored the issue of Christ.[47]

The more passive approach with reliance on prayer produced the desired effect. Before Will graduated from Yale in 1891, he was solidly in the faith and growing. He was so transformed that he gave up his dream of being a physician and promised instead to help his father preach, teach, and equip others to work with souls. "There is a far greater demand for good workers than the supply," Moody argued. William agreed and pledged his life to the cause of Christ.[48]

Moody as an educator may have been most effective as an instructor of his three children. By example, through one-on-one talks, and with his consistent stream of letters which they all cherished and kept, he helped rear a daughter and two sons who all became faithful spouses and parents, as well as dedicated disciples of Christ.

Paul, the Youngest Heir

Some of the most revealing and instructive of all of Dwight Moody's letters to his children were those he wrote to Paul. Born considerably later than the other children, Paul came into the family on April 11, 1879. Emma was nearly fifteen and Willie was ten. By the time Paul was in elementary school, Emma was grown and leading an adult life, and William was ready for Yale.

Paul experienced more periods of separation from his parents than the other children had at his age because he was not as sickly during childhood and adolescent years as Will. Furthermore, his big sister, a decade and a half his senior, was mature enough to care for him, freeing his mother to travel with Mr. Moody. Paul's big sister, except for the few times she was away at school—and most of her schooling was finished before Mrs. Moody was willing to leave Paul for even a few days—lived at home. She dearly loved Paul, played with him, and treated him more like a son than a sibling. Because she did not marry until Paul was fifteen, they developed a bond that would never be broken.[49]

Letters to Paul

During times of separation, D. L. Moody wrote to Paul weekly, regardless of the pressures of his schedule. At the same time he urged the boy to write regularly to him. Paul obviously loved his father and treasured the letters from him; he carefully preserved many of them and passed them on to his children.[50]

Cardinal Newman purportedly said that to live the gospel is to

be changed, and to be truly faithful is to change often. Few Victorian Americans made a more sincere effort to live the gospel than
Moody, and his letters to Paul—in contrast to his correspondence
with family from the 1860s and 1870s—reveal a phenomenally transformed man. To be sure, there were similarities and consistencies
over the years. Moody always remembered birthdays; he gave Paul a
pony, sent him a Magic Lantern with forty-eight pictures one year,
and one Christmas sent twenty dollars.[51] He always inquired about
health, and for Paul he urged outdoor work and cold baths as sure
ways of staying healthy.[52] To Paul, as to the other children, there
were given occasional assignments—pass on a kiss to the others, or
tend to the hens and cows.[53] Moody focused attention on all of his
children—telling them of his love for them, celebrating their accomplishments, and never glorifying himself or his ministry. He did
mention his own homesickness from time to time, but it was always
in a context of love for family rather than self-pity.[54]

Paul Moody

Evidences of a transformed Dwight Moody are present, however, and his letters used increasingly positive tones and an ever-growing emphasis on reaching out with love to others. Letters to Paul, both when he was a student at Mount Hermon and when he went on to Yale, were filled with encouragement to do loving things rather than to avoid certain behaviors. When Moody indirectly learned of Paul's unhappiness with one of his Mount Hermon teachers, he did not scold or reprimand him for his critical remarks. Instead he explained that the teacher had a difficult spot to fill. "Do all you can to help him," Moody urged. "Your influence should be on his side at all times."[55] In a similar way he urged the lad to look for ways to encourage lonely or troubled boys at school. "You will soon be sixteen and old enough to help any of the boys in Hermon." He especially sought Paul's help in reaching a troubled boy on the verge of being sent away: "Treat him kindly if you have a chance. . . . You can do a world of good if you [learn of any troubled boy, or one] inclined to go wrong . . . help him and do all you can to get him to do right."[56]

When the proud father learned of Paul's involvement in a Northfield Christian Endeavor Society, he responded with elation. Dashing off a letter of praise, he urged him to keep up the good work. Moody particularly delighted in learning that Paul gave a talk there one night. "Keep it up," he counseled. It is the way to learn to "think on your feet." He admitted that "when I commenced I could hardly get a sentence straight & I could not speak more than a minute or two at any one time."[57]

Paul at Yale

While Paul was at Yale, his father came to speak in chapel. Paul recalled that he had spoken at Yale every year while William was there between 1887 and 1891. After William graduated, however, he declined continual offers to speak at the Ivy League school. He maintained that his schedule was simply too crowded. As soon as Paul matriculated, however, he went back to New Haven and spoke in the college chapel. Paul remembered being "morbidly anxious" that his father should do well:

> In those days it was a serious misdemeanor to exceed the time of the service. The remark that "no souls are saved after twenty minutes" is said to have originated at [Yale's] Battel Chapel. Father preached for nearly half an hour over the time, but there was no shuffling of feet. I suffered so acutely that I was ill the rest of the afternoon with nervous indigestion. Yet the fact that he was forgiven was evidenced by the

largest crowd I had seen at the evening service, which differed from that of the morning in that it was not compulsory. Twice as many came to the old assembly room of the Dwight Hall of those days as could get in.[58]

Dwight was as proud of his son at Yale as Paul became of his father. Whereas he had been concerned about William's going to the famous but sometimes controversial Connecticut institution, he pushed Paul to study and be ready for the challenge. "Paul," he wrote a year before his application to Yale, "there is one thing I want you to do & that is to be thorough in all your studies do not leave any studies untill you have understood it. I am not anxious that you should rush through so to say you have got through. I want you to enter collage with out any conditions & to understand all you have gone over," so do not be in a hurry.[59] Paul remembered that "when word was received that I had passed enough subjects to be admitted to Yale, I think Father's satisfaction was fully as great as my own."[60]

Mr. Moody's lighter approach to dos and don'ts for this younger son, as well as his evident enthusiasm for Yale, produced rich dividends. In October 1898 he could write, "I thank God you have been chosen Deacon of your class[;] it is a great compliment to you & it cheers your Father & Mother more than we can tell. . . ."[61]

Gifts to Paul

Dwight Moody did a splendid job of teaching Paul about being a good steward of what God entrusted to him. "He was the most consecrated man I have ever known," wrote Paul. "He was not ascetic, not 'pious.'"[62] Father Moody gave him twenty dollars one year for a gift when he was ten years old. With the gift came the counsel, "I hope you will spend 1/2 of the $20 on the poor." Several years later Moody gave Paul an extremely generous gift: "I am sending you a telegram & saying the Chutter House is your Birthday present. I think you can sell it for $2,500 & invest the money . . . and bring you in something."[63] This time Paul was nineteen. Moody saw no need to tell him how to be a good steward. In the birthday letter that year D. L. wrote:

> You will be 19 in a few hours & I am thankful you have been spared to us another year. . . . I am so thankful you have taken so good stand in collage & I think you have three grand years of usefulness . . . for you in Yale & I am in hopes your influence will increase as the years go by. . . [64]

Mr. Moody sent Paul to Yale for an education, but he could personally provide some invaluable lessons from his own process of learning. Those who assumed Moody to be anti-intellectual or too practical to learn from reading books did not know the man. Once while he was in Texas he wrote to Paul and said, "I am going to send you Abbot's Life of Napolan [Napoleon]. I have read it sense I cam a way I think it will help you to see how he maid people love him & then thay would die for him." Just look at what he was able to do for "his country [this is] what you can do for Christ make man love you be constantly whatching for opertunity to bind men to you by some unselfish act for them & if you find a boy that does not like you make him do so by some kind act & if there is a poor boy—show him kindness." He urged Paul to read about how well Napoleon did with this—and he "did not have much light [or] some godly mother to start him. What a mighty power he might have [be]come. I think you will get some lessons from the life."[65]

His Father's Dream

Dwight Moody never attempted to hide his deep ambition for his boys to become preachers. He wrote to Paul on his sixteenth birthday, thanking him for bringing "joy and sunshine" to his parents. He confided, "I shall be so glad if you should become a preacher and take the field when I leave it. I would be glad if there should be some one of my family in the pulpit for all coming time. I am so thankful I ever went in to the field to do Christian work if I had a hundred lives I would shurley consecrate them all to the service of my lord and master."[66] He revealed to Will the same hopes. As soon as the elder son graduated and revealed a desire to preach, Mr. Moody used his influence to open a few pulpits for him, in the same way he recommended Whittle, Cole, Torrey, and others during earlier years. "I want to keep Will speaking as much as possible can you not get him some Sabbath do so if you can but do not say anything I have written," was typical of Moody's behind-the-scenes efforts to promote Will and thereby see one more preacher trained up for the field.[67]

D. L.'s Dreams for His Sons

Moody's dream for his sons became reality. Before D. L. died, Will did a lot of preaching. Although he, like his father, never sought ordination, he accompanied the senior Moody on many of his travels, serving as secretary, administrative assistant, inquiry room and

Bible reading leader, and sometimes stand-in teacher and preacher. Paul did not graduate from Yale until 1901, a year and a half after his father's death. He too did plenty of preaching. He studied theology in the early 1900s at New College, the Free Church of Scotland's school in Glasgow. He also attended Hartford (Connecticut) Theological Seminary. Ordained to the Congregational ministry in 1912, he held pastorates in a Congregational Church in St. Johnsbury, Vermont, and at Madison Avenue Presbyterian Church in New York City, and he served as a chaplain in World War I.

Both sons eventually turned from preaching and spent most of their mature years in education—encouraging young men and women to serve the Master in ministry, missions, or areas of Christian service. Paul taught at Mount Hermon for six years, and eventually became president of Middlebury (Vermont) College. William became the chief executive officer of both Northfield Seminary and Mount Hermon School—overseeing their merger into one institution in 1912.

There was something appropriate about Paul and William becoming educators. Paul Moody put it quite aptly—as Dwight Moody himself matured, he placed an increasingly greater value on education: "The growing emphasis on Education to which he gave more and more of his time . . . is evidence, if any is needed, that necessary as he considered conversion, it was not enough. As the newborn babe needs care and nurture, so the newborn soul needs training."[68]

MOODY'S INTEREST IN PUBLISHING

A burning desire to see souls saved, converts nurtured, and Christian disciples maturing and reproducing consumed D. L. Moody. Two nonformal educational avenues became tremendously important to him during the 1880s and 1890s. Moody continually sought innovative ways to fulfill Christ's great commission to make genuine disciples. Two methods he found effective were the publication and distribution of Christian literature and the promotion of Christian conferences to motivate and equip pastors and laity for wider usefulness.

Dwight Moody's vision of using Christian publications in his ministry actually went back to the Civil War. As soon as he discovered that his brother Warren had enlisted, he wrote to their mother and inquired about the location of Warren's training camp so he could send some spiritually edifying books. He also used hymnals and New Testaments quite liberally among the troops.[69] After the war, when Moody poured himself into YMCA and Sunday school work, the importance of getting solid training materials into the hands of lay workers and teachers became to him a matter of urgency.

Toward that end Moody had a long conversation with his brother-in-law, Fleming Hewitt Revell, in late 1868. Emma Moody's brother, three and a half years her junior and nearly thirteen years younger than D. L. Moody, maintained enormous respect for his increasingly renowned in-law. Because the Revell family suffered a financial setback in the late 1850s, young Fleming (his father carried the same name) ended his formal schooling at age nine, going to work to help support the family. This educational handicap notwithstanding, he had learned the three Rs quite well.[70]

Dwight Moody urged Revell to give up his position as drugstore clerk and do something with his life that would more directly help build the kingdom of God. Still only eighteen years old, the impressionable clerk exuded a vibrant Christian faith, but he confessed to no sense of calling to preach. Moody's ministry actually intimidated Revell. No matter to Moody. He explained to Fleming that a great need existed for a religious monthly magazine to edify Christians and help them mature in the faith. There simply was no inexpensive reading material available to the average Christian. Besides that, Sunday school teachers were in dire need of interesting, illustrative material.

THE BEGINNING OF REVELL'S PUBLISHING VENTURE

A praying man who also trusted Moody's instincts, Revell took a large step of faith and resigned his drugstore job. With Dwight and Emma's help, in January 1869 the first issue of *Everybody's Paper* appeared; and a few months later the first book with the Revell imprint was published. Entitled *Grace and Truth*, this book was written by William P. Mackay and urged upon Revell by Moody. According to Moody, the manuscript contained invaluable material for people who wanted to witness but had little or no formal training in basic Christian doctrine. To Moody's way of thinking, the nation was filled with potential Christian workers and teachers who were held back by lack of training. Revell could help fill this void.

An old pocket account book that remained in the Revell family for years revealed how Fleming, not yet twenty years old, traveled through the middle states selling subscriptions to *Everybody's Paper* and copies of *Grace and Truth*. Going from town to town with Christian literature, just like his brother-in-law had done years earlier with boots and shoes, the young Chicagoan's accounts show that he would sell five subscriptions in one town and ten in the next, until he built up a respectable subscription base. He also sold a large supply of books.

Unmarried until autumn 1872, Revell traveled widely, expanded his readership, and managed to make a living after expenses. Amazingly undaunted by the Chicago fire of 1871, even though it destroyed his headquarters, Fleming Revell started over again. His decision eventually proved to be one of the most astute choices of his life.

PUBLISHING AFTER THE BRITISH CAMPAIGN

If Revell thought Moody maintained serious interest in Christian publishing by the early 1870s, it must have seemed like a minor flirtation compared with the passion he exuded after 1875. The British campaign of the 1870s gave Moody ideas and created circumstances that transformed Christian publishing and accelerated nonformal Christian education. He witnessed firsthand how R. C. Morgan's periodical, *The Christian,* served to advertise meetings and drum up interest. Beyond that, Morgan's printing of sermons and talks promulgated Moody's messages to audiences who could never hear him preach, and these published versions helped those who hoped to study and remember the details of what they heard.

During the same campaign, Moody and Sankey learned of the mighty demand for hymnals. Ultimately millions of the "Moody-Sankey" songbooks got into the hands of people on both sides of the Atlantic. Quite soon these hymnals were enthusiastically adopted as effective instructional tools, even if one granted the limited scope of the biblical doctrine proclaimed in the texts. Moody and Sankey encouraged Morgan to take an initial risk and publish the songbooks, because they predicted that these books would advance the kingdom. The spread of hymnbooks, after all, encouraged musical worship and understanding of the gospel.[71]

When Moody returned to America from the 1870s British campaign, he promoted the sale of hymnals, being careful that neither he nor Sankey personally profited from the sales. Moody also urged Revell to expand his list of Christian periodicals, having seen the market possibilities and instructional usefulness of such works in the United Kingdom, where no fewer than ten weeklies and numerous monthly journals covered his meetings in detail—often reproducing his entire sermons.[72]

Despite pleas from Revell and others, Moody maintained a reticence to put himself forward by allowing books of his own messages to be published. This well-intentioned attempt to be humble and refrain from all appearances of pride or profiteering was set aside by the late 1870s—and none too soon.

Once Moody became famous during the British campaign, plenty of profiteers came forward who showed no reluctance to make money from his name and words. Dozens of superficial and inaccurate biographies were published in Britain and America during and in the wake of the British campaign. Even more distressing to Moody was the tidal wave of books and pamphlets of his messages—none authorized, and most inaccurate. Brimming with understandable righteous indignation, the world-famous evangelist protested this rank piracy. He asked people not to buy the works, but they did anyway.

Authorized Moody Books

This outright theft of and profit-taking from Moody's messages became a blessing in disguise that caused him to surrender to Revell's wishes and authorize the publication of his own words. In 1876 Revell published the first of his long line of D. L. Moody works with a pamphlet, *How to Conduct an Inquiry Meeting.* This was followed up by *The Second Coming of Christ, How to Study the Bible,* and *The Way and the Word.* By 1880 these little paper-covered books were followed by a hardbound volume entitled *Twelve Select Sermons,* as well as another hardback book of sermons labeled *Heaven: Where It Is; Its Inhabitants, and How to Get There.*

Fleming Revell, within a decade of starting his business with one periodical and one book, was the only authorized publisher of the works of D. L. Moody. Because of Moody's massive popularity, Revell immediately emerged from relative obscurity to prominence, becoming the largest publisher of religious books in North America.[73]

A glimpse of Revell's list of publications between 1880 and Moody's death in 1899 makes it obvious that Mr. Moody, his popularity, his contacts, and his areas of interest set the tone of the Fleming H. Revell Company. Revell's advertising—seen in his catalogues and the advertising pages at the front or back of books—led off with a listing of "Works of D. L. Moody." Even inside a book not written by Moody, his writings were given top billing.

The Moody titles, if studied in the order of publication, provide a clear picture of Moody's own agenda and show how new topics became important to him over time. The earliest titles were all evangelism—sermons and helps in witnessing and working with new converts on a personal level. Concomitant with these were works in the late 1870s on the Bible, its importance, and how to use it—for example, *The Way and the Word* and *The Second Coming of Christ.* By 1880 there was new emphasis on *The Full Assurance of Faith,* and in 1881 the doctrine and work of the Holy Spirit emerged as a major theme, as seen in his 116-page book *Secret Power; or, The Secret of Success in Christian Life and Christian Work*. These latter subjects, both increasingly dear to Mr. Moody, were followed by his passion for ministry revealed in *To the Work! To the Work!* and prayer in *Prevailing Prayer, What Hinders It?*[74]

Dwight Moody grew excited about Christian publishing rather quickly. By 1880 more than 350,000 of his own titles had sold, and he found demands for them wherever he spoke. Hoping to flood the market with his own books, and thereby drive out pirates, he proclaimed that "many books have been published in this country in my name, but none of them with authority unless the name Revell appears as publisher." He also made perfectly clear that "the only motive inspiring" his books "is that souls may be helped."[75] In Revell's advertising, which celebrated "The Works of D. L. Moody," for several years the ads carried the notice that "all former books published in Mr. Moody's name have been mere compilations, issued without his consent and notwithstanding his protest. The following are the only AUTHORIZED PUBLICATIONS BY *D. L. MOODY*." Revell, of course, sold foreign rights to several publishers, among them Hunter Rose in Canada. He brought out many Moody titles, including *Heaven* and *The Way to God*. These sold extremely well when Moody spoke in Toronto in 1884.[76]

Recruiting Other Authors

Moody had always recruited others to join him in soul work, so it surprised no one when he began to recruit some of his most talented fellow workers to add books to the list. Besides the leading line of Moody books, Revell, who had offices at 148 and 150 Madison Street in Chicago, published a large line of books in these categories: "Helps in Bible Study," "Helps in Christian Work," "Helps for Enquirers," and "Popular Works for All Classes."

Moody assisted Revell by bringing in the authors. D. W. Whittle, for example, did a booklet, *The Use of the Bible in Inquiry Room Meetings*, and a "Helps for Enquirers" work called *Life, Warfare and Victory*. Whittle also edited a wide-selling volume entitled *The Wonders of Prayer*. This topic was dear to Moody's heart, and he urged Whittle to get out a book of true stories about answered prayer, designed to encourage people to be more purposive in prayer. *Wonders of Prayer* appeared in the "Popular Works" area, and it went through several printings and an expanded edition.[77]

MOODY'S BELIEFS AS SEEN IN HIS BOOKS

It is significant that *Wonders of Prayer,* which originally appeared in 1881, had a lead essay by D. L. Moody, entitled "A Wonderful Answer to Prayer and Proof of the Existence of the Holy Spirit." Moody's own book on the believer's need for empowerment by the Spirit, *Secret Power,* came out simultaneously. The second article in the Whittle book contained a dramatic story by Emma Dryer about two women who experienced physical healing through "The Prayer of Faith."

It is neither surprising nor coincidental that a book that Revell brought out in 1882 was written by Moody's close friend and fellow preacher, the Boston Baptist A. J. Gordon. The Gordon book that made quite a sales stir in its day was titled *The Ministry of Healing; or, Miracles of Cure in All Ages.* It went through three editions by 1885 and was in part an attempt to undercut a growing new cult—Christian Science.[78]

Moody's interest in promulgating the doctrine of the Holy Spirit is seen in his sermons, books, and exhortations to preachers like R. A. Torrey. It is also seen in the Revell line that Moody so obviously helped shape. His interest in divine healing was not as boldly proclaimed, but it is apparent that Emma Dryer was correct when she told Charles Blanchard that Moody, later in his life, came to embrace a wider view of healing grace.[79]

Divine Healing

Moody never wrote a book on divine healing, but his relationship with men who did is revealing. A. J. Gordon and Moody were extremely close and they ministered together increasingly until Gordon's death in 1895. Moody also became a friend and admirer of A. B. Simpson, author of *The Gospel of Healing* and founder of the Christian and Missionary Alliance, which stood on "Christ as Healer" for one of its four foundational pillars. D. L. Moody was also close to Andrew Murray, author of *Divine Healing.* It is difficult to imagine that a combination of Dryer's exhortations and the fellowship of these authors of classics on divine healing had little impact on Moody, given some of the evidence.

Besides giving Dryer's article a prominent place in *The Wonders of Prayer* and encouraging publication of Gordon's *The Ministry of Healing,* Moody sent a letter to a former Northfield student, Joshua Gravett, whose wife had been diagnosed with terminal tuberculosis.

Moody learned that Charlotte Gravett had been urged to go to the
dry climate of the territory of New Mexico or to seek a cure with a
German physician in New York. These options were supposedly her
only avenues of hope. On January 13, 1891, Moody sent a special delivery letter to Gravett in a response to the young man's plea for
prayer:

> My dear Gravett:
>   Got your letter yesterday, and I am sorry for you and will do all I
> can for you. Enclosed find $100 to help out. Now if your dear wife
> does not feel like taking the German medicine, why not go see A. B.
> Simpson, if she has faith, and let him annoint her as God is able to
> raise her up. We here will all be praying.
>   I know New Mexico, and you would not like it. It is so desolate,
> you would both of you be homesick, I am sure.
>   You will find Rev. Simpson near . . . 6th Ave. [in New York]. Most
> any Christian can tell you. Keep me posted.[80]

A. B. Simpson, according to his own testimony, experienced
miraculous healing of a heart ailment. He wrote *The Gospel of Healing,* and he manifested an apparent gift from God to bring people
into the healing presence of Christ. The Gravetts took Moody's advice and attended "a simple anointing service" held on a Wednesday
evening at Simpson's church. A. B. Simpson spoke on Romans 8:11,
laid hands on Charlotte Gravett, and prayed. She lived for fifty-three
more years and never again showed a trace of tuberculosis.[81]

D. W. Whittle, perhaps Moody's closest friend and fellow laborer in the Revell publishing enterprise, recorded in his diary a
conversation in the early 1890s with Moody on divine healing.
Moody said,

> I believe as much as I believe anything that God hears our prayers and
> heals the sick. The only thing is to be led by the Spirit of God in the
> cases for which we pray. The passage in James 4, says the Elders of the
> church are to pray. But where now can we find Elders who are men of
> God and of faith as it is implied in the passage? We have no such el-
> ders in our church as a body and so it seems to me we know so little
> of the Lord's healing power. My fear in praying for one dear to me
> would be that my affection and intense desire to have God heal would
> mislead me as to knowing the mind of God and that I might be mis-
> taken in thinking that I had the answer. Thousands of Christians in
> America were mistaken when they prayed for Garfield [President
> James A. Garfield who was shot by an assassin in September 1881]. It

shocked me very much at that time to hear believers say they were as certain he would not die as they were of their own salvation. We cannot dictate to God. The prayer of faith is not to make myself believe that just the very thing I ask will be done and done in just my way . . . but a trust in God's power to do what I ask and a trust in His love that if He does not do it it is because it is better not to have it done and to leave the decision with Him.[82]

Moody went on to tell Whittle that he knew that some people have a healing gift. "Dr. Cullis in Boston" had such a gift and "case after case" was healed. Moody did not believe he had such a gift, despite the time Julius J. Estey of Vermont sent for him to pray for a dying child. Moody recalled he knelt by the baby's bed and prayed, and the child recovered. But others have a gift of healing, he said, and "I have not this gift of faith."[83]

Moody did not take as strong a position as A. J. Gordon, A. B. Simpson, Andrew Murray, or Emma Dryer; and perhaps that is why he let them write on a subject that he had sympathy for but about which he felt his own faith and understanding were too limited and even tentative.

Premillennialism

Moody exhibited no such tentativeness over the doctrine of premillennialism. By the early 1880s Revell had an entire line of books under the heading "Premillennial Works." Moody himself had written an earlier pamphlet, *The Second Coming of Christ,* and he helped recruit his St. Louis pastor friend, J. H. Brookes, as well as A. J. Gordon and George Mueller, to help fill out a list of nearly a dozen titles.[84] Premillennialism, like the Holy Spirit, Bible application, personal work and evangelism, became the hallmarks of Moody's teachings, and these themes were reflected in Revell's lists as long as Moody lived.

INCREASING THE MARKET FOR BOOKS

As Moody traveled to twenty-five or thirty communities each year during the 1880s and early 1890s, he enjoyed promoting books and putting them in the hands of friends, new Christians, donors, and pastors. Always careful not to keep royalties for personal use, even when money was tight at home, he channeled the funds into buying books to give away, or he used it for scholarships for students at each of the four schools. In autumn 1886 he wrote to one of his administrative aides that "I could not afford to go [to California] last

A. P. Fitt

year. I was south and I did not get much and for six months nothing has come in."[85]

Financial squeezes neither slowed down Moody's ambition to get out the truth, nor constricted his holding resources with an open hand. He constantly gave away his own books that he faithfully paid for from his own earnings.[86]

The Scarcity of Christian Books

Several factors transpired in the early 1890s that caused Moody to make another innovation in Christian publishing. First of all, as he traveled the nation, he was increasingly convinced that Christian books were too expensive. Poor people whom he met, as well as some who wrote to him, simply could not afford the price of most Christian books, including his own. Second, as he occasionally tried to find copies of his own books in local bookstores to buy and give away, he discovered that most bookstores carried no Christian books whatsoever. Indeed, he conducted a survey of Wisconsin bookshops and learned that only one store in the state had even a limited assortment of Christian books. The book dealers reported frankly that they did not receive calls for such literature.[87]

The Expense of Christian Books

The best deals on Moody's books, and the place of easiest access, were the Montgomery Ward catalogs. Among the twenty-five or thirty pages of book offerings was a modest selection of religious books—mostly Bibles, prayer books, and hymnals. Most book space was devoted to widely read secular novelists such as William Dean Howells and Mark Twain, but a few Christian authors were featured, among them Henry Drummond, Andrew Murray, and Dwight L. Moody. Montgomery Ward and Company carried boxed sets of four hardbound volumes of Moody's works published by Revell. If you did not buy the entire set, you did not get any Moody. Each volume contained two books, so eight of Moody's books were presented in four handsomely bound volumes. The $4.00 retail price, slashed to $2.80 by Wards, still cost $3.32 with 52¢ postage. A good deal by retail standards, the price still equaled or exceeded the cost of a pair of shoes or a pair of ordinary oil lamps. To typical wage earners who made well under $700–800 a year, Moody's books were luxuries.[88]

The Competition from Other Sources

Several other factors stirred Mr. Moody to action. Beginning in spring 1893 the stock market plunged. The American economy went into a downward spiral that lasted until autumn 1896. The resultant depression caused unemployment and reduced wages, leaving money even tighter than before. So the market for books at a dollar apiece for hardbacks and thirty to forty cents for paperbacks was quite out of reach for most breadwinners. Moody discovered, however, that the so-called "dime novels"—secular fiction for adults typically set in a context of western adventure—sold quite well. They were printed on the increasingly popular, highly acidic wood-pulp paper that yellowed quickly but was cheaper than the higher quality rag-content paper than remained supple and white for decades. Published in great volume to keep unit costs low, these pocket-sized little books were sold in the bookstores and were also sold door-to-door by ambitious salespersons. Dime novel characters like Deadwood Dick and Jesse Jones were better known and more talked about than Jesus or Paul.[89]

All of these factors caused Moody to want to push his own books, as well as the books of Whittle, Gordon, and other Christian preachers and teachers, into the mass market and into the hands of poor and middle-income Americans. In short, Moody decided to vault Christian books into as great a fashion as the phenomenally successful dime novels.

When Moody returned to Northfield in June 1894, after an extensive tour of Washington, D.C., and the South, he broached the idea to several friends, including Fleming Revell. Then in October he made a trip to Chicago and tried to get Revell committed to the concept. But no one believed this dream could be profitable. After a November 1894 tour of Montreal and Toronto, where Christian books were even rarer and harder for people to afford, Moody went home to Northfield, organized the data he had been gathering, and committed the issue to prayer in the cold, snow-laden solace of the western Massachusetts hills.

MEETING WITH REVELL: THE PLAN

By January 1895 Moody had a plan. The light he received signaled full steam ahead. The only enthusiastically supportive person, besides son William and his wife, was his son-in-law A. P. Fitt. Percy, as everyone now addressed the Irishman, lived in Chicago with Emma and helped out as assistant treasurer of the Bible institute in the headquarters at Institute Place close to Revell's office on Madison Street. On Saturday, January 19, Dwight and Emma arrived in Chicago. They had little time, but Moody wanted to talk book publishing before they started a deep southern swing into Texas and Mexico.[90]

Moody possessed a powerful sense of peace and urgency about his plan, and he came armed with some remarkable statistics. Despite economic recession and high-priced books, Revell sold 3,000 books a day in November and 2,500 per day in December by mail order. One of Moody's students sold 10,000 books between September and December, going door-to-door and presumably selling to many city churches.[91] On top of that, Moody had collected data showing that most penitentiaries and jails—where he often stopped to preach—maintained very small libraries. Furthermore, Moody observed that the penal institutions that did have books had few that were in any sense Christian or even edifying. Moody had a raft of testimonies from prisoners who told him, when he asked if there was anything he could do for them, "that if they had something to read it would help kill time." At one prison Moody asked "if they would read sermons or religious books," and "they replied that they would."[92] He sent some books to that prison, and he had learned at Christmastime that the books were a big hit in the prison.[93]

Moody's evangelistic and teacher's heart throbbed. "The price [of books] must come down," he proclaimed. Christian books—at least his books—must be made available at ten cents a copy.[94] Moody, with Fitt in lockstep beside him, talked again to Revell. George Doran, who worked for Revell and would one day launch his own religious publishing house, got in on the discussion as well. To Revell, who held the rights to all of Moody's books, the challenge of printing 100,000 copies of cheap paperbacks was too risky. On purely business grounds it was not feasible; furthermore, to reprint in cheap editions books he already had in print in paper and cloth was to compete with himself. To Moody good business had nothing to do with the plan. Souls were at stake, and Fitt and Moody said the underlying issue was benevolence, not profit.[95]

A Compromise

A compromise was finally reached, but there was tension between Moody and Revell for the next few years. The arrangement was for Revell to publish a series of uniformly sized books designed to combine five features: popular style, well-known authors, undenominational content, low price, and high quality workmanship. Moody, for his part, would advertise and distribute the books. The tension came over publishing 100,000 per title, with a selling price of ten cents a copy. Revell said he needed more profit than he could make from this venture that was, to his mind, quite foolish and risky.[96]

It is tempting to see Fleming H. Revell as a faithless and ungrateful man. After all, Moody persuaded him to go into Christian publishing, and without Moody's books, friends, and promotional activities, Revell would have been nowhere. A kinder view of Revell is probably the truer one. After all, the nation was in the throes of a major depression. No one knew when it would abate. Also, Revell had been privy to some of Moody's earlier visions, and he knew from experience that Moody had enthusiasm for some schemes he could not possibly bring to fruition. Revell, for instance, was a close friend of Emma Dryer. Throughout the 1880s Revell attended a prayer group with her and Farwell, and the threesome stormed heaven for help in keeping her women's work and deaconess project alive.[97] In short, Revell heard Moody urge the creation of a Bible institute in Chicago years before he was able to put his own shoulder to the wheel. He saw Moody leave others to do the work. Finally, Fleming Revell had a wife and two children to support, and, for better or worse, he could not think in the grandiose ways of his ebullient brother-in-law.

The Bible Institute Colportage Association

Once again Dwight L. Moody's vision, enthusiasm, and ability to attract talented people paid fabulous dividends. The Northfield dynamo used the Chicago Evangelization Society and its Bible institute as his base for his cheap paperback book operations. Before leaving for Texas, he informally organized the Bible Institute Colportage Association (BICA). Not formally incorporated until October 1899, the BICA took on the full responsibility of storing, selling, and distributing the books named The Colportage Library. Moody himself was president of BICA, with Fitt as superintendent and editor. A. F. Gaylord became treasurer, and eventually William H. Norton came on the team to serve as general manager.[98]

All of this brought added responsibilities to Moody and Revell, as well as to Fitt and Gaylord, who continued in their roles as assistant treasurer and business manager, respectively, of the Bible institute. Despite their already demanding schedules, all of these men rose to the task.

The First Colportage Titles

Like Martin Luther who covered Germany with tracts, the French Reformers who sent peddlers throughout the countryside with Christian books, and John Wesley who tried to put religious pamphlets in everyone's pockets, Dwight L. Moody—with the heroic assistance of Fitt and Gaylord—inaugurated the first standardized series of Christian "pocket books" in North America.[99] The first two volumes printed were a book of Moody's previously printed sermons, *The Way to God,* and Charles Spurgeon's messages, *All of Grace,* a title Moody acquired during a trip to Great Britain. Soon eleven titles, at 100,000 copies each, were available for distribution and sale. The famous and still highly in demand D. L. Moody was the author of seven of the eleven titles. These were mostly compilations of Moody's sermons carefully edited for publication by Fitt.[100]

By the time of Moody's death in December 1899, the Bible Institute Colportage Library boasted nearly ninety titles. Although the price had been raised to fifteen cents per volume in order to give colporters a fair commission, these highly successful mass-market paperbacks were still selling for about a third of the price standard-market paperback books commanded and at a small fraction of the selling price of hardcover books.[101]

By any publishing standards of the late nineteenth century, the

Colportage Library was a great success. Soon after Moody's death nearly one and a half million books in the series had been sold. The series became one of the most inexpensive and most effective evangelistic and educational tools ever devised.

The Ministry of BICA

The Colportage books were no sideline in Moody's busy life. His correspondence from 1895 onward demonstrates utmost zeal for publishing, selling, and giving away these books. Nothing could dissuade him from the belief that these books would lead throngs of men and women to Christ and assist in the disciple-making and maturation process of millions more. Between 1895 and 1899 he wrote hundreds of letters to Fitt, Gaylord, and Norton about Colportage books. These letters reveal how Moody persuaded friends such as Nettie McCormick to donate substantial contributions to subsidize the work. Moody himself gave money, and he sent Fitt an occasional gift of $100 in gratitude for all the work he performed.[102]

Moody gave away books to people when he campaigned in Canada, Mexico, and the western parts of the United States. He also took orders for books, and he acquired lists of names of people he thought would buy books. He likewise urged the free distribution of books to some folks—rather like seeding the soil he had broken while preaching. In brief, his preaching campaigns in the 1890s took on a weighty new dimension—the sale of Colportage books to be used in follow-up evangelism and disciple-making.[103]

Mass distribution of Christian literature flowed quite naturally into everything Moody undertook. At his four schools, he recruited students to work as colporters—selling books on holidays and during the summers as a way to support themselves, earn tuition money, and serve the Lord.[104] He also urged students and Christian workers to use bookselling as a natural way to call on people, get in the door, and then find an opportunity to witness and invite them to evangelistic meetings or church. To keep the workers motivated, Mr. Moody went to the campuses and offered a $100 prize to the student who sold the most Colportage books by the next term.[105] One of Moody's workers at Northfield summed up the way the promotion of books and Moody's students were naturally interconnected. "He used to urge the students" to sell books for many reasons. "The financial returns are liberal. A broad experience, necessary to balance up against isolation of student life, is obtained in moving from town to town, and coming into touch with all conditions of men and women. And all the time one is performing the best kind of missionary work and receiving training for Christ's service such as the schools can never give."[106]

Northfield and the BICA

In order to supply students who became colporters, Moody opened a BICA depot at Northfield, where thousands of books were stored and records were kept. Out in Chicago, where all of the editing and most of the administrative work and order filling was done, large facilities were opened, and more than a dozen people worked in an office, complete with five typists and several file clerks. Overseen by the Chicago office was a fleet of horse-drawn wagons, with the following sign emblazoned on each side:

Gospel and Colportage Carriage
D. L. Moody President
From
The Bible Institute
Chicago

The BICA sent these wagons all over the metropolitan area and into adjacent rural areas, selling books, witnessing to anyone who would listen, and passing out tracts. These gospel wagoneers cried out for more workers, advertising "The Bible Institute Colportage Ass'n, Publishers of Wholesome Christian Literature . . . Men and Women Colporters Wanted."[107]

Dwight Moody found markets open everywhere, but particularly in Canada and the western parts of the United States. These parts of North America had less access to inexpensive Christian literature, and the responses were outstanding when Moody did campaigns in Winnipeg and Brandon, Manitoba, in 1897, and several locations in Ontario the same year. When he preached in Texas in 1895, and Colorado, New Mexico, Arizona, California, and Utah in 1898 and 1899, the response was excellent as well. Interest from Mexico during Moody's extended campaign in 1895 was so strong that steps were taken to translate Colportage books into Spanish.[108]

Taking Books into Prisons

Moody became increasingly interested in prison ministry during the 1890s. He always had a heart for the poor and downtrodden, making efforts to speak in rescue missions, jails, and prisons when he conducted campaigns at home and abroad. In the 1890s, however, his interest was piqued once he learned that approximately 750,000 men and women comprised a criminal class who were continually in and out of jails and prisons.

Even before the BICA was formed he was sending New Testaments and packets of printed sermons to these institutions, urging the converted inmates to read aloud from the Gospels and sermons. He eventually learned that almost every one of the nation's 2,700 counties had a jail. In the wake of this discovery, Moody sent letters to every county sheriff and asked permission to get his literature inside. "Only one," according to Will Moody, "brought a disrespectful reply." Colportage books made their way to county jail and state prison libraries by the thousands. From Moody's angle of vision, as well as from those of many a philanthropist, it was important that Bible characters rival Deadwood Dick as household names and heroes.[109]

Using Books in Campaigns

The advent of Colportage books transformed the soul ministry that went on during Moody campaigns and the campaigns of men like D. W. Whittle and J. Wilbur Chapman. Inexpensive books were now on tables in the back of meeting halls. A donation was requested, but books were free to those who could not spare a dime. In the inquiry rooms, workers gave out books once they had discerned which type of work would be most useful. Pastors who participated in these union meetings purchased books too, using them to follow up with campaign converts, or simply using them with new and growing Christians in their congregations who were eager to learn. By the end of the century, there was abundant evidence to show that these Colportage books—in particular Moody's evangelistic sermons—had led countless souls from despair into productive lives as disciples of Christ.[110]

By the onset of the twentieth century, both regular Revell imprints and the less lucrative Colportage books had sold several million copies. Fleming H. Revell watched several of his imprints become top sellers in the 1880s and 1890s. To qualify as an official "best-seller" in those years, a book needed to sell a minimum of a half million copies in a single year. Hannah Whitall Smith's *The Christian's Secret of a Happy Life* became a top best-seller in 1883, twelve years before the advent of the Colportage Library. And in 1898 Ralph Connor's *Black Rock*, a novel, reached that sought-after list of towering favorites. Books by Moody were always big sellers— both as Colportage volumes or in hardcover or boxed sets as part of the standard Revell line—although no single work sold the magical 500,000 in any single year.[111]

D. L. Moody could have become a rich man, but he refused. Instead he invested his royalties into students' lives and the care of souls. Fleming H. Revell, sometimes reluctantly, allowed his brother-in-law to push him in new directions. As a result Revell became an extremely wealthy man whose company, before his death, had headquarters in New York with branch offices in Chicago, Toronto, London, and Edinburgh. Revell became a wise investor whose capital mounted, especially after he invested in the New York Life Insurance Company and became one of its directors. Living until 1931, Revell turned the management of Fleming H. Revell Company over to his son, F. H. Revell, Jr. Throughout his life Revell, Sr., served as a trustee of Moody's beloved schools in Northfield, and he served as a trustee of Wheaton College, the Christian college headed by his dear friend Charles Blanchard. He was known until his death as a philanthropist of the Farwell and Wanamaker stripe.[112]

To the credit of both Moody and Revell, they never had a falling out, despite some years of marked stress over the "competition," as Revell saw it, between BICA and Fleming H. Revell Company. George Doran helped keep them in a state of armistice, if not total peace. A. P. Fitt should be credited for resisting, until the year of Moody's death, the temptation and pressure to form a truly separate and competing company. But in 1899, the Colportage Association did declare its independence. Then in 1941, Moody Press was established, keeping the Colportage library but changing its name.[113]

MOODY'S INTEREST IN CONFERENCES

Most men would have been satisfied with preaching all over the world, having their books sell hundreds of thousands annually, and being the founder and spiritual leader of four schools that were equipping and sending Christian workers all over the world. But not Dwight L. Moody. It was said by a friend of Abraham Lincoln that Lincoln's "ambition was a little engine that knew no rest." In a sense, this was also true of Mr. Moody. After he surrendered his life to Christ, he began going after souls with an intensity that knew no bounds. In those early years after he gave up business to devote his full time to evangelism, he made it a point to witness to someone every day—never going to bed until he inquired of someone about his or her eternal destiny. This was ambition for souls, and it knew no rest.

As the years passed, especially after his profound experience with the Holy Spirit in New York in the early 1870s, Moody changed ministry methods. No longer did he grab the unsuspecting man and inquire about the condition of his soul. It was not that Moody had become indifferent, like so many Christians a few years after their conversion. No, he had merely decided to listen to the Holy Ghost and ask Him to point to the souls He had prepared for the message.[114]

Listening for direction to the ripe harvest field, rather than entering a field and asking God to ripen it, was a subtle but profound change in Moody's approach. One can debate his biblical strategy of fulfilling the Great Commission, but no one can deny the fruitfulness of Moody's new approach.

Throughout most of his life, from the days of his youth forward, Moody was a driven man—an ambitious man. The Holy Spirit seems to have harnessed and directed his personality rather than wrought a complete change in him. Moody zealously went forward into new fields, ones that widened from Sunday school work to mass evangelism, and on to purposeful personal work, the education of workers, and then to publishing materials to enrich these undertakings.

The Christian Conference Movement

One more field beckoned Moody before he could rest. Still part of his nonformal educational program, it was his own unique contribution to the Christian conference movement. Moody's keen interest in Christian conferences dated back to the early 1870s when he attended Pennefather's Mildmay conferences. While in England Moody also learned about the influence of the annual Keswick conferences in the western English Lake District, spearheaded by Evan Hopkins. Christians were healed, nurtured, and motivated at both places.

Back in the Unites States, Moody pondered and prayed, but he felt no leading to follow the steps of either Pennefather or Hopkins. If God wanted him to do something, it had to be a new thing. There were already conferences in the United States, the most popular being those at Niagara Falls and Clifton Springs, both in the religiously famous "Burned-Over District" of western New York. But these conference grounds were used rather eclectically, hosting everything from women's rights gatherings to Methodist holiness meetings.

What A. T. Pierson described as "the greatest sphere of Moody the educator"—his Northfield conferences—originated during a campaign in Cleveland, Ohio, in the fall of 1879. It was one of those inexpressible times when the Holy Spirit brings an illumination that only a person who has been graced by a similar experience can understand. Such a movement came to Moody when H. B. Hartzler, an Ohio minister, was speaking at a workers' meeting on "Prayer for the Church." Hartzler stressed "the absolute necessity of the power of the Holy Spirit in order to succeed" in ministry. While Hartzler was speaking, Moody sat attentively in the front row with his head bowed. "Suddenly," according to Hartzler, "he lifted his head, flashed a glance at me, as tho struck with a bolt, and then resumed his former position." After the meeting Moody rushed up to Hartzler, grabbed him by the arm, and pulled him into the pastor's study. With his usual abruptness he said, "I want you to come to Northfield next summer. Will you? I want to have a meeting to wait on God. I want you."[115]

The Announcement of Moody's Conference

Hartzler made no promises, and Moody did not write to him for several months. Then in early August a letter arrived from Moody, imploring Hartzler to come to Northfield for a conference from September 1 to 10, 1880. "I want you above any other man in this nation and I will pay all bills if you will come: Do not say me nay but come and let us wait on God together. . . . Enclosed you will find a circular that will explain itself."[116]

Moody sent the circular to hundreds of men and women, but it did not get mailed and posted until early August, making it difficult for many to change their schedules and get away to Northfield.

Despite the tardiness of the invitation, D. L. Moody's personal appeal to people to come and pray "for a new enduement of power from on high" resulted in more than three hundred men and women (not counting hundreds of local area people who did not sleep over) attending this first of a long line of Northfield conferences that became, to many people's way of thinking, the most effective educational enterprise launched by Moody.[117]

When the inveterate educator called the 1880 conference, he harbored no plan to inaugurate a new conference movement. Instead, he was responding to the nudge he had received from the Holy Spirit the previous November, plus confirmation that came from the Blaikies of Edinburgh, Scotland, who visited Northfield in spring 1880. Fellowship with Hartzler and Dr. William Blaikie finally helped convince Moody that a conference for Christian workers was needed for two reasons—to wait upon the Holy Spirit and to explore together the biblical doctrine of the third person of the Trinity.[118]

The 1880 meeting did, albeit slowly, lead to a unique confer-

A CALL TO BELIEVERS.

BY DWIGHT L. MOODY.

A Convocation for Prayer, and to wait upon the Lord for a new enduement of power from on high, at Northfield, Massachusetts, from September 1 to 10, 1880.

Grateful as all Christians should be, and are, for the revival of interest in the study of God's word,—manifest in many quarters,—and for the increase of personal and consecrated activity on the part of multitudes of laymen and women, there yet remains a profound sense of a still deeper need among us, namely, a fresh enduement of power from on high.

Without the presence of the Holy Spirit,—whose mission it is to convince, convict and convert men, by giving power to the preached word and sanctifying and making potent personal effort for the salvation of men,—the gospel of the blessed God itself may become, in a measure, a dead letter, and all Christian effort nothing more than the energy of the flesh.

It is Christ's presence in the gospel, by the Spirit, that makes it a living seed, and energizes it in the hearts and consciences of those who read and hear it. We may preach and teach the word, but he only can open the hearts of men to receive it; he only can make the word "quick and powerful"—living and full of energy; and it is his presence only in and upon believers which can enable them to do those "mighty works" which he promised they should do when he went away.

Therefore it was at his command that they tarried at Jerusalem, until they were endued with power from on high by the coming of the Holy Spirit; not *in* them as a living presence (for that they had), but *upon* them as an annointing power; so that when they preached and testified the gospel, it was, as Paul said of his preaching, "not in word only, but also in power, and in the Holy Ghost, and in much assurance" (1 Thess. 1:5). And therefore "they had favor with all the people, and the Lord added unto the church daily."

It is not only more knowledge and personal activity that we need in the ministry and among the laity, but the presence upon us and with us of the Holy Ghost. For he only can take the things of Christ and show them to us and by us to the world. It is, also, only by his presence in us and upon us, sanctifying our lives, that "we commend ourselves to every man's conscience in the sight of God," as living examples and illustrations of the saving and transforming power of the gospel.

Are we not at ease in Zion? Has not the church, both in the ministry and laity, lost that communion with God which is the condition of power with men? Are we not substituting outward appliances for inward life? In vain do we take the ark to battle unless the Lord himself go up with us. In vain is our learning and all our multiplied machinery if the Spirit of God is not present in power in the church.

Are we not too much engaged with questions of "mint and anise and cummin," when we should be on our faces mourning over our spiritual poverty, and seeking new power from God with which to do our Master's work among men?

Feeling deeply this great need, and believing that it is in reserve for all who honestly seek it, a gathering is hereby called to meet in Northfield, Massachusetts, from September 1 to 10, inclusive, the object of which is not so much to study the Bible (though the Scriptures will be searched daily for instruction and promises) as for solemn self-consecration, and to plead God's promises, and to wait upon him for a fresh anointing of power from on high.

Not a few of God's chosen servants from our own land and from over the sea will be present to join with us in prayer and council.

All ministers and laymen, and those women who are fellow-helpers and laborers together with us in the kingdom and patience of our Lord Jesus Christ—and, indeed, all Christians who are hungering for intimate fellowship with God, and for power to do his work,—are most cordially invited to assemble with us. Accommodations will be provided for all who may come. The expense of entertainment will in no case exceed one dollar per day. It is desirable that those who purpose meeting with us should send their names in not later than August 20, to insure accommodation.

It is to be hoped that those Christians whose hearts are united with us in desire for this new enduement of power, but who cannot be present in the body, will send us salutation and greeting by letter, that there may be concert of prayer with them throughout the land during these days of waiting.

Notice of intention to be present, and all letters of inquiry and fellowship, should be addressed to D. L. Moody, Northfield, Mass.

In accordance with the above call, there will be a

UNION MEETING IN THE BROADWAY TABERNACLE

Every Afternoon at 3 o'clock,

From Sept. 1st to Sept. 10th, inclusive.

Also, on WEDNESDAY AND THURSDAY EVENINGS, Sept. 1st and 2d, at 8 o'clock, at which times announcements of further Evening Meetings will be made.

All who are in sympathy with the call are cordially invited to attend these meetings.

"Press" Print, Paterson, N. J.

ence tradition that lasted many years after Moody's death. It would be misleading to ignore the impact of Keswick and Mildmay on Moody's thinking, but he never attempted to imitate either program. In fact, both Mildmay and Keswick stressed holiness and sanctification in ways that were too doctrinaire for Moody, and Keswick, in particular, was too rigidly structured for his taste.[119]

THE 1880 CONFERENCE–AND BEYOND

The Northfield conferences were not only unique, but they were also incalculably influential. Hartzler was amazed at the 1880 gathering. Workers from nearly every state, Mexico, Canada, and the United Kingdom were there. Even a wide array of furloughing missionaries from Africa, Asia, Greece, and other far-flung outposts made the pilgrimage to Northfield that fall. It was "like the Jerusalem Pentecost," the bishop declared; "there were present devout men of every nation under heaven." He said, "Pastors and evangelists, professors and editors, elders and deacons, devout women and earnest youth" gathered "in one accord, in one place" to meet and hear from the Holy Spirit. Perhaps three thousand letters and telegrams poured into Northfield from people who could not come, but who promised to pray for God's blessing on the gathering, and in return sought prayer for their own anointing.[120]

Much of the meeting was devoted to prayer. As described by one attendee, "From beginning to end it was a period of heart-searching, of consecration, and of humble supplication for an out-pouring of the Holy Spirit."[121] Moody occasionally tapped someone on the shoulder to go to the front and speak on the Holy Ghost—either testifying, presenting a devotional talk, or presenting a slice of biblical doctrine on the subject. Moody himself spoke little during the ten days, but he functioned as chairman and leader. Eventually the crowd begged him to speak on this topic so dear to his heart, and he finally obliged with several messages on God the Spirit.[122] The essence of these talks was published by Fleming H. Revell the next spring in *Secret Power*.

The thesis of Moody's talks and book was simple. The church lacked the power to change lives because it leaned too much on elements besides prayer, the Word, and the Holy Spirit. The late-nineteenth-century church, he argued, is like an army being defeated because it refuses to use its weapons. The church did not need new buildings, new organs, new choirs, or new measures. "That is not what the Church of God needs today. It is the old power that the

Apostles had." Moody insisted that the Holy Spirit will transform the ministers and enable them to use the "sword of the Spirit"—the Bible. "If a man is not filled with the Spirit, he will never know how to use the Book."[123] Moody stressed that Spirit-filled men preach the Word, not themselves, and that such workers must be continually filled with power from on high, rather than rely on any single experience from the past. "The fact is, we are leaky vessels, and we have to keep right under the fountain all the time to keep full of Christ, and so have fresh supply." Moody likened the Spirit-filled worker to an irrigated field in California's Sacramento Valley. The irrigated field is green and it stands in stark contrast to the non-irrigated field where the soil is dry, the vegetation is brown and dry, and no fruit will come forth.[124]

Moody stressed that all disciples—not just preachers and missionaries—need this grace, and it is freely offered to them. He continually stressed Jesus' promise of the Spirit in John 14, 15, and 16 as a promise to the church from the first century onward. Only the Comforter, Counselor, and Teacher—the Spirit—will give us wisdom, discernment, and power to do work that has eternal consequences. Work relying on anything but Him will ultimately be fruitless.[125]

Teaching on the Holy Spirit

Throughout Moody's lifetime the doctrine of the third person of the Trinity—with emphasis on His personhood and power for ministry—was stressed at every major conference held on Northfield soil. As Moody's friend and conference participant, T. J. Shanks, put it,

> Much of the attention of the convocation is always turned to the nature and offices of the Holy Spirit, His relation to preaching as a vital factor in its influence, and the importance of seeking His aid in abundant measure. All are led to engage in prayer for a special anointing of power for service, and on many sacred occasions earnest pleading has been answered by most awful and blessed visitations of the Holy Ghost. No one who has passed through such an experience will ever forget it.

Shanks, a New Yorker, knew firsthand that "to many the Massachusetts hill has become a very Mount of Transfiguration, and they have gone down into the world with faces glowing and with hearts burning in new-born devotion to their Savior-King."[126]

Hartzler called the 1880 conference a Jerusalem-like Pentecostal experience, and other people made similar comments about later meetings. A. T. Pierson went first in 1885, and he wrote that "the power of God pervaded the assembly from first to last. At times His presence seemed almost visible. Mr. Moody," Pierson continued, "rang out the motto: 'My soul wait thou only upon God for my expectation is from Him,' and from that moment all eyes seemed turned upward in expectation."

Pierson and others were deeply affected, and they especially sat in amazement over the absence of prearranged programs. "Think of it! no program—yet hundreds of believers hanging with deep interest on the lips of speakers." Pierson, a highly educated man with degrees from Hamilton College (1857) and Union Theological Seminary (1860), was Brooklyn born and raised. He marveled that Moody "simply looked to God from day to day for guidance and called on such speakers as he felt led to select." Moody himself acknowledged after the 1885 conference: "I have attended hundreds of conventions but never one like this for power." Pierson testified that "the Spirit's presence was felt in prayer, in song, in speaking, in hearing; not a break nor a blunder nor an inharmonious note nor an infelicitous speech."[127]

A. A. Bonar had a similar experience at Northfield in 1881, and this was at the one conference with rather more planning behind it. Bonar did prearranged Bible teaching, which he did with aplomb. But Bonar himself was powerfully affected. He later quoted Jeremiah 33:3 and celebrated the fact that God "has shown me great things which I knew not." F. B. Meyer, another Englishman, attended four successive Northfield conferences in the early 1890s, and he enthusiastically proclaimed that the emphasis on "the necessity of receiving the enduement of the Holy Spirit of Pentecost . . . caught up with great aridity, and from [Northfield] ministers, who had attended in large numbers, went to all parts of the States as those who had themselves passed through a baptism of fire."[128] This effect was precisely what Moody hoped and prayed for—workers freshly anointed to return to their places of ministry to pass on the good news to others.

Moody and the Conference Speakers

Moody had some other goals for these summer conferences, not the least of them being a time to further his own education. Whether Moody traveled through North America, to Mexico, or to Great Britain, he kept his ears open for men who spoke with anointing and

insight. He then urged the gifted ones to attend a Northfield conference. Of course he wanted many people to hear and learn from men
such as G. Campbell Morgan, F. B. Meyer, A. A. Bonar, Henry Drummond, George Adam Smith, A. J. Gordon, W. J. Erdman, R. C.
Morgan, George C. Needham, J. E. K. Studd, Hudson Taylor, and
dozens of others, but Moody also sat at the feet of these giants and
took copious notes to enrich his own sermons. To Moody, the Northfield conferences were times of first-rate education and spiritual
refreshment.

Besides spreading the good news of the Holy Spirit and fur-
thering the education of himself and others, Moody saw the summer
conferences as ideal times to promote and disseminate important
Christian books. He always had ample supplies of Fleming Revell's
books on hand, and after 1894 Colportage volumes were in equally
large supply. Mr. Moody pushed all of these works the same way he
had sold shoes a quarter century earlier. He also got many of his

D. L. Moody (circa 1890)

British speakers' books in print in America, being particularly helpful to British friends like F. B. Meyer, Henry Drummond, and A. A.
Bonar. And although C. H. Spurgeon and Andrew Murray were already widely read in America, Moody did what he could to make
them even better known.

Moody also saw the summer conferences as an avenue to
spread the knowledge of the three Northfield schools. He always impressed upon his visitors that "the schools are theirs as much as his";
therefore, they should tour the campuses, urge needy students to attend, and then consider supporting these institution that, after all,
belong to "the Christian public at large."[129]

COLLEGE STUDENT CONFERENCES

Finally, Mr. Moody used the summer conferences to achieve a
task that was an ever-increasing fire in his soul—the encouragement
of young people to become full-time Christian workers. "One of his
favorite principles," according to an associate, "is that it is far better
to set others to work than to try to do all the work oneself."[130]

This concern led Moody to call the first of many conferences for
college-age students at Northfield for July 7–31, 1886. Actually,
Moody planned to issue a call to college-age YMCA workers who
hoped to launch a major outreach to colleges. While preaching in
Georgia the previous April, Moody had met a Princeton student,
Robert P. Wilder, and urged him to help get all the college YMCA secretaries to the Mount Hermon campus for a time of encouragement,
inspiration, education, and renewed commitment. Wilder listened to
Moody, but he had a different idea. He told Moody that YMCA secretaries were sufficiently plied with conferences, but "an assembly of
college students" in general would meet a great need. Moody felt certain that Wilder's words were inspired. Immediately the young man
and the veteran preacher pooled their contacts and resources. It was
already April, but by July 7 they managed to attract more than 240 students, who descended upon the boys' school campus.[131]

The Students Who Came

This "College Students' Summer School" was enthusiastically
celebrated for its ethnic diversity and international flavor. In attendance were sons of missionaries who were intimately familiar with
China, India, and Persia; and there were "seven young men of divers
nationalities—an Armenian, a Japanese, a Siamese, a Norwegian, a
Dane, a German, and an American Indian."[132]

It is to Mr. Moody's credit that he let the young men (it was a conference for men only in 1886) shape much of the agenda. Moody liked to manage things his own way, to be sure, but he had infinite confidence in young people. He trusted their instincts and applauded their visions, particularly if they were serious Christians.

The first days began with Bible study led by Moody, followed by lunch and quiet time. Afternoons were given to sports and recreation, with everything punctuated by ample time for student interaction. The college men were especially stimulated by question-and-answer sessions offered by Moody each morning and evening. Moody also urged time for prayer "for a larger measure of the Holy Spirit." An attendee noted that after a few days, prayers were "most signally" answered. "The 'power from on high' fell in strange abundance. A peculiar tenderness of feeling and hallowed joy prevailed during the closing days." From then on Moody let the Spirit lead the men. The questions and focus began to shift, and "the most prominent outward expression of this experience [with the Holy Spirit] was a spontaneous convergence of attention upon foreign missions."[133]

By the time the benediction was pronounced on July 31, almost one hundred young men made commitments to overseas missionary work. There was also a shout of "Tell others the story!" Consequently two men were tapped, Robert P. Wilder and John N. Forman, both Princetonians, to spread the word to every college and seminary in Canada and the United States that the second "College Students' Summer School" would be held at Northfield June 30–July 12, 1887. Equally significant was the call to spread the word about a new organization formed at Northfield during the last days of the conference. When Dr. A. T. Pierson delivered what everyone agreed was "a thrilling address on missions," and urged that "all should go and go to all," he set even more men to praying about missions. His sermon became the impetus behind the Student Volunteer Movement, which raised as a banner these words from his lecture: "The evangelization of the world in this generation."[134]

Moody, nearly fifty years old by the time of this student conference, exuded as much enthusiasm and hope as the most zealous of the college men. He enthusiastically applauded both the organization that became the Student Volunteer Movement and the call for a meeting at Northfield in 1887. He promised to move the conference site to the seminary, inasmuch as it would accommodate more people, including women. He also promised to go after Henry Drummond to be one of the main speakers because the brilliant, magnetic Scotsman was the most effective communicator with college-age people that Moody knew.

Inasmuch as Moody had made a large sacrifice to go to Great Britain and Ireland twice between 1881 and 1884 at the insistence of clergy in those countries, he had some goodwill to cash in on over there. Through mail and telegraph Moody implored Drummond and several others to come. It was their turn to cross the Atlantic and bless North America. Drummond agreed.

Several people attended from England, including two Cambridge University students, and one man came representing the Emerald Isle. Fifteen Canadians registered, among them twelve college students from eight different institutions. American students filled most of the dormitories and tents that dotted the hillsides, coming from almost every Ivy League school, numerous liberal arts colleges, as well as universities and seminaries located in twenty-two states. In all, approximately 450 students came, including a scattered contingent of pastors, YMCA workers, and interested lay men and women. The YMCA general secretary for Scotland, William M. Oattes of Glasgow, came with his lay-leader wife. Mrs. William Oattes, the daughter of Glasgow's A. A. Bonar, led some well-received special sessions for women.[135]

Despite some venomous criticism of Moody for inviting Henry Drummond, who was writing about theistic evolution, the second students' conference was a phenomenal success. Besides the 450 or more registered boarding guests, anywhere from 1,000 to 1,500 more people from surrounding areas arrived on foot, horse, or in horse-drawn vehicles. Some folks came to hear the "heretic" Drummond, but the biggest local turnouts came when Moody, an honored prophet, spoke in a tent just a few hundred yards from his birthplace. One man recalled that he and two other students walked all the way from New Haven, Connecticut. D. L. Moody wrote to his daughter with the news that "72 colleges" were represented "and it was by far the most remarkable meeting ever held in Northfield."[136]

No one can calculate the worldwide effects of these meetings. Throughout the late 1880s and the 1890s, students gathered annually to "wait upon the Holy Spirit" and seek His will about missions. A. T. Robertson, a professor at Southern Baptist Theological Seminary, was in attendance during the summer of 1889. He reported that "hundreds" of young people, "tired and weary of college life, responded to Mr. Moody's call to meet him for twelve days at Northfield, Mass. What a compliment that so many" of the best young people of the world's "various schools should come gladly to his home among the hills! And they went joyfully, too." He said they came from all over the world, among them Scots, Irish, English, and Japanese, the latter "nimble . . . fellows with keen intellects [who] excited a great deal of interest in themselves and their country."

Robertson noted that no one was required to go to any of the sessions; therefore, "there is a beautiful spirit of abandon about everything. You don't know who will speak, since Mr. Moody so dislikes a set programme. Most of the lectures were worth hearing" and well attended, but "no one was so eagerly listened to as Moody himself." The Baptist professor was quite pleased that "the Students' Volunteer Movement for Foreign Missions had frequent meetings on the hill in the twilight, where much zeal was manifested, and many determinations reached to enter the missionary work." His colleague L. O. Dawson was thrilled to report that "few can realize the hold . . . the missionary spirit . . . has taken, and is taking, upon the young men of our colleges."[137]

Northfield as Conference Center

Thus Northfield, Massachusetts, had a well-deserved reputation as a conference center by the early 1890s. Starting with that first conference in 1880, a General Conference for Christian Workers took place every year except 1882 and 1883, when the Moodys were in Great Britain. Student conferences continued to meet yearly after 1886, and beginning in 1893 a women's conference was added to the menu. This rich educational and inspirational fare was enhanced still more in 1896, when Camp Northfield for Men became a regular selection on the summer agenda.[138]

By the 1890s Northfield, Massachusetts, had become an important year-round training center. Christians from all over the world, whose ages ranged from the teens to the seventies, found a wide range of formal and nonformal educational offerings to equip them for God's call on their lives. Several thousand men and women passed through the once quiet mountain village every year, and then they went forth with hopes and dreams to transform their world.

The extent to which these people affected souls, churches, and cultures cannot be measured, but one thing is certain. During D. L. Moody's lifetime, and for a season thereafter, those who tarried in Northfield were exposed to a rich view of the Holy Spirit and the urgency of the Great Commission. In Moody's words they were likewise exposed to the integral themes of "Christian unity, and the invitation is to all denominations and to all wings of denominations; but it is understood that along with the idea of Christian unity goes the Bible as it stands."[139]

If a complete assessment of the impact of Mr. Moody's Northfield programs cannot be made, an illustration reveals the significance of one piece of his educational enterprise. In 1911, on the twenty-fifth anniversary of the genesis of the Student Volunteer Movement for Foreign Missions, a celebratory convocation was held back at the Mount Hermon campus where it all began. SVMFM by then had spread to Europe and South Africa. During that silver jubilee, it was documented that five thousand student volunteers from America alone had become missionaries in foreign lands under the direction of a wide range of denominational boards and independent societies.[140] By any standard of measurement, Mr. Moody's vision had set in motion rivers that were irrigating many parched lands.

CHAPTER TWELVE

FINISHING WELL

D. L. Moody's Last Half-Decade

1895–1899

"God Is Calling Me; I Must Go."

The autumn of life brought Dwight Moody much joy. He was busy, as always, but this was his choice. He loved his work. Traveling, preaching, teaching, counseling, selling books, promoting four schools, and organizing summer conferences, Mr. Moody exuded boundless energy. Added to these pleasures, Mrs. Moody traveled with him much more of the time—freeing the inveterate traveler from the inner emptiness that comes with separation from the one you most dearly love. With enthusiasm and thanksgiving Moody wrote to A. F. Gaylord during an 1897 trip that he was being blessed in the work. In the same letter he expressed wonder that at age sixty, "I preached the same as I did twenty years ago."[1]

Still, Moody always longed to get home. "I am thinking next Wednesday morning I will look out on dear old Northfield," he wrote from St. Louis in spring 1897, "and will take a walk about and see things. I am just longing to see you all and to sniff the fresh morning air. It is a great joy to think that in so short a time I am to be free once again."[2] He also longingly exclaimed to an associate, "I will get to my home a little after 8 o'clock & will get my breakfast there in my home."[3]

To Moody, home in the summer was glorious and renewing. For him this meant rising at 5:00 A.M., followed by prayer and Bible study, and then going out and about the farm and schools. Breakfast was enjoyed by the whole family, including guests, and then they had a time of family prayers, with visitors invited to join in. Because Mr. Moody liked company, Paul remembered, "the house would be full.

Too full, I often thought as I surrendered successively one room after another to guests who were not always too fascinating to my
boyish fancy. . . ." The mid-mornings were filled with meetings or answering mail, and the big meal—dinner—"was in the middle of the
day." Moody believed it wasted precious time to linger over supper
because it "interfered with watching the sunset over his favorite hills,
and he would have moved the supper hour back to an indecently
early hour had it not been for my mother's protests."[4]

Either in the afternoon before supper, or in the summer twilight
after the evening meal, Mr. Moody often courted Emma as he had
done more than thirty years before in Chicago. The couple slipped
away from the house and guests; climbed into D. L.'s favorite, sturdy
black buggy; signaled Nellie Gray with the reins; and stole "away on
one of their beloved drives." The Moodys found time for frequent outings, especially leisurely walks through "Lover's Retreat." As a result
Dwight and Emma kept romance and freshness in their relationship.[5]

Paul Moody wrote with gratitude for a home that "seemed so ideal." He gave most credit to his mother, realizing that his father would
have agreed it was primarily her doing. Indeed, Mr. Moody's "admiration for her was as boundless as his love," and he "never ceased to
wonder" at her love for him. "My mother had seen in him in his raw
youth what others came to see, and her confidence in him and her
willingness to share his highly uncertain future gave him courage."[6]

THE MOODY CHILDREN'S MARRIAGES AND FAMILIES

Rich joy and satisfaction came to the Moodys during their latter years because of the marriages of the two oldest children. Emma's
May 10, 1894, wedding to A. P. Fitt pleased Mr. and Mrs. Moody
enormously. D. L. had "discovered" Fitt in Ireland in 1892 and knew
from the outset he was a dedicated Christian with splendid promise
for usefulness in the world of Christian work. Mrs. Moody wrote to
Emma soon after the wedding that she was "thankful . . . that you
have such a good, kind husband."[7] Fitt brought grace to the family,
plus diligence and good sense to the Bible institute and Colportage
ministry. No doubt the opening of an Eastern depot of the Colportage Association was, in part, Mr. Moody's scheme to get his
daughter and son-in-law back to Massachusetts in 1895.

William Revell Moody married an equally ideal mate, from the
vantage point of his parents. Mary Whittle, the daughter of Major
and Mrs. D. W. Whittle, became Will's wife on August 29, 1894. Besides being bright, attractive, and deeply committed to Christ and her

husband, Mary (some people called her May) encouraged an even closer bond between the Moody and Whittle families. By the 1880s D. W. Whittle had become one of Moody's intimate friends. Will had done more than find a superb wife; he helped assure frequent inter-family gatherings. To everyone's delight, Will and Mary lived nearby at Mount Hermon, and Will worked full-time with his father.

The grandchildren who quickly came from these unions brought more joy to Mr. Moody than most of the other delights of the 1890s. Irene was born to William and Mary on August 20, 1895, and Dwight (named for his grandfather), came two years later on November 7, 1897. The William Moody family enlarged their household again on November 11, 1899, when little Mary came into the family. The Fitts also were blessed with a child in these years, when Emma Fitt (named for her grandmother) was born December 16, 1895.

GRANDPA DWIGHT

Dwight Moody reveled in grandparenting. On the August morning of Irene Moody's birth, early risers among conferees saw Moody in his buggy, hailing everyone he saw: "Do you know I have a grand-daughter? I am taking a present over to her." Of course Irene could not even sample the basketful of donuts he carried for her, but the loving gesture became a celebrated piece of family lore, as did grandfather's second trip later that day. On this errand he still boomed the news to every friend and stranger, but his offering for Irene this time was a massive cauliflower, the largest his garden produced.[8]

Moody manifested enthusiasm for his grandchildren in numerous ways; most particularly charming are his letters to the little ones. When Emma Fitt was only a month old, Grandfather Moody wrote her this letter:

> This is my first letter to my dear little grandchild. I wanted to get a letter to you before your first tooth. Hurry up and get them all before the hot weather comes on, for I will get some candy, and you want teeth to eat it. I want you to hurry up and grow, so I can come early mornings and take you out riding when your father and mother are fast asleep. We will slip off over the river to see Irene, and have some good times.[9]

Just before Emma Fitt's first birthday her grandfather sent another endearing letter, treasured by the family over the years:

In six days you will be one year old, and your grandmother will make you a cake, and have it all frosted over with white sugar. . . . It will be one year ago Tuesday night I was sitting up for your grandmother, and when it got past midnight I thought I would go and see why she did not come home, and I heard you cry for the first time. The tears of joy came to my eyes, and I have thought a great deal of you ever since. Soon after my mother died, and you seemed to come to take her place, and you have been a dear, good little girl. . . .

I am going to steal up to your home next summer and take you out riding before your parents get up. Only think, of some fine June morning, we can go up Lovers' Retreat. The birds will sing you a beautiful song. What times we will have together! I get real homesick thinking about it. . . .

And now, my dear Emma, I am praying for you that the Lord will watch over you day and night, and keep you from all harm. You will never know how much your grandfather loves you. I shall be glad to get you in my arms again.[10]

A family friend observed that Mr. Moody "has learned to perfection the art of being a grandfather. I saw him one morning driving

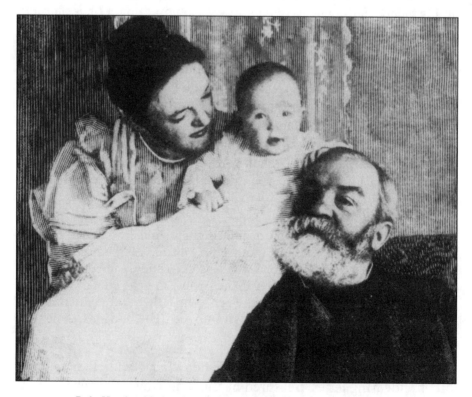

D. L. Moody with daughter Emma and granddaughter Irene in 1896

with his little four-year-old granddaughter [Irene] into the yard of his house. The child had gone to sleep in the buggy, leaning against him. Rather than disturb her, he had the horse gently unharnessed and taken away, while they sat on. Presently he, too, was overcome with sleep."[11]

MOODY'S LIFE AND FRIENDSHIPS

On one level, Moody lived a charmed life by the late 1890s. The schools were doing well with ever-expanding facilities and student bodies. Moody's books, as well as those of others published for the Colportage Association and Revell's regular lists, were selling extremely well, despite the effects of the depression of the 1890s.

Moody's circle of good friends widened ever larger, and the list of those whom he persuaded to speak at the schools and the summer conferences looks like a lineup of "Who's Who" in late-nineteenth century British and American Christianity. Among the speakers were Lyman Abbott, William Blaikie, Charles Blanchard, A. A. Bonar, John Broadus, Phillips Brooks, S. P. Cadman, Lewis Sperry Chafer, Jacob Chamberlain, J. Wilbur Chapman, Henry Sloane Coffin, Russell Conwell, Henry Drummond, William Erdman, Washington Gladden, A. J. Gordon, James M. Gray, Evelyn Hall, William Rainey Harper, O. O. Howard, Alexander MacKenzie, John McNeil, F. B. Meyer, G. Campbell Morgan, R. C. Morgan, John Mott, L. W. Munhall, Andrew Murray, George C. Needham, Francis L. Patton, George Pentecost, A. T. Pierson, Margaret Sangster, Ira Sankey, C. I. Scofield, George Adam Smith, Robert E. Speer, James Stalker, George Stebbins, Josiah Strong, C. T. Studd, J. Hudson Taylor, R. A. Torrey, L. D. Townsend, Henry Clay Trumbull, Henry Van Dyke, Booker T. Washington, Henry Watson, H. W. Webb-Peploe, and D. W. Whittle.

These made pilgrimages to Northfield, Massachusetts, because they loved and admired D. L. Moody. Through years of campaigning in Canada, Mexico, Britain, Ireland, and the United States, the jovial preacher of God's redeeming love and Christian unity had made numerous friends, and he had been instrumental in encouraging, teaching, and moving them to higher ground. Without question, Mr. Moody stood out as the foremost figure in late nineteenth-century evangelicalism. No other Protestant leader had so many friends, from so many places, representing nearly every denomination, from the most primitive Brethren to the highest church Anglicans. With gratitude he returned the friendship and esteem of a diverse body of fellow preachers, ministers, missionaries, and educators.

MOODY'S PROTÉGÉS

By the sunset decade of the century, Moody savored still another blessing—watching the successes of those he had singled out, mentored, and encouraged to serve the Master in full-time ministry. Few people could celebrate such good fortune as befell Moody. He saw many Timothys excel in the Lord's work. First and foremost, all three of the Moody children were safely in the fold and glorifying God in their individual spheres of influence. Paul was at Yale—a spiritual leader and his class deacon. William was working alongside his father, and Emma was a helpmate to another disciple, Percy Fitt, who was performing a herculean task as administrator for the Bible institute and editor of the Colportage paperback book enterprise. Nephew Ambert, a young man D. L. loved and nurtured almost like a son, was a local church leader who directed the business side of the Northfield Hotel and sometimes accompanied his uncle on trips. And then there were, among others, D. W. Whittle and Ira Sankey— two men Moody had urged to enter full-time ministry because he sensed God was setting them apart for the gospel ministry.

If Moody had done no more than encourage his own family, Whittle, and Sankey, he would have lived a markedly productive life and been the envy of many who had much less to show for forty years of service.

THE JOYS AND THE PRIVILEGES

In some ways, Dwight Moody appeared to have everything a Christian could desire. To the superficial observer, he and Emma lived glamorous lives. They had three healthy children; they traveled throughout the world. In the 1890s alone they went to Great Britain, Ireland, and Israel, with brief stops in western Europe and Egypt. They enjoyed rewarding campaign trips to Canada, particularly Ontario and Quebec, and to several parts of Mexico, most notably Mexico City. Everywhere they traveled people begged them to return; and places where they had never been, such as Japan, Australia, New Zealand, and Tasmania, issued invitations of the most sincere and urgent nature.[12] Besides these privileges, the Moodys had a large if rather plain home located in one of America's most scenic and tranquil spots.

Those people closest to the Moodys knew that their joys and privileges were genuine and truly exceptional, yet they were subject to pressures and pains that sometimes made their lives unbearably exhausting and stressful. The romance of living in hotels passed quickly, even if the accommodations were in first-class ones like Denver's Brown Palace; the Russell in Ottawa, Ontario; two of Manhattan's finest—Murray Hill and Park Avenue; and the elegant Parker House in Boston.[13] The Moodys certainly enjoyed their trips across the North Atlantic on modern steamships, but the stress of Moody's being a passenger on a sinking ship in icy November waters rather symbolized the ecstasy and agony of their challenging lifestyle.

THE VOYAGE ON THE *SPREE*

D. L. Moody and his son William were on board the German steamer, *Spree,* when it left Southampton, England, bound for New York on November 23, 1892. Mrs. Moody had already taken the family home in August, but Mr. Moody stayed for several weeks and did more preaching while waiting for Will, who was finishing a course of study in Germany. The twosome boarded the *Spree* with high expectations for a restful cruise, and they were particularly pleased to see General O. O. Howard on the same liner with his daughter-in-law and granddaughter in tow. Mr. Moody dreaded nothing but seasickness—a malady that frequently plagued him on even the calmest of sea voyages.[14]

Dwight Moody did experience a slight case of seasickness, but it was inconsequential, given the crisis that befell the ship and its 750 passengers. Three days and about 1,100 miles into the voyage, sometime after midnight in the early hours of Saturday, November 27, the main shaft of the propeller broke. Two large fragments exploded through the bottom of the steamer. Water immediately filled half of the ship's compartments, and the pumps could not pull water out as fast as it flowed in. The floundering vessel drifted for several hours with no electrical power, leaving the passengers huddled on deck in total darkness with full knowledge that the ship was beginning to sink. General Howard wrote that "the gloom and terror that followed the accident cannot easily be described."[15]

At daybreak D. L. Moody beckoned the general to join him and Will in their stateroom. Moody "knelt down by his berth and prayed, saying: 'O Lord, when Thy disciples were on the sea and in trouble, Thou didst save them. Are we not Thy disciples? Please smooth the waves so that we shall not be drowned, and please send us a ship.'" General Howard and Will also prayed, and then Mr. Moody read Psalm 91, which he suggested "seems made for just this occasion, doesn't it?"[16]

By nightfall Saturday, in the words of Moody, "the ship's bow was now high in the air, the stern seemed to settle more and more. The sea was very rough, and the ship rolled from side to side with fearful lurches." The captain had tried to keep people hopeful by predicting the *Spree* would drift into the course of another ship by sunset Saturday. When darkness fell and there was not a sign of a ship, the passengers experienced "an awful night, the darkest in all our lives! [Everyone was] waiting for the doom that was settling upon us! No one dared to sleep. . . . Rockets flowed into the sky, but there was no answer. We were drifting," wrote Moody, "out of the track of the great steamers. Every hour seemed to increase our danger."[17]

Sunrise on Sunday came with still no ship sighted and no new reason to hope. Moody rose to the occasion by asking the captain if he could hold a religious service in the First Cabin Saloon, the only safe place on board and the spot where everyone had gathered. "Most certainly; I am that kind, too," replied the captain. Moody reported that a call went forth and to his surprise, everyone came, except crew members who faithfully stayed by their posts. Moody read Psalm 91 and Psalm 107:20–31. General Howard spoke some God-centered words of hope, and his remarks as well as the Psalms were translated into German. A South American Catholic woman sang a solo, "Nearer My God to Thee," and prayers were offered to God, beseeching Him to keep the sea calm and to send a vessel of rescue.[18]

At about three in the morning on Monday, Dwight Moody was fast asleep in his stateroom. "I was aroused from my sound sleep by the voice of my son. 'Come on deck, Father,' he said. I followed him, and he pointed to a light, rising and sinking on the sea. It was a messenger to deliver us." A Canadian freighter, *Lake Huron,* came to the rescue, towing the mortally wounded *Spree* for eight days by two steel cables back to Queenstown, Ireland. Once the passengers touched land at Queenstown they made their way to the nearest church. It was Methodist in persuasion. Moody climbed to the pulpit, fervently praised God and offered thanks, and then delivered a message on the theme "God Is Love."[19]

Moody never forgot the *Spree,* its cracked hull, and God's great mercy. He often spoke of the rescue, the courage of her crew, and the miraculous escape. As difficult as those days must have been at times, Moody suffered more agony and sleeplessness over the wounded church than he did over the wreck of the *Spree.* He labored tirelessly to bring unity among Christians, inviting people from every conceivable regiment of God's army to help rescue and nurture souls. He continually urged unity in the celebration of the essentials of the Christian faith, liberty in the nonessential doctrines, and charity in everything toward all people. Only his family and closest friends understood how he suffered when the factionalism of Christianity began to widen and harden during the late 1890s.

UNITY AND DISUNITY OF CHRISTIANS

Moody was terribly distressed when men who disagreed on such things as modes of baptism, when Christ would return, divine healing, authorship of books of the Bible, and understanding of the sacraments/ordinances could not set aside their differences and reach out to the lost and feed the flock. His deep pain notwithstanding, splits were coming, and many people were bent on separation. Sometimes conservative biblical literalists pulled away and called a halt to platform and pulpit fellowship with those who did not agree with them. Moody grieved when hundreds of letters and telegrams flooded Northfield, declaring him a heretic for allowing Henry Drummond or George Adam Smith to speak to students and conferees. These two men were unfit to speak at a Christian gathering, according to these critics, because of Drummond's attempts to synthesize Darwin and Genesis and Smith's attempt to prove that more than one person wrote Isaiah. On one occasion a delegation of angry conservatives went to Northfield to reprimand Moody, and there was at least one ugly scene at a meal when harsh and hurtful words were spoken to Moody and a more liberal guest.[20]

Pressures from Conservatives and Liberals

Moody's correspondence suggests that some major donors to the Northfield and Chicago schools withdrew support by the late 1890s, causing a good bit of gossip and tension. Moody wrote a letter to Torrey and said "one of your students . . . heard that our friends were falling off. One person who had been giving 12000 a year had withdrawn their support. I wish you would find out who has been talking. It would be a great mistake to have our students talking about our finances and I am sure it would please some parties to hear that statement and I hope you will tell the faculty to keep still."[21]

The more liberal element could dish out an equally bitter broth. Where Moody experienced the most opposition from liberal quarters was in the area of the doctrine of the Second Coming. Moody was a premillennialist, he never apologized for it, and Revell published an entire list of books on the subject. But even here Moody never demanded that anyone side with him. In any case, as the nineteenth century drew to a close, many Christians were determined to fight over the issue, and Moody became a target of reproach. In 1898, for instance, according to the *Chicago Daily News,* the YMCA leadership in Chicago removed R. A. Torrey from his prominent role as the YMCA trainer of teachers.

For several years Torrey had offered a large class for Sunday school teachers on Saturday afternoons in the Central YMCA auditorium, and many people came out to hear him. But in October 1898, YMCA General Secretary L. Wilbur Messer abruptly dismissed and replaced Torrey—and he gave no reasons for his actions. According to the *Chicago Daily News,* "the removal of the Rev. Torrey at the central department and the substituting of another is looked upon as a direct slap at Dwight L. Moody and the friends of the great evangelist. . . ." The evidence suggests that the YMCA was weary of Torrey and Moody's doctrine; according to the *Chicago Daily News,* "the old fashioned gospel was not quite what the YMCA people wished."[22]

Moody was accustomed to critics who assailed him for being concerned for the eternal destiny of souls in an age when many social gospelers and universalists were primarily concerned with social reform, but the discerning New Englander recognized the marks of other issues this time. He wrote to Torrey after receiving a copy of the *Daily News* article, and inquired: "Do you think it is the second coming or Divine Healing" that precipitated this? There is no record that Torrey had an answer. In a way, it made no difference. Both doctrines were anathema to the liberal community, and it was determined not to associate with ministers who held such positions.[23]

Moody's Attempt to Bring Unity

In the face of growing opposition to his call for Christian unity, Moody tried to turn the other cheek, ignore the growing signs of warfare, and keep moving forward in what he considered to be a positive, Christ-centered way. His stance continued to bear fruit. Conservatives like C. I. Scofield and James M. Gray loved Moody and worked alongside him, never insisting that he desert more liberal friends and work only with conservatives like themselves. Many liberals, too, among them Henry Drummond, George Adam Smith, and William Rainey Harper, enjoyed fellowship and collegial relations with Moody despite the marked differences in the way he and they saw Scripture. Indeed, Harper, president of the University of

Chicago by the late 1890s, wrote to Moody in September 1899 to ask that he would please "come down to the University and speak, at least once," when he went to Chicago in November. Harper assured Moody

> There is every reason you should do so. Our common friend, George Adam Smith, was a great power with us this summer. I wish you could have heard him tell here of his feelings about yourself. I can understand how it is not possible for you to have men like George Adam Smith and myself speak at Northfield. We, fortunately, are in a different position, and the University is most anxious to have all sides represented. I do not understand, of course, that you, as a matter of fact, represent any other position than that which is actually maintained here at the University. The differences between us are merely differences of detail. We are all working for one common purpose. I write, therefore, to ask you to help us in this work.[24]

Men like Moody and Harper were bridges—powerful connections between increasingly polarized factions. What Moody must have grieved over was the reference to Smith and Harper not being able to speak at Northfield. They had, of course, spoken there in the past. But the tide of differences was raging higher and higher. No longer would it be possible—or at least politically wise—to invite them back again. Harper knew it, and so did Moody. The reality made Moody sad, and he saw no easy solution.

Harper and Moody were both men of good hope. Nevertheless, neither seemed to foresee that for better or worse they were traveling in opposite directions. Harper's optimistic comment that "the differences between us are merely differences of detail," and that "we are working for one common purpose" was simply not true. The University of Chicago was on a path leading away from its Christian foundation, and before long Moody would not be welcome there to speak. And the very fact that Drummond felt it best not to speak at Moody's schools on his last trip to America in 1893 showed Moody's institutions were traveling a divergent path too.

Moody, like Harper, either could not see or would not acknowledge the increasingly deep divisions within Christianity. Although men and women of charity from both sides could still get along, their goals were growing farther apart. The unity that Moody celebrated and fought so gallantly to maintain would not survive much longer. This reality deeply troubled his soul.

Stress at Northfield

If Moody had a difficult time grasping the widening gulf in English-speaking Christian circles, he had an even tougher time facing the factionalism in the Northfield schools. Moody apparently had a hand in C. I. Scofield's appointment as pastor of Northfield's Trinitarian Congregational Church, a position he held from 1896 until early 1903. What Moody could not seem to do was bridle the ambitious preacher's determination to impose his control over the Northfield schools.

In many ways Cyrus I. Scofield is an enigmatic figure. Born in Michigan in 1843, he was six years younger than D. L. Moody. His family moved to central Tennessee when he was a boy. Eighteen years old when the Civil War began, Scofield immediately enlisted and served with distinction as an enlisted man in General Robert E.

C. I. Scofield

Lee's army. After the war this man of medium build and height, bushy eyebrows, piercing dark eyes, and dark wavy hair with a middle part, moved to Kansas, studied law, passed the bar examination, and served in the Kansas legislature. In 1879 Scofield's life took a dramatic turn. By then a thirty-six-year-old lawyer battling alcoholism, he converted to Christianity through the witness of a fellow attorney. Within a few months he was in St. Louis, volunteering for YMCA work in Missouri's largest city, and involved in a mentoring relationship with the Reverend James H. Brookes, a superb pastor, Bible teacher, and close personal friend to D. L. Moody. In 1882 Scofield was ordained a Congregational minister, and he accepted the pastorate of the First Congregational Church in Dallas, Texas.[25]

Moody first met Scofield while doing the St. Louis campaign in late 1879 and early 1880. James Brookes and Moody became close friends during that extended series of meetings, and Brookes brought Scofield along to many sessions so he could watch the master evangelist in action. Moody met Scofield again during the February to May 1895 campaign in Dallas and Fort Worth. It was then that the two men probably discussed the recently vacated pastorate at Northfield that Scofield filled in 1896.

Scofield had no sooner arrived at Northfield than his ambitions to take an active role at the three schools became apparent. This man who would edit the famous *Scofield Reference Bible* (1909), and who popularized John Nelson Darby's seven-era dispensational framework, became a pastor to the Northfield and Mount Hermon students. He also did his best to impose his Darby-inspired dispensationalism on Moody and the schools. At one point during one of the 1898 summer conferences, he and several Brethren sympathetic to this hermeneutical approach tried to get Moody to rid the conference of speakers with whom they disagreed. Moody ignored their pressures.[26]

Moody should have seen a widening gulf in his own backyard. Scofield offered himself to the Northfield Bible Training School to teach a course on the Holy Spirit. This was soon followed by a course called "Dispensations." Correspondence between the pastor and Miss Lila S. Halsey, the principal of NBTS, makes clear that Scofield wanted increasing Bible teaching responsibilities in the school. Miss Halsey evidently found his style and angle of vision incompatible with her own, so she put him off by claiming lack of funds. Scofield persisted. Finally he wrote to her, "Pray understand—there is *no* question of remuneration involved in anything I have had in mind about the training school. I only want to invest my life where it will bring the best return for Christ. I believe my extension work accomplishes more than would be wrought by giving up and giving six months to Bible work in the Training School *unless* a free hand were given for its increase and up building."27

This was read by Miss Halsey as an attempted takeover of her school. She held Scofield off—even after Moody died when Scofield's pressure increased. He finally gave up and moved to more promising pastures back in Dallas.

Conflict Avoidance

Moody certainly witnessed these great divisions inside conservative Christian circles, but he was unable or unwilling to do much about them in the place where he had the most influence—Northfield, Massachusetts. That he understood the depth of some of the divisions is apparent from a letter he wrote to a Christian acquaintance in Australia: "Destructive theology on the one side, and the no less evil spirit of extreme intolerance on the other side, have wrought wide dissensions in many communities in America. Instead of fighting error by the emphasis of truth, there has been too much 'splitting of hairs' and only too often an unchristian spirit of bitterness."28

Moody was back to his old position of avoiding conflict. He stood back, begged for unity, and hoped the problems would go away. At worst, this was weak or naive. In any case it was hurtful and ultimately destructive. To put a better light on it, he might actually have believed that many of these differences could be bridged. One reason for such hope was the arrival at Northfield in February 1899 of a bound volume of letters labeled "1898 Petition From Australasia to Mr. D. L. Moody." This book contained a petition and letters signed by 15,831 Christian leaders in Australia, New Zealand, and Tasmania. These men, many of whom had been at great odds with one another at home over doctrinal differences, overcame their hostility long enough to unite for a Moody campaign, joining in common hope for revival and their belief that D. L. Moody would be God's channel.29

Such flattering expressions of confidence in Moody's ability to perform near miraculous deeds could certainly have tempted him to carry notions of his own omnipotence. If any darkness of this sort crept into his heart, new circumstances swiftly reminded him of his limitations. He clearly saw that God's ways were not his ways.

A NEW ENEMY: DEATH

A series of deaths rocked the Moody family. D. L. was markedly saddened by the unexpected death of his dear friend A. J. Gordon, who was only fifty-eight years old at the time of his passing in 1895. Moody was away in Texas and learned of the event too late to get back to Boston for the funeral. Moody shared so many spiritual intimacies with Gordon. The Boston Baptist pastor was far better educated than Moody, having attended Brown University and also Newton Theological Seminary. This gulf aside, they became close in the late 1870s when Moody did his campaign in Boston. Gordon and Moody shared common goals. Both men were passionate about reaching the lost, especially the poor and those broken by alcohol, drugs, and other abuses. Both preachers burned with a desire to educate young people, and each grew increasingly excited about foreign missions.

By the middle 1880s Gordon was a regular fixture at the Northfield conferences. He often spoke at the schools. He also lectured and oversaw much of the administrative work of the summer programs.[30] When Moody learned of Gordon's death, he wrote to A. T. Pierson, "Dear man, he has got home & left a bright light behind him," and "I had said to my wife on the day of his funeral we will have a memorial service this summer in the same place where he spoke on the Resurrection."[31]

Betsy Moody

A. J. Gordon's passing was only the first of a series of deaths that Moody reckoned with in the late 1890s. Betsy Holton Moody died on January 26, 1896, just a few days before her ninety-first birthday. Her passing caused the expected sadness because of the separation, but little deep grief. She was, after all, quite aged; and she had maintained a sharp mind and relatively good health right up to the end. Mr. Moody said at her funeral, "It is not a time for mourning. We are proud that we had such a mother. We have a wonderful legacy left us. . . . God bless you, Mother; we love you still. Death has only increased our love. Good-by for a little while." She had become a believer under his influence and preaching in 1876, so he spoke confidently of her destiny.[32]

Henry Drummond

Moody reacted quite differently when Henry Drummond died

D. L. Moody's mother, Betsy Moody, age 90 (1895)

at Tunbridge Wells, England, on March 11, 1897, at the age of forty-five. Drummond was snatched away too early, it seemed, and Moody suffered deeply. Preaching a three-week series of meetings in Cincinnati at the time, Moody was visiting his preacher friend, Charles F. Goss, a few hours after he learned the dreadful news. Goss said, "That evening at my table he laid his knife and fork down and cried like a child. 'He was the most Christlike man I ever met. I never saw a fault in him,' he said over and over again through his sobs."[33] Moody was still reeling from a horrid series of events involving Drummond that had occurred less than three years earlier. According to Goss, Moody recalled "how violently Drummond was attacked in Northfield [1893] during Moody's absence, for his advocacy of views which were regarded as erroneous in that supremely orthodox place."

Goss remembered that "Mr. Moody was in the midst of his campaign in Chicago at the time, and many of his most generous supporters wrote and telegraphed that 'if he did not denounce Drummond they would abandon him.' Instead, he destroyed their messages, and, sending for Drummond, said 'I want you to take part in my meetings.'" Drummond was too kind to cause Moody more injury. "I should only injure *you* instead of your *sustaining* me." Moody begged him, "Preach one of your old sermons." Drummond said he would rather not. Moody's reply, according to what he told Goss, was, "Well, wherever you go or whatever you do, I am your friend, and I will stand by you with the last drop of my blood." Moody stayed faithful to his old friend, even to the point of getting a volume of Drummond's *Addresses* published as part of the Colportage Library.[34]

Grandson Dwight

Drummond's death made Moody heartsick, but this grief served as a mere prelude to a more staggering blow. Moody had only one grandson. His name was Dwight Moody. Born to William and Mary on November 7, 1897, he died without warning on November 30, 1898, just weeks after his first birthday. Dwight and Emma Moody were in Florence, Colorado, when little Dwight died. Will Moody had sent a telegram on November 29 saying Dwight was ill, but "was passing through a crisis." The next day a wire came notifying the grandparents that the baby was dead and the funeral and burial would be within twenty-four hours. Mrs. Moody wrote to her daughter Emma—"we were unprepared for it by what Will sent us [yesterday. Now] we hear he has gone. Dear little fellow his life here was not long but he must have had a mission & has finished it. He was sent for a purpose. . . ." She inquired why the funeral was so soon. "I wonder if the nature of his trouble necessitated the funeral so soon."[35]

Eventually the grandparents learned that little Dwight died from a virulent case of spinal meningitis. It was highly contagious. With few embalmers available in those days, especially in rural areas like Northfield, it threatened the health of others to hold off the burial until the grandparents could come.

Mr. Moody wrote two letters on the afternoon of the funeral, asking others to offer the comfort he and Emma were prevented from giving. To A. P. Fitt he confessed his thoughts had been at Northfield all day. "I have prayed several times for poor Will and Mary. . . . I hope you will do all you can to comfort them." He also wrote to Miss Varley, a close faculty friend who served at Northfield Seminary: "Take our place comforting Will & Mary Poor Father and Mother How they will feel the loss. . . . Glad you are there to comfort them."[36]

Dwight Moody wrote a long letter to his grieving son and daughter-in-law, offering up more hope and light for them than he had found for Fitt and Varley. "I know Dwight is having a good time, and we should rejoice with him. What would the mansions be without children? And he has gone to help get things ready for his parents. . . . God does not give us such strong love for each other for a few days or years, but it is going to last forever, and you will have the dear little man with you ages and ages, and love will keep increasing." He concluded the lengthy and tender epistle with these words: "My heart goes up to God often for you, and the word that keeps coming to my mind is this: 'It is well with the child.' Only think of his translation! Thank God, Dwight is safe at home, and we will all of us see him soon."[37]

Granddaughter Irene

The deep sense of loss—the darkness of relentless grief—had only just begun for the Moody family. The fulfillment of ministry notwithstanding, they were learning that the rain ravages the justified as well as the heathen. Less than nine months after Dwight died, Mary and Will lost their firstborn, Irene. Two days after her fourth birthday, Irene's death came with a tenacious and persistent case of pneumonia. The doctors said it turned, at the last, into consumption—a name commonly used in those days for tuberculosis.

The grandparents were close by in New York when Irene took a serious turn for the worse. Immediately they were at the bedside to watch, pray, and comfort the benumbed parents. The youngster displayed strength and alertness enough to ask her grandfather to take her riding at 6:30 A.M. on August 14. This he did with thanksgiving and gusto. "She never looked more beautiful," recalled Moody. She was to be gone in eight days, and "she was just ripening for Heaven. She was too fair for this earth." Just before the close of her funeral service, he arose and spoke: "I would like to say a few words, if I can trust myself." With breaking voice he said:

> I have been thinking this morning about the aged prophet waiting in the valley of the Jordan, so many years ago, for the chariot of God to take him home. The chariot of God came down to the Connecticut

valley yesterday morning at about half-past six, and took our little Irene home. The one was taken at the end of years of active service; the other at the early dawn of youth. But the service of the prophet was no more complete than that of the little handmaid of the Lord, for God called both, and He never interrupts the service of His own.

Irene has finished her course. Her work was well wrought on earth. She has accomplished more than many in their threescore and ten. We would not have her back, although her voice was the sweetest voice I ever heard on earth. She never met me once since she was three months old, until the last few days of pain, without a smile. But Christ had some service for her above. My life has been made much better by her ministry here on earth. She has made us all better. . . . I thank God this morning for the hope of immortality. I know I shall see her in the morning, more beautiful in her resurrection glory than she was here.[38]

Emma Manning Revell

A month later Emma Revell Moody's mother, Emma Manning Revell, died in Chicago. Mrs. Revell had not been in good health for several months. This loss was no great shock. She was already quite elderly, so it was not out of the expected order of things. But standing by another open grave, and laying to rest one more loved one, made 1899 the most difficult year the Moodys had endured.

By early November Emma and Dwight were back to a rather normal life. They submerged their pain in diligent work among the living. D. L. made preparations for a three-week series of meetings scheduled for Kansas City, Missouri, a thriving, booming city of more than 100,000 on the western edge of the Show Me State. His plans included a brief stop in Philadelphia to see his friend John Wanamaker. Moody also planned to see the progress on the building being erected in the City of Brotherly Love for a series of meetings scheduled there in 1900. After Philadelphia he promised to stop for several hours in Chicago. He would not be there long enough to meet Dr. Harper and speak at the University of Chicago, but there would be enough time for two lectures at the Bible institute with some Colportage and institute business tucked in.[39]

D. L.'S LAST CAMPAIGN

No one in the family sensed that Mr. Moody was ill. He handwrote piles of letters throughout October and early November, and he dictated many more.[40] His appetite remained good; his routines seldom varied. He issued forth an image of vigor and robustness—

Mr. Moody in the late 1890s

even an aura of indestructibility—while other people fell by the way-side.

His son-in-law noticed one problem—Moody gained thirty pounds over the summer and early autumn of 1899. No one thought much about it, according to Fitt, because all the illness and death of the past months had interfered with Moody's usual roustabout exercise.[41]

Both Dwight and Emma put on weight during the 1890s, but many people wrote this off as normal, given their ages and the fact that for nine months out of most years they traveled extensively and were obligated to dine with local dignitaries. But for a disciplined man like Moody to add thirty pounds in a few months was not the result of lack of exercise or overeating. To be sure, people who knew him often commented on his eating habits. He would drink as many as five glasses of water during a meal, but never a beverage with calo-ries. In eating, as in other things, Moody behaved in unstaged but naturally humorous ways. One of his friends insisted Moody was never obsessive in eating habits, but he usually "ate with the greatest rapidity" and discarded "Mr. Gladstone's rules of chewing each mouthful seventy times—with humorous contempt." One evening, after a busy day, he entered his friend's house and inquired if he could have something to eat. "A large dish of pork and beans (of which he was very fond) was placed before him. He sat down, murmured a silent prayer, and without interrupting his repast by a word, emptied the entire dish as fast as he could carry the food to his mouth. And yet this was done with a certain indefinable grace! He ate voraciously, but never like an animal nor even like an epicure."[42]

In truth, D. L. Moody's rapidly growing girth developed in tandem with a weakening heart. Although hardly anyone knew his condition, he fell ill in London in 1892. The doctors who attended him diagnosed a bad heart and prescribed more rest and avoidance of stress. No doubt the increased portliness so apparent in the middle and late 1890s was, in part at least, edema (water retention) caused by a malfunctioning heart.

No one knew he was a sick man. Despite the corpulence, one man commented he did not appear "sluggish" or "gross." On the contrary, "he was light on his feet as a boy," and able to deliver many messages on any given day.[43]

Emma in Northfield

Emma Moody suspected nothing. Indeed, because Mary Whittle Moody was expecting a baby any day in mid-November, Emma decided, with Dwight's hearty approval, to stay in Northfield to help her and let Mr. Moody make this relatively short trip alone. On Wednesday, November 8, she bade her husband good-bye as he headed for Kansas City, with intermittent stops in Philadelphia and Chicago. That evening she wrote a letter to Paul at Yale. "Father left us this morning and is going to try to come back to us on Thanksgiving day, three weeks from tomorrow. . . . It seems now as though we were getting ready for the winter, now that Father has gone & I am getting ready for my storm windows."[44]

The wintry feeling quickly passed. Warmth and joy flooded Northfield three days later. Mary gave birth on November 11 to their third child—a healthy girl whom they named Mary Whittle Moody. The family rejoiced. They thought the tide of gloom had finally rolled away.

On the day Mary Whittle Moody was born, Grandfather Moody wrote the following words to four-year-old Emma Fitt, his oldest surviving grandchild:

> My dear Emma: I am glad that you have a little cousin. Will you kiss her for me, and will you show her your grandfather's picture? I do not think she will know me, but you can tell her all about me, so she will know me when she gets older, and we will play together with

her. I am going to send her a little kiss, just one little one.
 Your grandfather,

 D. L. Moody

 I will put the kiss in a little box, O , and you can take it to her.[45]

He also sent a telegram to Will and Mary: "Thankful for the good news. May she become famous in the kingdom of Heaven is the prayer of her grandfather." He followed this with a letter to Will: "I am full of praise and thanksgiving today. . . . Dear little child, I already feel my heart going out to her! Kiss the mother and the dear baby for me. . . . Thank God for another grandchild."[46]

The Kansas City Campaign

 Mr. Moody's visit to Philadelphia went well, and the lectures to the students in Chicago "were marked by unusual power."[47] Upon arrival in Kansas City, Moody was expansive—buoyed by the visits with associates and students on the way to Missouri. News of the safe delivery of Mary Moody caused the melancholia from so many days in sickrooms and at funerals and gravesides to fade for the time being.

 On the evening of November 11, Moody met with C. C. Case, the musician picked to lead the thousand-voice choir. They had a good visit in Moody's comfortable quarters in Kansas City's finest hotel, the New Coates House. Everything went well on Sunday and Monday, as Moody plunged into his messages with energy and apparent anointing. Case observed that Moody "enjoyed his work in Kansas City as well as any he ever did from what he said." Case said they were both encouraged by the size and openness of the crowds, and Moody enjoyed the massive choir. An "Old Men's Quartet" especially caught his fancy. Comprised of men who ages ranged from sixty-seven to eighty-two, he delighted in announcing their selections by saying, "I want my *boys* to sing so and so."[48]

 Moody's keen sense of humor in Kansas City masked a serious ailment. The family later learned that he had suffered heart pain all summer and fall, but he told absolutely no one lest they worry. He told no one in Kansas City either and behaved as if he were stronger than ever.[49]

Moody's Confession

 On Tuesday, November 14, Moody shed his disguise. Case met him for breakfast and noticed that "he looked pale and ate little. I asked how he rested, and he said 'I slept in my chair all night.'" Case immediately discerned the gravity of the situation, and he badgered Moody into confessing he had suffered chest pains for two weeks. Moody told Mr. Case: "I did not let my family know it, for they would not have let me come on here." It took two hours before the music director could persuade Moody he needed a physician. The doctor came, examined the ailing preacher, and applied a mustard plaster to his chest. This prescription immediately relieved the pain, so the valiant warrior went forward and preached six more sermons.[50]

Case recalled, "I could see that he was all the time growing weaker, and the last two days he had to be taken to the hall in a carriage, although [his hotel] was only two blocks away" from the large convention hall. Moody spoke twice each on Tuesday, Wednesday, and Thursday. "When he began speaking he did not show his weakness, but preached with old-time fire and spirit; but when he got back to his room I could see that he was very much exhausted."[51]

Moody's messages in Kansas City were biblical, powerfully illustrated, and decidedly evangelistic—typical of sermons he had delivered for decades. In retrospect one difference permeated his last few sermons—an emphasis on earthly death and the hope of heaven.

> We say this is the land of the living! It is not. It is the land of the dying. What is our life here but a vapor? A hearse is the most common sight. Families broken into. Over there is one who has lost a father, there a mother, there is a place vacant, there a sister's name is no more heard, there a brother's love is missed. Death stalks triumphant through our midst, in this world. Only yesterday I met a mother who had lost her babe. Death in front of us, death behind us, death to the right of us, death to the left of us. . . . But look at the other world. No death, no pain, no sorrow, no old age, no sickness, no bending forms, no dimmed eyes, no tears. But joy, peace, love, happiness. No gray hair. People all young. River of life for the healing of the nations, and everlasting life. Think of it! Life! Life! Life without end! And yet so many men choose this life on earth, instead of the life in Heaven. Don't close your heart against eternal life. Only take the gift, only take it. Will you do it?[52]

His very last sermon, delivered on Friday night, November 16, in the western Missouri city's packed convention hall, was on the invitation the heavenly Father is giving to every person to attend the great marriage banquet of His only-begotten Son. "Hasten to reply" to this "pressing invitation." Respond with, "By the grace of God I will be present."[53]

Moody never preached again. When he returned to his room the Kansas City doctor who had attended him since Tuesday insisted he notify his family and take the late train home.

On the Way Home

Early on November 17 Emma Moody received the first warning of her husband's condition. The telegram read: "Doctor thinks I need a rest. Am on my way home."[54]

Never a slacker, never despondent long, Mr. Moody sent two more telegrams from the train during his journey home: First, "Improving rapidly. Have not felt so well for a week." Next, "Have had a splendid day. No fever. Heart growing better all the time. No pain. Am taking good care of myself, not only for the loved ones, but for the work I think God still has for me to do on earth."[55]

This time Mr. Moody's vision was not inspired. When the train pulled into Greenfield on November 18, twelve miles below Northfield, several members of the family met him and drove him up to the big white house with green shutters. He climbed the stairs to the bedroom without assistance, apparently experiencing no difficulty. His plan was to wash up and then come down for tea. But he never walked down the stairs again.

Over the next few weeks, Moody sat up in a chair, but he spent most of his time in bed. Each day his breath shortened and strength diminished, but his mind stayed alert and he managed some good chats with family and friends. He allowed a doctor to tend him, and he also called for the elders to anoint him with oil and pray. Despite advice from doctor and family, he insisted on examining a new issue of one of the Christian periodicals he had inaugurated.

THE LAST WORDS ON EARTH

Moody's beloved son-in-law sat up with him all night on December 21. At 3:00 A.M., Will came in to take the next bedside watch. Around 6:00 A.M. the ailing preacher roused from sleep and in slow, measured words announced: "Earth recedes; Heaven opens for me." Will assumed his father was dreaming and attempted to awaken him. "No, this is no dream, Will. It is beautiful. It is like a trance. If this is death, it is sweet. There is no valley here. God is calling me, and I must go."[56]

The nurse summoned the family as well as the doctor, who was sleeping nearby. When everyone gathered round, the venerable sixty-two-year-old patriarch pronounced a blessing: "I have always been an ambitious man; ambitious to leave no wealth or possessions, but to leave lots of work for you to do. Will, you will carry on Mount Hermon. Paul will take up the Seminary, when he is older; Fitt will look after the Institute, and Ambert will help you in the business details."

After a pause, he exclaimed, "This is my triumph; this is my coronation day! I have been looking forward to it for years." Then with face illumined he cried out, "Dwight! Irene!—I see the children's faces."

After a few moments he turned to his beloved Emma: "Mamma, you have been a good wife to me." He slipped into unconsciousness, only to rally again a few minutes later. "This is a strange thing. I have been beyond the gates of death and then to the very portals of Heaven, and here I am back again." Then he made a few more assignments, telling Percy and daughter Emma about some things he would like for them to do at the Chicago Bible Institute. Emma received her assignment and inquired of her father, "What about mother?" He replied, "Oh, she's like Eve, the mother of us all."

At that moment Mr. Moody decided to get up and sit in his chair. "I'm not at all sure but that God may perform a miracle and raise me up. I'm going to get up." After a few minutes in the chair, he sank quickly and allowed the doctor to help him back to bed. Once settled in, he turned to Emma and apologetically whispered, "This is hard on you, Mother, and I'm sorry to distress you in this way. It is hard to be kept in such anxiety." The doctor then approached with another nitroglycerin injection, but the fading giant brushed him away—"It's only keeping the family in anxiety."[57]

In just a few moments he slipped quietly into eternity. According to Will Moody's calculation, "To the world, Friday, December 22d, was the shortest day of all the year, but for Dwight L. Moody its dawn ushered in that day that knows no night."

Many years before, Mr. Moody had offered what he called his "autobiography" to the public:

Some day you will read in the papers that D. L. Moody, of East Northfield, is dead. Don't you believe a word of it! At that moment I shall be more alive than I am now. I shall have gone up higher, that is all—out of this old clay tenement into a house that is immortal; a body death cannot touch, that sin cannot taint, a body fashioned like unto His glorious body. I was born of the flesh in 1837. I was born of the Spirit in 1856. That which is born of the flesh may die. That which is born of the Spirit will live forever.[58]

D. L.'S FUNERAL

The funeral was Tuesday, December 26, a gloriously sunny day. Patches of snow still lingered around the Moody home and seminary grounds, and a thin blanket of the first snow of winter still covered the nearby southern mountains of New Hampshire and Vermont.

Emma Revell Moody insisted on everything being done in accordance with her husband's wishes. No dirges. No black crepe draped the doors or windows. The shutters were open on the house, and sunlight was allowed to stream in. Everything must point to Christ and the Resurrection. Mr. Moody was laid out in a simple, gray cloth-covered casket, adorned with a few flowers and a spray that said "Grandpa."

After a brief service for the family in the house, thirty-two Mount Hermon students carried Mr. Moody's remains on a bier the half mile over to the Congregational church. This was what he wanted. Only four months earlier he had helped plan little Irene's service. Her small white casket was placed on a bier. Twelve Mount Hermon boys, friends of hers, carried her remains to the Northfield cemetery. At that time Mr. Moody told Will, "This is just as I would want it. No hearse and no mourning, but just let the Mount Hermon boys bear me to my resting place."[59]

The family honored his wishes. At the public funeral at the church following the private family service in the house, Scripture

Mr. Moody's funeral

The D. L. Moody gravesite at Northfield, Massachusetts

was read, prayers were offered, some of Moody's favorite hymns, including "Immanuel's Land," were sung, and brief messages were spoken by C. I. Scofield, R. A. Torrey, John Wanamaker, H. G. Weston, and A. T. Pierson. Next came the obligatory closing hymn and benediction, and then the Mount Hermon boys carried Mr. Moody's body back up the road, past his house, around behind his birthplace, and up to Round Top. The coffin was lowered into the ground on this highest point of the Northfield campus—the sacred place from which he loved to survey the river with its majestic mountain backdrop—the point from where he frequently preached during the summer conferences, and the very spot where A. J. Gordon delivered his stirring message on the Resurrection.

After a closing prayer by R. A. Torrey and a benediction from C. I. Scofield, someone broke forth singing one of Dwight L. Moody's favorite hymns, "Jesus, Lover of My Soul." As the mourners began making their way off the hill, the sun set just beyond the river.[60]

EMMA AND THE CHILDREN

With dignity and simplicity, Emma Charlotte Revell Moody carried on with the business of living. She devoted much time to her children and grandchildren. She also accompanied Paul (he did not marry until 1904 at age twenty-five) to Scotland after his graduation from Yale in 1901. The youngest Moody son spent several months at

Dwight and Emma Moody's tombstones at Northfield, Massachusetts

Emma Moody with her family in 1901. Back row: Mrs. Moody with Constance, Will Moody.
Front row: A. P. Fitt, Emma Moody Fitt, Emma IV, Mary, May Whittle Moody, Paul Moody

New College, Edinburgh, and Free Church College, Glasgow, studying theology. His mother went along to be with him, and the change of scenery was good for her soul. The opportunity to visit old friends also proved a solace and a welcome tonic.

One friend described Emma Moody as a "wife and mother of the old school, giving her best time and strength to her home. Her three children rise up and call her blessed."[61] Even so, Mrs. Moody found time and energy to do more than serve her family. After 1899 she continued in her roles as inveterate letter writer, trustee of the Northfield Seminary, treasurer of the Student's Aid Society, and "constant adviser to the principal" of the seminary. She taught a popular Sunday school class that was attended by more than ninety students plus many others from outside the student body.

Her devotion to the work in Chicago never waned. Indeed, like her husband, she continued to be a member of the Chicago Avenue Church, and she continued to support it quite liberally. Mrs. Moody also played active roles in the Colportage Association (she was vice president) and the Bible institute's advisory board, and at the time of her death she had a trip planned to Chicago, where she looked forward to speaking to students.

Emma Moody continued "the work," as they labeled it, with energy and devotion. Mrs. Moody's health declined markedly after Mr. Moody's death. She lost considerable weight—perhaps thirty-five pounds—and was diagnosed with Bright's disease, a kidney ailment, in 1901. A combination of this disease and her chronic heart condition slowed her down, but did not end her usual schedule: early to bed, early to rise, and a time of devotions after breakfast. She would then spend much of the day driving neighbors on errands and dispensing gifts and kindness to folks throughout the Northfield community.

On Saturday morning, October 10, 1903, Emma Moody rose early as usual. She collapsed while dressing. Death came in the afternoon. She was only sixty years old. It was said that "she left a trail of glory and kindly memories behind her in the hearts of her townspeople."[62]

Like Mr. Moody, Mrs. Moody finished well. So did all of their children.[63]

CHAPTER THIRTEEN

IN RETROSPECT
Some Keys to D. L. Moody's Effectiveness

In 1942, forty-three years after the death of Dwight L. Moody, a nineteen-year-old private in the United States Army sent a letter to Mr. Moody via the Colportage Association. It never occurred to this soldier, embroiled in the massive effort of World War II, that Moody was dead. Stationed at an undisclosed base in the South Pacific, J. H., a young enlisted man, had just read one of Moody's books. The words spoke so powerfully to the soldier that he assumed Moody to be alive and speaking directly to him. "Dear Mr. Moody," he wrote, "I've read your book The Way to God. I just want to say its wonderful, that I have accepted Christ as my Savior and my name has been entered in the Book of Life. I'm a private in the Army. I can't say where I'm at, but you can guess." With comely zeal, he continued, "Mr. Moody, believe me when I say this. I want to be a preacher. I'm not goin a sit here and say I'll try to be a preacher. But I'm gonna sit here and say I will make my stand for Jesus at the foot of the Calvary's cross." J. H. trusted Moody and felt constrained to reveal personal details concerning his mother, father, and sister. He demonstrated enough discernment to understand "people is gonna laff and make fun and try to discourage, but I WILL keep it and strive and fight on no matter what they say or do." He concluded his letter with these words: "Mr. Moody, *I love Christ*. I want to be his servant. I must close now. So answer soon. I'm anxious to hear from you."[1]

A generation earlier this young man could have been patiently counseled by Moody in an inquiry room or invited to attend the Chicago Bible Institute. Moody would have liked him—rough edges and all. The world famous preacher would have encouraged J. H. He would probably have expressed utmost confidence in him, because of a deep assurance that Jesus Christ had confidence in him as well as a plan for his life.

D. L. Moody (circa 1895)

How can Dwight L. Moody's extraordinary effectiveness—still strong long after his death—be explained? Uncovering reasons for a person's effectiveness, especially in the spiritual realm, is difficult at best. Nevertheless, it is as much a part of the historian's task to grapple with "hows" and "whys" of history as it is to discover the less elusive "whats" and "whens."

KEY #1: COMMITMENT

An initial key to unlocking the secret of Moody's influence is recognizing his all-encompassing—some said obsessive—*commitment*. Everyone close to Moody observed his enthusiasm for Jesus Christ and for doing what he believed the Lord called him to do. He wrote to D. W. Whittle from England in 1874, "I have done one thing, and the work is wonderful. *One thing* is my motto." His son Will maintained that "nothing could swerve him from this deep-rooted purpose of his life, and in all the various educational and publishing projects to which he gave his energy." Will said that for his father, "There was but one motive—the proclamation of the Gospel through multiplied agencies."[2] In brief, Moody, like all great men, had a single focus.

If ever a man in modern times determined to experience the truth of 2 Chronicles 16:9 ("For the eyes of the Lord range throughout the earth to strengthen those whose hearts are fully committed to him"), it was Dwight L. Moody. From the day he heard British evangelist Henry Varley say, "It remains for the world to see what the Lord can do with a man wholly consecrated to Christ," this idea took a powerful hold upon Moody. He could not get it out of his mind. It captured his heart. It became the foundation for all he did.[3]

KEY #2: A WILLINGNESS TO TAKE RISKS

Moody's commitment, with concomitant trust in God to supply the needs of those He called out, led to a second key: a willingness to take *risks*. To Moody's mind, God never worked mightily through people until they were willing to risk everything for His glory. Abraham had to leave Ur to become the patriarch of a chosen people; Esther had to risk her life to be an instrument in saving her people; Moses had to march the people to the Red Sea before it parted; and the Virgin Mary had to risk her reputation to become the most blessed of women.[4] Moody never found risk-taking easy. He wrestled with God for months before he quit his lucrative career and entered full-time ministry. This was an especially courageous move, considering he had absolutely no foreknowledge of how he would support himself. Then came the sense of leading to Great Britain, without enough money even to cover the ocean passage, and this too appeared foolish to some people. Finding support for four schools and underwriting mass-market paperback books also put his reputation at risk; still he stepped out in faith before he could see the provisions.

KEY #3: VISION

Closely interwoven with commitment and risk was his *vision*. Dwight Moody was always at his best when he was confident he had been in God's presence. The hills of Northfield were occasionally like Mount Sinai or the Mount of Transfiguration to him. Sometimes he climbed up on Round Top or went three miles north into New Hampshire. There he would ascend to a vantage point where he could survey Northfield, look at the Connecticut River Valley, and then call upon the Lord for guidance. He did not always sense a clear response to every one of his questions. On the contrary, he would often say in a time of agonizing choice: "Oh, I wish I could see Christ face to face for five minutes and ask Him what He would do!"[5] He read the Scriptures, prayed, and listened to God. Then, as soon as he had a vision, he went forth with confidence that a path would open and provisions would follow. Thus he started the Northfield schools, and it is the way other enterprises like publishing ventures and conferences were launched.

Strategy for the World's Fair

Vision not commonly shared by all Christians led Moody to use the 1893 World's Columbian Exposition in Chicago as a way to reach millions of people with the gospel. His son said he had "a peculiar genius for recognizing opportunities. On no occasion was this gift better illustrated than in the evangelistic campaign conducted in Chicago during the World's Fair in 1893." His idea for making "such a carnival the scene of a wide-spread evangelistic effort was as novel as it was daring."[6]

Moody's vision for ambitious evangelism at the World's Columbian Exposition came to him while praying on Olivet in Israel in 1892. Looking down on Jerusalem, his mind journeyed to Chicago where many people lived without knowledge of Jesus the Messiah. He imagined millions of people flooding into Chicago in 1893—from every state and territory of North America and from every nation on earth. He envisioned them coming to see the grandiose architecture and art of the magnificent White City, built on Lake Michigan's shore to celebrate the exposition. Moody foresaw people streaming in to be tantalized by all of the consumer wonders on display. But these people, he sensed, would quietly cry out: "No man cares for my soul!" Moody felt compassion for these masses because he knew they would see more than the White City and the latest in technological innovations. They also would see the "places of sin and sorrow, the closed church doors and open saloons, the darkened house of God and the brilliantly lighted devil's den." All this, recalled William Moody, "burdened his soul."[7]

Christians, Moody insisted, must take the initiative as God has taken the initiative. They must reach out to the visiting legions because others will not come to them. Consequently, he left Israel and went back to Britain before returning to the United States. In the United Kingdom he recruited workers and evangelistic preachers to help at the fair—among them A. P. Fitt. Once home, Moody recruited dozens more evangelists, including veterans J. Wilbur Chapman and R. A. Torrey and a young man named Billy Sunday.[8]

Chicago's Christians failed to see the mission possibilities of the fair until Moody prodded them with his illumination from Olivet.

Most Chicago believers argued for negative strategies. "Let us boy-cott the Fair because it is going to be open on Sundays"; or "Let us appeal to the law, and compel them to close on Sundays." But not Mr. Moody. He counseled against negativism, and he suggested they bypass the Parliament of Religions that was designed to parade examples of the world's great religions for everyone to contrast and compare. Moody also opposed a fiery Christian apologetical approach. Instead, "I would come to . . . the World's Fair [and] preach the Gospel with all the power that He would give me."9

Success of the World's Fair

With commitment to his evangelistic calling and obedience to his vision, Moody took risks, garnered his administrative skills, and executed one of the greatest evangelistic crusades in Christian history. People who doubted the efficacy of Moody's plan reeled in astonishment. For the last six months of the fair, Moody raised between $60,000 and $70,000—almost $800 per day—to rent the auditorium, theaters, halls, and tents. He and his hundreds of associates, with the Bible institute as headquarters, never criticized the fair or anything else. Going on the offensive, they organized speakers and singers, and then dispatched them to churches, halls, auditoriums, and tents all over downtown Chicago to preach and sing "the old Gospel [in] the power of the Holy Ghost." Moody and his co-workers advertised widely. They told the throngs that they had something of more interest and relevance than other shows or programs. To reach as many people as possible Moody recruited preachers from Germany, Poland, Russia, and France. These men went to Chicago and held services in their native languages for foreign visitors. Moody found Americans who could assist those who ministered in German and the Bohemian and Scandinavian languages. He even had songbooks in European languages. For instance, he used to splendid effect a German edition of Sankey's songs translated and published by social gospeler Walter Rauschenbusch.10

In an interview at the close of his World's Fair campaign, Moody was asked to assess the results. "Millions have heard the simple Gospel preached by some of the most gifted preachers in the world; thousands have apparently been genuinely converted to Christ, and Christians all over this land have been brought to a deep spiritual life and aroused to more active Christian effort for the salvation of others." When asked what was the most effective thing he and his colleagues did, he responded: "The preaching and singing of the old Gospel and the power of the Holy Ghost."

Thomas Spurgeon, a preacher son of the late Charles Spurgeon, was asked to offer his impressions of the outreach. Spurgeon credited Moody for the way he tackled the objective "with all his strength, and organized and inspired his noble army of workers most marvelously." The Londoner expressed amazement at the outreach's effect on non-Christians: "How many converts were gathered in at these mighty meetings, who can say? The Day will declare it. But we may rest assured that the slain of the Lord were many. . . . I love to think that from all parts of the world men came to Chicago to get saved, though they knew it not, and that they went to their distant homes to tell, not so much of the wonders of the Fair, as of the great things the Lord had done for them."[11]

KEY #4: MOODY'S SENSE OF THE HOLY SPIRIT

Inextricably tied to vision as a key to Moody's extraordinary effectiveness was his keen sense of the *personal reality and presence of the Holy Spirit*. After 1871 Moody staked everything on the application of John 14, 15, and 16 to his life and the life of every believer. He tenaciously held to his proclamation that "the existence of the Holy Spirit is to the child of God a matter of Scripture revelation and of actual experience." Moody believed with his whole heart and mind that the third person of the Trinity is indeed a person—One who wants to counsel, guide, comfort, and teach those whom He has convicted of sin and regenerated with new hearts. When ignored or insulted, this person is sorely grieved.[12]

Moody battled fearlessly against two widely entrenched worldviews of his time. First, he made a purposeful assault on the naturalistic philosophy of his age—a materialistic mind-set that belittled the spiritual reality as taught in the Holy Bible. Moody crusaded with equal zest against a widespread unbiblical reaction to naturalism—spiritualism. This latter movement was markedly strong in New England, and it spread all across the continent. Within the spiritualist movement, mediums sprang up like mushrooms at night, supposedly to put people into touch with loved ones or to connect people with spirits that would tell their future and guide them in daily choices. To Moody, the center of truth was found in the Bible, which promises a person to illumine the Scriptures and guide, instruct, and comfort us.[13]

Moody continually encouraged Christians to enter into a intensely personal relationship with the Lord Jesus Christ through the fellowship of the Holy Spirit. He likewise encouraged men like Torrey and Whittle to teach this doctrine wherever they went. The promulgation of the good news about God's presence with us today through His Spirit was heralded at summer conferences and published by Revell. This teaching on the Holy Spirit also towered front and center in the curriculum and devotional life at Moody's four schools. In this vein, Moody always credited the Holy Spirit as the source of anything and everything effective about his ministry.[14]

In 1881 he asserted "one man may have 'zeal without knowledge' while another may have knowledge without zeal. If I could have only the one, I believe I should choose the first." He went on to say that with "an open Bible, no one need be without knowledge of God's will and purpose." Nevertheless, the doctrine of the Holy Ghost "has been too much overlooked, as though it were not practical, and the result is lack of power in testimony and work. If we would work, 'not as one that beatest the air,' but to some definite purpose, we must have this power from on high." From experience Moody could say that "without this power, our work will be drudgery. With it, it becomes a joyful task, a refreshing service." This was his "secret power"—and he prayed for all Christians to understand this truth and personally appropriate it.[15]

KEY #5: A HIGH VIEW OF SCRIPTURE

If fellowship with the Holy Spirit was one of the keys to Moody's influence, closely tied to it was his *view of the Bible*. Because Moody unquestionably assumed the Bible to be God's special and direct revelation, he relied upon Scripture to serve as his standard for all priorities and guidelines for living. People might disagree with Mr. Moody's trust in the Bible and his interpretation of the sacred Scriptures, but they could neither deny that he had something to stand on besides the winds of consensus, nor could they fault the consistency behind his life and teaching. "It is the Word of God, not the word of man" that we must stand on. The word of man is ever-changing, but "the Word of God . . . is true. . . . This book is God's Word, and it will stand," despite the shifting fashions and opinions of humankind.[16]

According to R. A. Torrey, God used D. L. Moody powerfully because he was "a deep and practical student of the Bible." Moody explained to Torrey that he needed to study the Bible daily and apply its truths to his ordinary life experiences. To this end, "If I am going to get in any study, I have got to get up before the other folks get up." Once when Torrey spent the night at Moody's Northfield home, Moody tapped gently on his door at five in the morning, whispering, "Torrey, are you up?" When telling about that incident, Torrey said, "I happened to be; I do not always get up at that early hour but I happened to be up that particular morning. He said, 'I want you to go somewhere with me,' and I went down with him. Then I found out that he had already been up an hour or two in his room studying the Word of God."[17]

KEY #6: A CHRIST-CENTERED LIFE

Moody drew his nearly boundless energy for work from the Bible, and the richest fare he consumed from the Bible was a steady diet of the Lord Jesus Christ. Indeed, Moody's *Christ-centeredness* was another fundamental cause of his tremendous effect on his time and beyond. Moody took literally Jesus Christ's own statement recorded in Luke 24:27 that beginning with Moses and going through all the Prophets, the Scriptures point to the Messiah. Moody believed this without a doubt. He taught that "Christ was the key to the Old Testament" and then he would delight in saying, "And now I will show that Jesus is the key to the New."[18] Moody's close friends, among them F. B. Meyer, A. T. Pierson, and G. Campbell Morgan, taught the same interpretation of the Bible, and they applauded him for his faithfulness to this hermeneutic.

Moody's Christ-centeredness was the vital center of his schools as well as his Bible teaching. Keep "Christ pre-eminent in all you do," he told graduating classes at the Northfield and Mount Hermon schools in 1898. He predicted that he would soon turn the schools over to their generation. When that happened, he warned, people would tell them that a large endowment would be required to keep the institutions vital. But he insisted that if "we keep Christ pre-eminent we will have" all the friends needed to support the schools. "Make Christ first," he exhorted. "Destroy the Bible and we should crumble to nothing. Make Christ the cornerstone of your lives. These schools would never have existed if it had not been for Christ and the Bible. Live in Christ and the light on this hill will shine around the world."[19]

KEY #7: A CONFIDENCE IN YOUNG PEOPLE

It is significant that despite the demands on his time and countless opportunities to speak to large crowds of people who were generally considered "important," Mr. Moody spent so much time with young people like the economically disadvantaged students at

Mount Hermon and Northfield. There is no way to grasp Moody's effectiveness without recognizing his almost boundless *confidence in young people,* and especially the poor, the downtrodden, those people others wanted to turn away from.

Moody's ministry began among the poorest of the poor children in Chicago in the 1850s. When he opened his four schools they were first and foremost for the poor—and he raised tuition for most of them because they could do little to provide it themselves. In this spirit he called for the Chicago Bible Institute to be established on a tuition-free basis. In deference to Mr. Moody's vision it remains so, more than a century after its founding. John Farwell wrote that Dwight Moody was much like one of his heroes, President Abraham Lincoln, in his admiration for the poor and his supreme confidence in their ability to rise to great heights. Moody indeed shared this Lincolnian ideal so prevalent in his lifetime, but he also took his cues from the Bible. Moody lived out a commitment to the poor in part, at least, because the Scriptures call God's chosen people to care for the poor. Likewise, Jesus had a special calling to proclaim the Good News to the poor, so Moody divined that a true disciple must follow the same path.[20]

Moody's confidence in young people was by no means restricted to the poor. He comfortably and purposefully bridged the classes. He spoke often at Yale, especially when Paul was there, and he made memorable and influential talks at Princeton, Edinburgh, Oxford, and

Mr. Moody with a grandchild and college men

Cambridge.[21] The Northfield summer conferences for college students were packed with men hanging up banners of their schools—prominent among them Princeton, Harvard, Yale, Brown, Dartmouth, Columbia, and Cornell.[22] Moody had a profound impact on John R. Mott, for instance, the son of a wealthy lumberman, a 1888 graduate of Cornell, and a future evangelist and president of the World's Alliance of YMCAs. Mott provided a glimpse of what Moody's investment in young people accomplished during those summer conferences:

> In response to Mr. Moody's invitation students have come to North-field meetings from nations in all parts of the world. The world's student conference idea has been taken up in North America, Great Britain, Germany, Scandinavia, Holland, France, Switzerland, Australia, New Zealand, South Africa, Japan, China and India. Moody had worked among the students of Oxford, Cambridge, Edinburgh, Yale, Princeton, and the University of Virginia. The secret of his influence with students, is his uncompromising courage, aggressive warfare against sin, perfect honesty, frankness, rich sympathy and conquering love, whole-souled hospitality, matchless knowledge of the human heart, reality, absolute freedom from all cant, originality in speech and method, leadership, and abounding spiritual life."[23]

KEY #8: TEACHABILITY

That D. L. Moody always remained *teachable* is another key to his usefulness. From his earliest days as an evangelist, when he would ask ministers questions around a dinner table, down to his later years of gathering speakers in Northfield so he could pick their brains and take notes on their messages, Moody remained the learner. He picked out certain men to learn from. For example, on his first trip to Britain in 1867, he longed to meet George Mueller and Charles Spurgeon. He learned much from these men in 1867 and in the years to come. Moody helped bring Mueller to America in 1877, and he took notes feverishly as the venerable preacher spoke in Chicago. Moody also studied at Spurgeon's feet whenever he visited Britain, and Spurgeon generously gave Moody a complete bound set of his messages as a way to assist an American brother who was so hungry to learn. Moody learned all he could from Spurgeon about training men for ministry. Spurgeon, too, must have gleaned much from Moody because their correspondence reveals that he urged Moody to preach in his church—even on Sundays—and he rearranged schedules so that the ebullient American could dine in the Spurgeon home.[24]

Both of Mr. Moody's sons stressed his teachableness, finding it one of the most magnetic aspects of his personality. Paul Moody revealed that his father thought very highly of C. H. MacIntosh's commentaries and used them often as he prepared messages for campaigns. "MacIntosh was one of the leading Plymouth Brethren and to the leaders and teachings of this group Father owed much." Nevertheless, Paul insisted his father never became stagnant. Although he always remained loyal to old friends, he moved in the directions he felt led to go. "Very soon [Mr. Moody] became too liberal for them [the Plymouth Brethren] and, while never a member, he had less and less to do with them. Their separatist doctrines he could not follow."[25]

Moody, of course, learned most from the Scriptures. He never tired of the Word, and daily—barring emergencies or other exigencies—he immersed himself in the Bible both devotionally and for sermon preparation. He believed the Holy Spirit would meet him when he prayerfully opened the Word, granting insights to be passed to people whose hearts and minds were being prepared.

KEY #9: HUMILITY

D. L. Moody's *humility* must be remembered to help account for his impact on lives. Manifestations of this trait can be seen in his openness to learn from others and to submit to God, but it is also present in his attitude toward others. In Philippians 2, the apostle Paul exhorts the church to "consider others better than yourselves." Dwight Moody seems to have been able to apply this to himself in a way that is seldom seen in Christian leaders. Henry Drummond marveled at Moody's servanteartedness. In a biographical essay written for the widely-read *McClure's* magazine, Drummond underscored how, when a person first visits Northfield, an "astounding discovery" greets him. "For when you ask the clerk [at the Northfield Hotel] whether the great man himself is at home, and where you can see him, he will point to your coachman, now disappearing like lightening down the drive, and—too much accustomed to Moody's humor to smile at his latest jest—whisper, 'That's him.'"[26]

R. A. Torrey maintained that D. L. Moody "was the humblest man I ever knew in all my life." Torrey stressed the remarkability of Moody's humility, considering "the great things he did, and the praise that was lavished upon him." At conferences, Moody "loved to put himself in the background and put other men in the foreground." He would bring in a battery of speakers and keep pushing these men to speak before the crowds. "The only way we could get him to take any part in the program was to get up in the convention and move that we hear D. L. Moody at the next meeting. He continually put himself out of sight."[27]

KEY #10: LOVE FOR SOULS

Perhaps the reason D. L. Moody continually and sincerely put others forward can be seen in an underlying key to his effectiveness—his *love for souls*. Beginning with the way a young Irishman—a Plymouth Brethren evangelist named Henry Moorhouse—taught Moody to preach evangelistically by stressing the love of God for sinners, this "love them in" proclamation theology set the tone for his ministry.[28] Moody came to trust God's love for him—personally and unconditionally—and he wanted everyone in the world to learn this good news. Because Moody knew he was loved by the only person who finally mattered, he was constrained to love others out of deepest gratitude. Drummond celebrated the "sheer goodness and love" Moody exuded, and said "none can stand beside him" with this quality.[29] Moody loved to preach on the Prodigal Son and the Good Shepherd who sought a lost sheep; and he reveled in hearing Sankey sing "The Ninety and Nine" with this theme. Moody thoroughly understood and celebrated the biblical revelation that God has been on a magnificent wooing mission ever since the Fall. To Moody this love story was liberating news. It was Truth that could only be discovered through divine revelation.[30]

Living and resting in this glorious love—what Drummond called "The Greatest Thing in the World"—created in Moody what a friend described as his "master passion," his "love for all classes" of people.[31] Rich, poor, educated, ignorant, male, female, they were as one to Moody. In England he hobnobbed with nobility and factory workers; in America he moved as comfortably in prisons as he did at Ivy League colleges. Stations in life or the places people lived gave Moody no pause except to be careful to communicate. He was able to reach men and women at all levels of society because he truly cared about their souls—and they sensed it.

The Crucial One-to-One Touch

Mr. Moody spent much of his life preaching to large crowds. He did this better than anyone in his era, and in a fashion superior to most preachers in any age. This work was important and he knew it; otherwise he would have given it up. This preaching, however, was a prelude—an essential one, to be sure—to the crucial effort of one-to-one personal contact. At a convention where he spoke on "The Importance of Personal Work," he said, "Personal dealing is of the most vital importance." No one can tell how many souls have been lost through lack of following up the preaching of the Gospels by personal work. He went on to admit that "people are not usually converted under the preaching of a minister. It is in the inquiry meeting that they are most likely to be brought to Christ." Moody claimed there was nothing new about inquiry rooms. The approach of working with each person individually, as the Spirit directs, is set forth in the Bible. Jesus did most of His work on an individual basis, and he treated Nicodemus differently from the woman at the well. Ananias worked personally with Saul, and Philip was sent to have a meeting with the Ethiopian. From such examples Moody concluded: "We must have personal work—hand-to-hand work—if we are going to have results." He told a group of young men that "plenty of men are willing to preach to get on a platform, and preach and exhort, and do that kind of work; but workers are scarce who will labor with a drunkard, or deal with men one at a time."[32]

Dwight Moody did not believe it was effective to preach and then dismiss the congregation without an invitation. At the same time he did not think it wise to urge people to take an "anxious seat" in the room where the preaching was being concluded. This later approach, promulgated by Charles Finney a generation earlier, worked effectively in giving people an opportunity to talk to someone and receive prayer, but it also put seekers on display and created an atmosphere of conspicuousness that frightened away some people, caused others to feel compelled by appearances, and no doubt became a stage for those who enjoyed making spectacles of themselves. The inquiry room was not absolutely free from all of these problems, but it was more private and, therefore, more personal than the other prevalent methods.

Moody used the inquiry room because he longed for an opportunity to talk to people face-to-face. He wanted to care for the soul by asking pointed questions, in love. He then listened to the response with a discerning and patient ear—all in the presence and guidance of the Holy Spirit. Moody was spectacularly effective because he grasped with his mind and heart that all men and women need to confess sin. He knew too that people need to be told that Scripture promises that when we confess our sins and truly repent, God is faithful to forgive us and cleanse us from all unrighteousness (1 John 1:9).

The Need for Soul Doctors

Moody probably never saw just how he fit into the larger scheme of Christian history, but if he had, he would have seen that in the wake of the Protestant Reformation the biblical mandate to "confess your sins one to another" had all too often been thrown aside in an understandable but unfortunate overreaction to the rank abuse of the confessional. If gifted Protestant pastors like Englishman Richard Baxter recognized the need to encourage a return to personal work by visiting the home of each parishioner at least once a year, this practice was disappearing again by the nineteenth century.[33] In rural areas the country doctor all too often took the place of the visiting country parson. Indeed, as one perceptive observer of late nineteenth-century culture phrased it, "The role of the priest has been largely assumed by the family physician. How many, many strange, pitiful, and terrible secrets have been poured into the country doctor's ears, and how many people have received from him not only the relief of confession but the further benefit of wise and strengthening guidance."[34]

Perhaps Moody would not have liked the rhetoric of this observation, but he surely would have understood the biblical concept. In effect, Moody restored the role of priests to an urban society where most people had no one to turn to. Pastors and lay leaders—at least in most big cities—had neither the time nor the training to work with souls. Moody recognized this and made valiant efforts to correct it.[35] Furthermore, if country doctors filled the gap with the disappearance of the pastor-confessor, Moody knew urban physicians were too busy and increasingly too specialized to provide people the individual time they craved, not to mention the fact that they were not trained as soul doctors.[36] In the midst of these changes, Mr. Moody stood in the gap. He ministered personally as a soul physician and soul guide. He also trained a generation of pastoral men and women in the time-honored ministry of the care of souls.

With Moody's passing there was a gradual disappearance of his vision for soul work. Mass evangelist Billy Sunday reverted to preaching to large crowds. He invited people to walk forward and shake his hand if they desired to follow Christ. He also attempted to connect the respondents with a local church. But this was at best a flawed arrangement inasmuch as many people grew spiritually indifferent over the days and weeks that frequently intervened between conviction and follow-up.[37]

In more recent times Billy Graham has preached to massive crowds, and then issued an invitation for people to come forward if they would like to follow Christ. Trained counselors at the front of the hall do personal work with the inquirers. Something of a cross between Moody's and Sunday's approach, the Graham system is far more intimate and private than the path insisted upon by Sunday. If Graham differs from Moody it is because, to Graham's way of thinking, Christ called men publicly, so he must do the same. Graham insists that people need an opportunity to make a public confession of their faith in Christ.[38]

Dwight Moody would never have criticized Finney, Sunday, or Graham. That was not his style. But Moody did train those who worked with him to be careful not to insist on a premature public disclosure of faith. To Moody, public testimony more appropriately followed a time of talking, soul-searching, and prayer.

In the late twentieth century, the kind of love and nurture of souls advocated by Dwight Moody is extremely rare, especially in large metropolitan churches where the pressure is on the pastor to be a polished speaker who attracts large numbers. Pastors of large congregations do not have time to work with souls on an individual basis. Besides, it is now fashionable to refer soul-sick people to Christian counselors who are usually trained in psychology rather than the traditional methods of the care of souls.[39] In many churches, if the souls are not overly troubled, the work of their spiritual counsel and nurture is assigned to small groups rather than to pastors who are called, gifted, and trained in the nurture of souls.

In brief, the intimate, Spirit-saturated, personal work for the care of souls that made Dwight L. Moody so effective has nearly faded away a century after his death. Only time will tell if small groups and professional psychologists can take the place of a true doctor of souls.

OTHER ISSUES

Looking back over the life of Dwight L. Moody and the keys to his extraordinary effectiveness, it is tempting to romanticize him. It is essential to remember that he had his flaws and sometimes made mistakes. First of all, Moody was virtually unaccountable to any human being except his wife. To be sure, he counseled with friends like Farwell and Whittle, but by and large he lacked accountability. Unlike Billy Graham, he had no evangelistic association. Moody had no group of people hold him accountable and pay him a regular salary.

Although Moody never abused money, and although he left only a few hundred dollars and a house to his wife upon his death, he nevertheless answered to no one about what he did receive in gifts or how he spent it.[40] If all his royalties went into a general fund and never touched his pockets, no one knows how much money was given to him by friends, business leaders, and campaign organizers in various cities.

It is quite possible that Mr. Moody's unaccountable approach to finances contributed to Billy Sunday's irresponsibility with donations. Sunday admired Moody and certainly studied his ways for himself, and, like Moody, no one held him accountable. Unlike his predecessor, Sunday could not manage funds, and he succumbed to the temptations to live too lavishly and spoil his children. This behavior nearly destroyed his ministry and it devastated his family.

D. L. Moody could be abrasive. He sometimes ran roughshod over the boards of his schools, trying to bully them to his mode of operation, even threatening to resign if he could not get his way. Some people found amusing Moody's quip that he had no use of committees because if Noah had relied upon one, the ark never would have been built. People who worked with Moody did not find this humorous. They chafed under the yoke of his sometimes high-handed individualism.[41]

Moody's propensity to want to hide from problems often led to results that were destructive to the very goals he so diligently sought to accomplish. As noble as his desire to embrace all truly Christian traditions appeared to be, his schools sometimes floundered due to lack of direction. Moody's refusal to endorse or reject for the schools the dispensationalism of H. N. F. Marshal led to the loss of an excellent Northfield Seminary principal. Later Moody's ambivalence on the issue led to C. I. Scofield's resignation from the pastorate of the Northfield Congregational Church over the same issue that drove an earlier Northfield Seminary principal away. To be sure, Scofield was never on the seminary staff, but it is clear that he accepted the pastorate as a way to enter the community and offer his services at no charge to the seminary.[42]

Similarly, Moody's desire to keep men like George Adam Smith and Henry Drummond on his Northfield speakers' roster confused many people, especially after Drummond drifted from the mainstream of Christianity a year or so before his death in 1897.[43] Moody died leaving a cloud of uncertainty hanging over Northfield. This fact certainly played a role in marked tensions that developed during the next three decades between William and Paul Moody. William remained quite conservative and certain his father would have kept the schools in a mold that the more moderate Paul rejected. All things considered, Dwight L. Moody must take some of the responsibility for erosion of the biblical and Christ-centered focus of the Northfield and Mount Hermon schools over the years.[44]

Squabbles at the Chicago School

The Chicago Bible Institute, renamed Moody Bible Institute after the founder's death, is still biblically based and Christ-centered as Mr. Moody intended. The preservation of that institution's original design, however, is more to the credit of R. A. Torrey's and James M. Gray's leadership than to Moody's hands-on direction. Indeed, Moody clearly supported Torrey, who was an ardent conservative, yet obviously quite interested in emphasizing the person and work of the Holy Spirit, including divine healing. James M. Gray, on the other hand, Torrey's successor, also admired and supported by Moody, moved the school away from those emphases, especially divine healing, as soon as Torrey resigned in 1908. MBI's historian, Gene Getz, concludes that James M. Gray's leadership guided the school through a difficult time when it "may have moved in one of two directions— either toward fanaticism with an emphasis on 'healing' and 'emotional demonstrations' or toward theological liberalism, as happened in the Northfield Schools."[45]

If Torrey had stayed he would have shielded MBI from liberalism. After all, he was a major player in the Fundamentalist movement of the early twentieth century. But would there have been a different attitude toward some of the gifts of the Spirit under Torrey? It is impossible to say. But one thing is evident. Tensions existed between Torrey, on the one hand, and the board and Gray on the other. Part of this tension resulted from Torrey's frequent and extended absences. He often felt led to conduct evangelistic services all over the world. But there were other problems as well.

James M. Gray, born in 1851, was nearly fifty years old when Moody died. Educated at Bates College, Gray distinguished himself early in his career as a superb Bible expositor. Gray, a balding man who sported a neatly trimmed goatee and mustache, was a conservative evangelical of sacramental persuasion. Ordained in the Reformed Episcopal denomination, he held the senior pastorate of Boston's First Reformed Episcopal Church and served on the faculty of his denomination's theological seminary in Philadelphia. Moody admired

James M. Gray

his ability to teach the English Bible, and he had persuaded this impeccably groomed man who always dressed in black suits, shoes, and ties to oversee the Chicago Bible Institute in 1898 when Torrey was away on an extended campaign.[46]

R. A. Torrey was actually five years Gray's junior and was quite domineering. Torrey had neither the inclination nor the desire to defer to his elder. And Gray, for his part, was equally secure and certain of his abilities and interpretation of God's Word. To make matters more stressful, Torrey's absence and Gray's willingness to stand in as director constantly clouded the matter of who was in charge at CBI.

This was precisely the kind of problem Moody artfully avoided. He likewise had no heart to settle some of the tensions arising out of Torrey's emphasis on the Holy Spirit and divine healing on the one side, and Gray's gradual but marked movement into C. I. Scofield's cessationist camp. (Gray, for example, became a consulting editor for Scofield's Reference Bible.) Put bluntly, if Moody had continued to wield a powerful influence at CBI in the early twentieth century, either he would have had to take a firm stand on one side or the other of some issues, or the institute would have been torn apart from internal dissension. CBI might not have survived an extended era of Moody ambivalence.[47]

Willingness to Face Controversy

Although D. L. Moody had flaws and shortcomings as well as strengths, and if these liabilities and assets are relatively easy to identify, he took strong stands on several issues that sparked controversy. To evaluate his positions as right or wrong, or to assess his positions as strengths or weaknesses, is largely a matter of personal opinion, biblical interpretation, theological persuasion, or philosophical presupposition, because strong cases can be made for more than one interpretation. One issue of controversy is fund-raising for Christian work and enterprises. In the 1860s Moody read George Mueller's autobiography, *A Life of Trust*. Then in 1867 the Moodys met the famous Brethren Bible teacher who ministered to English orphans. Mueller and his wife housed, fed, clothed, and led to Christ thousands of orphans and street urchins, and they never asked anyone but God for money to carry on the work. D. L. Moody was impressed by Mueller's faith. Consequently, the American evangelist concluded that he would never ask anyone for personal support for himself or his family. On the other hand, D. L. Moody determined that God wanted him to make direct appeals for funds for Christian work, and enterprises.

There is no evidence that Moody ever solicited funds for himself or his family. He did not even insist that his personal expenses be met when he agreed to minister someplace for one day or several weeks. What he did do, however, was make bold and frequent appeals for funds to construct buildings for Christian work, such as a YMCA facility or a building for an orphanage. He likewise solicited funds in a most open manner to support other Christian workers such as deaconesses, and he never hesitated to ask for money to underwrite something like the publication of Christian literature or the distribution of books for prison ministry. In fact, D. L. Moody became a pioneer and an innovator in the field of religious fund-raising in the United States.

During the early years when he was trying to get a YMCA building or a mission school constructed, he made personal appeals to his wealthy friends and associates like John Farwell and Cyrus McCormick. By the early 1870s he handwrote hundreds of letters to

Christian friends, associates, and acquaintances, urging them to help him put up a facility or underwrite a project that promised to bring souls to the Lord Jesus Christ. After his ministry became diverse—especially once he had his schools to support—Moody employed secretaries to write form letters, which he signed, to an ever-growing list of potential donors. When the typewriter came into common usage by the late 1870s and early 1880s, Moody had fund-raising letters typed and he and Emma often spent many hours signing these appeals. In 1887, for example, Emma wrote that she and D. L. were extremely busy: "We have been sending off begging letters." She explained to Willie, "I have directed over 1000 letters [perhaps] 1500 and we are sending by post today 4000 so you can see we are busy."[48]

Moody often sent one of his books to a potential donor. In 1889, for instance, he sent a two-page typed appeal soliciting money to underwrite another summer conference for college students. He explained the importance of these meetings for bringing seekers to Christ, for encouraging "aggressive Christian work among their fellow students" and causing "many of them also deciding for the ministry." Then in a P.S. to the personally signed appeal, Moody explained, "I send you a copy of the book, 'College Students at Northfield,' giving an account of the students' meeting here last summer, and some of the addresses. I shall be glad to receive whatever you feel that you can give."[49]

Moody also sent personable, talented, and well-known emissaries to call on wealthy donors, assuming the personal touch would yield superior results. Either he or T. W. Harvey, for instance, made personal calls in Chicago, and on one occasion Moody sent D. W. Whittle all the way to Glasgow, Scotland, from Chicago to solicit 1,000 pounds (British sterling) from a man who had given an equal sum before.[50]

As Mr. Moody perfected his techniques by the 1880s, going from handwritten letters to typed letters with gift books, he developed additional techniques by the 1890s. Using a Christian weekly newspaper, *The Christian Herald and Sign of Our Times,* he had the editor do a full-page story on the effective work of the Chicago Bible Institute. The editor inserted in the middle of the article—blocked off in bolder print—a copy of a thank-you letter Moody wrote to a man who gave $1,000 to CBI. The article's end included an appeal for more donations to be sent directly to the newspaper office. The financial plea then led into a list of dozens of donors, complete with their names, hometowns, and size of gift. This tactic was effective, and the published lists reveal what a wide donor base of small contributors Moody relied upon.[51]

Dwight L. Moody's fund-raising techniques were extremely advanced and creative for the 1880s and 1890s—an era when advertising as business was in its infancy. To many people Moody was becoming crass. He was a materialist who manipulated people to fund his pet projects. To others he was an able fund-raiser who knew how to inform Christians of how they might help build the kingdom of God in gilded-age America. Everyone, whatever his perspective, admitted Moody was a trendsetter. Soon numerous churches and parachurches would adopt his techniques to bankroll their programs. Whether people liked his innovative tactics or not, they admitted Moody was extraordinarily effective at raising money. The amazing thing about the amount of money he raised during the 1893 World's Fair is that a devastating depression hit the United States in fall 1893, and it lasted until 1896. Moody was able to squeeze water out of the desert sand, or so it appeared to people who were making $400 to $500 a year, if they could even find work.[52]

This ability to raise large sums of money even during a depression caused some observers to point out that Moody drew his closest friends and supporters from the economic power elite. To be sure, he became friendly with extremely wealthy families in both America and Great Britain. People such as Lord and Lady Kinnaird stayed in the Moody home at Northfield, and they gave liberally to his causes, as did the powerful John Wanamaker family of Philadelphia.[53] These connections were always controversial, especially in times of economic depression, labor unrest, and confrontations between workers and owners of factories.

Labor-Management Disputes

D. L. Moody seldom took sides in labor-management disputes when he preached or when he wrote books. But his sympathies were well-known. In spring 1886 he revealed his attitude toward labor unrest and strikes in a widely circulated periodical, *Record of Christian Work:* "Either these people [striking workers] are to be evangelized or the leaven of communism and infidelity will assume such enormous proportions that it will break out in a reign of terror such as this country has never known. It don't take a prophet or a son of a prophet to see these things. You can hear the muttering of the coming convulsions even now, if you open your ears and eyes."[54]

Moody saw the storm clouds clearly. Massive labor unrest was already evident, with strikes in rail-center Chicago already under way. Then in May 1886 an Anarchist-Communist rally at Chicago's Haymarket Square turned into a riot. A bomb was thrown into a company of policemen. Seven lawmen were killed and seventy wounded. Although no one ever proved who threw the bomb, eight radical agitators were arrested, tried, and convicted. Seven men were sentenced to death and one to fifteen years in prison. Large and noisy demonstrations were held to protest the convictions of men who had little evidence presented against them except their radical political views.[55]

Moody remained silent. He advocated a religious solution rather than a political solution to these problems. Christian Socialists like celebrated novelist and critic William Dean Howells disagreed. Howells felt confident that Jesus would have confronted the owners of factions and taken the side of the poor. Howells and those who agreed with him said Christ would have thrown the money changers out again, but Moody maintained that Jesus never advocated political solutions to problems rooted in human sin. Moody's critics answered by saying he was siding with his friends like George Pullman and Cyrus McCormick. They were his supporters and they were major targets of strikes and agitators.

Violence erupted across the United States again in 1894, with most of the action in Chicago. The famous Pullman strike pitted workers against George C. Pullman and his railcar manufacturing business. This strike brought every Midwestern railroad to a standstill and paralyzed transportation in Chicago. Over the protests of Illinois governor John Peter Altgeld, President Grover Cleveland sent federal troops to break the strike. The trains had to run again, the president argued, because the U. S. mail must be delivered.[56]

Again, Moody's friends in railroad, meatpacking, farm equipment, lumber, and dry goods industries were on the side of law and order rather than the laborer. Moody was silent in public, but everyone knew he favored a spiritual rather than a political solution. He worked incessantly for the poor from the 1860s through the 1890s—building schools, raising money for orphanages, and distributing food, fuel, and clothing to the destitute, reaching out to prisoners and children of alcoholics. He preached the gospel to the poor and equipped countless women and men to do the same thing. He was convinced that everyone's greatest need was a personal relationship with Christ—a relationship that would bring with it new hearts, eternal life, and the ability to build a decent life in the land that offered equality of opportunity. Moody's critics accused him of being at best naive or at worst a downright partisan of rich men who exploited the poor. Opportunities, after all, were dwindling in an increasingly urban America. The nation was only 18 percent urban in 1860, but 44 percent urban by 1900. People simply could not find economic opportunity in the changing order. Therefore, according to those who advocated political action, the government must step in and regulate the economic and social order to bring about justice.[57]

Christian advocates of the social gospel urged followers of Christ to push for local, state, and federal intervention. The government, they said, should usher in justice for the poor. Moody, on the other hand, said that they had the biblical order reversed. When God becomes the center of people's lives, He leads them to lives of righteousness. Justice flows from righteousness, and only then will poverty be abolished and peace restored to the cities.

Some of Moody's critics argued that his premillennialist stand caused him to ignore poverty and other urban problems inasmuch as he expected Christ to return at any time. Social gospel advocates, however, who tended to be postmillennialists, did not expect Christ to return until one thousand years of peace and justice had been established. But Moody and most of his premillennialist friends did not use their beliefs as an excuse for inactivity. They indeed believed Christ could return at any moment, but they still planted churches, opened orphanages, took the gospel to jails, and trained young people to be ministers and missionaries. Moody's son Paul acknowledged that his father "believed in the Second Coming, loved to preach on it, and one of his favorite poems was on this theme. Yet he built his schools on a sound and enduring basis, [with] brick and mortar," never encouraging his followers "to be improvident" like the Thessalonians of old.[58]

The controversy over Moody's determination to hold to his priority of working with souls rather than striving for political change seemed less important to social gospelers and Christian Socialists of his day than to historians and social scientists in the last sixty or seventy years who have been disturbed that he did not devote his life to what they have perceived as a clear-cut class struggle. As a matter of fact, while Moody's contemporaries, men like Josiah Strong and Washington Gladden, did not always share Moody's agenda and presuppositions, they did not criticize him. Instead, they got on with their work and let him pursue his. And when he invited them to come and speak at Northfield, they came and enjoyed the fellowship and interaction.[59]

HIS PART IN PARACHURCHES
AND INDEPENDENT CHURCHES

Where Moody's contemporaries were not as silent was in the area of his contribution to the rise of two trends—parachurches and independent churches. This movement, for better or worse, undermined the Christian religious status quo for the next century. First, Mr. Moody was never ordained and never wanted to be. Likewise, at his schools he helped train a generation of lay leaders who became a mighty force in world Christianity. Not only did he train workers who were originally intended to assist pastors and stand in the gap where ordained ministers could not or would not go, but he also eventually trained people who, like their mentor, planted their own churches or filled pulpits where congregations wanted men with different backgrounds and expertise. Along with the rise of independent churches that inevitably competed with denominational churches, Moody and his co-workers promoted all types of parachurch organizations such as the YMCA and other independent home and foreign mission agencies. Despite contrary intentions, these institutions eventually supplanted rather than complemented existing structures.

Moody did much to calm troubled waters of unrest from traditional denominations. He astutely avoided holding Sunday morning union meetings in the cities where he held campaigns, preferring instead to urge the people to attend their own local churches. If he preached on Sunday morning, it was in a local church. To blunt the sharp edge of the critics who argued that he was still undercutting mainline churches and seminary-trained ministers, in each city where he campaigned, beginning in the 1880s, he gave at least one special talk designed to support pastors and local churches. "If our meetings here would unsettle the people, or have the effect of keeping them from attending their houses of worship—rather than constitute to take part in them, I would go back to Chicago, and settle down there at business of some kind or other." He would then point out how hard pastors worked and that they needed to be respected, prayed for, and fully supported. To the new converts he said, "Let me urge young converts to join the minister in his work, and not to be unsettled in regard to his duty." He continued that "the dearest thing to the heart of the Son of God on this earth is—the Church. . . . [and] take care to do nothing that would cool or kill his influence and efforts." Finally he maintained that if there had been "success of our meetings here," it is largely due to the fact that "your pastors [have] been sowing the seed here for years."[60]

HIS ROLE IN SENDING MISSIONS LABORERS

Do what he would, Mr. Moody could not dispel the obvious. By the end of the nineteenth century, a massive army of lay men and women were roaming the cities of Britain and America and the mission fields of the world. They represented every conceivable denomination, but increasingly they identified with their independent organizations and demonstrated decreasing loyalty to the old mainline traditions.[61]

Mr. Moody's multifaceted ministries were a significant—perhaps the most significant—impetus in bringing about the domination of Christian home and foreign missions by lay people and independent organizations, and this trend, for better or worse, accelerated another major trend that rocked the Christian status quo.

While the laity and independents asserted themselves in urban and foreign ministry, there was also a growing movement away from the Calvinistic theology that had dominated many of the major denominations in the decades up to the Civil War. Presbyterians, Congregationalists, as well as most Baptists and Episcopalians, had Calvinistic antecedents. Indeed, doctrines of election, total human depravity, and mankind's helpless sinfulness were lifted high. To be sure, a combination of the democratic tendencies of the American frontier, plus a heavy dose of Methodism, conspired to bring new emphases on free will and human ability to make a decision to follow Christ.[62]

Besides this essentially rural and frontier-based movement of the "democratization of theology," Dwight L. Moody and his large following began to stress an understanding of God who loves all people and wants no one to perish. Far from being universalists who claimed all will be saved, a "love them in" theology dominated Moody's ministry and the ministry of those he mentored and trained. The result was that by the time of Moody's death a more Arminian or Wesleyan view of God spread through the training programs and ministry command posts of urban and foreign missions. It seeped into the major denominations, and early on it took root in many independent churches. Consequently, the emphasis on individual initiative and responsibility that spread throughout rural America because of the New England revivals of the eighteenth century, the Finney revivals of the mid-nineteenth century, and the rapid spread of Methodism from the Atlantic seaboard westward became a com-

The Moodys with grandchildren (circa 1897)

plementary reality in the cities. Thanks to the ministerial and educational efforts of Dwight L. Moody, the Calvinism that dominated much of American Christianity as late as the 1870s was powerfully undercut within a quarter century, and, of course, this theological persuasion spread to the foreign mission fields as well.[63]

In retrospect, Dwight L. Moody looks rather similar to other strong religious leaders who have emerged across the centuries of Christian history. He possessed a wealth of natural talents, plus apparently supernatural gifts of vision, discernment, and power. Along with these extraordinary assets Moody carried an ample assortment of imperfections—all troublesome enough to remind his followers that he was in no way divine. As he fulfilled his mission, he left a powerful wake rich with transformed lives, new institutions, innovative trends, and a host of younger people trained up to take his place. Such a man as Mr. Moody made many friends and not a few enemies. Wherever he went he set fires of controversy—some of them smoldering to this day.

Late in life Mr. D. L. Moody uttered a prophetic statement. It is perhaps his most accurate epitaph: "I am thankful to tell you that I have some splendid men and women in the field. My school work will not tell much until the century closes, but when I am gone I shall leave some grand men and women behind."[64]

MOODY AND THE HISTORIANS

A nother rather large book would be required to summarize and evaluate the historical and biographical literature on Dwight L. Moody. Indeed, in 1948 Wilbur M. Smith published a 221-page book entitled *An Annotated Bibliography of D. L. Moody* (Chicago: Moody Press, 1948). Dr. Smith performed a superb service by gathering, listing, and sometimes summarizing and quoting from, the books and articles written on or by Mr. Moody. An updating of this work would be a welcome addition to Moody historiography because much has been published in the last half century.

For the reader who is interested in debates among historians, I am presenting this brief survey of selected literature. No attempt is made to offer a complete overview. Instead, I have set forth a few trends with references to representative books.

I. Biographies:

When Paul D. Moody published his reminiscences entitled *My Father* (Boston: Little, Brown, 1938), he noted that almost sixty biographies had been written about his father. Most of these early books were superficial, hastily written, error-filled, and overly sympathetic works that appeared in the middle 1870s when Moody became internationally renowned. Of the threescore books appearing before Paul Moody's memoir, several deserve special mention, and each one should be consulted by serious students of Moody's life. The first is W. H. Daniels, *D. L. Moody and His Work* (Hartford: American Publishing Co., 1875). Daniels was a friend of Moody and his family. He was their neighbor in Chicago, and he was pastor of Chicago's Park Avenue Methodist Episcopal Church. This book of more than 450 pages is full of primary sources, especially Daniels's own recollections and those of other Moody contemporaries. Daniels was an early-day oral historian. He interviewed many people in Chicago and Great

Britain. Although this work is extremely favorable to its subject, there is marked objectivity in the story, and there is no hint of hero worship.

Another biography replete with personal recollections is *Echoes from the Platform and Pulpit* (Hartford: A. O. Worthington & Co., 1900). Pages 33–111 comprise a surprisingly informative and insightful portrait of Mr. Moody by Charles F. Goss, who served as pastor of Moody's church for several years. Goss, like Daniels, admired his friend, but he made no attempt to turn him into a demigod.

Another biography that is based largely on personal reminiscences is A. P. Fitt, *A Shorter Life of D. L. Moody* (Chicago: Bible Institute Colportage Association, 1900). Fitt was Moody's son-in-law and a great admirer of the evangelist. Nevertheless, this slender book is an intimate portrait full of rich pickings from family letters and lore. He is especially good on Moody's relationship to his family.

For people at the turn of the century who are willing to read a larger biography by a family member, William R. Moody's *The Life of Dwight L. Moody* (Chicago: Fleming H. Revell, 1900) is nearly six hundred pages long and full of personal information, insights, and stories that only someone like this oldest son could have known. William Moody hastily wrote this book at the time of his father's death because he wanted to get an accurate biography in print before the profiteers saturated the market with books full of half-truths and outright fiction. Despite his haste, William Moody wrote an extremely valuable book. It is a rich primary source, and it was revised in a 1930 edition. The latter edition shows stylistic improvement, but it omits many important details of Mr. Moody's life covered in the 1900 volume.

Among other useful biographical works by men who knew Moody are John V. Farwell, *Early Recollections of Dwight L. Moody* (Chicago: Winona Publishers, 1907); R. A. Torrey, *Why God Used D. L. Moody* (Chicago: Bible Institute Colportage Association, 1923); and Charles R. Erdman, *D. L. Moody: His Message For Today* (New York: Revell, 1928).

One of the best portraits of Moody ever written is Gamaliel Bradford's, *D. L. Moody: A Worker in Souls* (Garden City, New Jersey: Doubleday, Doran, 1928). A three-hundred-page impressionistic portrait, it is the only serious attempt at a psychobiography of Moody. Bradford was not a professing Christian, but he wrote a balanced, sympathetic, and brilliantly insightful book that is indispensable to understanding Moody.

Paul Moody's *My Father* is full of previously unpublished

glimpses into Moody's life and character. Paul Moody is more willing than his brother to note his father's shortcomings, and he is eager to show why Moody distanced himself from separatistic Christians, especially the Plymouth Brethren.

Although several biographies came out about the same time as Paul Moody's book—all to celebrate the centennial of D. L. Moody's birth—none besides *My Father* makes a significant contribution to our knowledge of the man and his ministry.

Not until the 1960s do any biographies worthy of careful attention appear. In 1963 John C. Pollock published *Moody: A Biographical Portrait of the Pacesetter in Modern Mass Evangelism* (New York: Macmillan). Publication of Pollock's *Moody* is important for two reasons. First, the author was the first biographer to have complete access to the Moody family papers owned by Mrs. Emma Moody Powell and those of Mrs. William R. Moody, including the latter's invaluable diaries of her father, D. W. Whittle. Pollock, a well-known English writer, also had access to Moody correspondence collected in the 1940s and 1950s by Moody Bible Institute. Second, Pollock's biography is a well-written book, enriched with quotations from previously unused primary sources. It is ideal for a general reader of evangelical persuasion.

In 1969 James F. Findlay, Jr., published *Dwight L. Moody: American Evangelist, 1837–1899* (Chicago: Univ. of Chicago). This is, by all measuring devices, a first-rate book. Findlay had access to all of the sources Pollock consulted, but his book differs in significant ways. First, Findlay's *Moody* is based on extensive research into a vast range of primary sources that relate to both Moody and his era. Second, Findlay carefully and judiciously places Moody in a wider historical context, demonstrating how the evangelist was shaped by and influenced his times. Third, although the author is sympathetic to Moody, he is writing for an audience wider than evangelicals. This well-crafted book of more than four hundred pages is written for an educated, general readership. Findlay also places Moody squarely into the context of revivalism, and he passes balanced judgment on the historiography relating to Moody and revivalism. Finally, this 1969 biography is enhanced by careful, detailed, and extremely illuminating documentation. This book is replete with footnotes—something none of Moody's other biographers (except Gamaliel Bradford) offer the reader.

II. Church History:

Among the histories of American revivalism, William Warren Sweet, *American Revivalism: Its Origin, Growth and Decline* (New York: Scribner, 1945) is outdated in many respects, but it is still useful. Particularly impressive is the author's willingness to admit supernaturalistic causes to Moody's effectiveness. Two other books, Bernard A. Weisberger, *They Gathered at the River* (Boston: Little, Brown, 1958) and William G. McLoughlin, *Modern Revivalism: Charles G. Finney to Billy Graham* (New York: Ronald Press, 1959), treat Moody fairly and thoughtfully, but both explain him in large part as a representative of a conservative religious response to the rise of industry, the growth of cities, and the massive immigration movement of the late-nineteenth century. Although there is much to be said for their socioeconomic interpretations, neither author sees the larger complexity of factors that shaped and motivated him. (See McLoughlin's *Revivals, Awakenings, and Reform* [Chicago: Univ. of Chicago Press, 1978].)

Both Mark Noll, *A History of Christianity in the United States and Canada* (Grand Rapids: Eerdmans, 1992) and George Marsden, *Fundamentalism and American Culture: The Shaping of Twentieth-Century Evangelism: 1870–1925* (New York: Oxford Univ. Press, 1980), modern historians of American church history, include Moody in their thoughtfully conceived and well-written overviews. Neither author attempts to say anything particularly new about Moody, but they do place conservative Christians in a more favorable, prominent, and, therefore, clearer light than some earlier historians of American religious history who mainly celebrated the liberal tradition. See, for example, Henry May, *Protestant Churches and Industrial America* (New York: Harper, 1949); C. Howard Hopkins, *The Rise of the Social Gospel in American Protestantism 1865–1915* (New Haven: Yale Univ. Press, 1940).

III. General:

Unfortunately, much American religious history and general American history until recent years has been dominated by the grossly oversimplified assumption that the central theme of American history, at least in the period since 1860, has been the struggle between the business community, on the one hand, and oppressed groups on the other. Some of this historiography has been shaped by Marxism, and some of it by New Deal and post-New Deal liberalism with its commitment to governmental intervention as the best means of ensuring equality of opportunity for all people. Many of these historians consider Moody too insignificant to mention, but those who do grant him a place in their histories marginalize him as a pawn of the economic elite. See, for example, George Adam Smith, who quite early noticed and bemoaned this class-struggle theme as the way many people interpreted conservative Christian leaders, in *Life of Henry Drummond* (London: Hodden & Stoughton, 1899); Chester Destler, *American Radicalism, 1865–1901* (New London: Connecticut College Press, 1946); Charles and Mary Beard, *The Rise of American Civilization* (New York: Macmillan, 1930); Ray Ginger, *Altgeld's America* (New York: Funk & Wagnalls, 1958).

Other historians, although concerned with class conflict, have disparaged Moody as a man who was part of a conservative, middle-class group attempting to impose Christian values and order and their moral equivalent—rural virtues—on a disorganized, new, urban-industrial order. See, for example, Anne M. Boylan, *Sunday School: The Formation of an American Institution, 1790–1880* (New Haven: Yale Univ. Press, 1988); Paul Boyer, *Urban Masses and Moral Order in America, 1820–1920* (Cambridge: Harvard Univ. Press, 1978); James Gilbert, *Perfect Cities: Chicago's Utopias of 1893* (Chicago: Univ. of Chicago Press, 1991). Marsden, cited above, is much more balanced in his view of Moody, but he sees Moody's social views as primarily a product of his American middle class, individualistic values.

Historians such as Boylan, Gilbert, and Boyer are typical of most American historians. They interpret Moody as a well-meaning but reactionary man. To them, he was part of a rear guard action movement designed to protect a decidedly archaic culture and worldview.

IV. British and Canadian Church History:

If historians like Mark Noll and George Marsden have attempted to show that Moody and the evangelicalism he represented played a significant role in shaping American culture of the twentieth century, perhaps no one has argued as persuasively as British historian David Bebbington, *Evangelicalism in Modern Britain: A History from the 1730's to the 1980's* (Grand Rapids: Baker, 1992) that Moody helped spur on an evangelical movement that has been a powerful force in modern Britain. Although he does not say so, this is no doubt equally true in the United States.

The recent outpouring of Christian history monographs in

Canada is impressive. One of the striking trends is the seriousness with which D. L. Moody is taken. Brian J. Fraser, *The Social Uplifters: Presbyterian Progressivism and the Social Gospel in Canada, 1875–1915* (Montreal: Wilifred Laurier Univ. Press, 1988) demonstrates Moody's impact on bringing Canadian Presbyterians to embrace a moderate form of revivalism.

Michael Gauvreau, *The Evangelical Century and Creed in English Canada from the Great Revival to the Great Depression* (Montreal: McGill-Queenly Univ. Press, 1991) shows Moody's impact in Scotland in the 1870s, on men such as A. B. Bruce and Henry Drummond, being carried over to Canada some years later with transformational strength. He also shows how Moody helped stem the tide of liberalism. In Phyllis D. Airhart, *Serving the Present Age: Revivalism, Progressivism, and the Methodist Tradition in Canada* (Montreal: McGill-Queenly Univ. Press, 1992), we see marked evidence that Moody and Sankey helped "vindicate" Methodist revivalism that had been disparaged by other conservative Christians.

Ramsay Cook, *The Regenerators: Social Criticism in Late Victorian English Canada* (Toronto: Univ. of Toronto Press, 1985), in a judiciously written manner, makes clear that Moody's impact in Canada in the 1880s and 1890s was powerful enough that it could not be ignored, and that humanists of the late nineteenth century had to take him on from the platform and press. John W. Grant, *A Profusion of Spires: Religion in Nineteenth-Century Ontario* (Toronto: Univ. of Toronto Press, 1988), reveals Moody's profound impact on Ontario, especially by inaugurating a custom of pairing a singer and a preacher. Moody also helped cause the spread of premillennialism. David B. Marshall's splendid book, *Secularizing the Faith: Canadian Protestant Clergy and the Crisis of Belief, 1850–1940* (Toronto: Univ. of Toronto Press, 1992), among many other things, argues that Moody's Canadian revival campaigns had a strong impact on the churches, especially Presbyterian and Methodist.

Moody's books of sermons were reprinted and widely disseminated in Canada, and his biblical-based, Christ-centered preaching helped revitalize lethargic and dying churches. Finally, one of the most important additions to understanding the impact of Moody's ministry is an unpublished M.A. thesis by Eric Robert Crouse, "An American Evangelist in Canada: D. L. Moody and the Canadian Protestant Community, 1884–1898," M.A. thesis (History), University of Calgary. Crouse maintains that Moody's message had an inner spiritual dynamism that gave revivalism and evangelicalism respectability and staying power they might not have developed without Moody's leadership.

V. Unpublished Works:

If some of the most interesting historical writing that takes Moody seriously as a shaper of culture is coming out of Britain and Canada, it is also true that some of the most original contributions have appeared in unpublished theses and dissertations that one hopes will soon be published. Besides the splendid Crouse thesis noted above, Mark J. Toone, "Evangelicalism in Transition: A Comparative Analysis of the Work and Theology of D. L. Moody and His Proteges, Henry Drummond and R. A. Torrey," Ph.D. dissertation, St. Mary's College, University of St. Andrews [Scotland], 1988, is a brilliantly argued study of Moody as a bridge between liberal and conservative positions. Moody, Toone maintained, was owned by neither side.

Two unpublished works written in the United States deserve a wider audience. Donald A. Wells's 1972 work, "D. L. Moody and His Schools: An Historical Analysis of an Educational Ministry," is slightly dated. Nevertheless, it is a first-rate piece of scholarship that should be in print. Also Martha M. Goetzman, "Anomalous Features in the Chicago Prayer Meeting Revival of 1858: The Nature of the Revival as Revealed in Contemporary Newspaper Accounts," M.A. thesis, Trinity Evangelical Divinity School (Church History), 1985, is an impressive revisionist work that shows much revivalism scholarship to be oversimplified about the time and cause of the 1858 revival. This scholar's findings at least need to be in a major article so that future scholars will see that the old socioeconomic causal interpretations are inadequate.

NOTES

Abbreviations Used in the Notes

DLM	Dwight L. Moody
EM	Emma (Revell) Moody
Daniels, *Moody*	W. H. Daniels, *D. L. Moody and His Work* (Hartford: American Publishing Co., 1875).
Dedmon, *Great Enterprises*	Emmett Dedmon, *Great Enterprises: 100 Years of the YMCA of Metropolitan Chicago* (New York: Rand McNally, 1957).
Farwell, *Moody*	John V. Farwell, *Early Recollections of D. L. Moody* (Chicago: Winona Publishing Co., 1907).
Findlay, *Moody*	James F. Findlay, Jr., *Dwight L. Moody: American Evangelist, 1837–1899* (Chicago: Univ. of Chicago Press, 1969).
Fitt, *Moody*	A. P. Fitt, *The Life of D. L. Moody* (Chicago: Moody Press, n.d.).
Goss, *Echoes*	Charles F. Goss, *Echoes from the Pulpit and Platform* (Hartford: A. D. Worthington, 1900).
Gundry, *Love Them In*	Stanley N. Gundry, *Love Them In: The Proclamation Theology of D. L. Moody* (Chicago: Moody Press, 1976).
McDowell, *What D. L. Moody Means to Me*	John McDowell, et al., *What D. L. Moody Means to Me: An Anthology of Appreciations and Appraisals of the Beloved Founder of the Northfield Schools* (E. Northfield, Massachusetts: The Northfield Schools, 1937).
Moody, *Glad Tidings*	D. L. Moody, *Glad Tidings: Sermons & Prayer Meeting Talks* (New York: Treat, 1876).
Moody, *Moody*	William R. Moody, *The Life of Dwight L. Moody* (New York: Fleming H. Revell, 1900).
Moody, *My Father*	Paul Dwight Moody, *My Father: An Intimate Portrait of Dwight Moody* (Boston: Little, Brown, 1938).
Pollock, *Moody*	John C. Pollock, *Moody: A Biographical Portrait of the Pacesetter in Modern Mass Evangelism* (New York: Macmillan, 1963).
Powell, *Heavenly Destiny*	Emma Moody Powell, *Heavenly Destiny: The Life Story of Mrs. D. L. Moody* (Chicago: Moody Press, 1943).
Torrey, *Why God Used D. L Moody*	R. A. Torrey, *Why God Used D. L. Moody* (Minneapolis: World Wide Publications, 1992 Reprint).

Introduction

1. Woodrow Wilson is quoted in John McDowell, et al., *What D. L. Moody Means to Me: An Anthology of Appreciations and Appraisals of the Beloved Founder of The Northfield Schools* (E. Northfield, Massachusetts: The Northfield Schools, 1937), 23. On the same page as this reminiscence there is a copy of a letter from President Wilson to Doctor Bridgman dated 26 October 1914 where he says, "This is not a legend; it is a fact; and I am perfectly willing that you should publish it. My admiration and esteem for Mr. Moody was very deep indeed."
2. Wilfred Grenfell, *What Christ Means to Me* (London: Pilgrim Press, 1927), 21–23.
3. See Wilfred Grenfell, *A Labrador Doctor* (Boston: Houghton Mifflin, 1919); *Forty Years for Labrador* (Boston: Houghton Mifflin, 1932); and *What Christ Means to Me*, 23–27.
4. See the three books cited in note 3.
5. Luther D. Wishard, quoted in Joseph B. Bowles, *Moody the Evangelist: A Character Sketch with Original Sayings* (Chicago: Moody Bible Institute, 1926), 3.
6. Robert L. Dufus, "The Hound of Heaven," *American Mercury*, Vol. 5, April 1925, pp. 424–32, quoted in Gamaliel Bradford, *D. L. Moody: A Worker in Souls* (Garden City, New York: Doubleday, Doran & Company, 1928), 16.
7. Wishard in Bowles, *Moody the Evangelist*, 21.
8. Quoted in Moody, *Moody*, 502.
9. DLM to Mrs. MacKinnon, 12 November 1899, quoted in Moody, *Moody*, 546.
10. Quoted in McDowell, *What D. L. Moody Means to Me*, 9.
11. Moody, *My Father*, viii.
12. William Warren Sweet, *American Revivalism: Its Origin, Growth and Decline* (New York: Scribner, 1945), 169.
13. F. F. Bruce, In *Retrospect: Remembrances of Things Past* (Grand Rapids: Baker, 1993), 154.

Chapter One

1. Moody, *Moody*, chap. 1.
2. Ibid., 17.
3. Ibid., 33.
4. Daniels, *Moody*, chap. 1; Moody, *Moody*, chap. 1; Pollock, *Moody*, chap. 1.
5. Moody, *Moody*, 20.
6. Ibid.
7. Moody, *Moody*, 4–5.
8. Moody, *Moody*, 21.
9. Daniels, *Moody*, chap. 1; Moody, *Moody*, 21.
10. Daniels, *Moody*, 5.
11. Ibid., 5–6.
12. D. L. Moody, one-page document titled *Autobiography*, Moody Bible Institute archives (hereafter cited MBI).
13. Moody, *Moody*, chap. 1; Daniels, *Moody*, chap. 1.
14. Daniels, *Moody*, 6–7.
15. Goss, *Echoes*, sermon on 601.
16. Pollock, *Moody*, 5.
17. Goss, *Echoes*, 35; Moody, *Moody*, 30–31.
18. Goss, *Echoes*, 490–95.
19. Ibid.
20. Ibid.
21. Moody, *Moody*, 26.
22. For example, see the letters housed in MBI that were written in 1854 from D. L. Moody (hereafter referred to as DLM) to various family members.
23. Moody, *Moody*, 17–35.
24. Daniels, *Moody*, 13.
25. Moody, *Moody*, 35.

Chapter Two

1. U.S. Census of 1850, Statistics of Massachusetts.
2. Adna F. Weber, *The Growth of Cities in the Nineteenth Century* (Ithaca: Cornell Univ. Press, reprint, 1967), 25.
3. Brattleboro's population went from 2,600 to 4,000. See *Gazetteer and Business Directory of Windham County, Vermont, 1724-1884* (Syracuse, 1884).
4. Some fascinating train stop information is in Henry Drummond, "Mr. Moody: Some Impressions and Facts," *McClure's Magazine*, 1894, 55.
5. Daniels, *Moody*, 16.
6. Population, immigration, and historical information are in U.S. Census of 1850, Statistics of Massachusetts; Census of 1880, *Social Statistics of Cities,* Boston.
7. DLM to Brothers, 9 April 1854, Yale Divinity School archives (hereafter cited as Yale).
8. Goss, *Echoes,* sermon, 172; Moody, *Moody,* 34–36 (photo on 34).
9. Daniels, *Moody,* 16–17.
10. Quoted in Moody, *Moody,* 36.
11. Ibid., 36–37.
12. Daniels, *Moody,* 17–19.
13. Moody, *Moody,* 37–38.
14. Daniels, *Moody,* 17–19; Moody, *Moody,* 39.
15. DLM to Brothers, 9 April 1854, Yale; DLM to Mother, 5 June 1854, MBI.
16. DLM to Brother S[amuel], 4 May 1854, MBI.
17. See for example, DLM letter and copies of letters dated 4 May 1854; 9 April 1854, 22 August 1854, Yale; 5 June 1854, MBI.
18. DLM to Brother G[eorge], 4 May 1854, Yale.
19. DLM to Brother E[dwin], 4 May 1854, Yale; Daniels, *Moody,* 19.
20. DLM to Mother, 5 June 1854, MBI.
21. DLM to Mother, Brothers, and Sister, 11 October 1855, Yale.
22. DLM to Mother, 5 June 1854, MBI; and Dear Brothers, 9 April 1854, Yale.
23. Daniels, *Moody,* 21.
24. Material on Moody's relationship with Dr. Kirk, the pastor, and Edward Kimball, the Sunday school teacher, and the church in general can be found in Moody, *Moody,* chap. 3; Daniels, *Moody,* chap. 2; and Edward Kimball's "Reminiscences of Moody," a copy of which is on file at the MBI and Yale archives.
25. Kimball, "Reminiscences of Moody."
26. Ibid.
27. Moody quoted in J. Wilbur Chapman, *The Life and Work of D. L. Moody* (Philadelphia: American Bible House, 1900), 76.
28. Although many times he talked about being born of the flesh in 1837 and the Spirit in 1856, he evidently said it first to the reporter for the *Chicago Pulpit* in May 1872. See Wilbur M. Smith, *An Annotated Bibliography of D. L. Moody* (Chicago: Moody Press, 1948), 158.
29. Moody Papers, "Dwight L. Moody's experience 1855–56, Langdon S. Ward, deacon of Mt. Vernon Church," typescript, Yale archives.
30. Quoted in Moody, *Moody,* 44.
31. Ibid.
32. Kimball, "Reminiscences of Moody"; Findlay, *Moody,* 51.
33. Quoted in Joseph B. Bowles, *Moody the Evangelist: A Character Sketch with Original Sayings* (Chicago: Moody Bible Institute, 1926), 17.
34. Quoted in Moody, *Moody,* 42.
35. See Letters in September and October 1856, sent to several family members, Yale and MBI archives. See also Findlay, *Moody,* 52; and Moody, *Moody,* 45.
36. Letter to Mother, Brothers, and Sister, Yale.
37. Daniels, *Moody,* 27.
38. Betsy Moody to "My Dear Boys" 6 July [1856], Yale.
39. Moody, *Moody,* 46.

Chapter Three

1. His ambition to earn $100,000 is noted by his son William in Moody, *Moody*, 48. Likewise, D. L. Moody frequently recalled that after his conversion he had a deep longing to rescue souls. See Daniels, *Moody*, 26–27. For wages see U. S. Bureau of the Census, *Historical Statistics of the United States* (Washington, D.C., 1960), 92–93.
2. Tenth Census of the U.S., 1880, Vol. 19, *Social Statistics of Cities*, Chicago, 489–513. See also Bessie Louise Pierce, *A History of Chicago* (New York: Knopf, 1940), Vol. 2, 3.
3. *Historical Statistics of the United States;* see also *Railroad Maps of North America* (Washington, D.C., 1984), 45–51.
4. Pierce, *A History of Chicago*, Vol. 2; Harold M. Mayer and Richard C. Wade, *Chicago: Growth of a Metropolis* (Chicago: Univ. of Chicago Press, 1969).
5. Pollock, *Moody*, 17.
6. Daniels, *Moody*, 28–29.
7. For example, see DLM to Dear Mother, 28 August 1857(?), Yale archives; DLM to Dear Brother, 12 March 1857, MBI archives; DLM to Dear Luther, Pollock, *Moody*, 18–20; Moody, *Moody*, 47–50.
8. See for example DLM to Dear Mother, 28 August 1859, Yale archives; DLM to Dear Sister, 17 October 1859, MBI archives; DLM to Dear Brother, 12 March 1857, MBI archives.
9. Pollock, *Moody*, 17.
10. Edward Goodman, *The History of the First Baptist Church, Chicago* (Chicago, 1910), 25–26 quoted in Wilbur M. Smith, *An Annotated Bibliography of D. L. Moody* (Chicago: Moody Press, 1948), 83.
11. Pierce, *Chicago*, Vol. 2, 354. See 354–89 for a detailed overview of what she describes as "The Church and the Changing Order."
12. DLM to Mother, 25 September 1856, quoted in Moody, *Moody*, 47; Smith, *Moody*, 83.
13. DLM to George, 12 March 1857, MBI archives; another letter written in early 1858 is similar in love for money and God, quoted in Moody, *Moody*, 53.
14. Moral conditions as reported by the press in 1857 and 1858 are described and carefully documented by Martha M. Goetzman, "Anomalous Features in the Chicago Prayer Meeting Revival of 1858: The Nature of Revival as Revealed in Contemporary Newspaper Accounts" (Master's thesis, Trinity Evangelical Divinity School, 1985), 41–42.
15. DLM to Brother, 22 February 1858, Yale archives, describes the type of travel he has been engaged in. See also Moody, *Moody*, chap. 4, and the letter to Mother quoted on p. 53.
16. Moody, *Moody*, 47.
17. The best dated collections of Moody photographs are at Moody Bible Institute and the Museum and Archives of Northfield Mount Hermon Schools. William R. Moody has a splendid assortment of his father's photos in his biography. Chicago City Directories do not list Moody every year, but where his work and rooms are documented, he appears to be a mobile man. Moody, *Moody*, 73, carried a good summary of his personal and vocational patterns.
18. Daniels, *Moody*, 30–32; Smith, *Moody*, 83.
19. See DLM to Brother, 22 February 1858, Yale archives; DLM to Sister Lizzie, 19 November 1859; DLM to Mother, 28 August 1859, Yale archives. Goetzman, "Chicago Revival" maintains, with benefit of impressive primary evidence, that Chicago was not much affected by the Panic of 1857.
20. Moody's biographers disagree about his savings by 1860. Some say he had $12–15,000. No records are available, so I rely upon William Moody's account and that of Moody's friend, W. H. Daniels. They say he was worth $7,000 in 1860 and he was earning a regular salary of more than $5,000 per annum. Moody, *Moody*, 63; Daniels, *Moody*, 79–80.

21. For example, William G. McLoughlin, *Revivals, Awakenings, and Reform: An Essay on Region and Social Change in America, 1607–1977* (Chicago: Univ. of Chicago, 1978), William Warren Sweet, *The Story of Religion in America* (New York: Harper, 1950), and Bernard A. Weisberger, *They Gathered at the River: The Story of Great Revivalists and Their Impact Upon Religion in America* (Boston: Little, Brown, 1958). Goetzman in "Chicago Revival," however, shows that their thesis does not hold up in Chicago. The revival came earlier, the economy was not badly affected, and the effects were profound. She also notes that Timothy L. Smith's thesis on the 1857 Revival does not match the Chicago story.
22. Quoted in Moody, *Moody*, 48.
23. For example, DLM to George, 17 March 1857, Northfield archives; DLM to Luther, 6 June 1857, Yale archives; DLM to Lizzie, 17 October 1859, MBI archives.
24. Moody, *Moody*, 53; Goss, *Moody*, 479.
25. Stillson's recollections are recorded by Daniels, *Moody*, 33–55.
26. Ibid.
27. Moody's sermon quoted in Goss, *Moody*, 458–63; see also Daniels, *Moody*, 30–31, on his co-workers' recollections.
28. Daniels, *Moody*, 34; J. Wilbur Chapman, *The Life and Work of D. L. Moody* (Philadelphia: American Bible House, 1900), 92–93.
29. Ibid., 36–37.
30. Ibid., 38–39; Moody, *Moody*, chap.7.
31. Daniels, *Moody*, 37.
32. Moody, *Moody*, 51, 76. See also Farwell, *Moody*, 9–10.
33. "Mrs. D. L. Moody," *The Institute Tie*, November 1903, New Series, Vol. 4, No. 3; Emma Moody Powell, *Heavenly Destiny: The Life Story of Mrs. D. L. Moody* (Chicago: Moody Press, 1943), chap. 2.
34. Farwell, *Moody*, 7–8; "John Villiers Farwell," in Allen Johnson and Dumas Malone, eds., *Dictionary of American Biography* (N.Y.: Scribners, 1931), Vol. 6, 295–96.
35. Farwell, *Moody*, 8; F. Roger Dunn, "Formative Years of the Chicago Y.M.C.A.," *Journal of Illinois Historical Society*, Vol. 37, December 1944.
36. Ibid.
37. Daniels, *Moody*, 41–42.
38. Ibid.
39. Most of Moody's biographers give only sketchy accounts of the Moody-Farwell friendship. Indeed, most references are to Farwell's financial support of the Christian work with which Moody was involved. This mutually edifying friendship deserves deeper study than I can give. A place to begin is John V. Farwell, Jr., *Reminiscences of John V. Farwell* (privately published, 1911); Farwell, *Early Recollections of Dwight L. Moody;* James Gilbert, *Perfect Cities: Chicago's Utopias of 1893* (Chicago: Univ. of Chicago Press, 1991); Gene A. Getz, *MBI: The Story of Moody Bible Institute* (Chicago: Moody Press, 1969); "Farwell," *Dictionary of American Biography*, 295–96.
40. Daniels, *Moody*, 41–42.
41. DLM to Brother, 29 June 1860, Yale archives.
42. Farwell, *Moody*, 9.
43. Goss, *Moody*, 38.
44. Quoted in Goss, *Moody*, 310; see also D. W. Whittle, quoted in Moody, *Moody*, 75.
45. Quoted in Joseph B. Bowles, *Moody the Evangelist: A Character Sketch with Original Sayings* (Chicago: Moody Bible Institute, 1926), 17.
46. DLM to Mother, 10 February 1860, typescript, Yale.
47. Bowles, *Moody*, 17.
48. Moody quoted in Goss, *Moody*, 479–82.
49. Emma Moody Powell Papers, typescript, November 1860, Yale archives; Fitt, *Moody*, 34; Goss, *Moody*, 42.
50. Moody, *Moody*, 76; Goss, *Moody*, 42.
51. Goss, *Moody*, 42; Fitt, *Moody*, 34.

52. Moody, *Moody*, 76; Goss, *Moody*, 42.

Chapter Four

1. See, for example, DLM to Folks, 12 February 1861, Yale archives; DLM to Mother, 5 June 1861, MBI archives; Emma Revell to Mrs. Moody, 26 October 1861, Yale archives.
2. For evidence on the social mobility of well-educated pastors, see *Chicago Tribune*, 5 November 1886, and *New York Times*, 14 March 1876, quoted in Roger Dunn, "Formative Years of the Y.M.C.A." *Journal of Illinois Historical Society*, Vol. 37, Dec. 1944, 331; and Roger Finke and Rodney Stark, "How the Upstart Sects Won America: 1776–1850," *Journal for Scientific Study of Religion*, Vol. 28, No. 1, March 1989, 27–44.
3. DLM to Mother, 5 June 1861, MBI archives; Robert Weidensall, "Some Reminiscences of Early Days," a clipping in the Northfield archives. The phrase "dangerous classes" was common in the mid-1800s. See Charles Loring Brace, *The Dangerous Classes* (New York: Wynkoop and Hallenbeck, 1872).
4. Quoted in Moody, *Moody*, 113–14.
5. Quoted in Richard C. Morse, "Mr. Moody and the Young Men's Christian Association, His Contribution to the Work," *Association Men*, Vol. 25, No. 5, February 1900. Filed in the Papers of John R. Mott, Yale Divinity School Archives.
6. The best and most succinct account of the development of Chicago's YMCA can be found in Dunn, "Formative Years," 329–50. I have also benefited from Moody, *Moody*, especially chap. 11; C. Howard Hopkins, *History of the YMCA in North America* (NY: Association Press, 1951); Dedmon, *Great Enterprises;* Farwell, *Moody;* Goss, *Echoes*, 628; Morse, "Mr. Moody."
7. Quoted in Dedmon, *Great Enterprises*, 54–55. See also Dunn, "Formative Years," Notes 45, 46, p. 346.
8. Fitt, *Moody*, 38–39.
9. Ibid., 34.
10. DLM to Brother [Samuel], 13 January 1862, Northfield Archives.
11. Quoted in Daniels, *Moody*, 87–88.
12. Ibid., 83, 90.
13. Quoted in Dunn, "Formative Years," 338.
14. Ibid., 339.
15. "Mrs. D. L. Moody," *The Institute Tie*, November 1903, Vol. 4, No. 3, 77–79.
16. Hopkins, *YMCA*, 86–87.
17. "Mrs. Moody's Civil War Memo," Emma Moody Powell Collection, Yale archives.
18. DLM to Folks, 12 February 1861, Yale archives.
19. "Mrs. Moody's Civil War Memo."
20. George T. B. Davis, *Dwight L. Moody: The Man and His Mission* (Chicago: Boland, 1900), 80–81.
21. Quoted in Davis, *Moody*, 81.
22. Hopkins, *YMCA*, 90–91.
23. DLM to Samuel, 13 January 1862, MBI archives.
24. P. Smith, *Incidents of the U. S. Christian Commission* (Philadelphia: Lippincott, 1871), chap. 3; Lemuel Moss, *Annals of the U.S. Christian Commission* (Philadelphia: Lippincott, 1868), 75, 76, 122, 152, 308, 309, 459, 492; "Mrs. Moody's Civil War Memo"; Moody, *Moody*, chap. 8; Hopkins, *YMCA*, 90–92; Dedmon, *Great Enterprises*, 44–55. Unless otherwise noted the above sources were relied upon for the Civil War story as it related to Moody and the Chicago Christian Commission. For background, see Bruce Catton, *This Hallowed Ground* (Boston: Doubleday, 1956).
25. DLM to Mother, 4 March 1862, Yale archives.
26. Quoted in Davis, *Moody*, 81–85.
27. Moody, *Moody*, 90–91.
28. Daniels, *Moody*, 94–95.
29. D. L. Moody, sermon entitled "The Gateway into the Kingdom," in *The Way to*

God (Chicago: Revell, 1884), 38–39.

30. DLM to Mr. Farwell, 11 July 1862, printed in *The Institute Tie*, February 1906, typescript in Yale archives. See also DLM to Samuel, 11 June 1862, Yale archives.
31. DLM to Mother and Brother, 5 July 1862, typescript in Yale archives.
32. DLM to Mr. Farwell, 11 July 1862, Yale archives.
33. DLM to Samuel, 10 August 1862, MBI archives.
34. DLM to Samuel, 23 August 1862, MBI archives.
35. The dire economic conditions were reported in Moody's letters home. See, e.g., DLM to Folks, 12 February 1861, Yale archives. What little there is on the couple's courtship and marriage ceremony is summarized in Emma Moody Powell, *Heavenly Destiny*, chap. 2.
36. Emma Moody Powell Papers, typescript in 1862 and typescript labeled 28 August 1862; Powell, *Heavenly Destiny*, 44–45; Goss, *Echoes*, 49–50.
37. DLM to Mother, 5 June 1861, transcript in Yale archives.
38. EM to Mrs. Betsy Moody, 26 October 1861, Yale archives.
39. DLM to Mother, 13 September 1862, MBI archives.
40. EM to Mother, 1 December 1862, Yale archives.
41. Quoted in Powell, *Heavenly Destiny*, 44.
42. EM, "Civil War Memo"; DLM to Mother, 28 April 1863; Moss, *Annals*, 602f, lists the official delegates. Emma Moody is cited on p. 603.
43. EM to Mother, 1 December 1862, Yale archives.
44. EM to Mother, 1 December 1862, Yale archives; Pollock, *Moody*, 193; Powell, *Heavenly Destiny*, 46–47.
45. Samuel Moody to Folks, 24 October 1862, Yale archives.
46. DLM, added to Samuel Moody to Folks, 24 October 1862, Yale archives.
47. DLM to Hammond, 18 November 1863, Yale archives; DLM to Farwell, 11 July 1862, Yale archives.
48. Two typescripts in Emma Moody Powell Collection at Yale—undated but in her file on the 1860s—tell much about these personal struggles and family matters. The material was apparently family history that was in part, at least, from handwritten notes by Emma Moody. See also typed notes on letter DLM to Mother, 8 July 1864, Yale archives.
49. The material on D. W. Whittle comes from three sources: Elgin Moyer, ed., "Daniel Webster Whittle," *Wycliffe Biographical Dictionary of the Church*, revised and updated by Earle E. Cairns (Chicago: Moody Press, 1982), 433; Daniels, *Moody*, 495–99; Moody, *Moody*, 92–93.
50. Moody, *Moody*, 92–93.
51. Unless otherwise noted, the sources for General Howard's life and his relationship with Moody come from O. O. Howard, *Autobiography of Oliver Otis Howard* (N.Y.: Baker & Taylor, 1907), 2 vols. *Dictionary of American Biography* (N.Y.: Scribners, 1932) Vol. 9, 279–281; John A. Carpenter, *Sword and Olive Branch: A Biography of General O. O. Howard* (Pittsburgh: Univ. of Pittsburgh Press, 1964).
52. Carpenter, *Howard*, 25.
53. Quoted in John McDowell, et. al., *What D. L. Moody Means to Me* (East Northfield: Northfield Schools, 1937), 24.
54. Reverend Lloyd's report in Moss, *Annals*, 492.
55. Ibid., 279.
56. Catton, *This Hallowed Ground*, 425–26.
57. Moss, *Annals*, 481.
58. Ibid., 240.
59. A typed copy of a portion of Josephine Barbour's diary survives in the Yale Divinity School archives among Emma Moody Powell's materials labeled "Post War 1865." See also "Fleming Hewitt Revell (1849–1931)" in *National Cyclopedia of American Biography* (N.Y.: James T. White, 1937), Vol. 26, 442; *Dictionary of American Biography*, Vol. 15, 512–13.
60. Daniels, *Moody*, 105.
61. This "Golden Age" insight and thesis comes from Emma Moody Powell's notes

typed at the end of a typed letter: DLM to Mother, 4 February 1868, Yale archives.
62. DLM to Mother, 12 December 1864, typescript, Yale archives.
63. Mrs. Moody's "Civil War Memo," Yale archives.

Chapter Five

1. DLM to Annie Anderson, 27 July 1868, MBI archives.
2. DLM to Samuel, 13 February 1865, Yale archives.
3. Emma Moody Powell notes the Year 1866, Yale archives.
4. DLM to Mother, 28 April 1863, Yale archives.
5. Quoted in Pollock, *Moody*, 54.
6. Goss, *Moody*, 601.
7. Pollock, *Moody*, 52–54; Findlay, *Moody*, 107–10.
8. Daniels, *Moody*, 103.
9. Ibid., 103–8; Findlay, *Moody*, 110–12.
10. Daniels, *Moody*, 104; J. Wilbur Chapman, *The Life and Work of D. L. Moody* (Philadelphia: American Bible House, 1900), 101.
11. Pollock, *Moody*, 53.
12. Daniels, *Moody*, 107, 115, 119.
13. Dedmon, *Great Enterprises*, 79. This source is the one I relied upon for the data in the following paragraphs. See in particular chapters 3 and 4.
14. Dedmon, *Great Enterprises*, 62; Findlay, *Moody*, 105f.
15. Dedmon, *Great Enterprises*, 62.
16. "Oliver Otis Howard," *Dictionary of American Biography*, Vol. 9, 279–81.
17. Dedmon, *Great Enterprises*, 63.
18. DLM to Farwell, 11 July 1862, Yale archives.
19. Dedmon, *Great Enterprises*, 64–65.
20. DLM to Samuel, 10 April 1865, MBI archives. (This handwritten letter is dated 4/10/64 but the stationery has 1865 printed on top. Also, the baby Emma was born 24 October 1864, so DLM obviously made a mistake when he wrote 4/10/64.
21. DLM to Mother, 5 January 1865, MBI archives.
22. EM to Mother, 18 June 1866, Yale archives. Early letters in the collection show DLM's desire to take Emma to Massachusetts for her health.
23. EM to Samuel, 13 July 1866; EM to Mother, 30 August 1866; EM to Brother, 5 October 1866, Yale archives.
24. Farwell, *Moody*, 15; DLM to Samuel, 24 December 1866, MBI archives; Moody, *Moody*, 110.
25. The diaries of D. W. Whittle, which disappeared from the archives of Moody Bible Institute, are quoted in Findlay, *Moody*, 132. Partial typescripts of Whittle's diaries are in Powell papers, Yale archives.
26. Powell, *Heavenly Destiny*, 55f; Powell notes on 1867, Yale archives.
27. DLM to Mother, 19 March 1867; Yale archives; EM to Anna, 3 May 1867, Yale archives.
28. Ibid.; DLM to Farwell, 12 March 1867, Yale archives.
29. Quoted in Moody, *Moody*, 132.
30. Ibid.
31. EM to Anna, 3 May 1867, Yale archives; EM to Brother, 28 May 1867, MBI archives.
32. See Moody, *Moody*, 133, for the MacKenzie story. The Liverpool story is in George E. Morgan, *Mighty Days of Revival; R. C. Morgan: His Life and Times* (London: Morgan & Scott, 1922), 52 and note 3. For the YMCA prayer meeting subject, see Powell papers, typescript "May 1867," Yale archives.
33. Quoted in Moody, *Moody*, 136.
34. Quoted in footnote 2, pp. 70–71, in Morgan, *Mighty Days of Revival.*
35. Charles H. Spurgeon, *The Autobiography of Charles H. Spurgeon* (Philadelphia: American Baptist Publication Society, 1867), Vol. 4, 246–47.
36. DLM to Farwell, 12 March 1867, Yale archives.

37. DLM to Farwell, typescript attached to the 12 March 1867 letter, probably sent with that letter, Yale archives. See also Emma Moody Powell's notes at bottom of DLM to Mother, 19 March 1867, Yale archives. For background on Mueller, see Roger Steer, *George Mueller* (Wheaton: Harold Shaw, 1975), and A. T. Pierson, *George Mueller of Bristol* (London: Pickering, n.d.).
38. Moody's sermon in Goss, *Echoes*, 510–11.
39. A splendid brief summary of Darby and Moody's agreements and disagreements is in Findlay, *Moody*, 125–27. See also Gundry, *Love Them In*. The most recent biography of Darby by Max S. Weremchuk, *John Nelson Darby* (New York: Loizeaux, 1992), 143–44 contains the story of Darby's angry exit.
40. For details on Moorhouse and his influence on Moody, see Pollock, *Moody*, 68f; Moody, *Moody*, 137f; Fitt, *Moody*, 53f; and Goss, *Echoes*, 51, 294f; J. Edwin Orr, *Second Evangelical Awakening* (London: Marshall, Morgan, & Scott, 1949), 160; J. MacPherson, *Harry Moorhouse: The English Evangelist* (London, 1920) (Glasgow, Scotland: John Ritchie, n.d.).
41. Quoted in Moody, *Moody*, 138.
42. Ibid., 138–40; see also MacPherson, *Moorhouse*, 64–66.
43. Moody, *Moody*, 140. Note that the English historians spell Harry's name "Moorhouse." It is spelled Moorehouse or Morehouse by different American scholars. I have taken Orr and MacPherson's spelling.
44. Gundry, *Love Them In*, is superb on Moody's theology. An example of Moody's new theology is revealed in a sermon entitled "Love," published in D. L. Moody, *Glad Tidings: Sermons & Prayer Meeting Talks* (N.Y.: Treat, 1876), 240–51.
45. Goss, *Echoes*, 51.
46. Orr, *Second Evangelical Awakening*, 202.
47. Findlay, *Moody*, 128.
48. Torrey, *Why God Used D. L. Moody*, 14; Moody, *Moody*, 134.

Chapter Six

1. DLM to Mother, 24 August 1867, Yale archives.
2. Moody, *Moody*, 116–17.
3. Ibid., chap. 9. See also Anne M. Boylan, *Sunday School: The Formation of an American Institution, 1790–1880* (New Haven: Yale Univ. Press, 1988) is an important book that puts Moody in a context of the larger Sunday school movement.
4. Bessie Louise Pierce, *A History of Chicago* (New York: Knopf, 1940), Vol. 2, 359; Farwell, *Moody*, 77–78; Fitt, *Moody*, 64; Pollock, *Moody*, 69.
5. Dedmon, *Great Enterprises*, 65–66.
6. DLM to C. H. M. [McCormick], 15 April 1868, MBI archives.
7. Dedmon, *Great Enterprises*, 67–68.
8. Ibid., 68–69; see also DLM to C. H. McCormick, 26 November 1869, MBI archives.
9. DLM to Samuel, 7 January 1869, MBI archives.
10. EM to Mother, 17 June 1869, Yale archives.
11. DLM to Mother, 21 December 1869, Yale archives.
12. Dwight L. Moody, *Secret Power* (Chicago: F. H. Revell, 1881), 22–24, 31. Here he reflects on some of these struggles.
13. Moody, *Glad Tidings*, 471, contains a sermon where he comments on his struggles and the cure.
14. Ibid., 273.
15. Sarah Cooke, *Wayside Sketches: or, The Handmaiden of the Lord* (Grand Rapids: Shaw, 1895), 362.
16. Ibid., 363.
17. Torrey, *Why God Used D. L. Moody*, 45; Cooke, *Wayside Sketches*, 363.
18. Torrey, *Why God Used D. L. Moody*, 45–46.
19. Cooke, *Wayside Sketches*, 363.
20. Tenth Census of the United States, *Social Statistics of Cities 1880*, Vol. 19, 491–92.

21. Ibid., 491.
22. Ibid.
23. Goss, *Echoes*, 174.
24. Powell, *Heavenly Destiny*, 65–66.
25. Moody, *Moody*, 147–48.
26. Ibid., 148.
27. Powell, *Heavenly Destiny*, 69.
28. Dedmon, *Great Enterprises*, 72–73.
29. DLM to Dear Sir, New York, 24 November 1871, typescript in Northfield Archives; handwritten copy in C. H. McCormick Papers, Wisconsin State Historical Society; copy at MBI archives.
30. Fitt, *Moody*, 64–65.
31. Quoted in Fitt, *Moody*, 65.
32. A typescript in Powell papers, Yale archives, dated 1871 and labeled "D. L. Moody Anointing."
33. Quoted in Fitt, *Moody*, 65.
34. Whittle diary quoted in Findlay, *Moody*, 132–33.
35. Farwell, *Moody*, 51.

Chapter Seven

1. John Harries, *G. Campbell Morgan: The Man and His Ministry* (Chicago: Revell, 1930), 154–55.
2. Moody, *Moody*, 152.
3. Ibid., 152–53.
4. G. Campbell Morgan, *The Practice of Prayer* (London: Hodder & Stoughton, 1906), 125.
5. Ibid., 124–27.
6. Moody, *Moody*, 154.
7. Pollock, *Moody*, 100.
8. Ibid.
9. David Bebbington, *Evangelicalism in Modern Great Britain: A History from the 1730s to the 1980s* (Grand Rapids: Baker, 1992), 159–61.
10. Moody, *Moody*, 154.
11. Pollock, *Moody*, 101.
12. Quoted in Findlay, *Moody*, 131.
13. DLM to C. H. McCormick, 24 February 1873, MBI archives.
14. Bebbington, *Evangelicalism*, 159; Gene A. Getz, *MBI: The Story of Moody Bible Institute* (Chicago: Moody Press, 1969), 32.
15. My major source of information about Emma Dryer comes from an unpublished biographical essay on her by Sarah M. Peterson. A copy of this paper is in my personal library. Also I have relied upon materials in the Wheaton College Archives, especially correspondence between Dryer and Charles Blanchard. Also helpful are Getz, *MBI*, 34f; and W. H. Daniel, ed., *Moody, His Words, Work and Workers* (New York: Nelson, 1877), 503–5; Daniels, *Moody*, 187–88.
16. See Peterson, "Dryer"; see also the Dryer correspondence at Wheaton College Archives. For Dryer's account of three women who experienced miraculous healings, see Emma Dryer, "The Prayer of Faith" in D. W. Whittle, ed., *The Wonders of Prayer* (Chicago: Revell, 1885), 21–27.
17. Peterson, "Dryer"; Dryer correspondence, Wheaton College.
18. Daniels, ed., *Moody, His Words, Work and Workers*, 503–4.
19. DLM to C. H. McCormick, May 1873, MBI archives.
20. The sketch on Morton, as well as the ensuing one on Whittle, appear in Daniels, ed., *Moody, His Words, Work and Workers*, 495–503.
21. Quoted in Dedmon, *Great Enterprises*, 73.
22. DLM to Farwell, 7 June 1873, quoted in Farwell, *Moody*, 76–77.

Chapter Eight

1. A question is sometimes raised about Moody's speaking in tongues. I see no evidence that he did. He paid little attention to the topic. In *Secret Power*, 110, he likened tongues to choirs that sing in ways no one can understand. "Why is not that [choir] just as great an abomination?" Also, see Gundry, *Love Them In*, 154–56. "Mr. Henry Varley's Account of His Conversation with Mr. Moody in Dublin" in Wilbur M. Smith, *Annotated Bibliography of D. L. Moody* (Chicago: Moody Press, 1948), 155–57; Moody quoted in his "Prayer Meeting Talks," *Glad Tidings*, 471.

2. For details of Sankey's life, I have relied upon his autobiography, *My Life and the Story of the Gospel Hymns* (New York: Harper, 1907); and a sketch in the *Dictionary of American Biography*, Vol. 16, 352–53.

3. Sankey, *My Life*, 18–19.

4. Ibid., 19–24.

5. Moody, *Moody*, 154–55.

6. Sankey, *My Life*, 38–39; Pollock, *Moody*, 102.

7. Adna F. Weber, *The Growth of Cities in the Nineteenth Century* (Ithaca: Cornell Univ. Press, reprint, 1967), 43, 57, 64–67, 152–53.

8. David Bebbington, *Evangelicalism in Modern Great Britain: A History from the 1730s to the 1980s* (Grand Rapids: Baker, 1992), chap. 5.

9. Sankey, *My Life*, 39.

10. Ibid., 40.

11. Ibid., 40–41.

12. W. Y. Fullerton, *F. B. Meyer: A Biography* (Harrisburg, Pa.: The Christian Alliance Publishing Company, 1929), 30–31; J. H. Rushbrooke, "F. B. Meyer," *Dictionary of National Biography*, 582–83; F. B. Meyer, "Introduction" to W. R. Moody, *Moody* (1930 edition).

13. Quoted in Pollock, *Moody*, 107–8.

14. Rushbrooke, "Meyer," *Dictionary of National Biography*, 583.

15. EM, "Diary," 4–5 July 1873, Yale archives.

16. Sankey, *My Life*, 44–45.

17. Ibid., 46–47.

18. EM, "Diary," 25 August 1873, Yale archives.

19. John Hall and George H. Stuart, *The American Evangelists: D. L. Moody and Ira D. Sankey in Great Britain and Ireland* (N.Y.: Dodd & Mead, 1875), 22–23.

20. Sankey, *My Life*, 45–48; Sandra S. Sizer, *Gospel Hymns and Social Religion: The Rhetoric of Nineteenth-Century Revivalism* (Philadelphia: Temple Univ. Press, 1978), 4–5; 21.

21. Sizer, *Gospel Hymns*, 5.

22. "Ira David Sankey," *Dictionary of American Biography*, Vol. 16, 352.

23. Jane MacKinnon, "Journal of Mrs. Jane MacKinnon," 61, 95, Yale archives.

24. Ibid., 63.

25. Arthur T. Pierson, *Evangelistic Work in Principle and Practice* (New York: Baker and Taylor, 1887), 252.

26. Quoted in Hall and Stuart, *American Evangelists*, 33–34.

27. Pollock, *Moody*, 115.

28. Hall and Stuart, *American Evangelists*, 35–36; Pollock, *Moody*, 111.

29. Hall and Stuart, *American Evangelists*, 36.

30. Ibid., 36–37.

31. Pollock, *Moody*, 114.

32. Hall and Stuart, *American Evangelists*, 43.

33. Ibid., 44.

34. Jane MacKinnon's "Journal" is rich with details of every type and level of Moody-Sankey meetings. She and her husband followed Moody as Christian support-workers all over Scotland and Ireland. The Moodys stayed in their home at Campbeltown several days, and the MacKinnons frequently traveled with the Moodys. She kept a detailed journal and it is one of the richest sources imaginable

on how the work was conducted. The original is at Yale archives.

35. DLM to Brother, 9 April 1854, Yale archives.
36. MacKinnon, "Journal," 15.
37. R. A. Torrey sums up Moody's genuine humbleness and his desire to push others forward. See *Why God Used D. L. Moody*, chap. 5; see also Torrey, "D. L. Moody, The Unity of His Life," unpublished MS, Billy Graham Center Archives, Wheaton College.
38. See for example, Hall and Stuart, *American Evangelists*, 45, for an instance of this type of session; see also Daniels, *Moody*, 288, 299.
39. This theme of "God Is Love" is replete in Moody's sermons. Any "authorized" volume of his messages make this clear. Certainly the best and most in-depth assessment of Moody's proclamation theology is found in Gundry, *Love Them In*. See also Goss, *Echoes*, "Introduction" by Lyman Abbott.
40. Hall and Stuart, *American Evangelists*, 62.
41. MacKinnon, "Journal," 8, 58, 105.
42. Ibid., 16–17.
43. Hall and Stuart, *American Evangelists*, 47–49, 52.
44. EM, "Diary," 25 December 1873, Yale archives.
45. DLM to Farwell, 14 November 1874, Yale archives.
46. MacKinnon, "Journal," 91, 107; DLM to Cole, 5 August 1874, Yale archives.
47. MacKinnon's "Journal" is replete with such anecdotes and observations.
48. MacKinnon, "Journal," 135.
49. Ibid., 56.
50. Material on the English campaign is vast. I consulted *The New York Times; London Times;* Moody, *Moody*, chaps. 20–22; Hall and Stuart, *American Evangelists*, chaps. 6–8; MacKinnon, "Journal"; EM, "Diary," November 1874 to August 1875.
51. EM, "Diary," see entries from February through May 1874, Yale archives.
52. MacKinnon, "Journal," 40.
53. See for example, DLM to Hitchcock, 13 December 1873, MBI archives; DLM to Whittle, 7 March 1874, MBI archives; DLM to Farwell, 14 November 1874, MBI archives; DLM to Cole, 5 August 1874, Yale archives.
54. Pollock, *Moody*, 127.
55. Ibid., 127–29.
56. DLM to Farwell, 7 May 1874, MBI archives.
57. Ibid.
58. W. H. Daniels, a Methodist-Episcopal minister, was one of the signers of the letter. The story and a copy of the letter appear in his biography of *Moody*, 272–74.
59. Daniels, *Moody*, 274.
60. Ibid., 275.
61. Elgin S. Mozer, "Horatius Bonar," *Who Was Who in Church History* (Chicago: Moody, 1962) 49; Daniels, *Moody*, 275–76.
62. Ironically, on May 21, 1874, the date the Chicago men sent their letter to endorse Moody, ten thousand people came to hear him preach. See EM, "Diary," 21 May 1874, Yale archives.
63. See Daniels, *Moody*, 316–17.
64. Farwell, *Moody*, 173.
65. Daniels, *Moody*, 318.
66. Ibid.
67. See Daniels, *Moody*, chap. 7.
68. EM, "Diary," 26 October 1874 to 26 November 1874; Moody, *Moody*, 215.
69. Several issues of the *London Times*, January to August 1875 contain some of this anti-American sentiment.
70. MacKinnon, "Journal," 70–71.
71. See for example, DLM to Dear Sir, 31 March 1875, Billy Graham Center Archives.
72. Moody, *Moody*, 247–48; *New York Times*, 13–14 July 1875.
73. Moody, *Moody*, 251–53.
74. EM, "Diary," 18 August 1875.

Chapter Nine

1. Descriptive material on their arrival in New York comes from *The Times* [London], 15 August 1875; see also EM, "Diary," August 1875. For statistical data in the next paragraphs, see Moody, *Moody*, 251.
2. No reliable estimates for the entire twenty-five months of ministry exist. Statistics were not kept on these sessions. I have sifted data from newspapers and other contemporary accounts. The range of estimates is vast and there is no way to be certain. A. A. Bonar has some estimates in *James Scott: Laborer for God* (London: Morgan & Scott, n.d.), 8.
3. MacKinnon, "Journal," 80.
4. This reductionist thesis is presented in John Kent, *Holding the Fort: Studies in Victorian Revivalism* (London: Epworth Press, 1978), e.g., chap. 4.
5. Moody, *Moody*, 235.
6. *The Times* was hot and cold on Moody. Beginning heavy coverage in July 1875, this paper was never ardently behind Moody. It published letters that attacked and that defended the Americans, but it was quick to publish unfavorable stories even when they had to be retracted later. See January to August 1875.
7. MacKinnon, "Journal," 1, 62, 90.
8. Moody, *Moody*, 220.
9. Ibid.
10. A file of typed documents dated October 1874, including D. J. Findlay to William Moody, 16 April 1919; a typed copy of Moody's letter to the *Daily Times*, Yale archives.
11. Moody, *Moody*, 221.
12. Moody, *Moody*, 244–45; 465–66; Moody's role in raising money for YMCA buildings in several cities is in George E. Morgan, *R. C. Morgan: His Life and Times*, (London: Morgan & Scott, 1922), 285.
13. Ibid., 465; Dedmon, *Great Enterprises*, 109.
14. Jane MacKinnon's "Journal" has the Cotton story woven through the last half of the manuscript. It is apparent reading this Journal that Jane MacKinnon developed in much the same way.
15. By far the best treatments of Drummond are the 1899 biography written by George Adam Smith, *Life of Henry Drummond* (London: Hodder and Stoughton, 1899); and Mark J. Toone, "Evangelicalism in Transition: A Comparative Analysis of the Work and Theology of D. L. Moody and His Protégés, Henry Drummond and R. A. Torrey," Ph.D. diss., St. Mary's College, Univ. of St. Andrews, 1988. This latter work is simply first-rate and should be published. Also quite useful is Gundry, *Love Them In*. There is also helpful material in Moody, *Moody*. See also Emma Moody Powell's "Summer 1887" notes in Moody Papers, Yale archives, for material on Moody and Drummond.
16. Toone, "Evangelicalism in Transition," chap. 5.
17. Gundry, *Love Them In*, 48–50; Toone, "Evangelicalism in Transition," chap. 5; "Henry Drummond," Elgin Moyer, ed., *Wycliffe Biographical Dictionary of the Church*, revised and updated by Earle E. Cairns (Chicago: Moody Press, 1982), 123.
18. Toone, "Evangelicalism in Transition," 147.
19. Henry Drummond, "Mr. Moody: Some Impressions and Facts," *McClure's Magazine*, Vol. 4, 1894–95, 55–69.
20. Smith, *Drummond*; Moody, *Moody*, 204–6.
21. Moody, *Moody*, 204.
22. Quoted in Ibid., 204–5.
23. Ibid., 205–6.
24. Moody, *Moody*, 217.
25. Quoted in Moody, *Moody*, 215–16.
26. Morgan, *R. C. Morgan*, 78.
27. Norman Grubb, *C. T. Studd: Athlete and Pioneer* (Grand Rapids: Zondervan, 1933), see especially chap. 1 on Edward's conversion.

28. Joe Brice, *The Crowd for Christ* (London: Hodder and Stoughton, 1934), 11–15.
29. Lewis Drummond, *Spurgeon: Prince of Preachers* (Grand Rapids: Kregel, 1992), 308–9.
30. J. Edwin Orr, *Second Evangelical Awakening* (London: Marshall, Morgan, & Scott, 1949), 240–41.
31. John Lillyman, "Taylor of Down Under: The Life Story of an Australian Evangelist," Master's thesis, Wheaton College, 1994, 93, 102.
32. David McCasland, *Oswald Chambers: Abandoned to God* (Ann Arbor: Discovery House, 1993), 23–25.
33. Torrey, *Why God Used D. L. Moody*, 29–30.
34. Drummond, "Moody," 66.
35. Smith, *Drummond*, quoted in Moody, *Moody*, 203.
36. Bonar, *James Scott*, 49–50.
37. Morgan, *R. C. Morgan*, 57.
38. Patricia St. John, *Until the Day Breaks: The Life and Work of Lilias Trotter, Pioneer Missionary to Muslim North Africa* (Bromley: OM Publishing, 1990), 13–14.
39. Morgan, *R. C. Morgan*, 184.
40. David Bebbington, *Evangelicalism in Modern Great Britain: A History from the 1730s to the 1980s* (Grand Rapids: Baker, 1992), 162–64, 176.
41. Orr, *Second Evangelical Awakening*, 260–61; Morgan, *R. C. Morgan*, 179.
42. Moody, *Moody*, 171–72.
43. DLM to Farwell, 7 May 1874; Farwell to Dodge, 6 March 1876 in Farwell, *Moody*, 156. See also Findlay, *Moody*, 202–3; Pollock, *Moody*, 296–98.
44. Billy Sunday, for example, was hurt by his elegant lifestyle and the way he raised funds. See Lyle W. Dorsett, *Billy Sunday and the Redemption of Urban America* (Grand Rapids: Eerdmans, 1991).
45. DLM to Mother, 4 March 1876, Northfield archives; DLM to Hitchcock, 11 October 1878, MBI archives; DLM to Hitchcock, 12 October 1878, MBI archives; Farwell, *Moody*, 120; DLM to George, 22 March 1878, MBI archives.
46. Samuel Moody to DLM, 20 March 1878; DLM to SM, 30 March 1878, Yale archives.
47. DLM to Wanamaker 5 November 1877; 14 November 1877; 9 January 1878.
48. Farwell to DLM, 6 October 1875, quoted in Farwell, *Moody*, 131; MacKinnon, "Journal," 144–45; Moody, *Moody*, 234–35. The files, for example, of the *New York Times, Times of London*, and *Christian Cynosure* show great interest in Moody by 1875. Often he made the front page and frequently he was in the papers in every issue.
49. Moody told Farwell as early as 14 November 1874 that he could not possibly read all of the letters that came, "but I can assure you I read all American letters." Quoted in Farwell, *Moody*, 84. To get a sense of the growing scale of Moody's correspondence, all the researcher has to do is look at the volume of letters in the several archives, especially MBI and Yale. The number of Moody's responses to letters, as well as Emma's and William's responses, grow with each decade.
50. Emma Moody Powell, *Heavenly Destiny*, 99–100; Moody, *Moody*, 257.
51. Farwell to DLM, 6 September 1875 quoted in *Moody*, 128.
52. Ibid., 25 February 1875, 124–25.
53. EM to Mrs. MacKinnon 31 December 1875; Emma Moody's "Diary" contains several references to poor health and a stay in a health resort area.
54. A typescript dated October 1875 in the Emma Moody Powell papers, Yale archives.
55. Moody, *Moody*, 257.
56. The Whittle post-Civil War diary was lost thirty years ago. Quotations from it appear in Moody, *Moody*. See chapter 18 for entries relating to September 1875. Lengthy quotations from the diary also are available in typescript in the Powell papers, Yale archives.
57. Quoted in Moody, *Moody*, 258–59.
58. Ibid., 260.

59. Ibid., 261.
60. Ibid., 261–63.
61. Mr. Walter Osborn, reference librarian for Moody Bible Institute Library, has put together a booklet in typescript, titled "D. L. Moody's Travels." He has arranged Moody's travels chronologically, and also alphabetically by country, province, and state. I have relied upon this helpful resource for this and many other parts of the book.
62. *Christian Cynosure,* 23 September 1875.
63. *The New York Daily Tribune* put together a volume of Moody's sermons as they were delivered at Manhattan's Hippodrome. Titled *Glad Tidings* (N.Y.: E. B. Treat, 1876), this book has verbatim sermons and prayer-meeting talks as they were transcribed in the *Tribune.* There is also useful, introductory material in the beginning and sometimes in a preface to a message.
64. *Glad Tidings,* 13–14, contains Moody's words cited here. For a taste of the secular press, see *New York Times,* e.g., 23 February 1876; 25 March 1876; 12 February 1876; 14 April 1876.
65. Moody's sermon, "Love," in *Glad Tidings,* 331.
66. *The Tablet* is quoted in Moody, *Moody,* 284; the Northfield stories from a personal interview with Lawrence and Hazel Marcy, old timers who know Northfield lore, 27 May 1994, Northfield, Massachusetts.
67. Quoted in McDowell, *What D. L. Moody Means to Me,* 13, 28.
68. Ignatius of Jesus to DLM, 17 March 1875, Yale archives.
69. Moody's sermon, "Weak Things Employed to Confound the Mighty," in *Glad Tidings,* 11–12.
70. Ibid., 12–13.
71. Ibid., 14–15.
72. Quoted in Moody, *Moody,* 285.
73. Moody, *Moody,* 285.
74. Quoted from *Chicago Tribune* in Fowler, *Moody,* 497.
75. An example of a study of Moody's sermons is T. M. Hawes, "D. L. Moody As an Orator," *The Seminary Magazine* (published by the Southern Baptist Theological Seminary, Louisville, KY), Vol. 3, No. 2, February 1890. See Pollock, *Moody,* 189, for some excellent examples of imitators.
76. See U.S. Bureau of the Census, *Historical Statistics of Cities,* 1880.
77. Torrey, *Why God Used D. L. Moody,* chap. 8; Whittle is quoted in Moody, *Moody,* 261.
78. Quoted in Pollock, *Moody,* 186.
79. Ibid.
80. *New York Times,* see all April 1896 entries, especially 17 April and 20 April. See also Pollock, *Moody,* 186.
81. Pollock, *Moody,* 186–87.
82. Quoted in Moody, *Moody,* 277.
83. This episode made the *New York Times.* See 10 May 1876. See also Findlay, *Moody,* who does an excellent job of describing this Augusta meeting. He has some excellent quotations from Whittle's lost diary.
84. Whittle's Civil War diary is at the Library of Congress. It includes his time when he was in Sherman's army. Also see Pollock, *Moody,* 189.
85. Pollock, *Moody,* 188.
86. Moody, *Moody,* 288.
87. Ibid., 291.
88. Sankey, *My Life,* 77.
89. Quoted in Moody, *Moody,* 291.
90. Moody, *Moody,* 288.
91. DLM to Mother, 2 October 1876 and 12 October 1876, Yale archives.
92. Daniels, ed., *Moody: His Words, Work and Workers,* 489–94.
93. Ibid.; see also Pollock, *Moody,* 196.
94. Ibid.

95. Daniels, ed., *Moody: His Words, Work and Workers*, 510.
96. Ernest B. Gordon, *A. J. Gordon: A Biography* (Chicago: Revell, 1896); "Adoniram Judson Gordon," *Dictionary of American Religious Biography*, 176–77; see also Gordon entry in *Religious Leaders of America*, 355–56; see A. J. Gordon, *The Ministry of Healing*.
97. DLM to Durant, 28 May 1878, MBI archives; Moody, *Moody*, 320–21.
98. The Willard-Moody relationship can be found in Ruth Bordin, *Frances Willard: A Biography* (Chapel Hill: Univ. of North Carolina Press, 1986), 86–92; Daniels, ed., *Moody: His Words, Work and Workers*, 508–10; Anna A. Gordon, *The Beautiful Life of Frances E. Willard* (Chicago: WCTU, 1898) 102, 370–71, 386–87.
99. Willard to EM, 7 September 1877, quoted in Frances E. Willard, *My Happy Half Century* (London: Ward, Lock and Bowden, 1894), 261–68.
100. Pollock, *Moody*, 200.
101. Gordon, *Gordon*, 100.
102. Pollock, *Moody*, 198–200.
103. Emma Moody Powell, *Heavenly Destiny*, 115.
104. Whittle's diary is quoted in Pollock, *Moody*, 196.
105. Whittle's diary in typescript in Powell papers, 3, Yale archives.

Chapter Ten

1. EM to Jane MacKinnon, 11 September 1876; 25 May 1885, Yale archives.
2. Paul Moody, *My Father*, chap. 1.
3. Ibid., 16–17.
4. Ibid., 13–16.
5. For a succinct overview of the rural versus urban mentality, see Morton and Lucia White, *The Intellectual Versus the City* (Cambridge: Harvard Univ. Press, 1962). See also William Dean Howells, *The Landlord at Lion's Head* (New York: Harper, 1896) and *The Rise of Silas Lapham* (Boston: Ticknor, 1885), two realistic novels set in New England. These novels are written by Moody's contemporary and they depict a time and mind-set that was typical of Moody and those he lived with.
6. For example, see letters in April and May 1878 sent to George and Ambert (nephew), MBI archives; see also DLM to George and Ambert 3–4 February 1879; 1 April 1880; 10 April 1880, MBI archives; 28 February 1881, Yale; 8 March 1881, 17 May 1881, MBI archives.
7. DLM to George, 19 November 1880, Yale archives; DLM to Ambert, 21 February 1881, MBI archives.
8. Paul Moody, *My Father*, 47–48.
9. He never succeeded with Wanamaker, but Sankey, Whittle, Bliss, and others are examples of men who followed Moody's urgings and lead.
10. See Pollock, *Moody*, 196 for quotations from Whittle's diary regarding Emma's health. On Fanny Holton, see correspondence that shows she was employed for at least ten years (1876–86), Yale archives; Emma Moody Powell notes, December 1886; see also Fanny Holton to Moodys, December 1886.
11. Estimates from U.S. Bureau of the Census, *Historical Statistics of the U.S.*
12. For example, DLM to Hitchcock, 27 October 1878, MBI archives, DLM to Hitchcock, 30 January 1879, MBI archives.
13. Moody, *Moody*, 319–20.
14. This thesis is embraced by many historians, but the most impressive advocate of this point of view is James F. Findlay, Jr. See his biography of Moody, and also an article in *Christian History*, Vol. 9, No. 1, 1990, "The Northfield Schools," especially 30.
15. Moody family correspondence in the 1880s shows that he was invited to India, Palestine, and Asia; e.g., EM to Mother, 24 January 1883, Yale archives; DLM to Willie, January 1884, Yale archives. There is a scroll at the museum in DLM's birthplace that contains the names of more than 15,000 ministers in New Zealand and Australia. This massive display of unity was arranged to finally convince

Moody that he should do an extended campaign in their respective countries. For the successes of the 1881–83 trip to Britain, see Emma Moody's Diary for 1881–83, Yale archives; Moody, *Moody,* chap. 26; Morgan, *Mighty Days of Revival;* Pollock, *Moody,* chaps. 25–26. On San Francisco, see Douglas F. Anderson, "San Francisco Evangelicalism, Religious Identity, and the Revivals of D. L. Moody," *Fides Et Historia,* Vol. 15, No. 2 Spring, 1983.

16. DLM to Mr. MacKinnon, 13 September 1881, Northfield Archives contains this quotation that is typical of what he was saying between 1879 and 1885.
17. Drummond, "Mr. Moody," *McClure's,* 59.
18. Quoted in John McDowell, *What D. L. Moody Means to Me,* 24.
19. Quoted by Drummond in "Mr. Moody," *McClure's,* 59–60.
20. There are scores of letters at MBI archives and Yale from DLM to Samuel Moody from the 1850s until 1876, the date of Samuel's death, that support this thesis.
21. See Wilbur Smith, *An Annotated Bibliography of D. L. Moody* (Chicago: Moody Press, 1948), 73.
22. DLM to Officers; DLM to Hitchcock, 4 February 1878; 27 October 1878; 11 October 1878; 12 October 1878; 9 December 1878; 18 January 1879; 30 January 1879, MBI archives. These are examples of what he did for years. See also Charles Blanchard to A. P. Fitt, C. A. Blanchard Papers, 16 November 1910, Wheaton College archives.
23. See S. Peterson, "Dryer"; Dryer to Charles Blanchard, January 1916, C.A. Blanchard Papers, Wheaton College archives, and C. Blanchard to A. P. Fitt, 16 November 1910, Wheaton College archives.
24. See Peterson, "Dryer," and Blanchard Papers.
25. Letterhead, 1887, copies in MBI archives.
26. DLM to Mrs. McCormick, 18 July 1887, MBI archives.
27. Peterson, "Dryer," Dryer to Blanchard, January 1916, Wheaton College archives; DLM to Dryer, 27 July 1887, MBI archives.
28. DLM to McCormick and Dryer, 27 July 1887; DLM to McCormick, 15 August 1887, MBI archives; DLM to McCormick, 6 October 1887, Yale.
29. DLM to McCormick, 15 October 1887, Yale archives.
30. DLM to Trustees, 14 July 1887, MBI archives.
31. Original documents of incorporation quoted by Gene A. Getz, *MBI: The Story of Moody Bible Institute* (Chicago: Moody Press, 1969), 59–62.
32. I have located approximately 1,800 Moody letters in several archives. Many of these are handwritten and the volume of his output increased every year. Moody sent out thousands of form letters asking for money or urging people to attend conferences. Although he did not handwrite such epistles, he did sign most of them.
33. EM to Mrs. MacKinnon, 11 September 1876, Yale archives. This type of letter is not unusual after 1875.
34. Quoted in McDowell, *What D. L. Moody Means to Me,* 9.
35. Pollock, *Moody,* 202; Findlay, *Moody,* 308–9.
36. DLM to Durant, 28 May 1878, MBI archives. On prevailing notions of educating women, see Mary Dorsett, "The Women in Wheaton's Past," *Wheaton Alumni,* Vol. 57, No. 1, February 1987, 4–7.
37. T. J. Shanks, *D. L. Moody at Home* (Chicago: Fleming H. Revell, 1886), 14.
38. Ibid.
39. Moody, *Moody,* 320.
40. Ibid.
41. Pollock, *Moody,* 177; Findlay, *Moody,* 205.
42. John N. Haupis, Jr., *Brattleboro: Selected Historical Vignettes* (Brattleboro: Brattleboro Publishing Co., 1873), 20–26; *Gazetteer and Business Directory of Windham County, Vermont* (Syracuse, N.Y., 1884). See also Lyle W. Dorsett, "Town Promotion in Nineteenth-Century Vermont," *New England Quarterly,* Vol. 40, No. 2, June 1967.
43. Correspondence in Northfield Archives relating to scholarship aid to poor stu-

dents reveals that Moody frequently called upon Julius Estey to help impoverished New England women.

44. Moody, *Moody*, 320–21.
45. Powell, *Heavenly Destiny*, 128–29; Moody, *Moody*, 321.
46. Ibid.; Burnham Carter, *So Much to Learn: The History of Northfield Mount Hermon School for the One Hundredth Anniversary* (Northfield: 1976), 69–75; Walter Osborn, "D. L. Moody's Travels," unpublished chronology, Moody Bible Institute, 1979.
47. Moody, *Moody*, 321.
48. Carter, *So Much to Learn*, 74.
49. Shanks, *Moody at Home*, 18.
50. DLM to Camp, 21 July 1881, with attached photograph, MBI archives. See also, Moody, *Moody*, chap. 29; Pollock, *Moody*, 216f; Shanks, *Moody at Home*, 21.
51. Emma Moody Powell Papers, typescript of data on the Mount Hermon Land purchase; Shanks, *Moody at Home*, 20.
52. Moody, *Moody*, 321.
53. A first-rate unpublished Ph.D. dissertation by Donald A. Wells, "D. L. Moody and His Schools: A Historical Analysis of an Education Ministry," Boston University, 1972, is a thorough, objective, and indispensable resource on Moody's schools. See also Findlay, *Moody*, 315f; Shanks, *Moody at Home*, chap. 1; Moody, *Moody*, chap. 29. Besides these sources I have relied upon the rich historical archives housed in the Northfield Schools' Library.
54. Shanks, *Moody at Home*, 19.
55. DLM to Mrs. McCormick, 16 August 1886; George F. Magoun, "Mr. Moody's Schools," *Our Day! A Record and Review of Current Reform*, Vol. 9, No. 59, November 1892, 790–800.
56. *Northfield Echoes*, "Mr. Moody and the Mount Hermon Students," Vol. 7, No. 1, 1900, 76. This is the Moody Memorial issue.
57. Shanks, *Moody at Home*, 18.
58. The Zululand speakers are noted in *The Hermonite*, 26 March 1898. Photos of classes are in the schools' archives. Articles and photographs in *The Hermonite* are especially revealing on the minority issue, e.g., 28 November 1896; 15 June 1897.
59. See chaps. 3, 4; Daniels, *Moody*, 36; Dedmon, *Great Enterprises*, 63; *Hermonite*, 3 November 1894, 18 May 1895, e.g.
60. For material on anti-Semitism in the late 1800s, see John Higham, *Strangers in the Land: Patterns of American Nativism* (New Brunswick, N.J.: Rutgers Univ. Press, 1955); and Richard Hofstadter, *The American Political Tradition* (New York: Knopf, 1948).
61. *The Hermonite*, 29 March 1894; 22 May 1897.
62. Helpful on this topic are Yackov Ariel, "An American Evangelist and the Jews: D. L. Moody and His Attitudes Toward The Jewish People," *Immanuel*, Vol. 22–23, 1989, 41–49; David A. Rausch, *Fundamentalist–Evangelicals and Anti-Semitism* (Valley Forge, PA: Trinity Press International, 1993); George M. Marsden, *Fundamentalism and American Culture: The Shaping of Twentieth-Century Evangelicalism* (New York: Oxford Univ. Press, 1980). All three of these authors offer useful insights on this topic.
63. F. B. Meyer, "D. L. Moody: A Prophet of God," *Northfield Echoes*, Memorial Issue, Vol. 7, No. 1, 1900, 29.
64. Several favorable articles on Roman Catholics appear in issues of *The Hermonite* throughout 1893, 1894, and 1895. The essay on the monks is 25 February 1899.
65. Meyer, *Echoes*, 29.
66. *The Hermonite*, 15 June 1897.
67. *The Hermonite*, 15 June 1897; 14 June 1898. *Northfield Echoes* and *The Hermonite* both exude a nonsectarian bias. For examples of sectarian clubs see *The Hermonite*, 13 March 1897.
68. These names were gathered from student publications where chapel talks and spe-

cial lectures were reported. Both *Northfield Echoes* and *The Hermonite* are at the school library and archives.

69. This Bible is in the museum at Moody's birthplace in Northfield.
70. The Northfield Bible Training School Records, History Files, Northfield Archives, as well as many issues of *The Hermonite*, make it clear that the Holy Spirit was the subject of many talks by Moody, faculty such as Martha Hitchcock, and guests such as C. I. Scofield, F. B. Meyer, and R. A. Torrey.
71. *The Hermonite*, 25 June 1891.
72. McDowell, *What D. L. Moody Means to Me*, 35.
73. Ibid., 38; Margaret Hook Olsen, *Patriarch of the Rockies: The Life Story of Joshua Gravett* (Denver: Golden Bell Press, 1960), 14f.
74. McDowell, *What D. L. Moody Means to Me*, 36.
75. Ibid., 37.
76. Ibid.
77. Ibid.
78. Ibid., 38.
79. Ibid., 39.
80. Ibid., 40, 42. See Sheffield and Keener entries.
81. Evelyn S. Hall, "Mr. Moody Among His Girls at Northfield," *Northfield Echoes*, Vol. 7, No. 1, 1900, pp. 42–49.
82. James McConaughy, "Mr. Moody at Mount Hermon," *Northfield Echoes*, Vol. 7, No. 1, 1900, 75–83.
83. D. L. Moody, "On Music and Singing," *The Christian*, 6 January 1898.
84. D. L. Moody, "Losing Sight of Self," *Glad Tidings*, 491–92.
85. See Calvin Coolidge, *Autobiography of Calvin Coolidge* (Rutland, Vermont: Academy Books, 1929); John Almon Waterhouse, *Calvin Coolidge Meets Charles Edward Garman* (Rutland: Academy Books, 1984); R. A. Woods, *Preparation of Calvin Coolidge* (N.Y.: Houghton Mifflin, 1924), chap. 6.
86. D. L. Moody's letters to his sons, written while they were at Yale, span the late 1880s and 1890s. These letters are at MBI archives, Yale archives, and an excellent collection of Emma's and D. L.'s letters to Paul are in the possession of Paul's granddaughter, Margaret Stout. The letters reflect Emma and Dwight's loving concern for their sons' spiritual and physical well-being.
87. McDowell, *What D. L. Moody Means to Me*, 9.
88. "History Files," Northfield Bible Training School, Northfield Archives, contains records of the school. Among the files are boxes of correspondence arranged in alphabetical order. See, for example, files of Julia Gooding, Nellie Greeley, Nellie Green, and Mattie Haven. Women wrote from New England, California, and Canada.
89. DLM to Whittle, 24 May 1889, Yale archives; DLM to Gertrude Hulburt, 21 July 1890, Yale archives.
90. Photographs of "The Northfield" are in the Training School history files, Northfield Archives. See also Moody, *Moody*, 446.
91. Clippings from the Springfield, Massachusetts *Daily Union*, 31 March 1892, History File, NBTS, Northfield Archives. See Lila A. Halsey, "Training Christian Workers at Northfield," *Northfield Echoes*, Vol. 7, No. 1, 1900, 101–4; and annual *Reports* of the Principal of NBTS.
92. Halsey, "Training," 103; History File, NBTS, Northfield Archives.
93. Magoun, "Moody's Schools," 790–91; Halsey, "Training," 101–4.
94. Baines Griffiths to Julia Gooding, 15 June 1891, NBTS, Northfield Archives.
95. Clipping from a newspaper dated 13 September 1898, History File, NBTS, Northfield Archives.
96. J. Wilbur Chapman, *The Life and Work of D. L. Moody* (Philadelphia: American Bible House, 1900), 351.
97. See note #95.
98. Halsey, "Training," 103.
99. Report of the Principal, Martha A. Hitchcock, NBTS, 1902–1903, History Files,

Northfield archives.

100. DLM to Mr. MacKinnon, 13 September 1881, Northfield archives; the "Streams" quotation is in McDowell, *What D. L. Moody Means to Me,* 9.

Chapter Eleven

1. DLM to F. G. Ensign, 15 December 1888, MBI archives.
2. DLM to Ensign, 22 November 1888 and 30 November 1888, MBI archives.
3. DLM to Ensign, 15 December 1888, MBI archives.
4. DLM to Ensign, 20 January 1889, MBI archives.
5. DLM to Whittle, 24 May 1889, Yale archives.
6. Ibid.
7. DLM to Ensign, 8 June 1889 and 27 June 1889, MBI archives; W. G. Moorehead to DLM, 23 June 1889, MBI archives; Gene A. Getz, *MBI: The Story of Moody Bible Institute* (Chicago: Moody Press, 1969), 34, 35, 51.
8. Sketches on Torrey's life are in *Who's Who In Christian History* and *Dictionary of American Religious Biography.* See also the full-scale biography of Torrey, Roger Martin, *R. A. Torrey: Apostle of Certainty* (Murfreesboro, TN: Sword of the Lord, 1976).
9. Ibid.
10. Getz, *MBI,* chaps. 4 and 5. On the Dryer issue see Moody's correspondence, MBI archives, with T. W. Harvey in 1888 and 1889. See also T. W. Harvey to Ensign, 20 November 1888, MBI archives, where Harvey makes it clear several board members had "asked her to resign." Capron's difficult personality is set forth in Hurlbut to DLM, 12 July 1890, and T. W. Harvey to DLM, October 1890, MBI archives.
11. DLM to Ensign and Harvey, throughout 1888 and 1889, MBI archives, show the abilities of those men and the tasks they performed. See, e.g., DLM to Harvey, 26 October 1889, 20 November 1889, 5 December 1889, MBI archives.
12. DLM to Gentlemen (McCormick Company) 17 June 1887, Yale archives; DLM to Ensign, 27 June 1889, 13 October 1889, MBI archives; DLM to Smith, 8 November 1889, MBI archives; DLM to Ensign, 9 November 1889, MBI archives; DLM to Harvey, 5 December 1889, MBI archives.
13. Getz, *MBI,* 63. See also "Mr. Moody's New Plan" (1890), in Smith, *Annotated Bibliography of D. L. Moody,* 78–80.
14. See Torrey, *Why God Used D. L. Moody,* chap. 8. Also see Torrey's books, *The Person and Work of the Holy Spirit* and *The Holy Spirit.* The quotation on seminaries is from Moody, *My Father,* 190.
15. Torrey, *Why God Used D. L. Moody,* chap. 8, 47.
16. Getz, *MBI,* 63.
17. Two books by George Marsden throw some helpful light on this ever-widening gulf: *Fundamentalism and American Culture: The Shaping of Twentieth-Century Evangelicalism, 1870–1925* (New York: Oxford Univ. Press, 1980); and *Understanding Fundamentalism and Evangelicalism* (Grand Rapids: Eerdmans, 1991).
18. Osborn, "D. L. Moody's Travels."
19. DLM to Miss Strong and Gaylord (two letters), 24 November 1898, MBI archives. On fund-raising, see, e.g., DLM to Whittle, 24 May 1889, Yale archives.
20. DLM to Torrey, 10 December 1894, MBI archives; Charles R. Erdman, *D. L. Moody: His Message for Today* (Chicago: Revell, 1928), 133.
21. Osborn, "D. L. Moody's Travels."
22. EM to Jane MacKinnon, 1878, quoted in Powell, *Heavenly Destiny,* 118.
23. EM to Ensign, 19 March 1889, MBI archives.
24. Moody, *My Father;* Moody, *Moody;* Fitt, *Moody;* Powell, *Heavenly Destiny.*
25. Moody, *My Father,* 80, 142, 81.
26. Powell, *Heavenly Destiny,* 146, 174.
27. Emma Moody's correspondence, especially by the late 1880s, and through the 1890s, located at Yale and Moody Bible Institute, reveal her deep involvement in the various facets of D. L. Moody's ministry. DLM to Paul, 3 March 1895, Stout

Family Papers, tell of the Mexico books.
28. EM to Mother, 9 November 1877, Yale archives; Powell, *Heavenly Destiny,* 129.
29. Powell, *Heavenly Destiny,* 113–14, 115; EM to Mother, 9 November 1877, Yale archives.
30. Powell, *Heavenly Destiny,* 119–20.
31. Ibid., 118–19.
32. DLM to Emma, n.d., Northfield Museum.
33. DLM to Emma, 21 January 1885, MBI archives; 24 April 1887, Yale archives.
34. Powell, *Heavenly Destiny,* 112.
35. Ibid., 208.
36. DLM to Willie, 18 October 1884; 22 September 1888, Yale archives.
37. DLM to Willie, 3 January 1885, 6 January 1885, Yale archives.
38. DLM to Willie, 21 January 1885, 31 January 1885, Yale archives.
39. DLM to Willie, 20 March 1886, MBI archives.
40. DLM to Willie, 25 September 1886, MBI archives.
41. DLM to Willie, 8 December 1886, 10 December 1886, Yale archives.
42. DLM to Miss Ford, 6 January 1887; 9 February 1887, Yale archives.
43. EM to Willie, 25 February 1887, Yale archives.
44. DLM to Willie, 3 November 1887, Yale archives.
45. DLM to Willie, 26 November 1887, Yale archives.
46. DLM to Will, 4 December 1888, MBI archives.
47. DLM to Will, 7 January 1890, MBI archives.
48. DLM to Mr. M., 31 December 1890, MBI archives.
49. Letters from DLM to Paul, 16 February 1895, 17 February 1895, Stout Collection, reveal the bond and the depths of Emma's love for her brother.
50. Paul Moody's granddaughter, Margaret Stout, still has approximately fifty letters D. L. Moody wrote to his son. This family collection also contains some splendid letters written by Emma Moody to her younger son.
51. DLM to Paul, 4 November 1884, 9 April 1887, 11 February 1888, 25 December 1889, Stout Collection.
52. DLM to Paul, 25 January 1890, 5 September 1894, 3 February 1895, Stout Collection.
53. DLM to Paul, 25 January 1890, 23 January 1888, 4 February 1893, Stout Collection.
54. DLM to Paul, 11 December 1889, 16 March 1887, 23 January 1888, 6 June 1888, Stout Collection.
55. DLM to Paul, 16 February 1895, Stout Collection.
56. DLM to Paul, February 1895, Stout Collection.
57. DLM to Paul, 11 February 1895, Stout Collection.
58. Moody, *My Father,* 86.
59. DLM to Paul, 3 February 1895, Stout Collection.
60. Moody, *My Father,* 84.
61. DLM to Paul, 24 October 1898, Stout Collection.
62. Moody, *My Father,* 160.
63. DLM to Paul, 25 December 1889, 11 April 1898, Stout Collection.
64. DLM to Paul, 19 April 1898, Stout Collection.
65. DLM to Paul, 11 February 1895, Stout Collection.
66. DLM to Paul, 11 April 1895, Stout Collection.
67. DLM to Bishop, 22 October 1899, Syracuse Archives.
68. Moody, *My Father,* 190.
69. See chap. 4; see also DLM to Mother, 13 September 1862, Yale archives.
70. This paragraph, as well as the next paragraphs on F. H. Revell, come primarily from two biographical sources: *The National Cyclopedia of American Biography,* Vol. 26, 442; *Dictionary of American Biography,* Vol. 15, 512–13. Bernard R. DeRemer, *Moody Bible Institute* (Chicago: Moody, 1960), 25, reveals some evidence about Revell's prayer ministry.
71. See chapter 8 of this book.

72. Smith, *Bibliography of Moody,* xiv.
73. Allan Fisher, "D. L. Moody's Contribution to Christian Publishing," *Christian History,* Vol. 9, No. 1, 1990, 32–33.
74. See, e.g., the advertisement sections of early Revell publications such as *Twelve Select Sermons, Heaven,* and *Secret Power.* See also the last twelve pages of *The Wonders of Prayer* (Revell, 1885).
75. See DLM's inscription in the front of *Heaven* (1880).
76. See front inside of *Secret Power* (1881). On Canadian editions, see David Marshall, *Secularizing the Faith: Canadian Protestant Clergy and the Crisis of Belief, 1850–1940* (Toronto: Univ. of Toronto Press, 1942), 86.
77. *The Wonders of Prayer,* Revised Edition (1885) contains twelve pages of advertising arranged in categories.
78. See *Wonders of Prayer,* 19–20, 21–27 by Moody and Dryer respectively. See also advertising on the Gordon book in the back of this volume.
79. See chapter 7 of this book. See also Peterson, "Dryer," and the Dryer-Blanchard correspondence in Wheaton College Archives.
80. Quoted in Margaret Hook Olsen, *Patriarch of the Rockies: The Life Story of Joshua Gravett* (Denver: Golden Bell Press, 1960), 43.
81. Olsen, *Gravett,* 41–44. See also A. W. Tozer's biography of Simpson, *Wingspread: Albert B. Simpson, A Study in Spiritual Altitude* (Harrisburg, PA: Christian Publications, 1943).
82. Whittle's diary, typescript, Yale archives, 3.
83. Ibid. The Dr. Cullis referred to by Moody was Charles Cullis, a respected and powerful minister. See A. J. Gordon, *The Ministry of Healing,* chap. 8.
84. See p. 12 of advertising in D. W. Whittle, ed., *The Wonders of Prayer* (Chicago: Revell, 1885).
85. DLM to Rankin, 29 October 1886, Yale archives.
86. DLM to Rankin, 11 November 1887, Yale archives; DLM to McCormick, 13 January 1887, Yale archives.
87. Smith, *Annotated Bibliography,* 81, "The Bible Institute Colportage Association"; see also "Mr. Moody as Publisher and Author," *Northfield Echoes,* Vol. 7, No. 1, 90–91.
88. See, for instance, Catalogue no. 57, Spring and Summer 1895, 55–74, 516–19, 551.
89. Frank Luther Mott, *Golden Multitudes: The Story of Best Sellers in the United States* (New York: Macmillan, 1947) is an excellent overview of publishing trends and best-selling authors, including topics such as Dime Novels and D. L. Moody.
90. For itinerary see Osborn, "D. L. Moody's Travels." See also Getz, *MBI,* 230–31.
91. DLM to Jones, 5 January 1895, MBI archives.
92. Moody, *Moody,* 432–33.
93. DLM to Jones, 5 January 1895, MBI archives; Moody, *Moody,* 433.
94. Moody, *Moody,* 431.
95. Fisher, "Moody's Contribution to Christian Publishing," 32–33.
96. Ibid.; Moody, *Moody,* 432.
97. DeRemer, *Moody Bible Institute,* 25, tells about the prayer meetings of Dryer, Farwell, Revell, and others.
98. Getz, *MBI,* 230.
99. Ibid., 230–31; "Mr. Moody As Author and Publisher," *Northfield Echoes,* Vol. 7, No. 1, 1900, 89–95.
100. Getz, *MBI,* 231.
101. Ibid., 230–31; Fisher, "Moody's Contributions to Christian Publishing," 32–33.
102. The MBI archives has an A. P. Fitt collection of Moody manuscripts. It contains 350 items that reveal DLM's massive involvement in the work. See also N. F. McCormick to DLM, 6 March 1895; DLM to A. P. Fitt, 2 March 1895.
103. See Fitt Collection, e.g., DLM letters to Fitt/Gaylord, 27 April 1895, 27 March 1895, 29 January 1895, 18 February 1895, 13 & 15 April 1895, 10 October 1895; with similar letters in 1896, 1897, 1898, and 1899.
104. *The Hermonite,* 15 April 1895.

105. *The Hermonite*, 8 May 1897.
106. "Moody As Author and Publisher," *Northfield Echoes*, Vol. 7, No. 1, 1900, 93.
107. Photos in the MBI archives.
108. Moody, *Moody*, 432.
109. Ibid., 432–33.
110. See testimonies in "Moody As Author and Publisher," *Northfield Echoes*, Vol. 7, No. 1, 1900, 89–95.
111. Mott, *Golden Multitudes*, 310–12.
112. See Revell biographical sketch in *The National Cyclopedia*, 442.
113. Fisher, "Moody's Contributions to Christian Publishing," 33; Getz, *MBI*, 231.
114. Paul Moody makes a point of how his father changed his approach. See *My Father*, 187.
115. H. B. Hartzler to W. Moody, 22 February 1900, Yale archives.
116. DLM to Hartzler, 4 August 1880, Yale archives.
117. Moody, *Moody*, 361–63; Erdman, *Moody*, 140.
118. Moody, *Moody*, 361.
119. Bebbington, *Evangelicalism*, 159–61; Steven Barabas, *So Great Salvation: The History and Message of the Keswick Convention* (Westwood, N.J.: n.d.); John C. Pollock, *The Keswick Story* (Chicago: Moody, 1964).
120. Quoted in McDowell, *What D. L. Moody Means to Me*, 44.
121. T. J. Shanks, *D. L. Moody at Home* (Chicago: Revell, 1886), 33.
122. McDowell, *What D. L. Moody Means to Me*, 44.
123. Moody, *Secret Power*, 1–38.
124. Ibid., 45–46.
125. Ibid., 55–73.
126. Shanks, *Moody at Home*, preface, 33.
127. Quoted in Delevan Pierson, *Arthur T. Pierson: A Biography* (London: James Nisbet, 1912), 191–92.
128. M. Bonar, ed., *Andrew A. Bonar: Diary and Life* (London: Banner of Truth, 1960), 334; W. Y. Fullerton, *F. B. Meyer: A Biography* (Harrisburg, Pa.: The Christian Alliance Publishing Co., n.d.), 41.
129. On books, see Fullerton, *Meyer*, 41; on promotion of schools, see Shanks, *Moody at Home*, 32.
130. Ibid.
131. T. J. Shanks, ed., *A College of Colleges: Led by D. L. Moody* (Chicago: Revell, 1887), chap. 1.
132. Ibid., 16. See also Basil Mathews, *John R. Mott: World Citizen* (New York: Harper, 1934), 42–47.
133. Ibid.
134. Ibid., 17–18; See also David M. Howard, *Student Power in World Missions* (Downers Grove, Illinois: InterVarsity, 1979), 91.
135. Mark J. Toone, "Evangelicalism in Transition: A Comparative Analysis of the Work and Theology of D. L. Moody and His Protégés, Henry Drummond and R. A. Torrey" (Ph.D. diss., St. Mary's College, Univ. of St. Andrews, 1988), 3, 291; Shanks, ed., *College of Colleges*, 23, 280–88.
136. Shanks, *Moody at Home*, 38; DLM to Emma, 14 July 1887, Yale archives, and a document quoting W. L. Phelps labeled "Summer 1887," Powell Papers, Yale archives; J. Edwin Orr, *The Light of the Nations* (Grand Rapids: Eerdmans, 1965), 202.
137. A. T. Robertson, "Northfield Notes" (unpublished); L. O. Dawson, "Moody's School," *Seminary Magazine*, Vol. 2, No. 6, October 1889.
138. Fitt, *Moody*, 90.
139. Quoted in Moody, *Moody*, 497.
140. Pierson, *Pierson*, 198.

Chapter Twelve

1. DLM to Gaylord, 26 April 1897, MBI archives.

2. Quoted in Moody, *Moody*, 530.
3. DLM to Gaylord, 8 April 1897, MBI archives.
4. Moody, *My Father*, chap. 2. See also, Moody, *Moody*, chap. 44.
5. Powell, in *Heavenly Destiny*, records material on Emma and D. L.'s outings.
6. Moody, *My Father*, 52.
7. EM to E. Fitt, 22 May 1894, Yale archives.
8. Moody, *Moody*, 535.
9. Quoted in Fitt, *Moody*, 110; DLM to E. Fitt, 7 January 1896.
10. DLM to E. Fitt, 10 December 1896, quoted in Fitt, *Moody*, 109–10.
11. Quoted in Fitt, *Moody*, 111.
12. Moody was invited to Australia, New Zealand, and Tasmania. See the petitional scroll of more than 15,000 names in Moody Museum, D. L. Moody Home, Northfield. An invitation to Japan is recorded in a document at Yale archives, in the Powell Collection.
13. That Moody stayed in such places is apparent from the letterhead. See, for example, DLM to Gaylord, 31 October 1898, 16 October 1897, 30 January 1897, 3 October 1896, 8 May 1896, MBI archives.
14. Pollock, *Moody*, 279; O. O. Howard, *Autobiography of Oliver Otis Howard* (New York: Baker and Taylor, 1907), Vol. 2, 559–60.
15. Howard, *Autobiography*, 560.
16. Ibid., 561.
17. Moody quoted in Fitt, *Moody*, 102–3.
18. Fitt, *Moody*, 103; Howard, *Autobiography*, 563.
19. Howard, *Autobiography*, 563–64.
20. See George Adam Smith, *The Life of Henry Drummond* (N.Y.: Doubleday, 1898), 452–53; Findlay, *Moody*, 411–12; and both Mark J. Toone, "Evangelicalism in Transition: A Comparative Analysis of the Work and Theology of D. L. Moody and His Protégés, Henry Drummond and R. A. Torrey" (Ph.D. diss., St. Mary's College, Univ. of St. Andrews, 1988), 291, 294, and Moody, *My Father*, chap. 12, contain rich evidence.
21. DLM to Torrey, undated and filed in MBI archives in 1894 letter book. Because there is a reference to Will's sick daughter, the letter must have been written after August 1895, and probably in 1899.
22. A photocopy of the *Chicago Daily News* clipping in MBI archives, 1898 letter-book, filed in October 1898.
23. DLM to Torrey, 31 October 1898, MBI archives.
24. Harper to DLM, 22 September 1899, Yale archives.
25. Sketches of Scofield appear in the *Dictionary of American Religious Biography*, 399–400; *Who's Who In Christian History*, 616; see also Joseph M. Canfield, *The Incredible Scofield and His Book* (privately printed, 1984). Photos of Scofield appear in J. Wilbur Chapman, *The Life and Work of D. L. Moody* (Philadelphia: American Bible House, 1900), 457, 497; and Charles G. Trumbull, *The Life Story of C. I. Scofield* (New York: Oxford Univ. Press, 1920).
26. Canfield, *Scofield*, 153–65.
27. See "History" Box in NBTS files, Northfield Library Archives. The Scofield letters to Halsey are quite revealing. His final attempt to take over is in a letter dated 14 June 1900, written just a few months after DLM's death. She apparently kept Scofield at bay.
28. Quoted in Moody, *Moody* (1930 edition), 52.
29. This bound volume is in a display case, Moody Museum, Moody Birthplace, Northfield. Linda Batty, the archivist for the Northfield Schools, showed me this book, and she also told me that two Australian researchers saw this a few years ago. They told her they were amazed that letters were included from all the leaders of that era, including ones who had been at loggerheads with one another.
30. Ernest B. Gordon, *Adoniram Judson Gordon: A Biography* (Chicago: Revell, 1896); see also sketches in *Religious Leaders of America*, 177–78 and *Dictionary of American Religious Biography*, 176–77.

31. DLM to Pierson, 14 February 1895, MBI archives.
32. Fitt, *Moody*, 108–9.
33. Goss, *Echoes*, 86.
34. Goss, *Echoes*, 86; the book was pulled together in 1897 and available in 1898. See Colportage list on back of Norton to DLM, 29 November 1898, MBI archives.
35. EM to Emma Fitt, 30 November 1898, Yale archives.
36. DLM to Fitt, 1 December 1898, Yale archives; DLM to Miss Varley, 1 December 1898, Syracuse archives.
37. Quoted in Fitt, *Moody*, 111–12.
38. Ibid., 112–13.
39. Ibid., 115.
40. His letters at MBI archives and Yale archives are still numerous for this period.
41. Fitt, *Moody*, 120.
42. Goss, *Echoes*, 83.
43. George E. Morgan, *R. C. Morgan: His Life and Times* (London: Morgan & Scott, 1922), 184, reveals the discovery of Moody's heart condition in London in 1892. On his healthful appearance, see Goss, *Echoes*, 83.
44. EM to Paul, 8 November 1899, Yale archives.
45. Fitt, *Moody*, 113–14.
46. Ibid., 113.
47. Ibid., 115.
48. Quoted in Moody, *Moody*, 546.
49. Moody, *My Father*, 168.
50. Quoted in Moody, *Moody*, 545.
51. Ibid.
52. Ibid., 547.
53. Ibid., 548.
54. Ibid., 549.
55. Ibid.
56. Fitt, *Moody*, 122.
57. Moody, *Moody*, 552–55.
58. "The Autobiography of Dwight L. Moody." See Frontispiece and 554–55 of Moody, *Moody*.
59. Moody, *Moody*, 559.
60. Ibid., 559–70.
61. *The Institute Tie*, New Series, Vol. 4, No. 3, Chicago, November 1903, 77–80. See also a typed autobiography by Paul Moody. Original in the Stout collection.
62. Ibid.
63. William Revell Moody died 12 October 1933. Emma Moody Fitt died 17 September 1942. Paul Dwight Moody died in November 1947. All three were devout Christians, as were their spouses.

Chapter Thirteen

1. J. H. to DLM in 1942, Emma Moody Powell Collection, Yale archives. The copy of the letter I found is a typescript, with ellipses after the initials.
2. Moody, *Moody*, 502.
3. Goss, *Echoes*, 92.
4. Moody's love for risk takers is illustrated in his book *Bible Characters*, published as a Colportage book in the late 1890s.
5. Fitt, *Moody*, 92.
6. Moody, *Moody*, 409.
7. Quoted in Ibid., 410.
8. Ibid., 12–13; see also H. B. Hartzler, *Moody in Chicago* (New York: 1894); and Lyle W. Dorsett, *Billy Sunday and the Redemption of Urban America* (Grand Rapids: Eerdmans, 1991). Another important book is James Gilbert, *Perfect Cities: Chicago's Utopias of 1893* (Chicago: Univ. of Chicago Press, 1991), chap. 6.
9. Moody, *Moody*, 413.

10. Ibid., 416–19. See also Paul M. Minus, *Walter Rauschenbusch: American Reformer* (N.Y.: Oxford Univ. Press, 1988), 56–57. Although Rauschenbusch became a leader among social gospelers, he was markedly influenced by Moody as a young man.

11. Moody is quoted in Moody, *Moody,* 418–19. Thomas Spurgeon wrote "Memories of America" in *Sword and Trowel* (London) March 1894, 128–32.

12. Moody, *Secret Power,* see especially chaps. 10–12.

13. Ibid., 11–12, 60–63.

14. See, for example, R. A. Torrey, *Why God Used D. L. Moody,* chap. 8, as well as his book *The Holy Spirit.* Revell published both books. An example of the influence of instruction on the Holy Spirit and how it set the tone for the schools is typified in Martha A. Hitchcock's report about NBTS: "The Spirit-filled life is the normal condition of the Christian, and only in normal conditions can there be normal growth. It was because Paul knew the necessity that he prayed that we might 'be strengthened with might by His Spirit in the inner man' that He would work in us, 'according to the working of His mighty power,' which He wrought in Christ when He raised Him from the dead. So then, the thought that we take with us is that to be like our ideal we must live in the Spirit." Report of the Principal of NBTS, 1902–1903, Northfield archives.

15. Moody, *Secret Power,* preface. Typical of the way Moody preached on the importance of the Spirit was a message he delivered in San Francisco. See Anderson, "San Francisco Evangelicalism," *Fides,* 50.

16. Quoted in J. Wilbur Chapman, *The Life and Work of D. L. Moody* (Philadelphia: American Bible House, 1900), chap. 25. Gundry, *Love Them In,* 45, shows that it was Henry Moorhouse who taught Moody to preach the Bible rather than his own words.

17. Torrey, *Why God Used D. L. Moody,* chap. 4.

18. Quoted in Chapman, *Life and Work of Moody,* 387.

19. *The Hermonite,* 28 May 1898.

20. Farwell, *Moody,* 8–9.

21. Paul Moody reports on his father at Yale in *My Father;* Pollock, *Moody,* 182 contains good material on Princeton. See also the Studd/Moody letters in the 1880s, Yale archives, which contain material on Cambridge.

22. See, e.g., T. J. Shanks, ed., *A College of Colleges: Led by D. L. Moody* (Chicago: Revell, 1887), esp. "Catalogue of Delegates," 280–88.

23. Quoted in Powell, *Heavenly Destiny,* 166. A useful sketch of Mott is in *Current Biography* (1947), 453–56. See also B. J. Mathews, *John R. Mott: World Citizen* (New York: n.p., 1934), 42–48, and chap. 16.

24. See Spurgeon to DLM, Friday eve, 1884, Yale archives; see also the following letters from Spurgeon to Moody (typescripts in the Powell papers) dated 7 February 1884, 27 March 1884, 24 April 1884, 8 May 1884, 4 June 1884, 10 June 1884, 13 June 1884, Yale archives. See also C. H. Spurgeon's *Autobiography,* Vol. 4, 169–71, 246–48. On Mueller's visit to the United States, see Roger Steer, *George Mueller* (Wheaton: Harold Shaw, 1975), 243–55; 274–78.

25. Moody, *My Father,* 188–89.

26. *McClure's,* 1894–95, Vol. 4, 55–69, 188–92.

27. Torrey, *Why God Used D. L. Moody,* chap. 5.

28. Gundry, *Love Them In,* 45–46.

29. Henry Drummond, "The Greatest Human I Ever Knew," in J. Wilbur Chapman, *Life and Work of Moody,* xiii.

30. Gundry, *Love Them In,* 218.

31. Goss, *Echoes,* 85.

32. Quoted in T. J. Shanks, *D. L. Moody at Home* (Chicago: Fleming H. Revell, 1886), 41–42; see also the Moody lecture in Shanks, ed., *College of Colleges,* 152.

33. See Richard Baxter, *The Reformed Pastor* (Richmond, VA: John Knox Press, reprint 1956).

34. Gamaliel Bradford, *D. L. Moody: A Worker in Souls* (Garden City: Doubleday,

Doran and Co., 1928), 275. This book, especially chap. 8, offers the most insightful understanding of Moody and the care of souls. Bradford was not a Christian, but this sympathetic biography displays a keener understanding of Moody's work with souls than other biographies.

35. Quoted in Shanks, *Moody at Home,* 41.

36. Bradford, *Moody,* 275.

37. See Dorsett, *Billy Sunday.*

38. I, along with several hundred other people, was instructed in Billy Graham's methodology by Mr. Graham himself when he spoke at the Billy Graham School of Evangelism, Indianapolis, Indiana, May 1980.

39. The best history of this subject is *A History of the Cure of Souls* (San Francisco: Harper and Row, 1977) by John McNeill.

40. *N.Y. Times,* 5 February 1936, clipping in Stout Collection, says he left an estate of $500. This total evidently did not include the house.

41. Fitt, *Moody,* 95; see also chaps. 10 and 11.

42. See chapters 10, 11, and 12.

43. Mark J. Toone, "Evangelicalism in Transition: A Comparative Analysis of the Work and Theology of D. L. Moody and His Protégés, Henry Drummond and R. A. Torrey" (Ph.D. diss., St. Mary's College, Univ. of St. Andrews, 1988), chaps. 5, 7, 8.

44. Patty Stout, Paul Moody's granddaughter, explained to me that the brothers had a markedly strained relationship after their father's death. It was significant too that Paul never took over the Northfield Seminary despite his father's deathbed assignment. He taught there only a short time under his brother's leadership. The Moody brothers' books reveal some of their differences, but they conceal their disagreements rather well.

45. Gene A. Getz, *MBI: The Story of Moody Bible Institute* (Chicago: Moody Press, 1969), 77. V. Raymond Edman, *They Found the Secret* (Grand Rapids: Zondervan, 1960) contains a chapter on Walter L. Wilson with a story about James M. Gray. This story suggests a robust view of the Spirit on one level but not like the one that Torrey held. Torrey's biographer, Roger Martin, *R. A. Torrey: Apostle of Certainty* (Murfreesboro, Tenn.: Sword of the Lord, 1976), 69–76, shows how serious Torrey was about divine healing in this dispensation.

46. DLM to Gray, 5 March 1898 and 28 May 1898, MBI archives.

47. The subject of Torrey's departure from MBI is worthy of further study. The Torrey papers in the MBI archives, plus hints in Getz, *MBI,* suggest some growing rifts of the kind DLM hated to take sides on. A biographical sketch of Gray, as well as photographs of him, are in DeRemer, *Moody Bible Institute.*

48. EM to Willie, 29 October 1887, Yale archives. Examples of fund-raising letters are in Moody and Yale archives. Typical of these are: DLM to Gentlemen, 17 June 1887, Yale archives; DLM to Mrs. McCormick, 18 July 1887, Yale archives; DLM to Sir, 15 March 1889, MBI archives.

49. DLM to Friend, Spring 1889, Yale archives.

50. DLM to Mrs. McCormick, 26 April 1887, MBI archives; DLM to Whittle, 24 May 1889, Yale archives.

51. *The Christian Herald,* 25 July 1894, copy in MBI archives, Moody letters, July 1894.

52. Moody, *Moody,* 413–14. See also George Sweeting, "Blessed Are the Money Raisers," *Moody Monthly,* November 1988.

53. See, e.g., EM to Willie, 29 October 1887, Yale archives. This letter refers to the Kinnairds' visit at Northfield. And the Wanamakers were so close to the Moodys that a lake on the school land was named for them—Wanamaker Lake.

54. Quoted in Findlay, *Moody,* 327.

55. See Ray Ginger, *Altgeld's America: The Lincoln Ideal Versus Changing Reality* (N.Y.: Funk & Wagnalls, 1958).

56. See Stanley Buder, *Pullman: An Experiment in Order and Community Planning* (N.Y.: Oxford Univ. Press, 1967).

57. An excellent unpublished senior thesis on this topic is Harold J. Brewer, "The Contributions of the Christian Evangelist, D. L. Moody to Gilded Age Reform and Education," Princeton, 1974.

58. Moody, *My Father,* 192.

59. Findlay, *Moody,* 411; Brewer, "Moody."

60. A text of this address is Appendix No. 1, in A. A. Bonar, *James Scott: Laborer for God* (London: Morgan & Scott, n.d.), 109–12, titled "Mr. Moody's Sympathy with Pastors."

61. Kenneth Scott Latourette, *The Great Century in Europe and the United States of America: A.D. 1800–A.D. 1914* (New York: Harper, 1941), chap. 10, especially 371.

62. See Nathan O. Hatch, *The Democratization of American Christianity* (New Haven: Yale Univ. Press, 1989).

63. See Latourette, *Great Century,* 430–31; and Norris Magnuson, *Salvation in the Slums: Evangelical Social Work, 1865–1920* (Metuchen, N.J.: Scarecrow Press, 1977).

64. D. L. Moody quoted on the inside cover of *Moody Centenary Song Book* (Chicago: Moody Bible Institute, 1936).

A NOTE ON SOURCES

The endnotes for each chapter will show the reader precisely what sources I have relied upon for each portion of this biography. Nevertheless, I hope some general remarks will prove useful to serious students of Moody's life.

Primary source material is unusually voluminous and rich for a man who had so little formal education. Fortunately for the biographer, Moody was an inveterate letter writer from his teenage years until his death. I located approximately 1,800 letters written by D. L. Moody. The largest collection is housed in the Archives of the Moody Bible Institute, with the Yale Divinity School Archives running a close second in volume. Besides these two repositories, a substantial collection of Moody's letters is in the museum and archives at the Northfield schools. Smaller collections of Moody's letters are at the Library of Congress; Syracuse University; Wisconsin State Historical Society; Billy Graham Center Archives, Wheaton, Illinois; and the University of Wisconsin, Eau Claire.

Most of the archives noted here also contain papers of relatives and associates of Mr. Moody, as does the archives of Wheaton College's [Illinois] Buswell Library. Most of this material was quite helpful.

A private collection of approximately one hundred letters written by Dwight and Emma Moody to their son Paul is in the possession of Mrs. Margaret Stout, D. L. Moody's great-granddaughter. These are extremely illuminating letters, as are some of Paul Moody's autobiographical materials that Mrs. Stout has carefully preserved.

Besides these collections of unpublished papers, I have relied upon dozens of published primary sources. Among the most useful are the biographies of Moody written by family members and people who knew him well. These books were indispensable: W. H. Daniels, *D. L. Moody and His Work* (1875); John V. Farwell, *Early Recollections of Dwight L. Moody* (1907); A. P. Fitt, *The Life of D. L. Moody* (1900); Charles Goss, *Echoes From the Pulpit and Platform* (1900); Paul Moody, *My Father* (1938); William R. Moody, *The Life of Dwight L. Moody* (1900); Emma Moody Powell, *Heavenly Destiny: The Life Story of Mrs. D. L. Moody* (1943). I also made extensive use of Moody's own books, especially his published sermons.

Many newspapers and periodicals were consulted for this biography. Especially revealing were *The New York Times, The London Times, The Christian,* and *The Christian Cynosure.*

One source that saved me virtually weeks of digging and calculating is an unpublished guide to "D. L. Moody's Travels," arranged by Mr. Walter Osborn, Reference Librarian, Moody Bible Institute. Equally valuable is a book by Wilbur M. Smith, *An Annotated Bibliography of D. L. Moody* (1948).

Two modern biographies of Moody proved to be constant, useful, and admirable companions: James F. Findlay, Jr., *Dwight L. Moody: American Evangelist, 1837–1899* (1969); and John C. Pollock, *Moody: A Biographical Portrait of the Pacesetter in Modern Mass Evangelism* (1963).

INDEX OF PERSONS

INDEX OF SUBJECTS

INDEX OF PLACES

SINCE 1894, Moody Publishers has been dedicated to equip and motivate people to advance the cause of Christ by publishing evangelical Christian literature and other media for all ages, around the world. Because we are a ministry of the Moody Bible Institute of Chicago, a portion of the proceeds from the sale of this book go to train the next generation of Christian leaders.

If we may serve you in any way in your spiritual journey toward understanding Christ and the Christian life, please contact us at www.moodypublishers.com.

"All Scripture is God-breathed and is useful for teaching, rebuking, correcting and training in righteousness, so that the man of God may be thoroughly equipped for every good work."
—2 TIMOTHY 3:16, 17

MOODY
PUBLISHERS

THE NAME YOU CAN TRUST®

A PASSION FOR SOULS TEAM

ACQUIRING EDITOR:
Greg Thornton

COVER DESIGN:
Ragont Design

INTERIOR DESIGN:
Ragont Design

PRINTING AND BINDING:
Quebecor World Book Services